Modern Architecture in Berlin

Erich Mendelsohn, 1926

Modern Architecture in Berlin

466 examples from 1900 to the present day

selected and described by Rolf Rave

Edition Axel Menges

ISBN 978-3-936681-29-1

Third, revised edition

Printing and binding: Graspo CZ, a.s., Zlín, Czech Republic

Translation into English: Karl Edward Johnsen
Editorial work: Rebecca Chestnutt, Nora Krehl-von Mühlendahl, Robert Niess, Roosje Rave, Wolfgang Schäche
City maps: Julia Wolter, based on maps by Senatsverwaltung für Stadtentwicklung, Berlin
Book design: Rolf Rave
Cover design: Axel Menges
Cover photo: Daniel Libeskind, Jüdisches Museum, Berlin (photo: Bitter & Brett)

Some texts for older projects contributed by Hans Joachim Knöfel

What does a city consist of? Of everything that has been said, dreamt, destroyed, happened. The built, the vanished, the dreamt of that came to nothing. The living and the dead. The wooden houses that have been demolished or burned down, the palaces that might have been, the bridge that was drawn but never built. The houses that are still standing, in which generations have left their memories. But there is much more than that.

A city is all the words that have ever been said, an incessant, neverending murmur, whisper, song and clamour that has resounded over the centuries and then been blown away. It cannot have disappeared if it had not been part of it, even that which can no longer be recovered belongs, simply because it was once, here, at this spot, shouted or spoken on a winter's nigth or a summer morning. The field preaching, the tribunal's verdict, the cry of the flogged, the bidding at the auction, the decree, the proclamation, the demonstration, the pamphlet, the announcement of a death, the calling of the hours, the words of nuns, whores, kings, regents, painters, sheriffs, hangmen, shipmasters, lansquenets, lock-keepers and master builders, that ceaseless conversation in the living body of the city, which is the city itself.

Cees Nooteboom in: *25 Buildings You Should Have Seen: Amsterdam*

Preface

"It is a tragic blow of fate that Berlin, a Wendish fishing settlement, which evolved to a city with over a million inhabitants and capital of the German Empire, should be cursed for steadily outgrowing itself: to always become and never to be." Karl Scheffler, 1910.

Although Berlin's history encompasses more than eight hundred years and its beginnings reach back as far as the twelfth century, its present-day urban image is essentially characterized by structures and buildings dating from the nineteenth and twentieth centuries. Four "modern" development phases, whose respective qualities were vastly different, played a determining role in this image: during the second half of the nineteenth century, against the backdrop of industrialization, Berlin's rise from a comprehensible Prussian capital and residence to an expanding metropolis of the German Empire; the 1920 consolidation of the city with the surrounding ninety-three townships, rural communities and properties to form "Greater Berlin"; following the destruction of the Second World War, working "back to back" politically, territorially, and regarding the appearance of Berlin as a divided, urban structure until 1990; and from the reunification to the present day, the ongoing structural and spatial connections as well as architectural refinements required for Berlin's role as capital of the new Federal Republic.

What the development phases up to the reunification had in common was their unhesitatingly rigorous and result-yielding treatment of the existing city and its architecture. This was strongly supported by an impetuous and, in each case, zeitgeist-driven belief in progress. In this way, the emergence of the unrestrained building boom of "Berlin's middle class" during the reign of the German Empire wiped out the classical design of Karl Friedrich Schinkel's Prussian capital, while the architectural vocabulary of the new city, formed by industrialization, was forced to experience its crude, spiritual and physical dismantling during the period of the Weimar Republic, when Berlin advanced to the heights of a metropolitan city and, culturally speaking, became for awhile the "hub of the avant-garde world". Last but not least, thanks to its uncompromising and radical architectural concepts meant to establish a conscious break with the middle-class city of the nineteenth century, the "golden twenties" turned this pulsating metropolis into no less than a legend and proclaimed its "Neues Bauen" (new building) an expression of Modernism and social progress. During this period nearly every well-known architect associated with the avant-garde, whether inland or abroad, regarded Berlin as an intellectual focal point as well as a vanishing point. This was where one felt explicitly challenged to make an adequate contribution to the heated debates concerning the ideal architectural perspective for the twentieth century.

Following the period of the Weimar Republic, the coming to power of the Nazi regime, which lasted from 1933 to 1945, caused a further break in the previous development phase. With obviously different political motivations in mind, this phase, too, hoped to radically change Berlin's existing layout. It culminated in Albert Speer's plans, developed since 1936, for "redesigning the Imperial Capital", a mammoth project in anticipation of the wartime aggression of the National-Socialist state and meant to transform Berlin into "Germania", the future "Capital of the World". However, the planned destruction of the existing city, in the grip of such architecturally backward monumentality without a standard, was ultimately brought to its unplanned and horrific conclusion under the hailstorm of bombs which fell at the end of World War II.

The improvisations of the first postwar years were followed by a political "reconstruction" of the city that was divided in two parts. Yet, in the one or the other urban sector, this soon revealed itself to be a reorganization that had nothing in common with the cultural inheritance, since no serious thought was given to restoring what was damaged. Nevertheless, citizens of both urban parts believed that they were taking full advantage of the chance to develop the vision of a "new city" on the rubble of the old one. In the West this was pursued using theoretical measures and models and the design repertoire of the Modern age; in the East it entailed engaging at first a "Socialist urban planning" and a corresponding architecture of "national traditionalism". Until the reunification in 1990, architectural "rebuilding strategies" as unalike as these complied with the respective territorial affiliations of a good many socially predetermined changes in Berlin's overall framework. But while they occasionally brought about exemplary architecture, the same strategies failed to make the promised "city of tomorrow" a reality.

Urban structures which existed separately and internally fragmented for decades were spatially integrated thanks to numerous architectural programs initiated since the reunification. These stood out clearly for the first time among the countless vehemently placed twentieth-century models that preceded them, and, by virtue of their inherent conceptual approach, they supported the notion of rediscovering the historic city and its metropolitan typologies, which meanwhile had been thoroughly forgotten. At the beginning of the twenty-first century, the fact that critical reflection directed at cultural inheritance created a connection to Berlin's complex architectural history promoted a productive dialogue between the old and the new, while representing a supportive perspective for the future as well.

The contents of this architectural guide vividly stand out against the backdrop of Berlin's recent history – a course of events as multifaceted as it was, in part excessive, up until today. This publication focuses on the city's last one-hundred years when, generation by generation, Berlin daringly and almost obsessively rediscovered itself architecturally. The selected examples not only convey a visually impressive and representative longitudinal progression, but also the form in which the most provocative of social movements, changes and breaks presented themselves in the architecture of the city.

With texts and images, the following pages present 466 constructions built from 1900 to the present day. The author's choices support the greater intention to point out what can now be deemed contemporary, typical, and exemplary about every period of Berlin's diverse, uneven, and amazingly rich architectural history, while aspiring to individually illuminate and explain each one. That the examples offered here blatantly declare themselves products of the "Modern age" or "Neues Bauen" permits them to be understood as a "manifesto in images", which consolidates to a twentieth-century architectural collage, whose quality and wide range grant it an unquestionable uniqueness. Their spectrum contains all the essential phases of architectural development: from the programmatic entry into the twentieth century manifested in work by Alfred Messel, Hermann Muthesius, Peter Behrens, Alfred Grenander, Heinrich Tessenow, and the heroically received architecture of the 1920s, whose protagonists include Walter Gropius, Ludwig Mies van der Rohe, Erich Mendelsohn, Bruno and Max Taut, Hans Scharoun, but also Hans

Poelzig and Bruno Paul, as well as Hans Hertlein, the postwar and reconstruction period with buildings by Alvar Aalto, Le Corbusier, Egon Eiermann, Oskar Niemeyer, and Pierre Vago, to the beginning of the twenty-first century, embodied in architecture by Josef Paul Kleihues, Oswald Mathias Ungers, Jürgen Sawade, Aldo Rossi, Rem Koolhaas, Frank O. Gehry, Daniel Libeskind, Helmut Jahn, Hans Kollhoff, and next-generation architects such as Bernd Albers, Klaus Theo Brenner, Max Dudler, Petra and Paul Kahlfeldt, Jan Kleihues, and Walter Noebel, whose multilayered architectural statements were capable of leading to the present.

Despite conveying the simultaneity and asynchrony of different architectural approaches and forms of expressions, they reflect the indissoluble relationship of time, space, and architecture, and the urban-planning intentions determining this context. These notions of urban design and urban structuring, which characterize the respective time periods, connected with a series of Berlin's master builders, who created the urban preconditions upon whose basis great architecture could unfold. During the transition from the nineteenth to twentieth century, between 1896 and 1924, this was the case with Ludwig Hoffmann, head of the municipal planning and building control office. With caution and insistence, Hoffmann effectively shaped the cityscape and left his mark upon it. His successor was the individualistic Martin Wagner. Up until his 1933 dismissal, brought on by the National Socialists, Wagner steered, with sovereignty, the building and structural skills of the German capital at that time and oversaw the completion of landmarks that have endured to the present. Under Hoffmann's patronage, Berlin made the huge leap from a large city to the undisputed metropolis of the German Empire. Thriving in the early 1920s, under Martin Wagner's direction, to become Greater Berlin, the imperial capital advanced to a modern cosmopolitan city.

For a longer period of time, however, no successor managed to build on the accomplishments of Hoffmann and Wagner. On the strength of their will to design and clarity of urban vision, they granted Berlin its very own character. Still, due to the interchangeable nature of the comparatively short-lived planning approaches developed since the end of World War II, all traces of the results have been lost to the vastness and structural diversity of the city. Not until Josef Paul Kleihues, who applied himself to planning the newly-built areas of the International Building Exhibition (IBA), organized in West Berlin between 1979 and 1987, and Hardt-Walther Hämer, who, in the same framework, was responsible for the so-called old buildings' areas, did two exceptional protagonists once again concern themselves with the city plan. Both could be measured against the inspiring figures that shaped Berlin during the first half of the twentieth century. Linked with their work is redeveloping the historical city and the enduring structural qualities made available largely through the resulting planning strategies of the "critical reconstruction" on the one side, and the expression of a "cautious urban renewal" on the other.

Since the reunification, urban development was in the hands of Hans Stimmann, the Senate's Director of Urban Development between 1991 and 2006. Ultimately, one associates with his name the city's re-urbanization and the reclaiming of its identity, successively lost to war-inflicted destruction and distortions of the so-called reconstruction caused by the city's division.

Wolfgang Schäche, April 2012

Author's note

The intention of this book is to lead the reader toward 466 constructed examples from the history of twentieth-century architecture, revealing the beginnings of Modernism and the development from 1907, the influential 1920s to the present. Each object significant to us in this respect is depicted in a half-page-wide column. Arranged by object number (001 through 466), an accompanying image is shown for identification purposes, below which is either a ground plan or interior shot – the third dimension, as it were – as well as the project's title, construction period, location, architect, and client. This information is followed by a brief text which characterizes the object or places it within a specific context.

All the presented objects are arranged topologically. They follow a conceivable route, a route consistently developed from a prominent inner-city "Platz" or "square". There are 8 routes, 8 directions, and 8 "Plätze" (squares): for **N** (north) Pariser Platz, located in front of the Brandenburger Tor; for **NE** (north-east) Gendarmenmarkt; for **E** (east) Alexanderplatz; for **SE** (south-east) Mehringplatz, formerly the town gate in southern Berlin; for **S** (south) Potsdamer Platz; for **SW** (south-west) Lützowplatz; for **W** (west) Breitscheidplatz, near the Bahnhof Zoo; and for **NW** (north-west) Hansaplatz, located in front of the meanwhile 50-year-old city district Hansaviertel, where the **Interbau,** the first building exhibition after World War II, was held.

Presented in a list at the front of the book, these routes lead from the inner city toward regions on the outskirts, and toward respective districts on the periphery. The following page presents a stylized map of Berlin whose 8 sections appear, in turn, at the beginning of each route. In addition to the object numbers listed in both the map and the architect's specifications, the reader finds letters added as references to objects not depicted here.

An alphabetically arranged list at the back of the book names every featured architect, artist, and engineer, together with the respective object number. In conclusion, a second list names all the participating photographers and/or designers.

Because of its structure and both lists, this book not only functions as a guide but also as an easy to handle yet extensive reference work on Modern architecture of this century in Berlin. The opening text by Wolfgang Schäche describes the historical development of Modernism, the early beginnings and the turning away from Historicism, the radical breaks instigated by the Bauhaus in the twentieth century, the restrictive phase of fascism in the 1930s, the new start and postwar urban hostility in the 1950s, with the **Interbau** exhibition the building boom, the new self-awareness of the 1960s and 1970s, the large-scale building exhibition **IBA** with international participants in the 1980s, the end of the Communist regime, and ultimately the reunification of Berlin's two halves with newly conceived urban-planning guidelines put to use in the 1990s and at the beginning of the twenty-first century.

Hardly another city reveals so much history, so many breaks and new starts, to the extent that this one does; hardly another city possesses so much building history – or so rich a history of building.

Rolf Rave

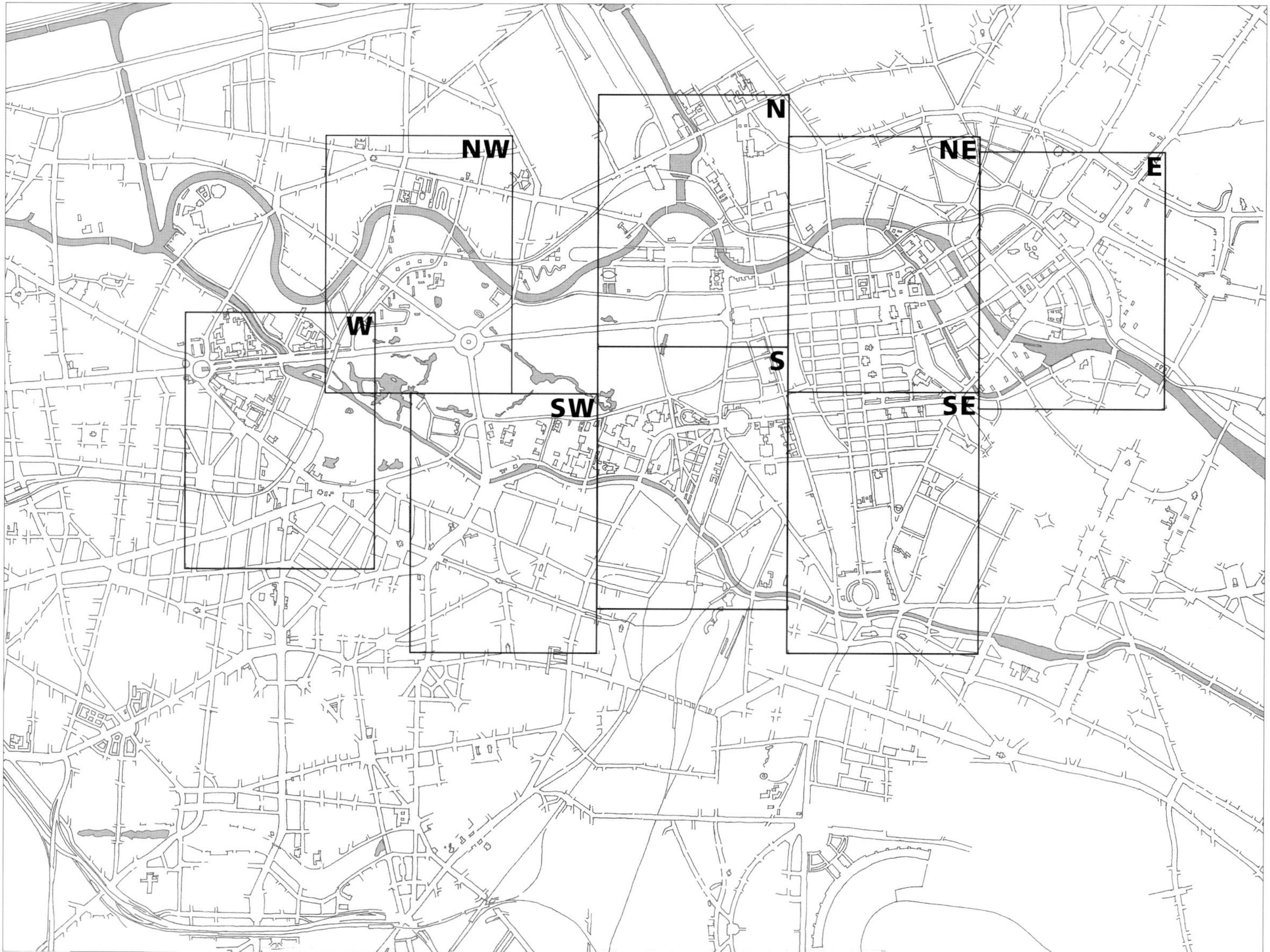
N
NW
NE
E
W
S
SW
SE

Each tour takes you from a midtown place in a different direction to the periphery of the city.

N Pariser Platz 001–061
North-east of Tiergarten, Wedding, north of Reinickendorf, Märkisches Viertel, Wittenau

NE Gendarmenmarkt 062–104
Spandauer Vorstadt, Prenzlauer Berg, Weißensee, Karow-Nord

E Alexanderplatz 105–128
Friedrichshain, Prenzlauer Berg, Lichtenberg

SE Mehringplatz 129–179
Südliche Friedrichstadt, Kreuzberg, Neukölln, Friedrichshain, Britz, Köpenick, Adlershof

S Potsdamer Platz 180–235
South-east of Tiergarten, Kreuzberg, Schöneberg, Tempelhof, Lichterfelde, Lankwitz, Buckow, Mariendorf

SW Lützowplatz 236–314
South-west of Tiergarten, Wilmersdorf, Steglitz, Dahlem, Grunewald, Zehlendorf, Wannsee

W Breitscheidplatz 315–410
Charlottenburg, Schöneberg, Westend, Siemensstadt, Gatow, Spandau

NW Hansaplatz 411–466
West of Tiergarten, Hansaviertel, Moabit, south of Reinickendorf, Wittenau, Borsigwalde, Tegel

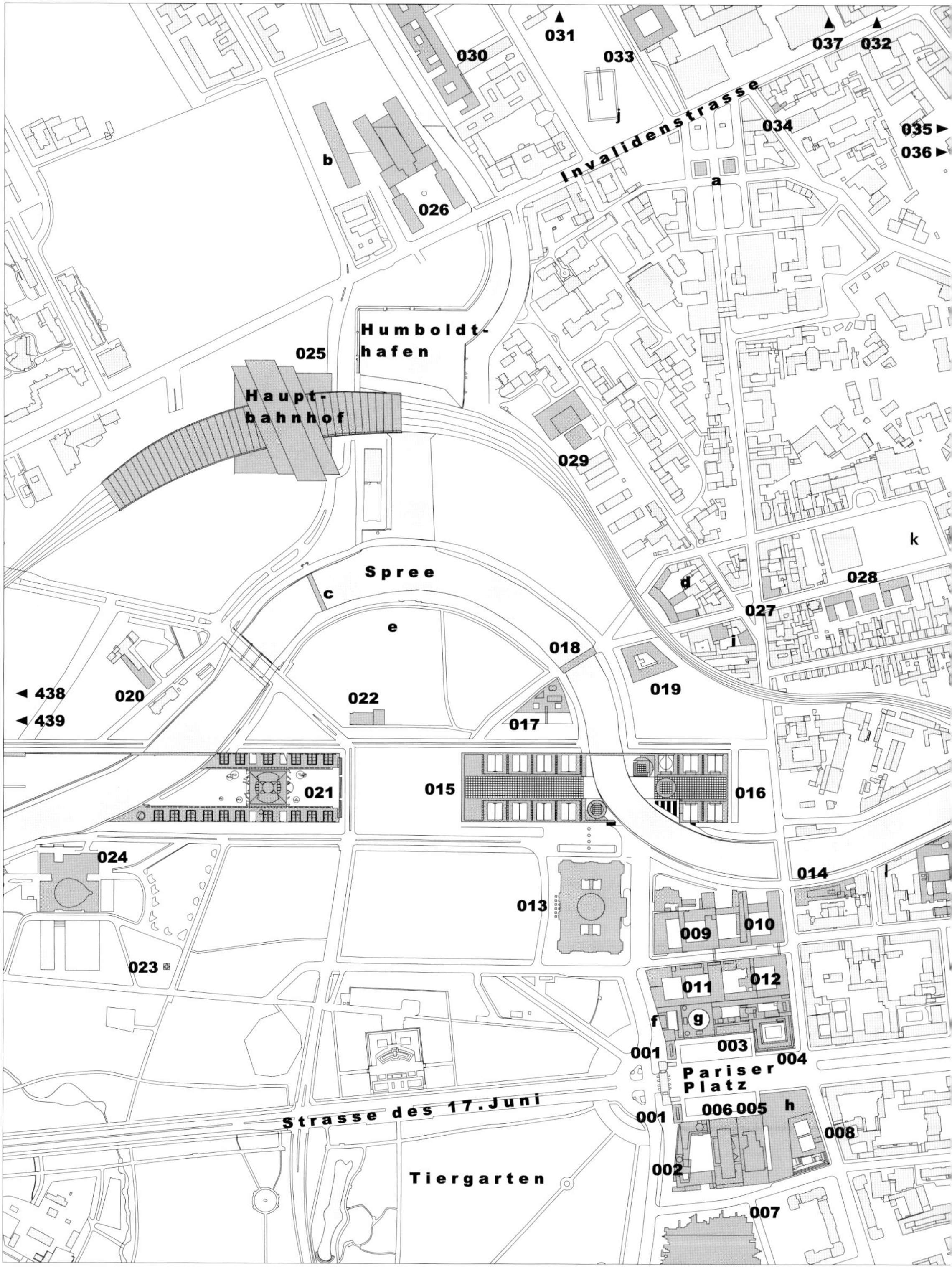
031
037
032
030
033
Invalidenstrasse
j
034
035
036
b
a
026
Humboldt-
hafen
025
Haupt-
bahnhof
029
k
Spree
c
d
028
027
e
i
018
019
438
439
020
022
017
021
015
016
024
014
013
009
010
023
011
012
f
g
001
003
004
Pariser
Platz
Strasse des 17. Juni
001
006
005
h
008
002
Tiergarten
007

Pariser Platz N

No.	Building	Architect
001	Haus Sommer / Haus Liebermann	Josef Paul Kleihues
002	Botschaft der USA	Moore Ruble Yudell
003	Französische Botschaft	Christian Portzamparc
004	Haus am Pariser Platz	Laurids Ortner, Manfred Ortner
005	Akademie der Künste	Günter Behnisch & Partner, Werner Durth
006	DG-Bank	Frank O. Gehry
007	Holocaust-Denkmal	Peter Eisenman, Richard Serra
008	Britische Botschaft	Michael Wilford
009	Jakob-Kaiser-Haus 1 and 2	Schweger Assoziierte
010	Jakob-Kaiser-Haus 3 and 7	Peter Busmann, Godfrid Haberer and others
011	Jakob-Kaiser-Haus 5 and 6	Pi de Bruijn, Peereboom Voller and others
012	Jakob-Kaiser-Haus 4 and 8	von Gerkan, Marg und Partner
013	Deutscher Bundestag	Foster + Partners
014	ARD Hauptstadtstudio	Laurids Ortner, Manfred Ortner
015	Paul-Löbe-Haus	Stephan Braunfels
016	Marie-Elisabeth-Lüders-Haus	Stephan Braunfels
017	Childcare center	Gustav Peichl, Rudolf Weber
018	Kronprinzenbrücke	Santiago Calatrava
019	Bundespressekonferenz	Gernot Nalbach, Johanne Nalbach
020	Fire and police station	Matthias Sauerbruch, Louisa Hutton
021	Bundeskanzleramt	Axel Schultes, Charlotte Frank
022	Schweizer Botschaft	Diener & Diener
023	Carillon	Bangert, Jansen, Scholz, Schultes
024	Kongreßhalle / Haus der Kulturen	Hugh A. Stubbins
025	Hauptbahnhof / Lehrter Bahnhof	von Gerkan, Marg und Partner
026	Museum für Gegenwartskunst im Hamburger Bahnhof	Josef Paul Kleihues
027	Haus am Karlsplatz	Walter A. Noebel
028	Residenz am Deutschen Theater	Krüger, Schubert, Vandreike, Bellmann, Böhm
029	Max-Plank-Institut	Hannelore Deubzer, Jürgen König
030	Bundesministerium für Wirtschaft und Technologie	Thomas Baumann
031	Bundeswehrkrankenhaus	Heinle, Wischer und Partner
032	New Media Center	Carlos Zwick
033	Bundesministerium für Verkehr, Bau- und Wohnungswesen	Max Dudler
034	bender/slender	Britta Jürgens, Matthew Griffin
035	Borsig-Areal	Hilde Léon, Konrad Wohlhage, Siegfried Wernik
036	Edison-Höfe	Manuel Alvarez
037	Kapelle der Versöhnung	Rudolf Reitermann, Peter Sassenroth
438	Kopfbau Spreeschlange	Jörg Pampe
439	Spreeschlange	Georg Bumiller

	Building	Architect
a	Torhäuser	Josef Paul Kleihues, 1996–98
b	Rieck-Hallen	Wilfried Kühn, 2004
c	Gustav-Heinemann-Steg	Max Dudler, 2005
d	Kronprinzenkarrée	nps tchoban voss, 2004/05
e	Spreebogenpark	Sauerer & Weber
f	Business premises	Bernhard Winking, 1996/97
g	Dresdner Bank	von Gerkan, Marg und Partner, 1996/97
h	Hotel Adlon	Patzschke, Klotz & Partner, 1995–97
i	Filling a building gap	Claus Kampmann, Rudolf Fiedler
j	Garten der Geschichte	Frédéric Giròt
k	Sammlung Boros	Karl Bonatz, 1942; Jens Caspar, Petra Petersohn 2005–08
l	Bundespresseamt	Engel, Zimmermann, 1996–2000

001

Haus Sommer

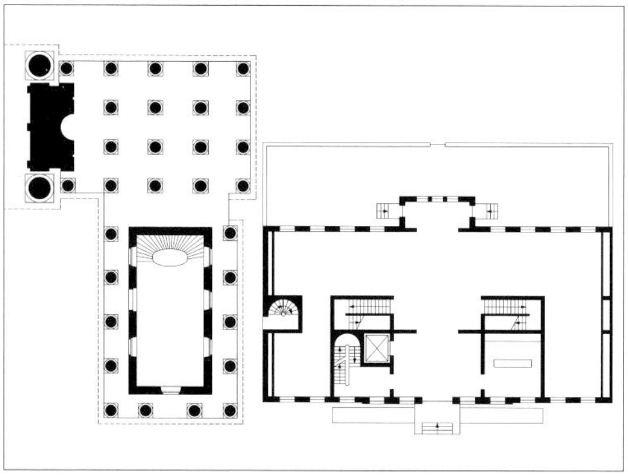

Plan of the ground floor of Haus Liebermann

Haus Sommer / Haus Liebermann
1995–99
Mitte, Pariser Platz 1 and 7
Architect: Josef Paul Kleihues
Client: Harald Quandt Grundbesitz

Originally built from 1788 to 1791 as lateral extensions of the Brandenburg Gate by Carl Gotthard Langhans, both new buildings reflect less the details and more the style of their historic classical models, which celebrate clearly designed and subdivided white structures. Today the "houses" no longer serve any residential purposes and function solely as representational and exhibition spaces. The indexed quote of both loggia was first inserted during a second building phase.

002

South-west side

Detail of the rotonda

Botschaft der USA
Embassy of the United States
2004–07, draft 1996
Mitte, Pariser Platz 2
Architects: Moore Ruble Yudell
Management: Overseas Buildings Operations

Following the complete destruction of the passed-down property (formerly Palais Blücher) purchased by the United States in 1931, a significant location for the American presence was created here. In the sense of ensuring the greatest possible security, the general planning was greatly delayed by 9/11 issues. Yet the building's inherent openness is fully guaranteed for its visitors: the entrance offers itself on Pariser Platz, the public square it faces; the grand inner-courtyard has a garden on two levels; and the three orientating sides (toward the square, city park, and Jewish memorial) are differently designed. The same applies to the construction of the rooftop elements crowned by a dome which, visible in the west, creates a strong reference to the rotonda of the Reichstag building **(013)**.

003

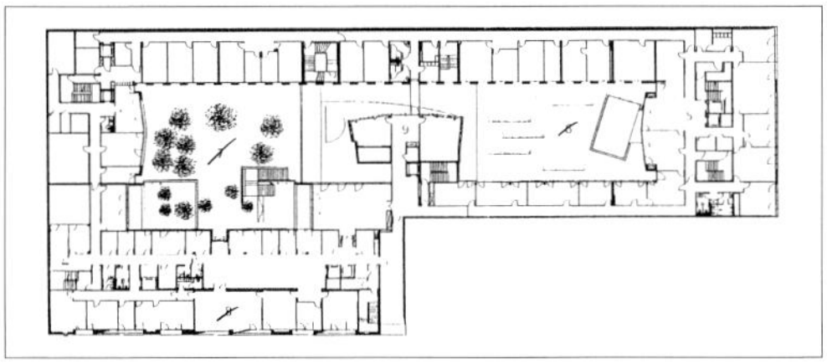

Plan of the ground floor

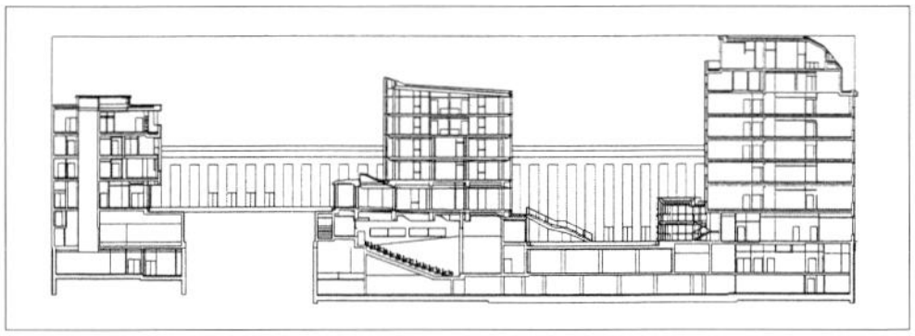

Longitudinal section

Französische Botschaft
French Embassy
1998–2002
Mitte, Pariser Platz 5
Architect: Christian Portzamparc
General planning: Steffen Lehmann
Client: The French Republic

The former building acquired by Napoleon III in 1860 for the French legation, today the building's playful and highly expressive façade also portrays France as a modern and liberal state while perhaps disrupting the homogeneity of the immediate space. The arrangement of its building parts – from offices, residential chambers, a consulate for altogether 200 employees spanning two courtyards, to the "English courtyard" and sunken "sculpture courtyard" – occupies 7 floors and reaches as far as the Wilhelmstraße.

004

Haus am Pariser Platz
1998–2001
Mitte, Unter den Linden 80
Architects: Laurids Ortner, Manfred Ortner
Client: Allgemeine Beteiligungs- + Gewerbeimmobilien Verwaltungs GmbH + Co

The basement storey of this residential and office building contains a large social space, the ground floor houses smaller shops, and the five upper floors accommodate office spaces. In the roof section are apartments with arcades, and included for their lighting are conspicuously tall battlement-like dormer windows. At this spot, the noble aura of the Trosselfeld travertine, tin-plated sheet-copper roof, and bronze fittings of the wooden windows justly compares with the representative Hotel Adlon (the brothers Patschke), and with the neighboring structure on the right (Hans Kollhoff).

005

North façade

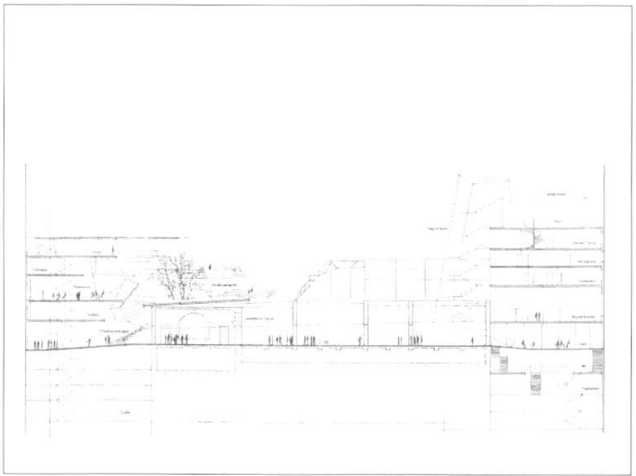

North–south cross section

Akademie der Künste
Academy of arts
1999–2002
Mitte, Pariser Platz 4
Architects: Günter Behnisch & Partner with Werner Durth, Ruth Berkthold and Franz Harder
Client: Akademie der Künste

The result of a 1994 in-house competition announced by the academy of arts, the building was erected where the academy's original building, 1905–07 by Ernst von Ihne stood, and incorporates the preserved exhibition hall with skylight. The new building respects the rigidity of the site's border. While spreading out in its depths as far as Behrenstraße, its open and transparent aspect is sustained throughout all its parts: foyer, exhibition hall, administration area, café, sun lounge, assembly hall, club rooms, sculpture garden, and basement storage areas. A financially tight spot could be alleviated by having the south wing taken over by the Hotel Adlon.

006

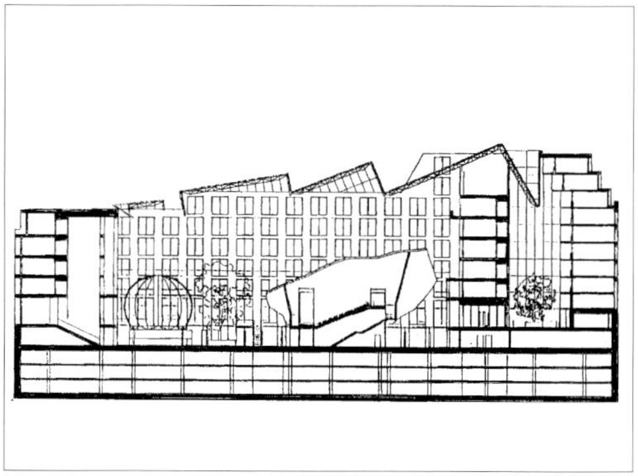

Longitudinal section

DG-Bank
1996–2000
Mitte, Pariser Platz 3
Architect: Frank O. Gehry
Client: DG-Bank

Viewed from its north façade facing the square, which Gehry himself refers to as an "urban backdrop", the building shows itself from a highly disciplined side, and displays the usual command of form and detail. Housing 40 apartments, its south side is divided from the main wing of the Deutschen Genossenschaftsbank (DG-Bank) by a large atrium with a conference hall inserted under glazed sheds and reflects, at the same time, the sculptor's well-known and computer-supported virtuosity.

007

Stele field with view of Potsdamer Platz

Holocaust-Denkmal
Memorial site of the Holocaust
2001/2002
Mitte, Ebertstraße at the corner of Behrenstraße
Architect: Peter Eisenman in collaboration with Richard Serra
Initiator: Lea Rosh
Exhibition design: Dagmar von Wilcken
Client: Stiftung Holocaust-Denkmal

On the occasion of a 1994/95 international competition, the call was made for proposals by artists and architects for creating a memorial site dedicated to the Holocaust. The submissions intended for this prominent site were examined from the standpoints of their adaptability and possible effects. In 1997, emerging from a second competition round with 7 participants, and from a series of subsequent revisions, as well as accompanied by the theoretical contributions of renowned personalities, the memorial site took on a clear form and is meanwhile a very impressive location for the people of the whole world.

008

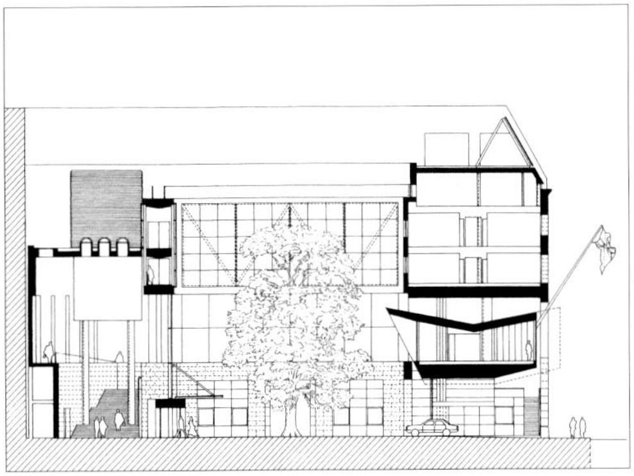

Cross section

Britische Botschaft
British Embassy
1998–2000
Mitte, Wilhelmstraße 70/71
Architect: Michael Wilford
Wall design: David Tremlett
Dancing columns: Tony Cragg
Client: Bilfinger und Berger / ARTEOS

Built at an historic site, the newly-built British Embassy interrupts the conventional building line both three-dimensionally and colorfully. It offers glimpses into the garden courtyard with an English oak tree. Behind this stands the "grand staircase", connecting the main level to the spacious "wintergarten" (sun lounge), conference room, and library. The architecture's large and energetic forms communicate with magnificent wall designs and sculptures. The actual world of the embassy's administration first commences on the 5th floor.

009

010

Courtyard toward the Spree River with artwork by Dani Karavan

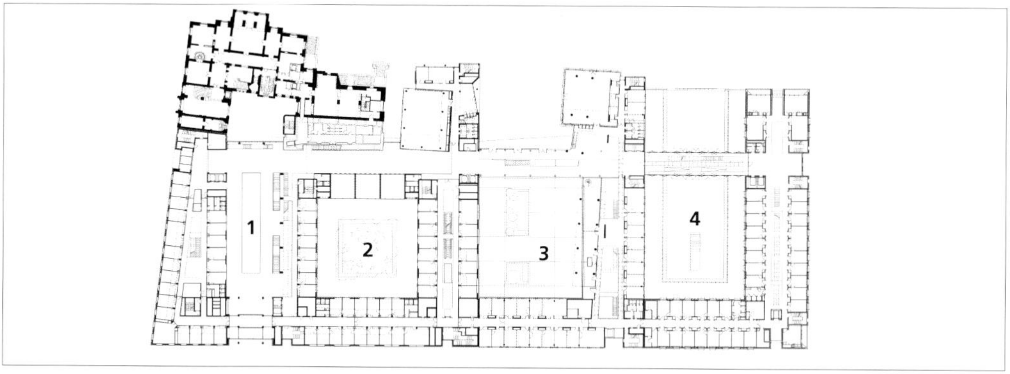

Northern street-border development

Jakob-Kaiser-Haus 1 and 2
1998–2002
Mitte, Dorotheenstraße 100
Architects: Schweger Assoziierte
Floating boats: Christiane Möbus

Standing nearest to the parliament building, but also in close proximity to the Palais of the Parliamentary President designed by Wallot in 1897, this building is the entree of the entire complex. On one floor it allows visitors access to all four connecting houses of the magistral seat. The arranged quarters for members of Parliament, located on both sides of Dorotheenstraße, are directly connected to the Bundestag (House of German Parliament) by way of a tunnel.

Jakob-Kaiser-Haus 3 and 7
1998–2002
Mitte, Dorotheenstraße 99
Architects: Busmann + Haberer with Alfred Bohl and Bruno Vennes
Artwork: Dani Karavan

In compliance with a general decision of the Berlin Senate's planning director, Hans Stimmann, unlike with the Paul-Löbe-Haus, the so-called "Dorotheen-Blocks", simultaneously used as offices for members of Parliament, were planned in unalike building units. What applied here, in the southern section of the complex, was to fully integrate the existing building structure. Its core formerly accommodated a venerable apartment building, and later a bank in the year 1910. Now, in order to attain a flourishing and successful ensemble effect, a brick sculpture was placed in front of one of the courtyard pediments.

011

012

"Sky ladders"

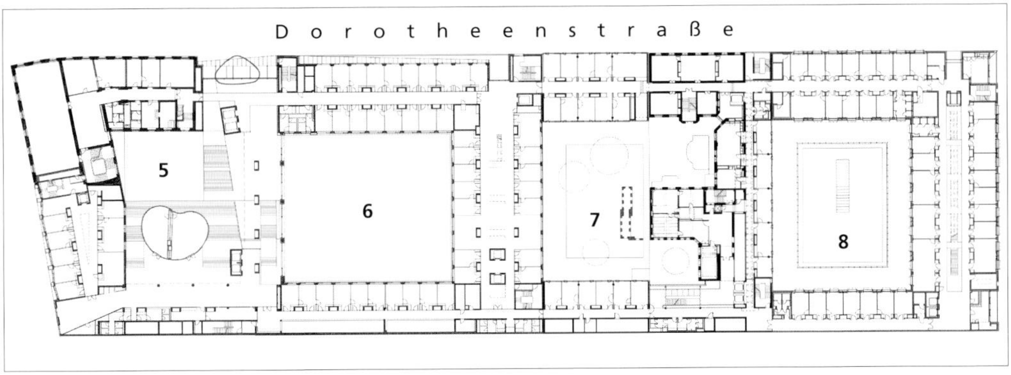

Southern street-border development

Jakob-Kaiser-Haus 5 and 6
1998–2002
Mitte, Dorotheenstraße at the corner of Ebertstraße
Architects: Pi de Bruijn, Jan Dirk, Peereboom Voller with Yushi Uehara
Project director: Marcel Campschroer
Client: Bundesbaugesellschaft Berlin

A second glazed skin not exactly following the building line gives the house a mysterious exterior. With finesse, this compositionally integrates the entire roof of a corner development devised for a building formerly the chamber of associated technicians in 1911. An access route from the building's west side was also developed here. This directs the visitor to a spacious foyer, which connects both structural rows by way of a cross-cut tunnel over the Dorotheenstraße.

Jakob-Kaiser-Haus 4 and 8
1998–2002
Mitte, Dorotheenstraße at the corner of Wilhelmstraße
Architects: von Gerkan, Marg und Partner with Hubert Nienhoff and Uwe Grahl
Project directors: Bernd Cossman, Henning Schlattmeier, and Beate King
Landscape planning: WES

On Wilhelmstraße, the building opens itself to the city. Located here are two shops, the Parliament's bookstore, and the visitor's entrance. In addition, a staircase the height of the building divides the two houses, which are connected by the second of two bridges, and the view extends as far as the Spreeufer. The garden courtyard is dramatically enriched by the erratic stone overhangs and rock formations arranged by Matthias Jackisch.

013

Deutscher Bundestag
House of German Parliament
1995–99
Tiergarten, Platz der Republik
Architects: Foster + Partners
Project management: Mark Braun
Client: Deutscher Bundestag

Emerging from numerous competition phases and the subsequent demand for a dome, the war-damaged Reichstag, designed from 1884 to 1894 by Paul Wallot, was cleansed of all its architectural detail work save the initials of its Russian conquerors. As early as the 1960s, Paul G. R. Baumgarten implanted the ascetic, parliamentary chambers in the building. The dome, somewhat lower than the one in Wallot's construction, both illuminates and ventilates the parliamentary chambers located directly below it – with two spiral ramps serving as the visitors' routes to and from the dome's interior.

014

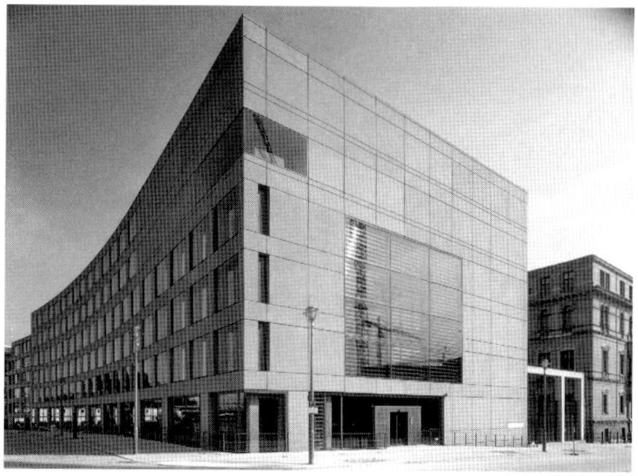

View of the north and west façades

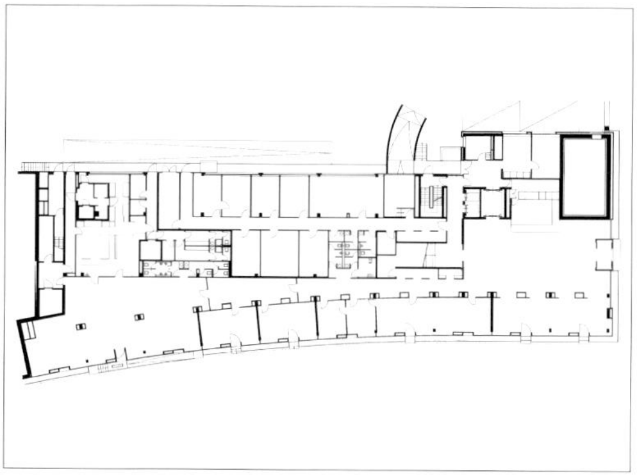

Plan of the ground floor

ARD-Hauptstadtstudio
Berlin studio of the ARD broadcasting network
1995–98
Mitte, Wilhelmstraße at the corner of Reichstagsufer
Architects: Laurids Ortner, Manfred Ortner, with Hans-Peter Wulf
Lighting design: Licht-Kunst-Licht
Client: SFB/WDR

The brick-red colored concrete panels dissipate in the foundation on Reichstagsufer and continue their path around the corner to incorporate a studio window flush with the façade, from which a direct view of the parliament is meanwhile obstructed by buildings. Opening from a tripled impost on the ground floor, a large glass-roofed staircase commences on the 1st floor.

015

Main hall

016

Façade facing the Spree River

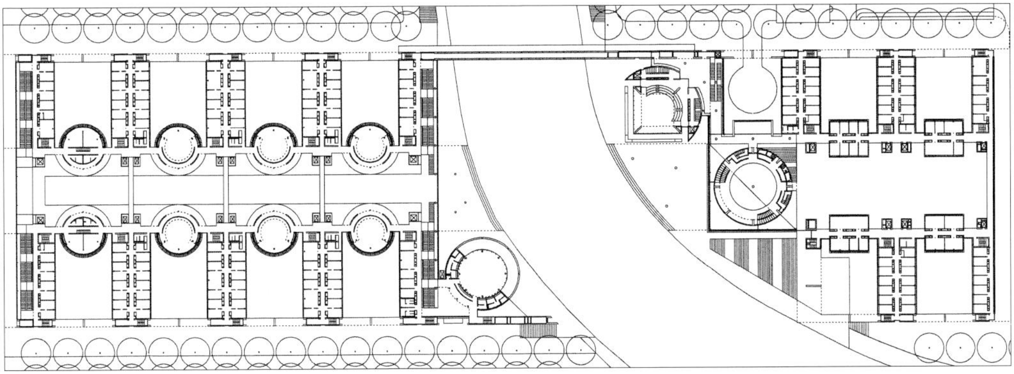

Plan of a standard floor showing both the houses left and right of the Spree River

Paul-Löbe-Haus
1997–2001
Tiergarten, Paul-Löbe-Allee 1
Architect: Stephan Braunfels
Project management: Günter Kaesbach, Philippe Vernin
Client: Bundesbaugesellschaft

Both building parts result from a 1994 competition. Their evident harmonizing also rests on their similar structural elements, for example their chamber-like floor plans and exposed concrete surfaces. By visually referring to the Federal Chancellery, they complete the "Band des Bundes" or "strip of national government structures" in an easterly direction. A street-level, glass-roofed main hall compiles all the design nuances leading to the building for the parliamentarians' offices. A detached restaurant and assembly hall (Eurosaal) are located on an open square – the so-called Spreebogen of the Spree River.

Marie-Elisabeth-Lüders-Haus
1998–2003
Mitte, Otto-von-Bismark-Allee 1
Architect: Stephan Braunfels
Project management: Karin Melcher, Ramsi Kusus, Philipp Jamwe
Client: Bundesbaugesellschaft

Connected with the building for the parliamentarians' offices (81,000 sqm for circa 276 million Euro) by a narrow bridge leading over the Spree River, the parliament's library (65,000 sqm for circa 170 million Euro) forms the east terminus of the Spreebogen. Also located here is the semi detached hearing room. As part of the "strip of national government structures", originally intended to find its center in a democratic forum, the relationship between the two buildings is further strengthened by large protruding roofs, under which lie the front steps to the square.

017

Childcare center
1998/99
Tiergarten, Konrad-Adenauer-Straße, Bismarck-allee
Architects: Gustav Peichl, Rudolf Weber
Client: Bundesbaugesellschaft

In an all-providing state like the Federal Republic of Germany is becoming – justifiably so – provisions are also made for working mothers by developing suitable childcare possibilities. With this objective in mind, the cheerful and carefree sky-blue triangle – a foreign species in its own right – effectively fills a spacious triangle of 3,635 sqm, magically created with yet another leap across the Spree River by the "strip of national government structures".

018

Guardrail detail

Kronprinzenbrücke
1997/98
Mitte, intersection of the Kapelle-Ufer and Schiffbauerdamm
Architect: Santiago Calatrava
Client: Brückenbauamt Berlin

Instead of his dome for the Reichstag, a bridge on the Spree River? This was by no means one of Calatrava's favorite projects – and posted among his international listing of successes, his Internet page describes it that way. Although the overall treatment of the bridge is impressive, the oversized guardrails closest to the river, and the primitive guardrail terminations at either end of the walkway harm the flow of energy throughout the construction's slender elements. Following Calatrava's contribution, farther down the river this is hardly the case with the new Gustav-Heinemann-Brücke by Max Dudler.

019

West façade

Bundespressekonferenz
Federal press conference
1998–2000
Mitte, Schiffbauerdamm at the corner of Reinhardtstraße
Architects: Gernot Nalbach, Johanne Nalbach
Courtyard garden: Cornelia Müller, Jan Wehberg
Client: Allianz Versicherung

The result of a competition: while on computer screens the building's wall surfaces appear to have reserved gray-blue tones, by day and by night its façade shimmers in the cityscape, a gleam with 5 different materials. On the 1st floor, the conference room takes on a special significance through prominently framed window sections. Intended as a meeting place for journalists, the restaurant is located at the building's ground-floor level. Floor area: 17,700 sqm; building costs: circa 51 million Euro.

020

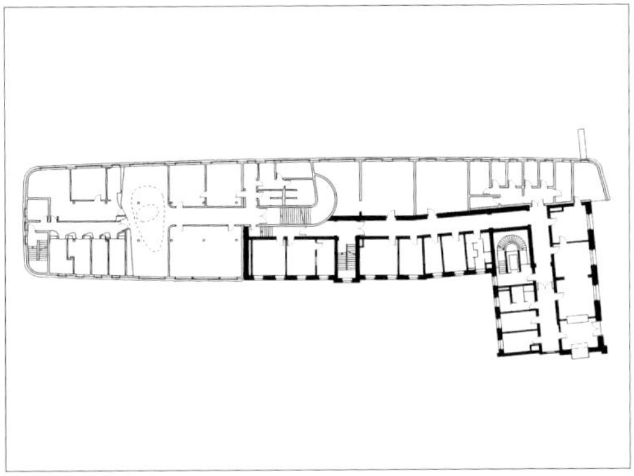

Plan of the 1st floor

Fire and police station
2002–04
Tiergarten, Alt-Moabit 143/145
Architects: Matthias Sauerbruch, Louisa Hutton
Client: Senatsverwaltung für Stadtentwicklung

At a former freight depot, the remains of a warehouse were both redesigned and structurally expanded with a longitudinal aisle whose outer skin consists of red (for the fire station) and green (for the police station) shimmering glass panels. Joined and curved, the panels not only reflect daylight; when interacting with artificial light, they also establish a relationship to the nearby Federal Chancellery similar to that of the Communs to the Neues Palais in Potsdam.

021

East façade

Central staircase

Bundeskanzleramt
Federal Chancellery
1995–2001
Tiergarten, Willy-Brandt-Straße 1
Architects: Axel Schultes, Charlotte Frank
Sculptures: Eduardo Chillida
Colored walls: Markus Lüpertz
Landscape: Cornelia Müller, Jan Wehberg
Structural engineers: GSE, Saar, Enseleit und Partner

The Federal Chancellery represents the completed portion of a 1993 east–westerly, urban planning competition in the "strip of national government structures". Developing westward, the H-shaped complex forms a courtyard garden extending over the Spree, and eastward a cour d'honneur. Its northern façade houses the actual entrance from which foyers, conference rooms, spaces for the press, a sky lobby, and the chancellor's apartment follow on 8 levels. Most of the office spaces are grouped on both flanks of the building around a "wintergarten" or sun lounge.

022

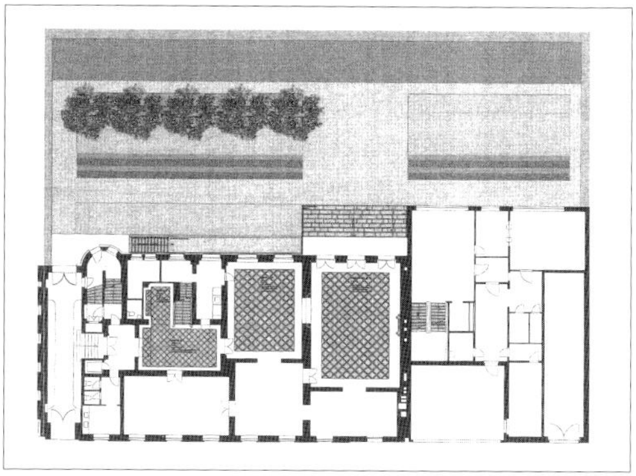

Plan of the ground floor

Schweizer Botschaft
Swiss Embassy
2000
Tiergarten, Otto-von-Bismarck-Allee 4
Architects: Diener & Diener
West pediment: Helmut Federle
Client: Bundesamt für Bauen und Logistik

Located for over five decades at a desolate spot, after the fall of the Berlin Wall the Swiss Embassy now stands in the immediate vicinity of the Federal Chancellery, in the heart of the government district, where it appears in a new splendor. The hypersensitive quality of the building's structural presence and form-related language – with extensions attached to the sides of its pediments – seems to almost shamefully rationalize its unique and unintentional position (costing 22 million Swiss francs).

023

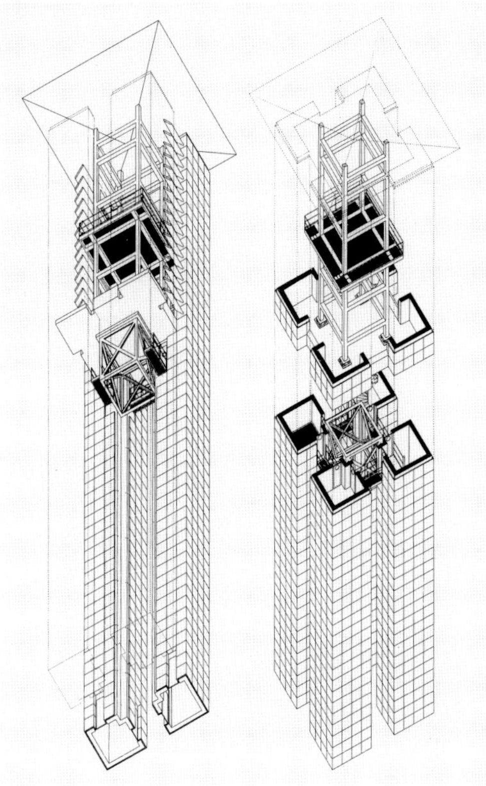

Carillon
1987
Tiergarten, John-Foster-Dulles-Allee at the corner of the Querallee
Architects: Bangert, Jansen, Scholz, Schultes
Client: Land Berlin

The decisive factor regarding this structure (the result of a group of short-listed competition contestants) was more so the expression of a musical instrument and not merely the designing of a tower. Financed by Mercedes and donated as a present on the occasion of the City of Berlin's 750th year celebrations, the bells were imported from Holland and the structure's concrete variants manufactured by Strabag Bau. Ranging from 8 kg to 7,8 tons, the Carillon's 68 bells, located above and below the control panel in the bell chamber, make it Europe's largest instrument. A computer stores up to 99 melodies for so-called everyday purposes.

024

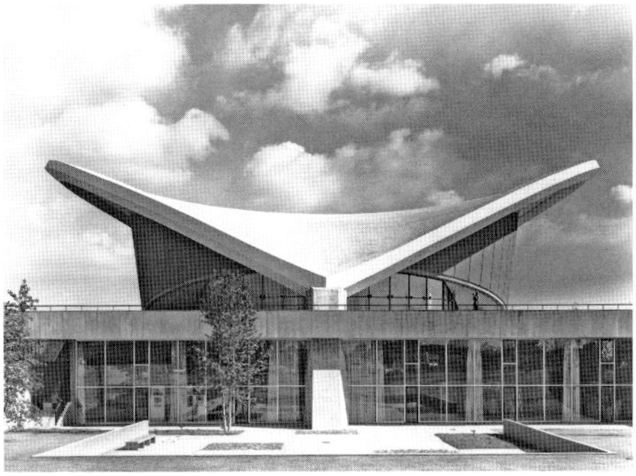

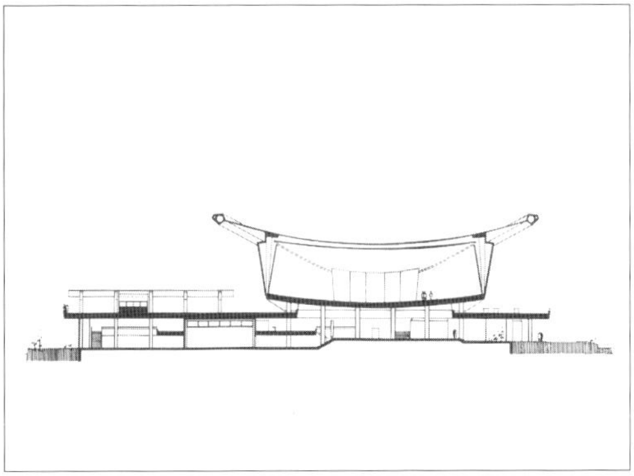

Cross section

Kongreßhalle – Haus der Kulturen
1958
Tiergarten, John-Foster-Dulles-Allee 10
Architect: Hugh A. Stubbins (Cambridge, Mass., USA)
Contact architects: Werner Düttmann, Franz Mocken
Client: Benjamin Franklin Foundation

The conspicuous roof construction seems suspended by a cable network and rests on only two vault abutments, serving as the stabilizing reinforcement and anchoring ring over the walls of the lecture hall, which dissolves as joined individual shells. Notwithstanding that a heavy concrete block crashed down – why ever – on 21 May 1980. The large auditorium seats 1,250 guests, and a smaller one offers seating for 400. The structure includes a conference hall, restaurant, and, located above the entranceway, a terraced staircase on a platform. Stubbins in former times was assistant of Walter Gropius.

025

Station roof

Hauptbahnhof / Lehrter Bahnhof
1998–2010
Tiergarten, Invalidenstraße
Architects: von Gerkan, Marg und Partner
Client: Deutsche Bahn

The station – rather a functional structure than architecture – is located where the war-destroyed station and the former municipal railway station originally stood. At the junction of the circle line and a new north–south underground connection, it creates a central hub in the form of two skyscraper segments imbued with a 430-m long platform area and 3 pairs of tracks. The station's roof is yet another step in the minimizing of support-free constructions made of steel and glass, with diagonally-arranged bottom chords flying outward from side supports. Unfortunately, for financial reasons the station's east terminus was decidedly shortened by 50 m.

026

Grand Gallery

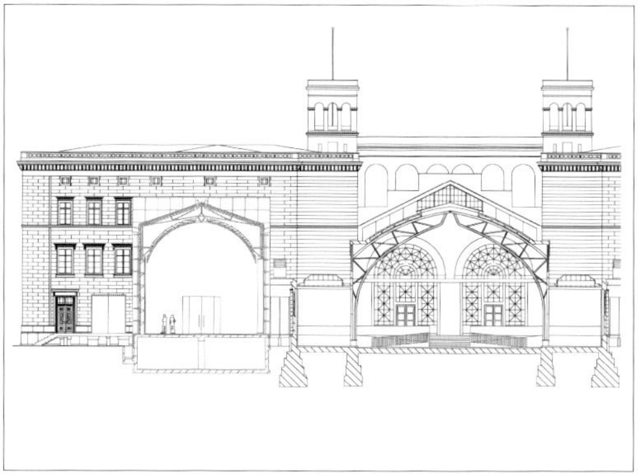

Cross section of the exhibition halls

Museum für Gegenwartskunst im Hamburger Bahnhof
1992–96
Tiergarten, Invalidenstraße 50–51
Architect: Josef Paul Kleihues
Project manager: Roger Karbe
Light object / entranceway front: Dan Flavin
Client: Senator für Bauen, Wohnen und Verkehr

This converted structure is the result of a limited competition process. Not long after its completion, the former train terminal was replaced by the Lehrter Bahnhof and rebuilt to a museum dedicated to transportation and technology. Through the sensitive treatment of its building substance, and by adding a "grand gallery", the resulting spatial offer proved multifaceted and multimedia-related enough for a "museum of contemporary art". Meanwhile – after restructuring the existing storage areas – the "Flick collection" as well enhances the museum's west side, designed by Johannes Kühn, Wilfried Kühn, Simona Malwezzi.

027

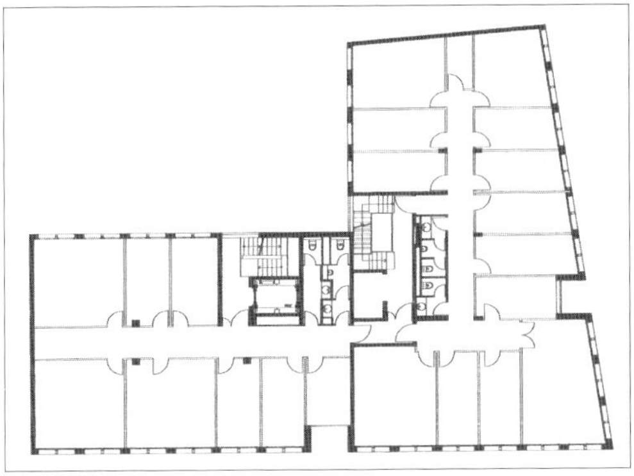

Plan of the 1st floor

Haus am Karlsplatz
1997/98
Mitte, Luisenstraße at the corner of Reinhardtstraße
Architect: Walter A. Noebel
Client: Bundesverband der Zementindustrie

Facing the Rudolf Virchow memorial statue by Fritz Klimsch, built from 1906 to 1910 and depicting *Titan conquering the Sphinx*, this building greatly accentuates the corner of the block. Through its structural division and staggered parts, it assumes a spot that compliments the finely detailed, urban scheme of the Luisenstadt quarter. The quarry-stone façade follows the principle of two levels in order to minimize the number of visible joints. The building's urban mix includes apartments, suites, and shops.

028

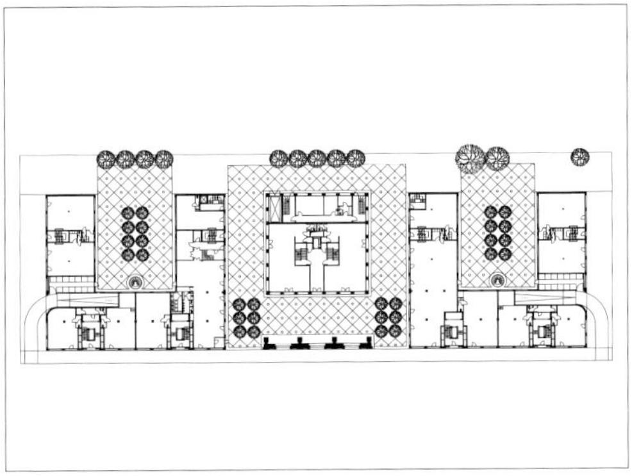

Plan of the ground floor

Residenz am Deutschen Theater
Residential premises at the Deutsches Theater
1993–99
Mitte, Reinhardtstraße 29
Architects: Torsten Krüger, Christian Schuberth, Bertram Vandreike; Götz Bellmann, Walter Böhm
Peripheral-space planning: Hans Loidl
Client: allbau GmbH

"In connection with the historic gate (from a former riding school), this diversely utilized complex – for residential and gastronomical purposes, as well as for public services and theater culture – creates here an enduring reflection of the multicultural lifestyle in the ambitious metropolis of Berlin." Two U-shaped residential buildings flank the recessed commercial cube, with a rehearsal stage for the Deutsches Theater. Together with the preserved gate, these help to produce an inviting, public space for a centralized site. The cube's significance is accentuated by horizontal wall bands made of metal.

029

View of the entrance side

Max-Planck-Institut
1998–2000
Mitte, Schumannstraße 21–22
Architects: Hannelore Deubzer, Jürgen König with Christa Kleine
Construction management in collaboration with Döpping Widell
Client: Max-Planck-Gesellschaft, Munich

On the main grounds of the Charité university hospital, the institute's building – also used by the German center for rheumatism research – encourages interdisciplinary collaborative work. The U-shaped construction is closed by an elaborately designed entrance hall made of red concrete blocks. Emerging from a 1994 competition, its design focuses on a long-term urban planning rearrangement meant to orient itself along existing axial references.

030

West façade

Attic-floor foyer

Bundesministerium für Wirtschaft und Technologie
1993–2000
Mitte, Scharnhorststraße 34–37
Architect: Thomas Baumann
Construction management: Dieter Schnittger
Landscape architects: Cornelia Müller, Elmar Knippschild, Jan Wehberg
Client: Ministerium für Bauen, Wohnen und Verkehr

Following severe destruction caused by war, the infirmary for the disabled was first the seat of the supreme court and later the government and diplomatic hospital. While establishing the concept for the greatest possible restoration of the structure – to accommodate 300 office spaces, conference rooms, a cafeteria, and printing works – traces of its different periods were preserved. Along the navigation canal in Spandau, the large and encompassing saddle roof, with its photovoltaic panels, forms part of a lighting and illumination concept.

031

Lobby

Bundeswehrkrankenhaus Berlin
Berlin army hospital
1997/98
Mitte, Scharnhorststraße 13
Architects: Heinle, Wischer und Partner; responsible partner: Christian Pelzeter
Client: Bundesbauamt Berlin III

"Incorporated into the spatial concept together with the first two floors of the original building substance, the new building creates a functional unity and leads to a separating of the areas for inpatients and outpatients. The new lobby is defined itself as the connecting element between the public space and hospital, and functions as the service center for patients and employees."

032

New Media Center
1998
Mitte, Chausseestraße 8, Novalisstraße 11
Architect: Carlos Zwick
Client: 1. GCN

Apart from the new building on Chausseestraße and different parts of the original structure, the project concerns the hall of a former locomotive manufacturer **(035)**. With foldable shading elements, the lattice units of the new building change the face of the façade, contrasting its wood and glass sections.

033

Inner courtyard

Bundesministerium für Verkehr, Bau- und Wohnungswesen
1997–99; old building, 2000
Mitte, Invalidenstraße 44
Architect: Max Dudler with Christian Bernrieder
General planning for old building (until 1998): Gerber Architekten
Client: Bundesamt für Bauwesen und Raumordnung

Following a 1996 competition, it was decided that the building formerly the "Geologische Landesanstalt" and "Bergakademie" (built by August Tiede from 1875 to 1878) would receive two structural additions. The larger of the two is already completed. Rising over a base, the clear lines of a skeletally-structured cube of gray-green trade granite is closed by an elaborate casement window of black anodized aluminum. It satisfies the demands for the spatial atmosphere and acoustics while inserting itself at the top floor. A glass-roofed courtyard houses 3 meeting rooms; the basement area accommodates 88 parking spaces.

034

bender/slender
2003/04
Mitte, Hessische Straße 5
Architects: Britta Jürgens, Matthew Griffin
Client: Jürgens, Jürgens, Griffin

In the immediate vicinity of the "Platz vor neuem Tor", where two cubes by Josef Paul Kleihues celebrate symmetry, the aluminum strip of a diagonally protruding bar of office and studio spaces devilishly interrupts the building line: "Bender strives for the future, and incorporates the past in dialogue with itsneighbors." A maisonnette apartment lies "slender" on the neighboring side wing. In any case: the harmonizing of client and architect gives birth to fantasy.

035

Site plan

Borsig-Areal
2000–03
Mitte, Chausseestraße at the corner of Schlegelstraße
Architects: Hilde Léon, Konrad Wohlhage, Siegfried Wernik
Client: Versorgungswerk der Zahnärztekammer

Before the former gates to the city, the only preserved element of the historic Borsig Werke facilities **(456 to 459)** is the carefully restored administrative building, while the block edge development connects with an existing apartment building, engaging in an interplay of Modern modules, floor-height French doors, and quarry stone slabs. The block becomes realigned through a new pattern continued by way of the façade's painted coat.

036

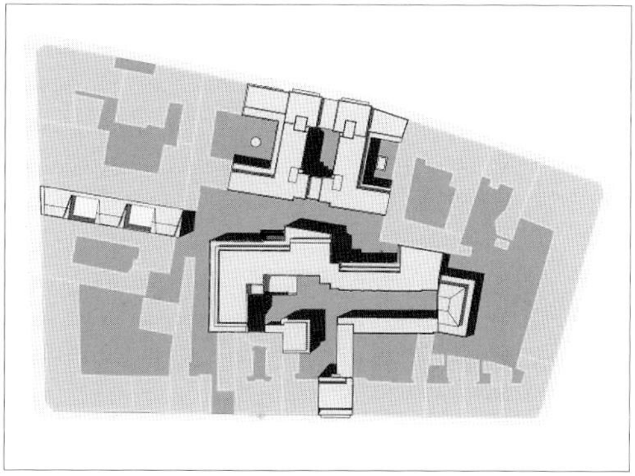

Site plan

Edison-Höfe
2002–05
Mitte, Schlegelstraße 26, Chausseestraße 18, Invalidenstraße 116–119
Architect: Manuel Alvarez
Client: HAVIKA Lofthouse

Apart from developing and reutilizing individual houses, in this case rehabilitating a block also means producing a coherent, block-integrated, and connecting network, which utilizes the existing courts and passageways in order to gain access to every spatial possibility for the presentation of exhibitions and events – like the "Design May 2005" cultural event.

037

"Oscillating field"

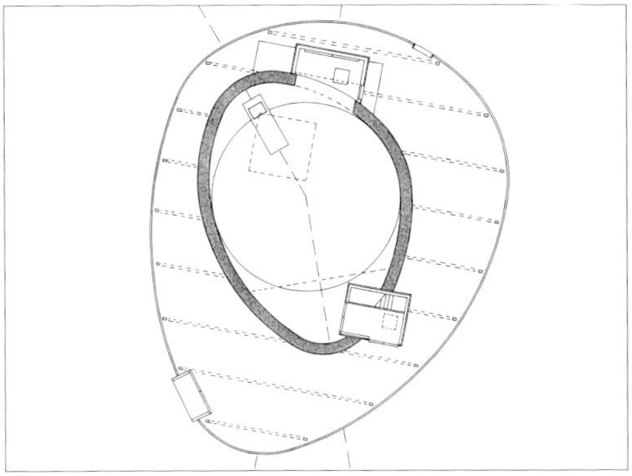

Plan of the ground floor

Kapelle der Versöhnung
Chapel of reconciliation
1999/2000
Mitte, Bernauer Straße at the corner of Hussitenstraße
Architects: Rudolf Reitermann, Peter Sassenroth
Loam construction: Martin Rauch
Client: Ev. Versöhnungsgemeinde

This new place of worship was built at a spot along the so-called "death strip" abutting the former Berlin Wall, where a church of conciliation was demolished in 1985. The chapel is a massive, egg-shaped space formed by a 60-cm-thick loam wall, and surrounded by a second skin – to which the roof also belongs – contained within a light, wooden construction. Both related forms – though differently perceived structural bodies – draw their intensity from the "oscillating field" that develops between them.

038

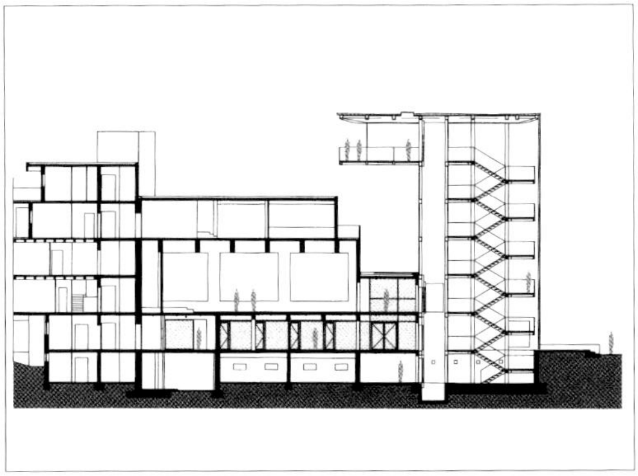

Section

Dokumentationszentrum Berliner Mauer
The Berlin Wall documentation center
2002/03
Mitte, Bernauer Straße 111
Architects: Andreas Zerr, Klaus Nieländer, Peter Hopka
Mirrored wall: Sven Kohlhoff, Claudia Kohlhoff

Regarding the fall of the Berlin Wall, many feel the desire for normalcy was fulfilled too quickly and too generally. Here a completely preserved portion of the Wall with "death strip and watchtower", among other pertinent details, can be viewed from the height of the visitors' platform and perceived as an annotated time period – like in the exhibition spaces of this former community center.

039

Reception hall – CAD model

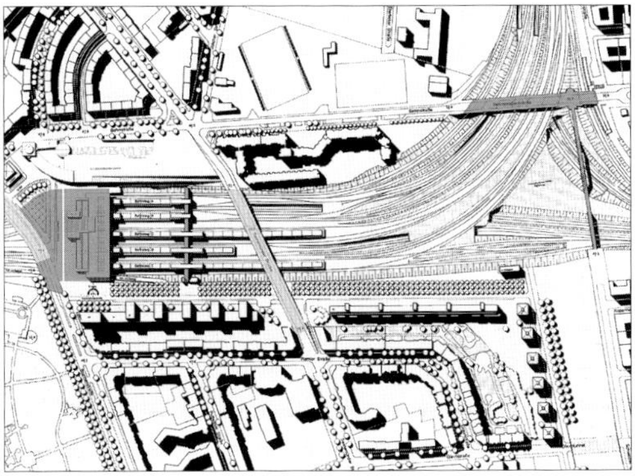

Site plan

Bahnhof Gesundbrunnen
Gesundbrunnen train station
1998–2002 / phase 3, 2006
Wedding, Badstraße/Brunnenstraße
Architects: Ingrid Hentschel, Axel Oestreich
Client: Deutsche Bahn

With its hub function for long-distance ICE and regional trains, as well as for suburban railway and underground lines, the train station at the Berliner Ring's new north–south crossing takes on a greater significance through the city's new north–south line. The street-level reception area provides for utter clarity with its 8-m tall glazing. Further structural connections include an access bridge and a tunnel to the U-Bahn platforms. The station's grounds cross a pedestrians' footbridge by the same architects.

040

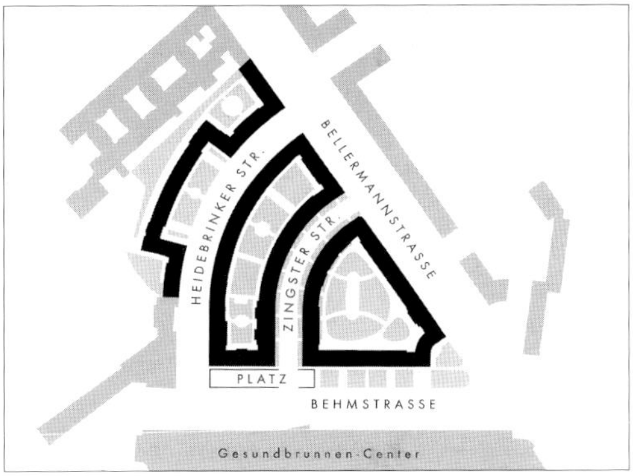

Site plan

Gartenstadt Atlantic
Atlantic garden city
1925–29
Gesundbrunnen, Behmstraße / Bellermannstraße
Architect: Rudolf Fränkel
Phantom Lichtburg: Benita Braun-Feldweg
Client: Atlantic AG / Karl Wolffsohn

The term "garden city" derives from a nineteenth-century ecological and social concept. In this case, it stands for a self-contained and health-conscious city district offering large open spaces alongside the district's metropolitan qualities. This made it possible to also create in the neighborhood a variety of commercial spaces, dance clubs, and what had been Berlin's largest movie theater, the so-called "Lichtburg". Temporarily rebuilt after the war, today this area serves as a shopping mall. From 2004 to 2006, however, the area devoted to living spaces was renovated with great charm by the architects Benita Braun-Feldweg and Matthias Muffert, who incorporated decorative details and color schemes in keeping with the previous period.

041

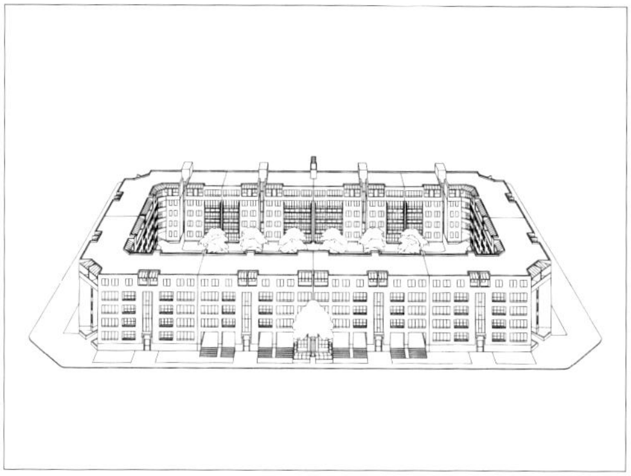

Perspective drawing

SWB Block 270
1971–76
Wedding, Vineplatz, Bernauer Straße and Wolliner Straße
Architect: Josef Paul Kleihues with Manfred Schonlau
Client: Degewo

The new building of this block is located on the old block perimeter and represents the first valid attempt since the war to create an homogenous, block-system plan. This is also what makes it a model structure for the urban renewal measures 20 years later. The length and lateral direction of the 5-storey block are exact reflections of one another. The building's red-toned exposed masonry is enhanced by wooden windows painted white, whose consistent size calm the façade. Positioned diagonal to the corners are large passageways leading to a partially public, interior courtyard area with greenery, where stairwells and elevator connections (at the entranceways) lead to the street, interior courtyard area, and underground garage.

042

Factory for small engines

High-voltage transmission facility

High-voltage transmission facility, assembly hall, and production factory for small engines of AEG
1910–12
Wedding, Hussiten-, Volta-, Brunnenstraße
Architect: Peter Behrens

The high-voltage transmission facility, the first structure built on the grounds at Humboldhain, consists of a large production factory and two 5-storey flanking wings serving as workshops and storage areas for materials, with a building part for office spaces connected at the east side. Erected as a reinforced concrete construction, the 120-m long and 70-m wide edifice is lined with handmade brick and iron clinker units. In 1911, with a projected length of 196 m, the production factory for small engines was completed as a corner development on Voltastraße. Its powerful, vertical subdividing develops in units, each of which has 8 axes. The last facility part, the assembly hall, is a three-hinged steel construction located on Hussitenstraße.

043

044

Mediaport

Brunnenstraße – tower spires

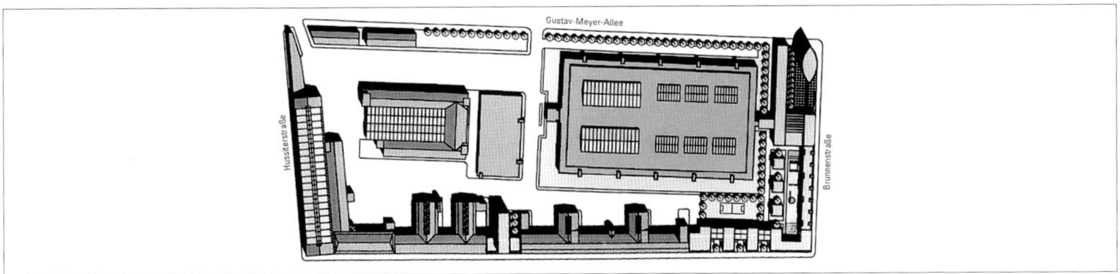

Site plan

Media Port Berlin
1994–96
Wedding, Voltastraße 6
Architect: Josef Paul Kleihues
Project manager: Andreas Hempel
Client: Media Port Berlin

During the firm of AEG's converting of the entire block into an industrial location based in northern Berlin, and its transformation into a modern "new media" location, a wide range of factory spaces were made available and restructured. The main emphasis was placed on a 12-storey skyscraper with two building parts that stand in contrast to the existing halls, as with the part that faces south – formerly a factory designed by Peter Behrens for manufacturing small motors **(042)**.

Block 240
1995/96
Wedding, Brunnenstraße at the corner of Voltastraße
Architect: Josef Paul Kleihues
Project manager: Michael Alshut
Client: Bavaria

At the corner to Gustav-Meyer-Allee, near the old entrance gate, stands a second, equally tall and ellipsoidal building. While accentuating the Brunnenstraße entranceway, its development houses 6 floors of residential spaces and, at Voltastraße, consolidates to 3 solitary structures in a comb-like arrangement in the courtyard along Brunnenstraße.

045

Education and research building
1990–97
Wedding, Augustenburger Platz 1, Seestraße
Architects: Hannelore Deubzer, Jürgen König; preliminary planning with Volker Cornelius
Awarded the 1996 architecture prize of the BDA Berlin

Built from 1899 to 1906, the clear and functional arrangement of the pavilion facility of the Rudolph-Virchow-Krankenhaus, designed by Ludwig Hoffmann, was typical for structures of that period. After as many as four of its ward blocks were torn down, along the middle of the thoroughfare the new buildings emerging from a 1987 competition provided the additional facilities for a university campus. With character, these satisfy the complex, instructional and research programs behind a well-ordered, curved construction made of gray precast concrete.

046

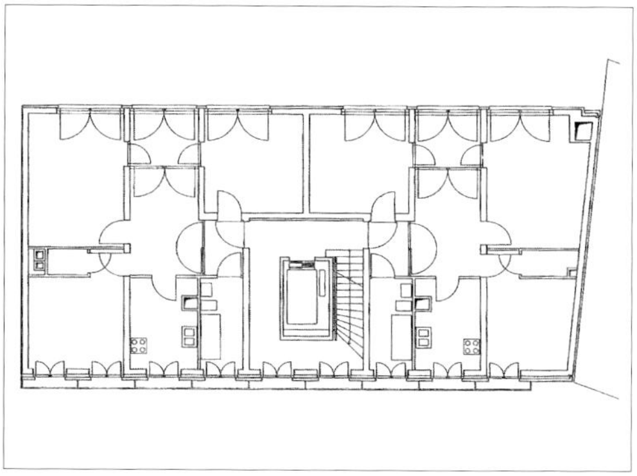

Plan of a standard floor

Apartment building
1994/95
Wedding, Drontheimer Straße 26, 23
Architects: Hans Kollhoff, Helga Timmermann
Project manager: Oda Pälmke
Client: DeGeWo

The building closes a constructional gap. The left pediment accommodates a passageway to a children's daycare center in the rear, and the right the entranceway to a underground garage. Apart from these openings, the building's middle part offers entranceways to the apartment house, and to shops enlivening the ground floor. Included are 2 semi-detached dwellings, each housing 13 apartments on 6 upper floors. Their stereotypical French doors facing the street hardly divulge the different, conventional services: bedrooms, kitchens, bathroom facilities, and staircases.

Buildings by Peter Mebes and Paul Emmerich

Buildings by Ludwig Mies van der Rohe of 1926/27

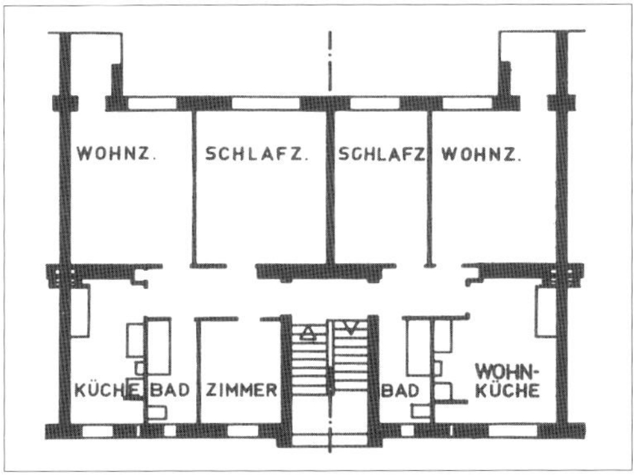

Floor plan of 2 and 2 1/2 room apartments

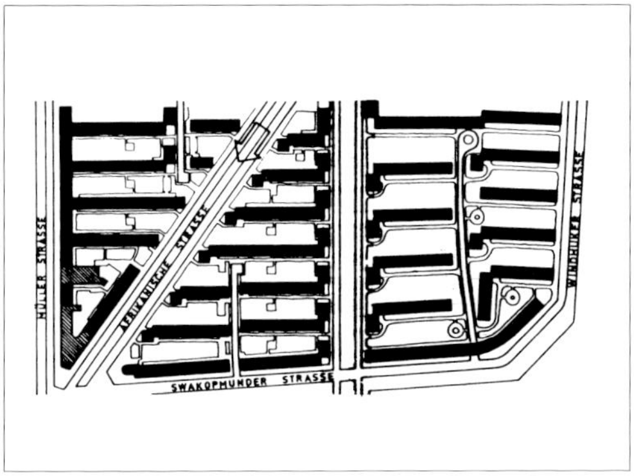

Site plan

Friedrich-Ebert-Siedlung
1910–12/1929–31
Wedding, Müllerstraße, Afrikanische Straße, Swakopmunder Straße
Architects: Peter Mebes, Paul Emmerich, Bruno Taut
Small-scale apartments: Mies von der Rohe
Client: "Eintracht" Wohnungsbau AG

Not only does this represent one of the earliest examples of row housing in Berlin, but also Mies' sole project in the area of social housing construction. Regarding its general approach, this development in the residential district Wedding greatly differs from Mies' villa-related and high-rise projects. What seems to be missing here is the sense of innovation and the cool elegance that the master architect endowed the Weißenhof housing colony in Stuttgart with. The floor plans of these 1- to 3-room apartments are conventional for a public housing development of this period. Because of the differently formatted windows kept flush with the walls, the design of the simple plastered façades remains reserved and pleasing. The four row structures are connected along the street by corner structures. Small apartments are housed in 4-storey row structures whose adjoining courtyards interconnect by footpaths, optically continue over bordering side-streets, and terminate at 1-storey commercial tract on Müllerstraße. The names of the streets give the quarter its nickname: "African quarter".

Very near in the Bristolstraße you will find the small settlement Schillerpark by Bruno Taut **(450)** in his expression total different.

048

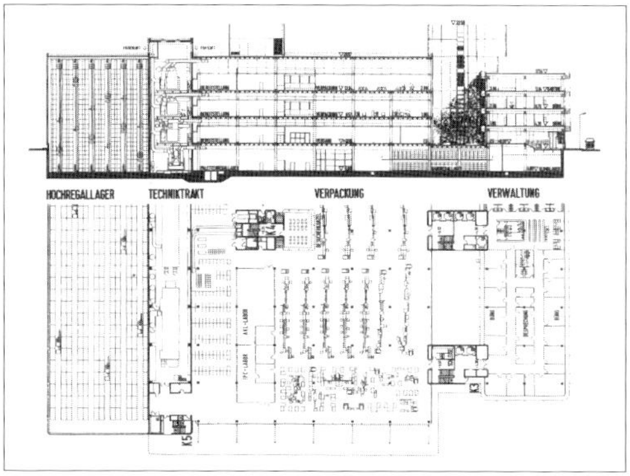

Cross section and partial plan of the 1st floor

Schering central packaging and services
1971–75
Wedding, Fennstraße 22–31
Architects: Klaus Hendel, Horst Haseloff, Wolfgang Hotzel
Client: Schering AG

Subdivided according to the concern's four functional areas, the building complex offers a social and administrative wing, a production wing, a wing for in-house technology, and a high-bay warehouse. The choice of materials, color, and furnishings were coordinated from the standpoint of their aesthetic aspects in order to achieve the concern's expressed goal – to create here a "humane factory". Evolved from the pharmacy of Ernst Christian Friedrich Schering in 1851, the pharmaceutical concern survived both World Wars and, despite tremendous damages, continually expanded. Even when major industry left the capital, Schering survived West Berlin's blockade period of 1948/49.

049

Hall on the 1st floor

Schering administration building
1970–78 (three building phases)
Wedding, Müllerstraße 175–181, Fennstraße
Architects: Kiemle, Kreidt and Partner
Design: Dietrich Kolb, Reinhardt Steinweg
In-house technology: Schmidt Reuter Partner Ingenieurgesellschaft für technische Gesamtplanung
Supervision: Herbert W. Kapitzki
Client: Schering AG

Result of an competition in 1968. "As a 'strip', the building stands in front of Schering's research and production facilities. Together with a pedestrian zone, four floors of offices bridge Fennstraße. To achieve a spatial expansion, the bulk of the main building is recessed. Support-free floors of office spaces, secured by the entire building depth and flush in three directions, allow for individual or service rooms when needed."

050

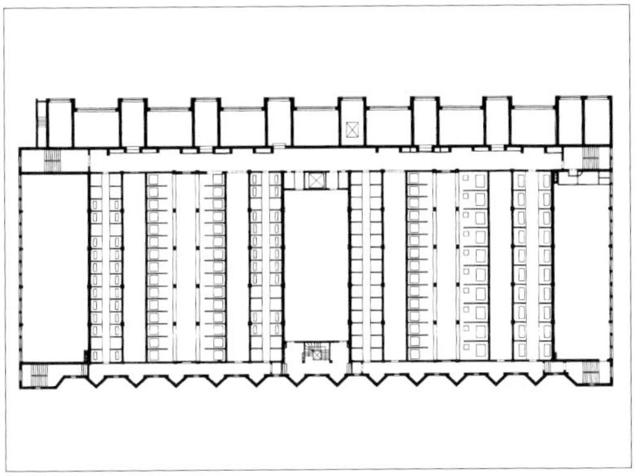

Plan of a standard floor

Scharnhorst transformer station
1928
Wedding, Fennstraße / Am Nordhafen
Architect: Hans Heinrich Müller
Client: Berliner Städtische Elektrizitätswerke

What can nowadays be handled by most small appliances had to be handled by so-called "Abspannwerke" or transformer stations in the 1920s – the downgrading of high-voltage electricity for household use. Müller knew how to give form to more than 40 facilities of this type without overlooking their location and function. For this building, he folds the expansive surfaces of the southern longitudinal wall and gives the industrial structure a certain degree of majesty by incorporating a temple-like architecture with rows of pillars. Today a vivid imagination is needed to arrive at ways of utilizing the empty, structural shells of old buildings – examples of this being the Metahaus **(341)**, or the Vitra Design Museum on Kopenhagener Straße, both planned by Paul and Petra Kahlfeldt.

051

Bibliothek am Luisenbad
Library at the Luisenbad
1992–95
Wedding, Travemünder Straße 2
Architects: Rebecca Chestnutt, Robert Niess
Structural engineer: Manfred Manleitner
Architecture prize of the BDA Berlin

The result of a 1988 competition, this project focuses on respecting the original building substance of the former Luisenbad recreation facilities located on the much praised though today heavily pipelined Panke River, rich with history since 1888. The façades of the older building could be exposed by cleverly attaching a lower level to the development. This incorporates essential parts of the library and creates a spacious open area. Floor area: 1,764 sqm; building costs: circa 12 million Euro.

052

Block by Otto Rudolf Salvisberg

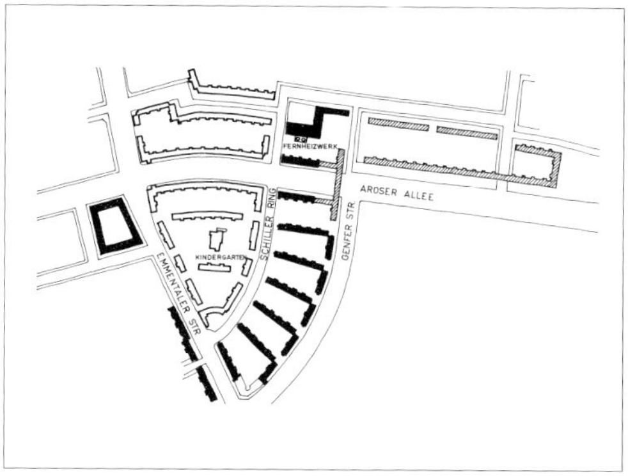

Weiße Stadt
The white city
1929/30
Reinickendorf, Aroser Allee, Emmentaler Straße, Schillerring, Genfer Straße
Architects: Wilhelm Büning, Otto Rudolf Salvisberg, Bruno Ahrends
Client: Heimstätten-Gesellschaft "Primus" mbH
Unesco world heritage since 2008

Because its 1,270 apartments are housed in buildings whose plastered brick surfaces are uniformly painted white, the colony was named "the white city". The balcony access block, which gives the colony a main focus and allows the wide boulevard to evolve to a functional space, is a reinforced concrete structure. West of this site is a district heating plant to which a commercial laundry is connected, and to the east a kindergarten. As visual signals, tower-like additions inserted in the old block edge development mark the point where the new city begins.

053

Animated site plan

Wilhelm-Sander-Haus
1984–87
Reinickendorf, Oranienburger Straße 285
Architects: Joachim Ganz, Walter Rolfes
Construction management: Hochbauamt Reinickendorf
Client: Senat von Berlin
Architekturpreis Berlin 1989

The concept of this new building for the Karl Bonhoeffer psychiatric clinic combines the facilities for the long-term housing of psychologically-disturbed offenders and the spaces used for their therapeutic treatment. The conceived system of interior and exterior spaces, and its utter clarity, make possible a full spectrum of restricted and unrestricted areas used in conjunction with the employed psychiatric measures. The building's structural presence and formal language reflect the historic substance of the entire clinic – a structure built in 1887 by Blankenstein.

054

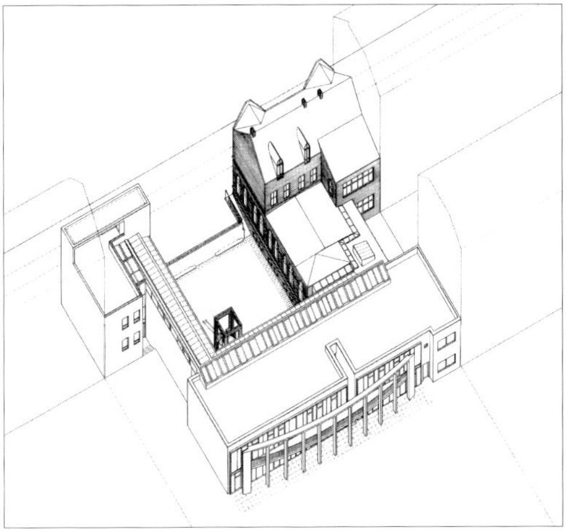

Child daycare center
1995–98
Reinickendorf, Letteallee 82–86
Architects: Rebecca Chestnutt, Robert Niess
Client: Hochbauamt Reinickendorf

The expansion of this small building protected by preservation laws intelligently uses the foundation's depth to form 2 unlike open spaces: forecourt and garden. Clear constructional forms correspond with powerful color accents, and the overall mood feels playfully creative.

055

East façade

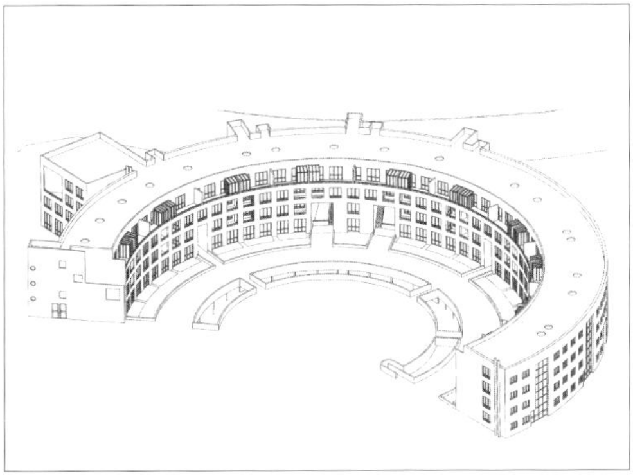

Axonomtric view from the south

Apartment development
1993–96
Wittenau, Dannenwalder Weg 70–78
Architects: Bangert und Scholz
Project manager: Andreas Kuhn
Client: GESOBAU

In 1992, a year before finishing the construction's circle for the Barnim-Gymnasium **(127)**, two-thirds of the circle were completed already for a residential court opening in a southerly direction and creating the continuation of a neighboring apartment complex. An attached, cubical structure, which houses gastronomical services, extends the development beyond the area of the Wilhelmsruher Damm. An underground parking lot in the courtyard follows the prevailing circle and accentuates the exterior facilities.

Märkisches Viertel

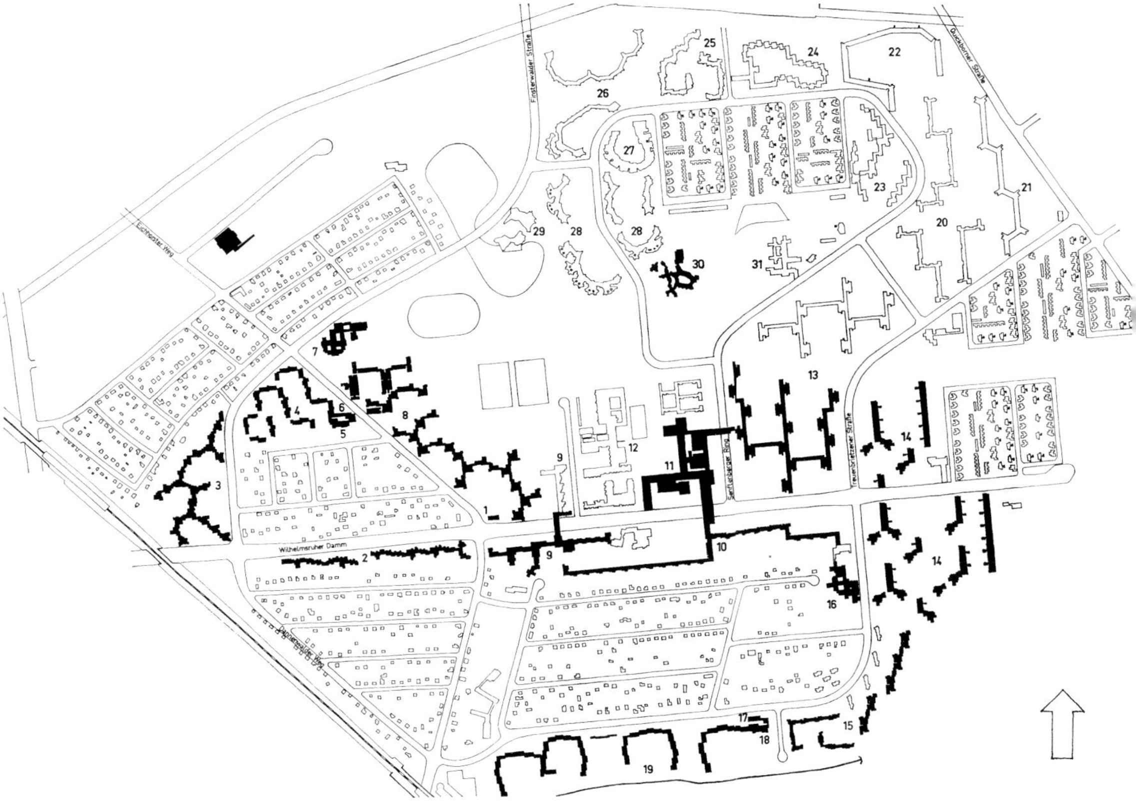

Conceived to accommodate 40,000 inhabitants and located in the rural area between Wittenau and the village of Lübars, the urban qualities of this large-scale housing colony make it stand out from the usual "dormitory housing projects", something made especially clear by a certain density regarding the block-system planning and by a shared, centralized location with social and "Märkisches"-related facilities. Extending from this core, three structural arms, sometimes made up of eighteen storeys, encircle a series of small garden settlements. So ultimately created was a visually sound and easily accessible large-scale sculpture. As thirty architects (some from outside Germany) participated, the most diverse concepts of "living" flowed one into the other but consistently demonstrated a high level of design. Werner Düttmann, Hans C. Müller, and Georg Heinrichs headed the overall planning and coordination, and the project's realization occurred between 1963 and 1974.

1 Former info-pavilion
2/31 Karl Fleig
3 Herbert Stranz
4 Hansrudolf Plarre
5/18 Fin Bartels, Christoph Schmidt-Ott
7 Harald Franke
8 Oswald Mathias Ungers (060)
9 Ludwig Leo (061)
10/21 Renè Gagès, Volker Theissen (059)
11 Dietmar Grötzebach, Gerd Neumann
12/15 Werner Düttmann
13 Hans C. Müller, Georg Heinrichs (058)
14 Ernst Gisel
16 Günter und Ursula Plessow
20 Astra Zarina Haner
25 Peter Pfankuch
26 Heinz Schudnagies
27 Anatol Ginelli
28 Chen Kuen Lee
29 Bodo Fleischer
30 Stephan Heise

056

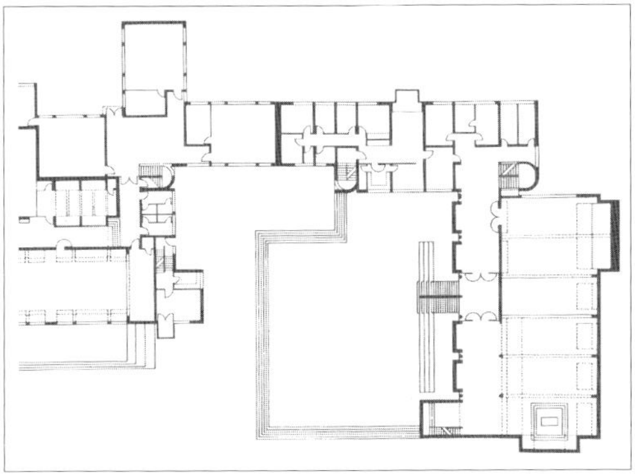

Apostel Johannes community center
1969–71
Wittenau, Dannenwalder Weg 167
Architects: Dietmar Grötzebach, Gerd Neumann, Günter Plessow with Eberhard Lucht
Client: Ev. Kirchenkreis Reinickendorf

In a gap between the Märkische Grundschule designed by Günter and Ursula Plessow (1966–70) and the building by René Gagès (**059**), this compactly structured community center claims a spot for itself with youth activity rooms and sisters' station on its ground floor, and a church, (combinable) hall, club rooms, and apartments for ministers on its upper floor. Consolidating measures of this kind further support the concept of an urban center for a far-reaching colony area.

057

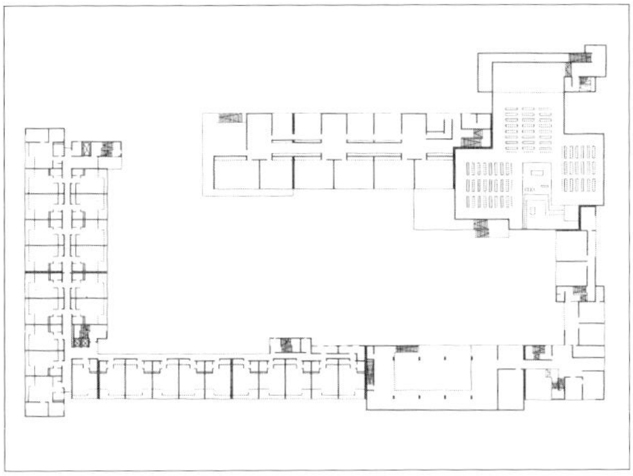

St. Martin community center
1970–73
Wittenau, Wilhelmsruher Damm 142
Architect: Werner Düttmann with Peter Münzing
Client: Ev. Kirchengemeinde St. Martin

"With the adjoining senior citizens home (architect: Werner Düttmann; client: DeGeWo), the community center forms its own block on the edge of the main center of the 'Märkisches Viertel' district. The northeast corner, which faces the market, is commanded by a church to which the community center connects to the south – with the starkly structured spaces of the church allowing the community to come closer in three groups. Connecting to the west is a childcare center, above which is located the branch of a school."

058

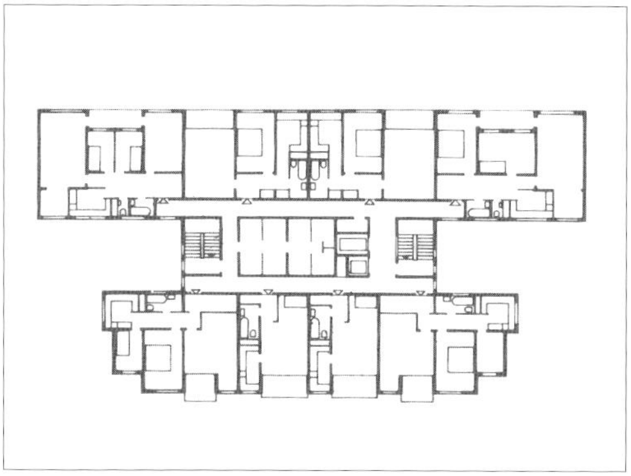

Plan of a standard floor

Apartment complex
1967/68
Wittenau, Wilhelmsruher Damm
Architects: Hans C. Müller, Georg Heinrichs with Peter Voigt
Client: DeGeWo

Both the building and its floor plan subscribe to the large-panel construction method derived of the Coignet system: long linear slabs develop through laterally employed staircase towers. In turn, these develop to 4 apartments, and to 4 more in the building part beside the staircase tower. Via structural junctions, they connect 5 times to the neighboring slabs while their color allows them to stand out from each other and the staircase tower. In addition, they form large courtyard areas. In the meantime several of the façades and windows have been altered, rigid insulation added and the original color scheme from Utz Kampmann with strong primary colors gave way to an arbitrary re-painting.

059

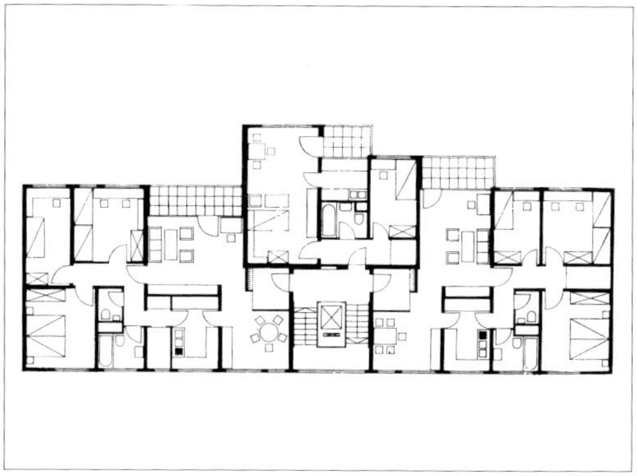

Plan of the 6-storey building

Apartment complex
1966–68
Wittenau, Wilhelmsruher Damm
Architects: René Gagès, Volker Theißen, Werner Weber
General color system: Utz Kampmann
Client: Gesobau
Implementation: Schälerbau – Allbeton

A 6-storey slab the length of the entire center forms a junction between the high building parts by the same architects and the part designed by Ludwig Leo. Recessed window bands, which develop the stairwells of semi-detached dwellings, combine with the windows of the apartments that emerge here. By comparison, the high building parts are vertically accentuated and accommodate altogether 978 apartments. After much criticism of the "Märkisches Viertel" district, slight modifications were carried out here. In this case, these involved the building's entranceways by Thomas Darboven

060

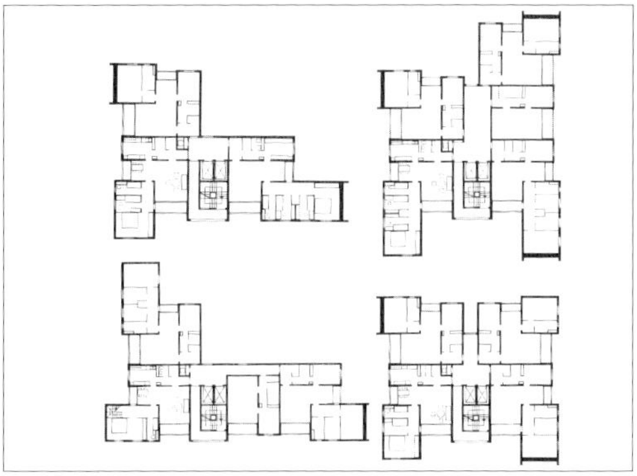

Plan of a combination example

Apartment complex and old people's home
1967/68
Wittenau, Eichhorster Weg
Architect: Oswald Mathias Ungers
Client: Gesobau

The "positive and negative space" concept addressed through combining structures and open areas is also the point of departure for the floor plan solution: the living area hangs between the vertical elements of sleeping quarters, entranceway, and kitchen, with each neighboring house docking at the sleeping quarters. The ground floor is large enough to accommodate the redundant stress development. The overall construction, offering 1,305 apartments and senior citizens home with care center, has an externally insulated and plastered, all-concrete façade

061

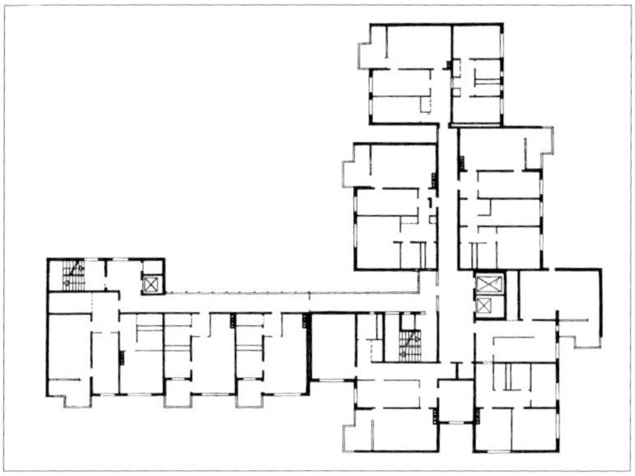

Plan of a standard floor

Apartment complex
1966/67
Wittenau, Wilhelmsruher Damm
Architect: Ludwig Leo
Client: Gesobau

With its greatly staggered structures ranging from 5 to 17 storeys, and a bridge erected over Wilhelmsruher Damm for telephone services, the complex marks the beginning of the central area. The same building configuration repeats itself three times around the partially glazed, balcony access block. Altogether 508 apartments exist here. The large-panel construction method derives from the Camus system. Further details include sand-colored, small-sized mosaics, and the powerful yellow tones in the exposed concrete surfaces of the attics and balconies

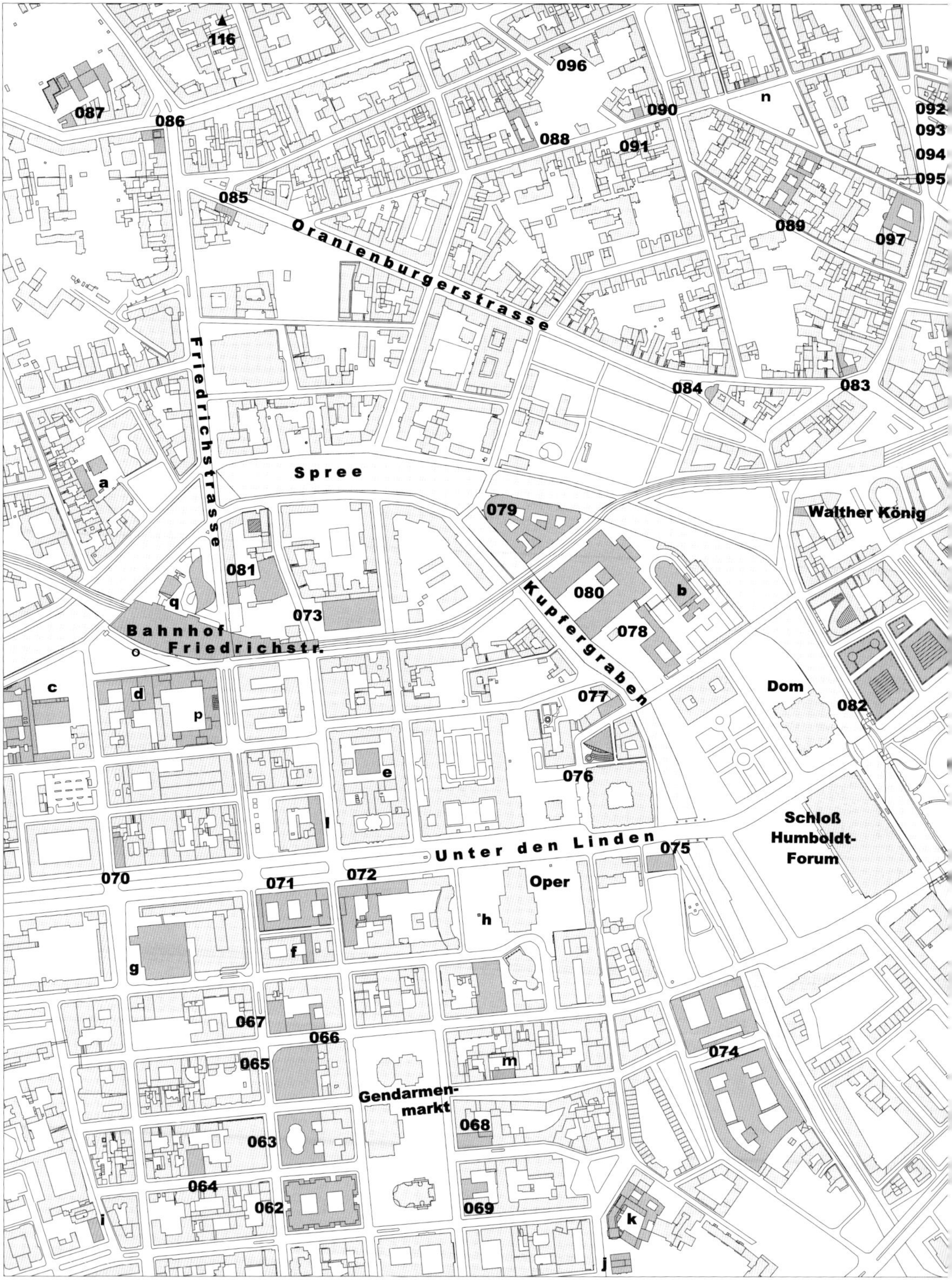

116
096
087
086
090
n
092
093
094
095
088
091
085
Oranienburgerstrasse
089
097
Friedrichstrasse
084
083
Spree
a
079
Walther König
081
080
b
q
Kupfergraben
073
Bahnhof
Friedrichstr.
078
o
c
d
p
077
Dom
082
e
076
l
Schloß
Humboldt-
Forum
Unter den Linden
075
070
071
072
Oper
h
f
g
067
066
065
m
074
Gendarmen-
markt
068
063
064
062
069
i
k
j

Gendarmenmarkt NE

062	Friedrichstadt-Passagen, Quartier 205	Oswald Mathias Ungers
063	Quartier 206	Pei Cobb Freed & Partners
064	Deutsche Treuhand	Christoph Mäckler
065	Quartier 207	Jean Nouvel
066	Office and apartment building	Jürgen Sawade
067	Hofgarten am Gendarmenmarkt	Hans Kollhoff, Helga Timmermann
068	Wisenschaftsforum am Gendarmenmarkt	Wilhelm Holzbauer
069	BEWAG-Haus am Gendarmenmarkt	Max Dudler
070	Unter den Linden office building	Jürgen Sawade
071	Lindencorso	Christoph Mäckler
072	Deutsche Bank	Benedict Tonon
073	Jacob-und-Wilhelm-Grimm-Zentrum der Humboldt-Universität zu Berlin	Max Dudler
074	Auswärtiges Amt	Heinrich Wolff, Thomas Müller, Ivan Reimann
075	Kommandantenhaus	Thomas van den Valentyn
076	Deutsches Historisches Museum	Pei Cobb Freed & Partners
077	Am Kupfergraben 10	David Chipperfield Architects
078	Neues Museum	David Chipperfield Architects
079	Bode-Museum	Heinz Tesar
080	Pergamonmuseum	Alfred Messel, Ludwig Hoffmann
081	Admiralspalast	Heinrich Schweitzer, Alexander Diepenbrock
082	Dom Aquarée	nps und partner (now: nps tchoban voss)
083	Office and apartment building	Armand Grüntuch, Almut Ernst
084	Office and apartment building	Armand Grüntuch, Almut Ernst
085	Arcotel Velvet	Eike Becker
086	Corner development at Oranienburger Tor	Hans Kollhoff, Helga Timmermann
087	Katholische Höfe	Thomas Höger, Sarah Hare
088	Café Bravo	Johanne Nalbach
089	Sophie-Gips-Höfe	Becker, Gewers, Kühn & Kühn
090	Apartment building	Florian Hoyer, Harald Schindele
091	Apartment building with shops	Jörg Ebers
092	Urbanes Leben	Jean-Marc Abcarius, Christian Burn
093	Apartments	Silvia Carpaneto, Christian Schoeningh
094	Loft building	Bernd Faskel
095	Corner house	Silvia Carpaneto, Christian Schoeningh
096	Haus Kicken	Hans Düttmann
097	SAP training center	Mark Braun
116	Loft building	Klaus Schlosser, Jean Lamborelle

a	Berliner Ensemble, conversion and extension	Hans Düttmann, 2003
b	Alte Nationalgalerie	HG Merz, 1992–2001
c	Bundespresseamt	Engel, Zimmermann, 1996–2000
d	Friedrich-Carrée	Thomas Müller, Ivan Reimann, 2000–04
e	Staatsbibliothek	HG Merz, 2005–10
f	Rosmarin-Karree	Paul Kahlfeld, Petra Kahlfeld, 1995–98
g	Komische Oper, foyer	Kunz Nierade, 1966–67
h	Library	Micha Ullman, Andreas Zerr, 1994
i	Landesvertretung Thüringen	Worschech & Partner, 2004
j	Childcare center	Volker Staab, Alfred Nieuwenhuizen, 2001/02
k	Haus zur Berolina	Grundei, Krämer, Pysall, Stahrenberg, 2002/03
l	Palazzo Italia	Axthelm, 2006/07
m	Belgische Botschaft	Röthnick, Planitzer, 1999–2001
n	Multi-generation house	Armand Grüntuch, Almut Ernst, 2007
o	Bahnhof Friedrichstraße	C. T. Brodführer, 1919–25; W. Weinkamm, 1999
p	Friedrich-Carrée	Walter A. Noebel, 1999–2002
q	Spree-Dreieck	Mark Braun, 2007–09

062

Friedrichstadt-Passagen, Quartier 205
1991–95
Mitte, Friedrichstraße at the corner of Mohrenstraße
Architect: Oswald Mathias Ungers
Project manager: Sebastian Klatt, Karl Heinz Winkens
Client: Tishman Speyer Properties

The southernmost edge of the quartier's three blocks measures 109 x 67 m, and extends as far as the Gendarmenmarkt. Its architectural language expresses the surrounding urban mixture more than it does the shopping center on Friedrichstraße, connected to the other two blocks by underground passageways. The coloring of the paneled, grid-pattern façade has consistently quadratic window openings of the same size, and differentiates between Berlin's standard building height and 4 attached floors.

063

Quartier 206
1994–96
Mitte, Friedrichstraße at the corners of Jägerstraße and Taubenstraße
Architects: Pei Cobb Freed & Partners
Client: Arc-Union-Bouygueas, Fundus-Gruppe

The middle of the three blocks of the Friedrichstadt-Passagen is a 1991 competition winner. It also offers the most sophisticated merchandise. This seemingly crystalline building has an expressionistic, folded façade whose endless arrangement of illuminated panels radiate light onto the street by night. Its interior – especially the main hall of the development with piano bar and escalator – showcases a wealth of floor patterns, overhead lighting, and wall designs, which decoratively correspond with the building's discriminating character.

064

View from Taubenstraße

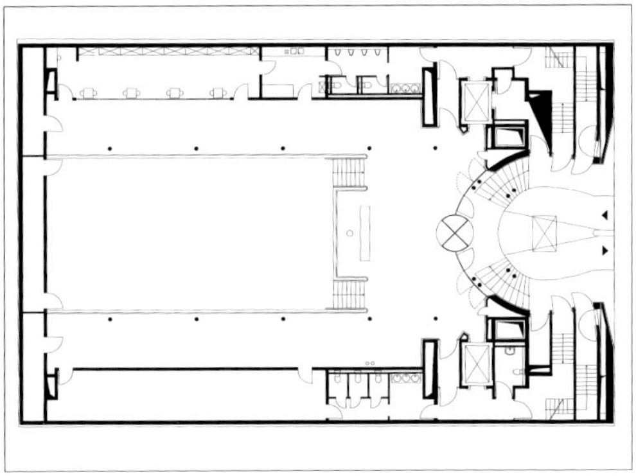

Plan of the ground floor

Deutsche Treuhand
1996–98
Mitte, Taubenstraße 44
Architect: Christoph Mäckler
Project manager: Jan Pieter Fraune
Client: KPMG

The administration building of the Deutsche Treuhand is situated on a plot closed in by its three-sided gable ends, so that obtaining sufficient natural lighting for the office spaces was only possible by way of the glass-roofed atrium and wall-high glazed sections. The entrances and exits are bundled together between massive walls and underneath powerful eaves, which contradict the building's lighter, interior world of glass.

065

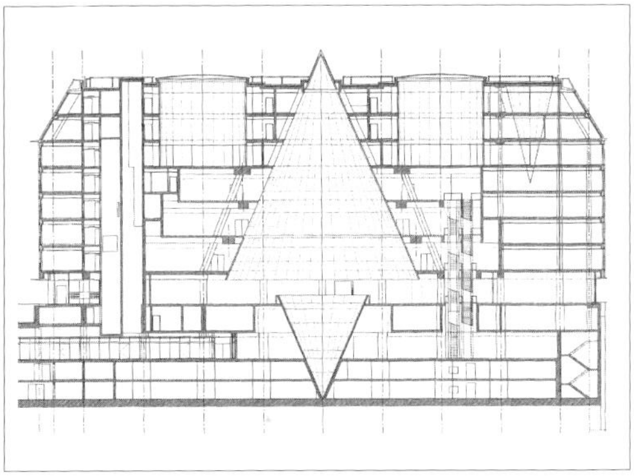

Cross section

Quartier 207
1994–96
Mitte, Friedrichstraße at the corner of Französische Straße
Architect: Jean Nouvel
Engineering specialists: Arup, Polónyi + Fink, HL-Technik, IBS Schalm
Client: EURO PROJEKT

Developed from a design completed for a 1991 competition, on a programmatic as well as factual level, it links the underground floors, passageway, and basement-level garage, in a southerly direction the block connects with both of the adjoining blocks. Strikingly different here are the curved façades and roof structures completely rendered in glass, and various "light cones" whose zenithal light reaches the floors of the department store and office spaces. Floor area: 39,585 sqm; building costs: circa 107 million Euro.

066

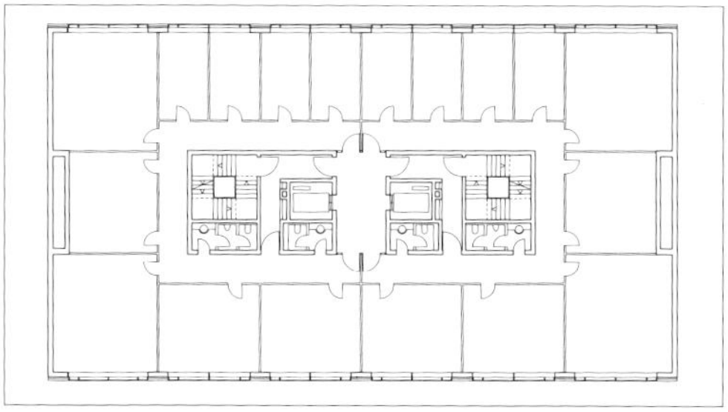

Plan of a standard floor

Office and apartment building
1994–96
Mitte, Französische Straße 48
Master plan for the site: Josef Paul Kleihues with James Akin and Dirk Blomeyer
Architect: Jürgen Sawade
Client: Hofgarten Real Estate

The clearly structured floor plan and façade of the 8-storey building stands on a newly arranged plot including a required 2-level underground garage. The two uppermost floors, recessed by 60 cm, sensitively take into account the opposite street profile, and their dissipating ascent is further emphasized by their flatness and highly reflective materials.

067

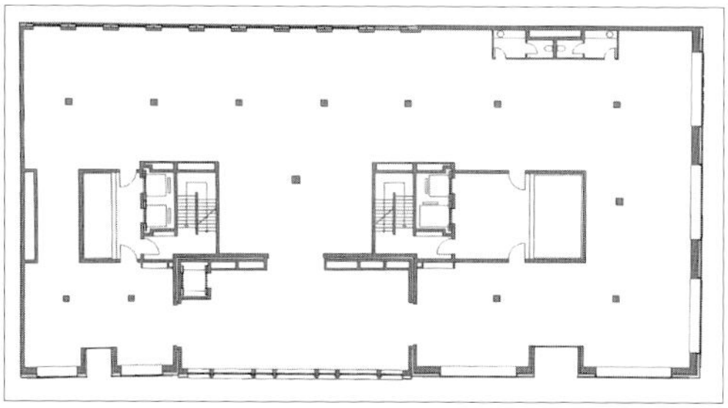

Plan of the 1st to the 4th floors

Hofgarten am Gendarmenmarkt
1994–96
Mitte, Friedrichstraße 78–80
Master plan for the site: Josef Paul Kleihues with James Akin and Dirk Blomeyer
Architects: Hans Kollhoff, Helga Timmermann
Client: Hofgarten Real Estate

The façade of a preserved building divides the longitudinal wing on the Friedrichstraße and reveals the former site allotment. The two-floor quality of the foundation, and narrow subdividing of the 4 upper floors and both stepped floors, favorably support this prominent, magisterial thoroughfare already an exclusive shopping and strolling mile in the early 1920s.

068

Entrance hall

Wissenschaftsforum am Gendarmenmarkt
1995–99
Mitte, Markgrafenstraße 37
Architect: Wilhelm Holzbauer
Client: VolkswagenStiftung

Regarding the building's extension and structural addition, the architect writes: "Reacting to the classical spatial composition ... the new building at the corner was to be given ... beside the Berlin-Brandenburgische Akademie der Wissenschaften, a block-like and uniform overall effect. The impressive series of pilasters were continued, and the roof's form readapted from the original ..." This creates a site-specific adaptation and up-to-date formal language, also displayed in the central, glazed hall with its reflecting blue tones.

069

Façade facing the square

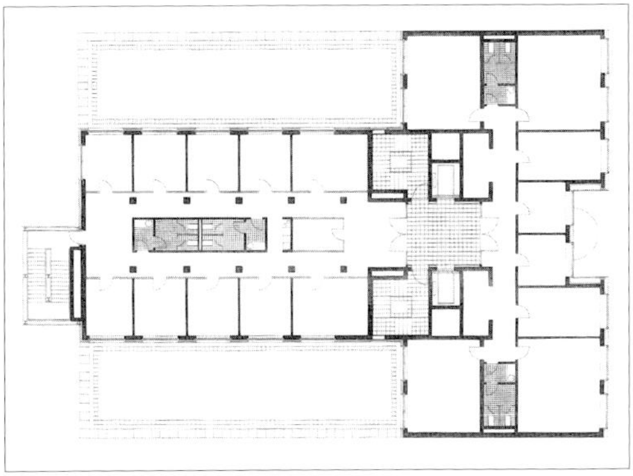

Plan of the 3rd floor

BEWAG-Haus am Gendarmenmarkt
1996/97
Mitte, Markgrafenstraße 35
Architect: Max Dudler with Manfred Kunz, Brigitta Weise
Façade planning: ATF
Client: Berliner Kraft- und Licht AG

At the historic spot where the first Berlin power station stood, near the block of buildings opposite the Deutscher Dom, the axiality is not only articulated through its façade, but also – void of pathos – through its T-shaped floor plan. This is achieved through the simple geometry of a razed table, the deep-set windows and subdivisions of the steel mullions, and dark field of stone made of ebony-black granite slabs. The uppermost floors house altogether 14 apartments – in a structure by the same architects responsible for the building located at Behrenstraße 27.

070

View from the south-west

Unter den Linden office building
1993–95
Mitte, Unter den Linden 42
Architect: Jürgen Sawade
Client: Unter den Linden 42 GbR

Visible from the street, the glazed gallery of the single loaded corridor office building is placed alongside the neighboring pediment, where it reaches a 7-storey height. It provides a fire wall ideal for hanging visual works, also making it perfectly suited to accommodate the Heiner Pietsch collection. "So the office spaces are situated in a zone of tension between a real exterior world and an artificial counter-world created indoors."

071

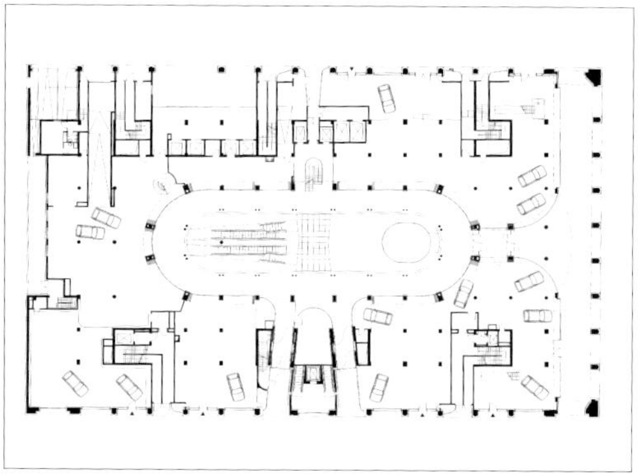

Plan of the ground floor

Lindencorso
1993–96, rebuilt 1999
Mitte, Unter den Linden at the corner of Friedrichstraße
Architect: Christoph Mäckler
Project management: Jan Pieter Fraune, Beate Grimm, Thomas Mayer
Client: D. Katz, K. Marks

This circa 92-million-Euro-heavy colossus with pronounced three-dimensional subdivisions, 3 foundation floors, 3 upper floors, and 2 attic floors, evolved from a 1992 competition. Through the representative firm presence of Volkswagen, the building's original and differentiated ground-floor offer is largely reduced to showroom areas for cars, which also applies to the basement level. But the highly impressive arcades on Friedrichstraße survive this just the same.

072

Entrance hall

Deutsche Bank
1995–97
Mitte, Unter den Linden at the corner of Charlottenstraße
Architect: Benedict Tonon with Novotny Mähner Assoziierte
Client: Deutsche Bank AG

This is an additional branch of the Guggenheim Foundation. By removing the elevated first upper-floor levels, the ensemble of two buildings located at Unter den Linden could acquire a high-walled exhibition space for changing exhibitions devoted to contemporary art on the one hand, and a spacious hall simultaneously an entranceway, lecture hall, and reception area on the other – in its entirety an excellent location for developing cultural life, and all the aspects of cultural patronage.

073

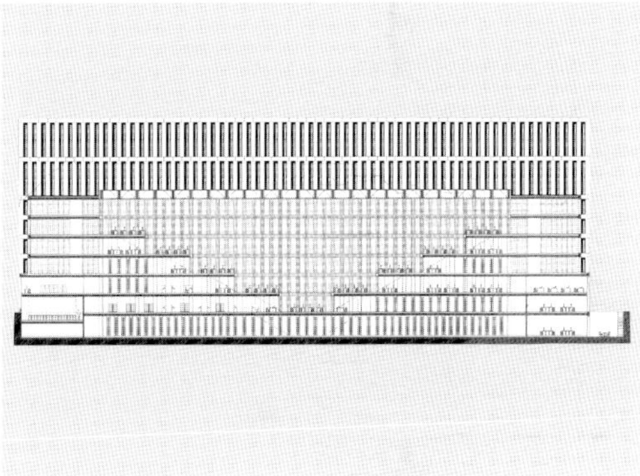

Longitudinal section

Jacob-und-Wilhelm-Grimm-Zentrum of the Humboldt-Universität zu Berlin
2006–08
Architect: Max Dudler with Jochen Soydan
Mitte, Geschwister-Scholl-Straße 3
Client: Humboldt-Universität zu Berlin

The winning competition design from 2004, "... well considered from the standpoints of its concept and urban-planning scheme, is a design of sculptural proportions. Not only does it express in the form of a building the wealth of tradition the Humboldt-Universität enriches Berlin with, but also the fact that the university ranks as an internationally recognized, modern and innovative institution for education and research. The new center develops as a theme its inherent similarity to the typology of a bookshelf, a form which, in turn, evolves from a book." Included here are a 70 m long, centralized reading room; a second reading room reserved for historical volumes; an archive for 2,8 million books, and a total of 20,000 sqm of floor area.

074

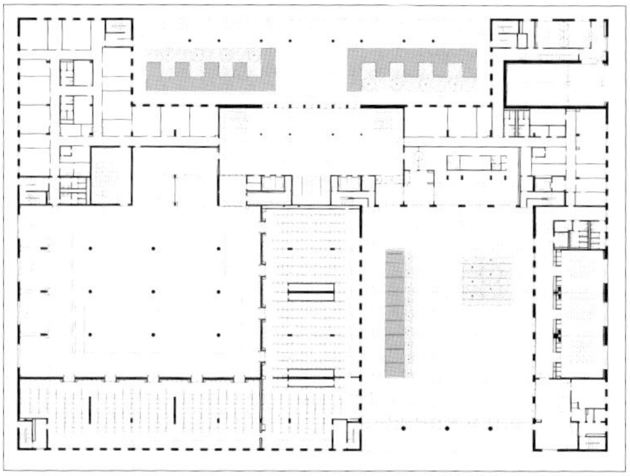

Plan of the ground floor

Auswärtiges Amt
Federal Foreign Office
1997–99
Mitte, Werderscher Markt 1
Architects: Thomas Müller, Ivan Reimann
Project manager: André Santer, Regula Scheibler
Light and glass object: James Carpenter
Client: Bundesamt für Bau- und Raumordnung

This was the preferred submission of an international competition, because it preserves the existing block corners on the one side, and resolves the complex with 3 courtyard spaces addressing the exterior space through glass façades on the other "... and literally pulls the city into the building". Bright Roman travertine, green gneiss, silver metal, and cherry wood give the building its light coloring. Floor area: 50,000 sqm; building costs: circa 135 million Euro. To the south the former Reichsbank 1934–40 by Heinrich Wolff was renovated for the foreign office by Hans Kollhoff.

075

South façade

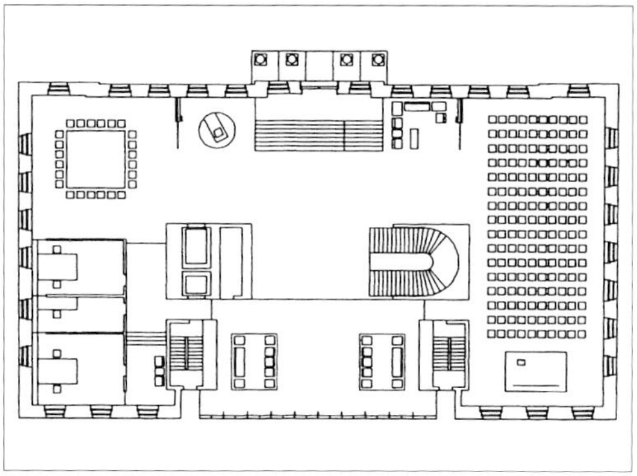

Kommandantenhaus
2003/04
Mitte, Unter den Linden 1
Architect: Thomas van den Valentyn with Matthias Dittmann, Johannes van Linn
Reconstructed façade: Stuhlemmer+Stuhlemmer
Client: Bertelsmann AG

This qualifies as an exemplary reconstruction case focused on a 1795 palace which, after its completion, was torn down and meticulously rebuilt, true to detail, facing the boulevard. At its southern side, the new design features the addition of a façade-high glazing, thus creating a visual connection between the interior and 3 upper floors of the publisher's representative seat.

076

Glazed inner courtyard, model

Deutsches Historisches Museum
1999–2002
Mitte, Hinter dem Gießhaus
Architects: Pei Cobb Freed & Partners
Client: Bundesamt für Bau- und Regionalgestaltung

Whoever could effectively place a glass pyramid in the courtyard of the Louvre in Paris was a welcome contender for the former Zeughaus, where master builders of the Baroque such as Nering or Schlüter had already left their mark. The project involved the planned extension to be used for temporary exhibitions, and a glazed roof for the magnificent inner court. In the process – with great sensitivity – the new structure merely docks itself underground. "Transparency and movement: both are essential for winning our attention and luring us deeper into a museum."

077

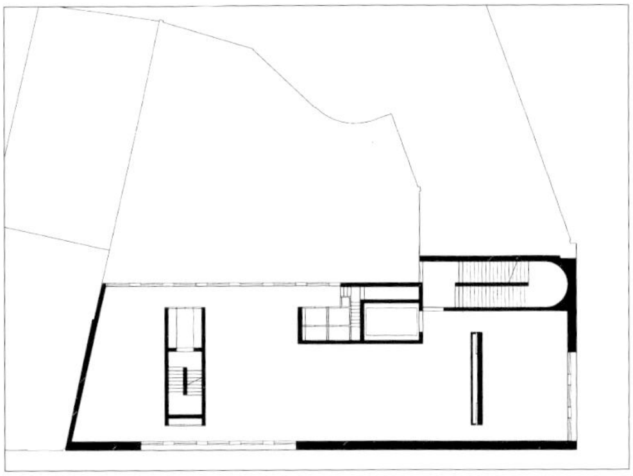

Plan of the 2nd floor

Am Kupfergraben 10
2003–07
Mitte, Am Kupfergraben 10
Architects: David Chipperfield Architects
Project architect: Alexander Schwarz
Client: Celine and Heiner Bastian

This building was consciously conceived to function as part of closing the block's perimeter and not to dissolve as a solitary structure within the museum ensemble. According to Chipperfeld, "To sit in the first row doesn't mean sitting on the stage." The building's "special normalcy" is expressed through the compactness of slurried, secondhand-brick masonry framed by bands of two-layered cast stone and the spacious well-placed openings, which also respect the order of the neighboring building on the right while integrating its corner pilasters at the same time. The interior space orients itself toward the generous proportions of a commercial loft used for the presentation of contemporary art.

078

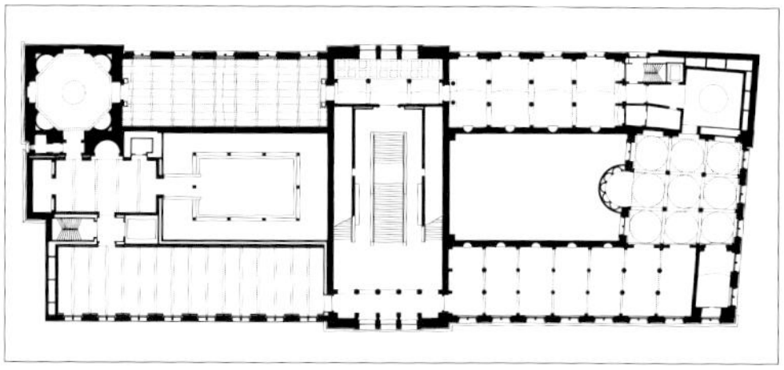

Floor plan of level 2

Neues Museum
2003–09
Mitte, Museumsinsel, Bodestraße
Architects: David Chipperfield Architects
Client: Staatliche Museen Preußischer Kulturbesitz

Thirteen years after erecting K. F. Schinkel's so-called Altes Museum, from 1843 to 1855, a second museum by F. A. Stüler was built on the famous "museum island". Severely damaged during the war, and threatened by the decision to have it torn down, the building could be elaborately restored and connected to its preserved parts through a synchronizing of colors and tonalities. Only the grand staircase represents a new architectural element. Planned at the Kupfergarten, a waterway on the museum's north side, is a centralized building, the James Simon Gallery, and entranceway intended to join all the museums on the island at an underground level.

079

Sculptures gallery on level 1

Space under the domed rotunda on the south-east side

Bode-Museum
1997–2006
Mitte, Museumsinsel, Bodestraße
Architect: Heinz Tesar
Client: Staatliche Museen Preußischer Kulturbesitz

Gottfried Knapp: "Heinz Tesar has carefully preserved the existing building, and provided it with highly unusual additional sections for the anticipated hordes of visitors. His work proved its extraordinary qualities even at the opening. There is scarcely anywhere else in the world where the contrasting styles arising from a museum's various building periods come together to form such an individual whole, at best comparable in its density with the Italian architect Carlo Scarpa's museum designs. The essential basis for this successful symbiosis of heterogeneous stylistic elements is the variable historical architecture that museum director Wilhelm Bode invited architect Ernst Eberhard von Ihne to develop around 1900 for the collections, which were very disparate in both style and genre."

080

Drawing by Messel

Pergamonmuseum
1911–30
Mitte, Am Kupfergraben
Architects: Alfred Messel, Ludwig Hoffmann

In place of the Schinkelesque park courtyard, and erected on relatively boggy building property, this construction was intended to complete the museum ensemble with its archeological collection. From the very beginning, the central piece here was the Pergamon Altar unearthed by Schliemann – a find which not only required a protective encasement but also a great deal of light. The overall construction concept, which included the connecting side-wings, evolved from the museum's glazed roof. Oswald Mathias Ungers emerged the winner of a competition focused on improving the entrance way situation. Still unresolved, however, is the plan for an underground walkway meant to connect all the buildings of the museum ensemble.

081

Admiralspalast
1910/11
Mitte, Friedrichstraße 101
Architects: Heinrich Schweitzer, Alexander Diepenbrock
Façade ornaments: Franz Naager

Subdivided by five dormitory pillars, the building's fin de siècle façade radiates an architectural magnificence as well as a marked festive quality between the East and West. The constantly changing utilization of the space ranged from swimming facilities, ice-skating rink, restaurant to a theater, later the well-known Metropol Theater. According to a plan devised by Assmann/Salomon/Scheidt, an entirely new forecourt to the railway station was developed on the station's opposite side.

082

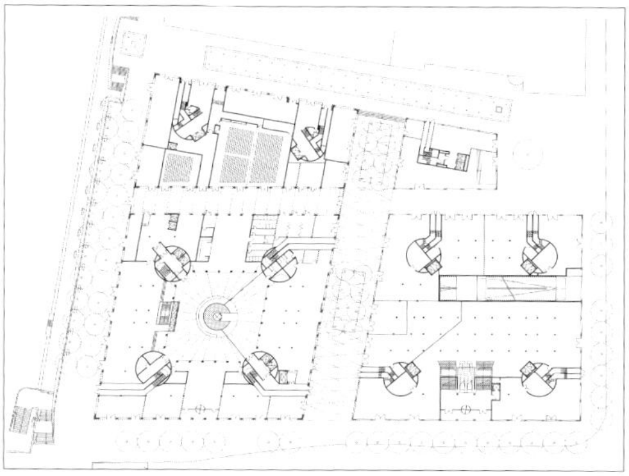

Plan of the ground floor

Dom Aquarée
2001–03
Mitte, Karl-Liebknecht Straße / Spandauer Straße
Architects: nps und partner (now: nps tchoban voss)
Project manager: Manfred Treiling
Torwächter: Stefan Balkenhol
Client: DIFA

Following the old city plan and situated where the chic SAS Hotel of the GDR period formerly stood, 4 new blocks were created. These extend in an east–westerly direction on the one hand, and north to south along the route of Heiliggeistgasse on the other – here as a pneumatic, film-roofed passage – and finally cross. In the largest block, at the southwest corner, unlike the area established by the Radisson Hotel for offices and apartments, the arrangement of parts surrounds a glass cylinder fishtank, the height of the building, serviced by an elevator – from which the area derives its name.

083

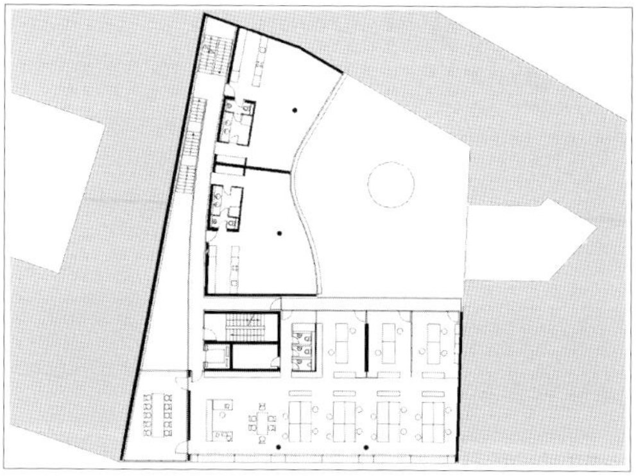

Plan of the 1st to the 4th floors

Office and apartment building
2000
Mitte, Hackescher Markt 2–3
Architects: Armand Grüntuch, Almut Ernst
Client: Gantenbrink GbR

With 4 storeys for office space and 9 apartments, the building incorporates the large-scaled floor height of the neighboring building by August Endell on the right. At the same time, through a nearly complete, double-shelled glazing, it develops a more homogenous façade with massive coverings for the heating, cooling, and electrical utilities, but without incorporating suspensions. What stands out is the building's detail work, and the use of valuable materials, especially in its development area and open surfaces. In 1906, Endell greatly enhanced the attractive multifunctional commercial spaces, restaurants, galleries, and two theaters of the Hackeschen Höfe with an extravagant façade design. Creating an additional decoration are the neighboring courtyards of the "Rosenhöfe" developed in 2003 by Hinrich Baller on Rosenthaler Straße 36.

084

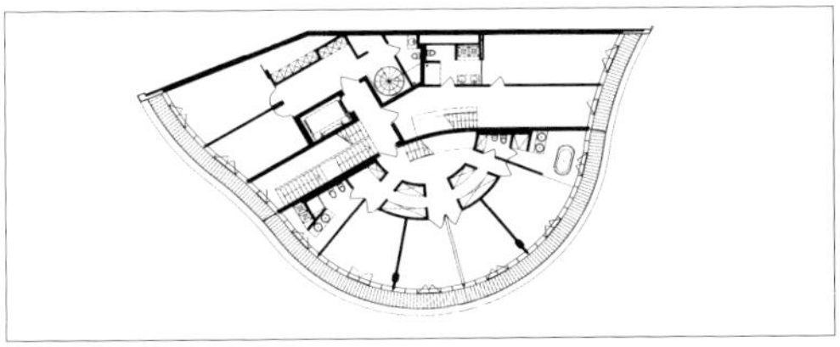

Plan of 5th floor

Office and apartment building
2001
Mitte, Monbijouplatz 5
Architects: Armand Grüntuch, Almut Ernst
Client: Grundstücksgesellschaft Monbijouplatz 5 GbR

The western tip of the small, triangular block located at Monbijoupark is closed by an elegant curve whose physical presence is heightened by powerful, horizontal bands. Like a pulpit, it places itself in the axis of Oranienburger Straße. The building has 5 full storeys with shops on the ground floor and 1st floor; office spaces on the 2nd and 3rd floors; and apartments, at times interconnected in a maisonnette-like fashion, on a slightly stepped, 4th floor.

085

Guest room

Arcotel Velvet
2002–04
Mitte, Oranienburger Straße 52
Architect: Eike Becker
Client: Matura Bauten

The design emerged from a 2001 competition and addresses the theme of a building's outward effects as a way of rethinking the rather lifeless, everyday image of hotels in the streetscape environment: "The basic motif of the façade's design is an expansive animation. The rooms' video equipment projects stirring images on the screens of the starkly structured, glass façade facing Oranienburger Straße. With a façade made of storey-height glazed frames, and room-height windows, this closes the gap beside the 'Künstlerhaus Tacheles' cultural center."

086

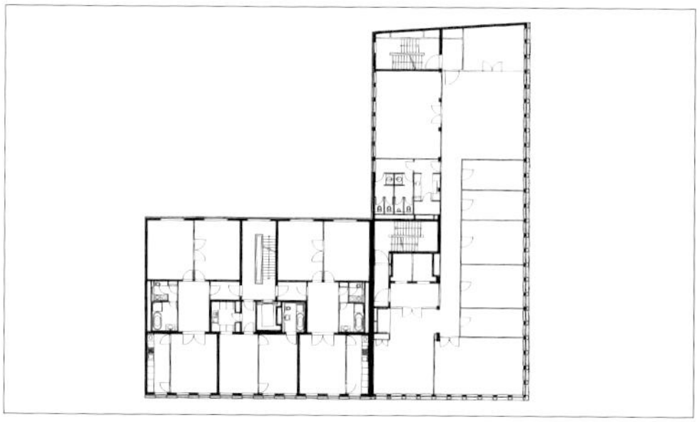

Plan of the 2nd floor

Corner development at Oranienburger Tor
1997–99
Mitte, Friedrichstraße 119
Architects: Hans Kollhoff, Helga Timmermann
Client: KapHag

Where the old eighteenth century city gate once stood, the building ensemble conceived for this location was intended to create an extension of one of the gate's lateral sides at a later date. While the apartment house on Friedrichstraße follows the standard height for Berlin structures, evolving from a 3-storey development, the following office building divulges a tower. The differently structured façades and attics, uniformly made of grayish-green pietra serena, with window sections made of bronze or bronzed aluminum, also have passageways revealing equally impressive interiors.

087

Diocese administration

Interior of the church

Katholische Höfe
1994–99
Mitte, Hannoversche Straße 5, Chausseestraße 128
Architects: Thomas Höger, Sarah Hare
Client: Erzdiözese Berlin

After deciding to erect a Catholic academy at this site, christened churchyard in 1777, built one after the other were a conference room (by architects Latta and Hölscher), a hotel, an auditorium, an office building, and the administration building for the diocese of German bishops. And finally the chapel was completed – cleverly inserted in the ensemble behind a row of columns in collaboration with the artist Norbert Rademacher.

088

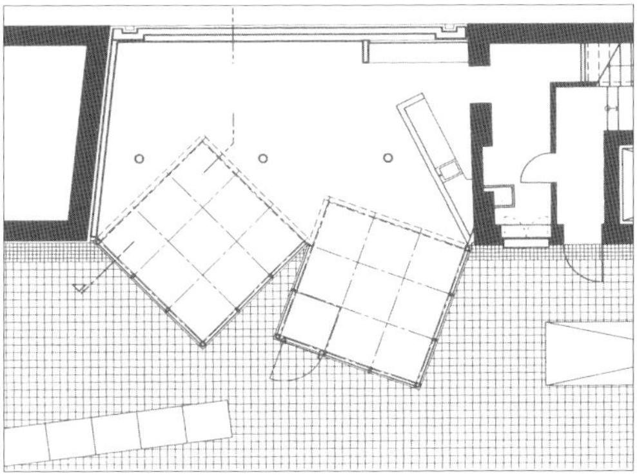

Plan of the ground floor

Café Bravo
1999–2000
Mitte, Auguststraße 67
Concept: Dan Graham
Architect: Johanne Nalbach
Client: Kunst-Werke-Berlin e.V.

Two glass-and-chrome cubes, which only seem indiscriminately arranged, are placed on Berlin-style courtyard cobblestones with the utmost precision. Gerwin Zohlen writes about this construction: "... architecture is one of many vehicles for Dan Graham. He orchestrates a free-for-all of perceptual signs directed at reflections, refracted surfaces, dissolving contours, visual disturbances, and corrected orientations ..." The exhibition spaces – located in the rear and designed by Hans Düttmann – were developed from the halls of a factory formerly used for producing margarine.

089

Sophie-Gips-Höfe
1995–97
Mitte, Sophienstraße 21, Gipsstraße
Architects: Becker Gewers Kühn Kühn
Project manager: Swantje Kühn
Client: Erika and Rolf Hoffmann

The rebuilding of a former factory that manufactured sewing machines, and the structural additions, align the passageway through three courtyards elegantly utilized for commercial purposes – sometimes with offices in lofts. In the middle courtyard is the attached, penthouse apartment of Mr. and Mrs. Hoffmann, whose private collection of contemporary art is located underneath it. On the ground floor is Barcomis Café. The apartment house on Gipsstraße concludes the series of courtyards at a newly built 5-storey construction which accommodates smaller apartments.

090

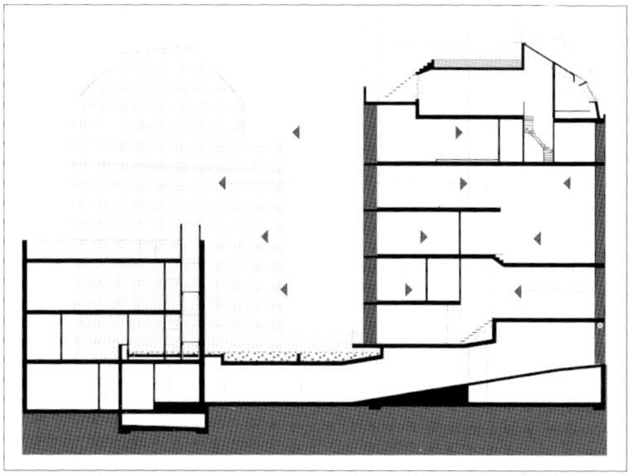

Cross section

Apartment building
1998–2001
Mitte, Auguststraße 62
Architects: Florian Hoyer, Harald Schindele
Client: Erika Schindele

"The building is fundamentally made up of multi-floored apartments, whose flowing floor plans frequently vary their living quarters. Without engaging a spatial division, bathrooms become coupled with bedrooms. On the one hand, the façade refuses closure by integrating the cityscape as a backdrop; on the other, via interior galleries and seen from the street side, they offer an image similar to that of a stage set for the 'play of living'. The possibility of collaborating with the future inhabitants led to a high degree of acceptance and individualization."

091

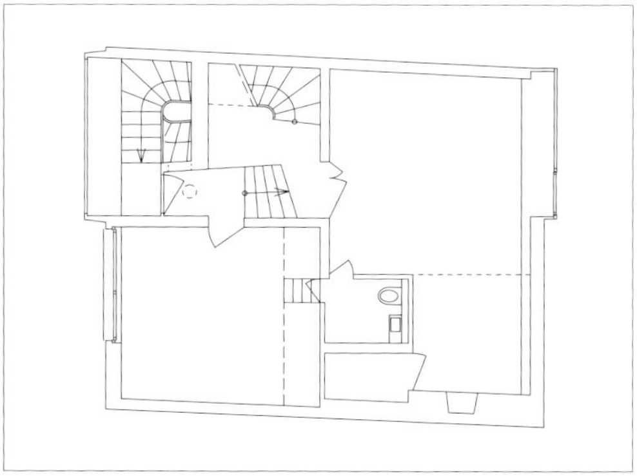

Plan of levels 2 and 3

Apartment building with shops
2004
Mitte, Auguststraße 26
Architect: Jörg Ebers with Daniel Buchheit

Another building block in the ensemble created in the attractive, suburban area of the Spandau district (Spandauer Vorstadt): unconventionally evolved from the floor plan and structural details – of a 7.80 m wide urban gap, and on a floor area of 154 sqm – the structure created here was planned to be used by 3 parties on 5 levels. The incorporated shops and studio-and-maisonnette apartments hardly limit the relaxed contact with the neighboring senior citizens.

092

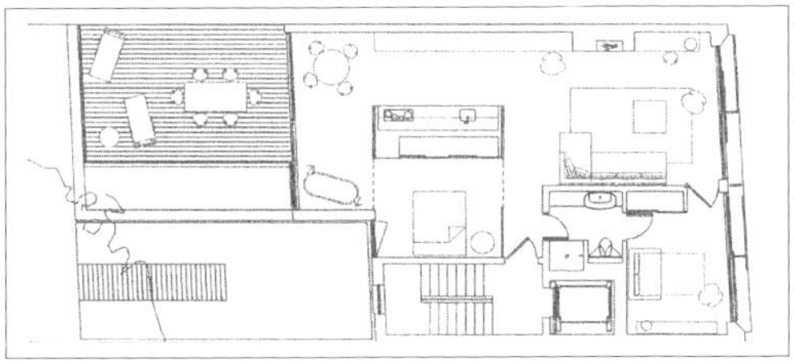

Plan of the 1st floor

Urbanes Leben
2003/04
Mitte, Mulackstraße 12 and Joachimstraße 5
Architects: Jean-Marc Abcarius, Christian Burns

This small project evolves directly from the concept of urban life: arranged over a shop on the ground floor is a decisive, 3-storey living area set behind a glass-and-slat paneling, above which the building staggers backwards. Yet the liveliness and lightness of the façade atmospherically harmonizes with the surrounding cornice-laden public housing from the nineteenth century.

093

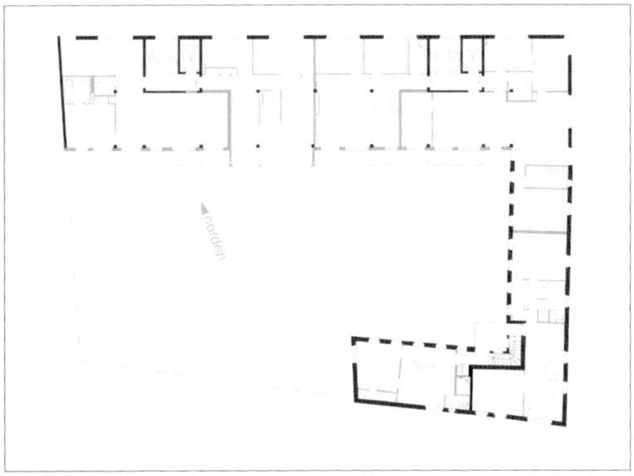

Plan of the 3rd floor

Apartments
2001–03
Mitte, Steinstraße 26–28
Architects: Silvia Carpaneto, Christian Schoeningh
Exterior facilities: Martin Erneth

Arranged in 3 building parts, the project included the participation of the future residents to create 22 spaces for apartments and 6 spaces for businesses as well as 12 parking spaces. Best understood in the view from the street, the plan incorporates both the courtyard's highly functional green areas as well as its greatly subdivided, colorful façade.

094

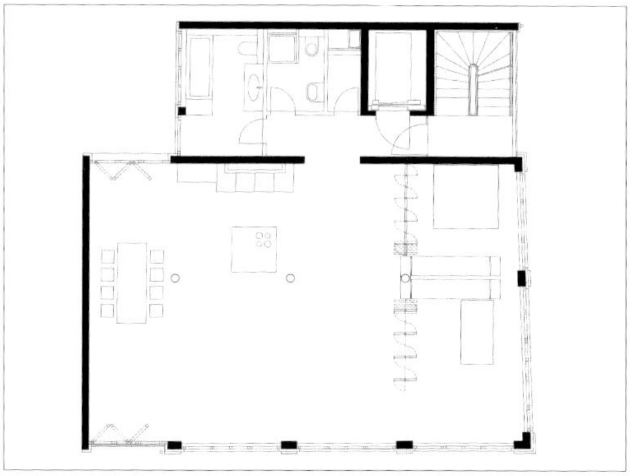

Plan of a standard floor

Loft building
2001
Mitte, Mulackstraße 24
Architect: Bernd Faskel
Client: S.A.R.F.

The possibility of residents designing the form of their own living and work spaces gains more popularity, encouraged here by the empty floors of unused commercial buildings. Combining this dream with all the comforts of a new structure was the obvious next step, especially when seen in relation to the attractiveness of the affordable prices of older commercial spaces – in this case, 1000 sqm for circa 2 million Euro.

095

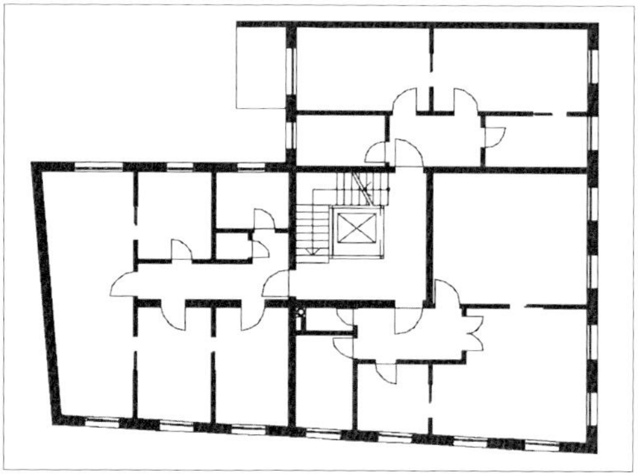

Plan of the 1st to the 3rd floors

Corner house
1999–2000
Mitte, Gormannstraße 24
Architects: Silvia Carpaneto, Christian Schoeningh
Client: Gormannstraße 24 Bauherren GmbH

"The corner house is divided according to the small-sectioned and true-to-size structuring found in the Spandau suburban area. Clearly visible here as a new building, it incorporates structural elements of the immediate vicinity's historic building substance. The subdivision of the street façades, using only a few serial elements, creates a sense of peace and consistency; at the same time, their suggested movements follow the house's rhythms and produces here a wide range of optical effects – self-confident in a dense, historical context." Above the commercial spaces on the ground floor are 3 upper floors, each housing 3 apartments, and an additional stepped, attic floor.

096

Courtyard façade

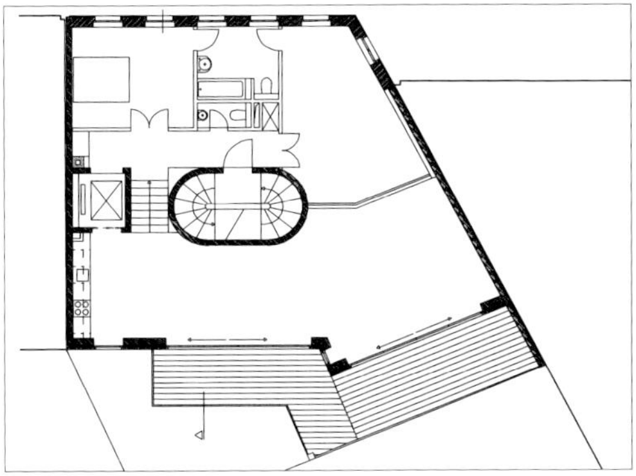

Plan of the 2nd floor

Haus Kicken
2003/04
Mitte, Linienstraße 161 A
Architect: Hans Düttmann
Client: Annette and Rudolf Kicken

The Kicken house is built on the 180 sqm floor area of a gap in the block, and offers 6 storeys that face the street. Utilizing a floor area of 650 sqm, the four storeys facing south and directed towards a playground, accommodate 3 split-level living units and gallery spaces on the same level. All the levels have access to an elevator. Both sides of the building are slightly staggered, moving towards the street in one direction, while withdrawing from the prominent neighboring building in the other.

097

Detail of the façade

SAP training center
2002/04
Mitte, Rosenthaler Straße at the corner of Gipsstraße
Architect: Mark Braun
Client: Rosenthaler Höfe Entwicklungsgesellschaft for SAP Deutschland

At a sophisticated site formerly occupied by a department store designed by Messel, the 6 storeys of the training center and office building were erected atop a 2-leveled underground garage. The total glazing, a sign of clarity and transparency, is structured by massive metal bands which incorporate the sun-shading and simultaneously signal the centralized entrance at the corner with a powerful swung form. The hall that follows this is spacious, bright, and subdivided in a lively manner. No differently than in the office areas, here, too, the architects intervened with a heightened sense of styling and developed lighting of their own design.

098

Wohnstadt Carl Legien
Carl Legien residential community
1929/30
Prenzlauer Berg, Erich-Weinert-Straße, Georg-Blank-Straße, Gerbitzstraße
Architects: Bruno Taut, Franz Hillinger
Client: GEHAG

Unlike most new-style housing development, this example of a modern quarter for a residential community is located in the inner-city. The building rows along the block's longer sides are realigned to open blocks with the shorter building parts, "making it possible to ideally combine here a convincingly compact metropolitan architecture with generously proportioned park-like areas of greenery" (Wolfgang Schäche). As usual, the adjoining color concept that Bruno Taut developed works with powerful yellow, turquoise, and signal-red tones. On Sodtkestraße, a few of the building parts were restored during 1995 renovating measures.

Because ot the excellent condition of this outstanding, intraurban example of a settlement with not a trace of individual privat proprietors and best maintenance this community got the label Unesco world heritage in July 2008

099

Buschallee housing complex
1928–30
Weißensee, Buschallee, Gartenstraße
Architect: Bruno Taut
Renovation and Modernization: Winfried Brenne

The lengthy, 3-storey constructions rows on both sides of the wide boulevard (Buschallee) have recessed attic floors of a contrasting red color. Their longitudinal presence is further strengthened by large loggia positioned in front of consistently small apartments bundled together in twos. The traffic noise, especially of the streetcars, made it necessary to build a glazing during the 1993–98 renovating measures.

100

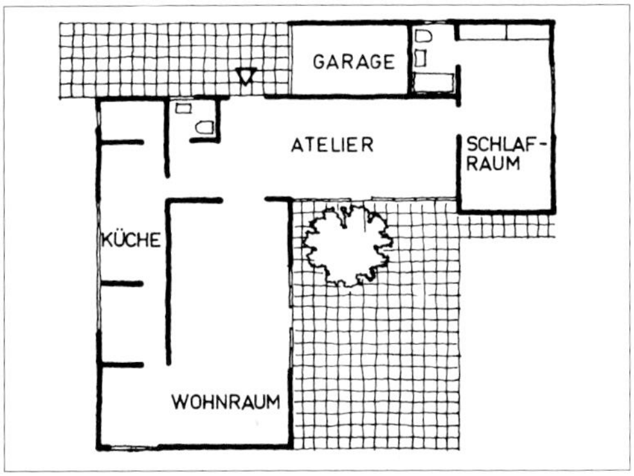

Haus Lemke / Mies-van-der-Rohe-Haus
1932
Weißensee, Oberseestraße 60
Architect: Ludwig Mies van der Rohe
Renovation: Winfried Brenne

On innumerable occasions – both in practice and in his teachings – Mies confronted the development of the "single-storey, flat-roofed, corner" building type. This house exemplifies the manner in which hallway and corridor resolve the development of spaces which merge on the same level. Despised by the Nazis, and wholly neglected during the GDR period, together with its brick walls and the slender, steel profiles of its large windows, the building had to be thoroughly renovated and now functions as an art gallery in the Pankow / Weißensee district.

101

Main entrance

Entranceway lobby

Elementary school
1994/95
Karow Nord, Achillestraße 31 at the corner of Bucher Chaussee
Architects: Axel Liepe, Hartmut Steigelmann
Open-area planning: Norbert Müggenburg with TOPOS
Client: Bezirk Weißensee

The result of a 1993 competition: the construction not only emphasizes the triangular site it stands on, which develops here to a point; it also turns this point into the location and main entrance for both 2-storey wings of classrooms with colonnade and gymnastics hall, stretching in a southerly direction as far as Bucher Chaussee. The building's contents are heightened by the disciplined yet lively interplay of brick façades engaged from the tip of the property, with its elevated projecting roof, to a youth clubhouse with the superintendent's apartment.

102

North-west side

Courtyard side

Housing
1994/95
Karow-Nord
Architects: Jan Rave, Roosje Rave
Garden planning: Ariane Rönz
Client: Gehag

Following an urban planning concept by Charles E. Moore, John Ruble and Buzz Yudell, the center of this area for housing estate at Berlin's city limits is an oval-shaped medallion, whose design is more like that of a Baroque castle complex, although it could also be compared to the horseshoe-shaped colony by Taut in the district of Britz **(169)**. In turn, the loggias, glazed on their east side, orient themselves towards this sophisticated open space and function as solarium. The absence of elevators for 4 plus 1 floors, as well as not having parking facilities meant exclusively for residents, make the apartments difficult to rent.

103

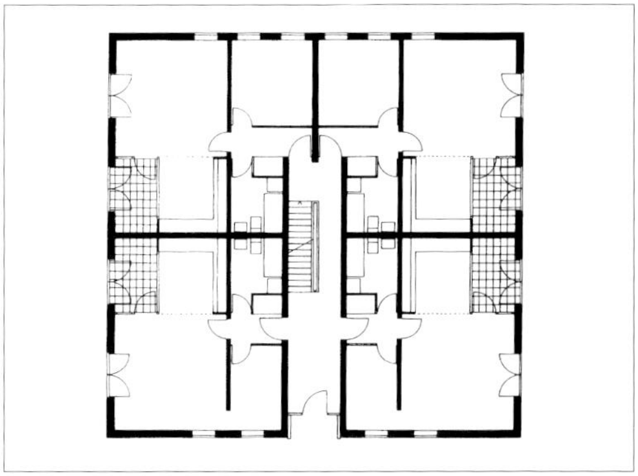

Plan of the ground floor

Two apartment houses
1994–96
Karow-Nord, Achillesstraße 34 + 36
Architect: Stephan Höhne with Christian Rapp
Client: Groth + Graalfs

Because of its dominating saddle roof (or "hung-fish roof") shrouding the 3 upper floors, this house built on a square floor plan is given a single direction. The roof causes the $1^1/_2$- and $2^1/_2$-room apartments of the doubled duplex to taper as they develop upward. This type of roof also appears in a few hall constructions and prefabricated houses from the 1930s. Another example of applying the theme of a heightened axis is used by the same architects for the child daycare center on Münchehagenstraße 43.

104

North façade facing the highway

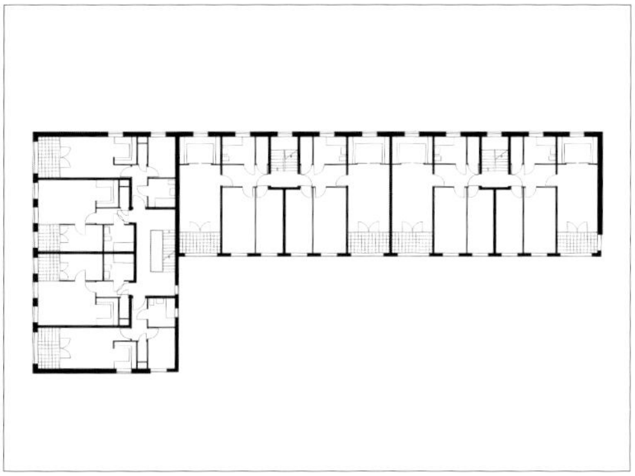

Plan of a standard floor

Apartment houses on the Ring
1996–98
Karow-Nord, Am Ring
Architects: Dieter Eckert, Hubertus Negwer, Detlef Sommer, Wouter Suselbeck
Client: Gehag

At the northern terminus opposite the motorway circulation, the morphological dimensions of these massive, barn-like buildings seem to defy the expressway with their practically closed walls, behind which lie sanitary facilities and staircases. But when facing south, in the direction of the apartment colonies, the same walls reveal large openings.

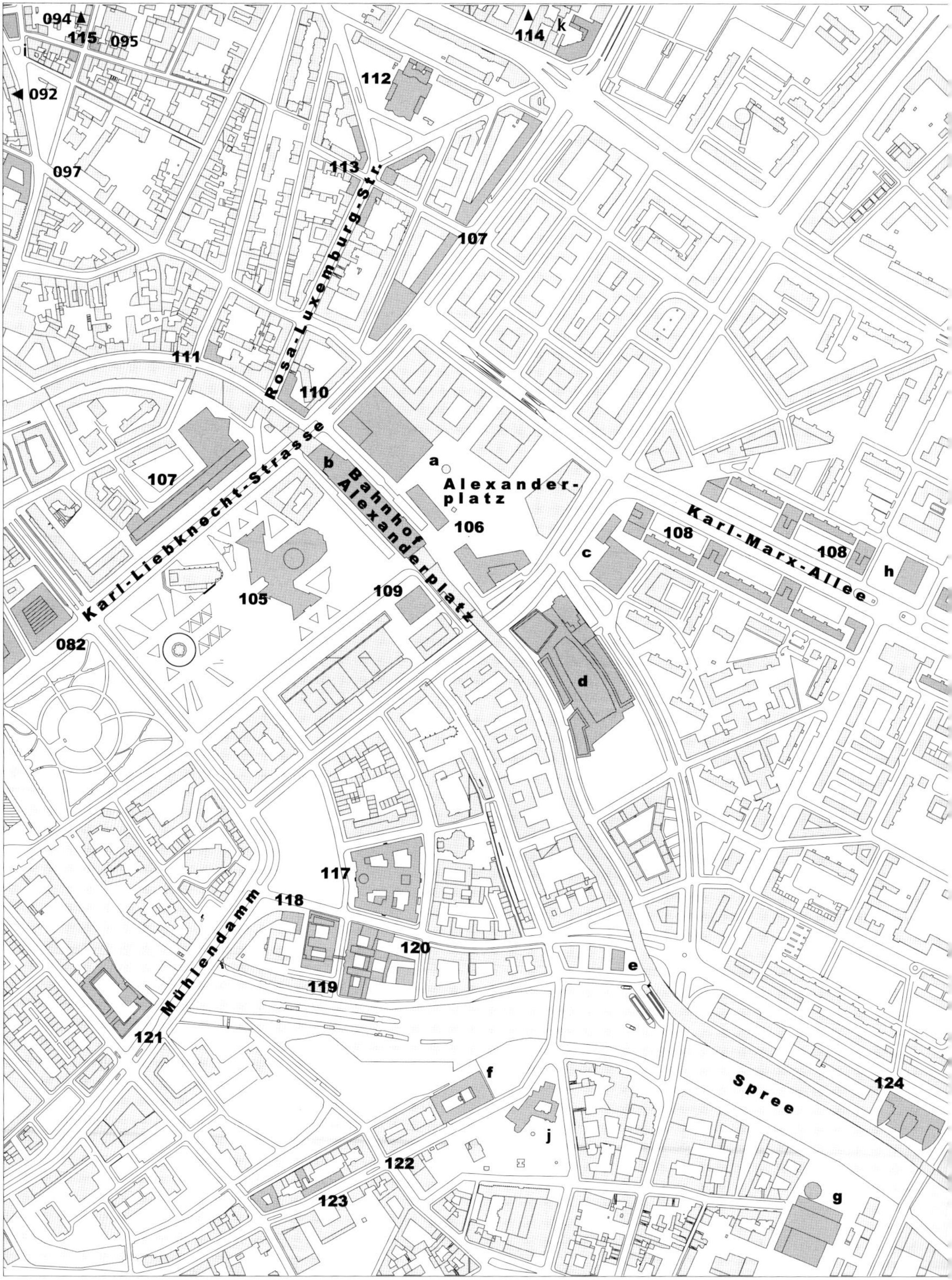
094
115
095
092
097
112
113
114
k
i
Rosa-Luxemburg-Str.
107
111
110
107
b
a
Bahnhof Alexanderplatz
Alexanderplatz
106
Karl-Liebknecht-Strasse
105
109
082
c
108
Karl-Marx-Allee
108
h
d
117
118
120
e
119
Mühlendamm
121
f
j
Spree
124
122
123
g

Alexanderplatz E

No.	Building	Architect
082	Dom Aquarée	nps und partner (now: nps tchoban voss)
092	Urbanes Leben	Jean-Marc Abcarius, Christian Burns
094	Loft building	Bernd Faskel
095	Corner house	Silvia Carpaneto, Christian Schoeningh
097	SAP training center	Mark Braun
105	Television tower	Fritz Dieter, Günter Franke, Hermann Hensel-mann
106	Berolina-Haus / Alexander-Haus	Peter Behrens
107	Karl-Liebknecht-Straße area	Wolfgang Radke
108	Karl-Marx-Allee	Egon Hartmann, Hermann Henselmann, Kurt W. Kurt W. Leucht, Richard Paulick, Karl Souradny and others
109	CUBIX	nps und partner (now: nps tchoban voss)
110	Administration building of the Wohnungsbau-gesellschaft Berlin-Mitte	Jochen Jentsch, Bernhard Brabetz, Klaus Bendler
111	Transformer station and commercial building	Alfred Grenander
112	Volksbühne	Oskar Kaufmann
113	Lichtspiel-Theater Babylon	Hans Poelzig
114	Königstadt-Brauerei	Thomas Müller, Ivan Reimann
115	ten in one	Christoph Roedig, Ulrich Schop
116	Loft house	Klaus Schlosser, Jean Lamborelle
117	Stadthaus	Ludwig Hoffmann, Gerhard Spangenberg
118	Office building	Christoph Langhof
119	Berliner Wasserbetriebe headquarters	Joachim Ganz
120	Niederländische Botschaft	Rem Koolhaas / OMA
121	Haus der Deutschen Wirtschaft	Schweger Assoziierte
122	Office building of the Allgemeiner Deutscher Gewerkschaftsbund	Max Taut, Franz Hoffmann
123	Art'otel Ermeler-Haus	Johanne Nalbach
124	Trias office building	Lucia Beringer, Günther Wawrik
a	Galeria Kaufhof, extension and façade	Kleihues + Kleihues, 2005–07
b	Bahnhof Alexanderplatz	Rebecca Chestnutt, Robert Niess, 1998
c	Haus des Lehrers	Hermann Henselmann, Bernhard Geyer, Jörg Streitparth, 1961–64
d	Alexa-Shoppingcenter	Laurids Ortner, Manfred Ortner, José Quintela de Fonseca, 2007
e	Sozialverband Deutschland headquarters	Hilde Léon, Konrad Wohlhage, Siegfried Wernik, 2002/03
f	Brasilianische Botschaft	Pysall, Stahrenberg & Partner
g	Thermal power station	Jochem Jourdan, Bernhard Müller, 1994–97
h	Kino International	Josef Kaiser, Heinz Aust & Kollektiv, 1961–63
i	ro 63	Fin Bartels, Christoph Schmidt-Ott, 2003/04
j	Märkisches Museum	Ludwig Hoffmann, 1900–08
k	Warenhaus Jonaß / Soho House Berlin	Gustav Bauer, Siegfried Friedländer, 1928; J.S.K. Architekten, 2009

105

Model

Television tower
1965–69
Mitte, Rathausstraße / Klosterstraße
Architects: Fritz Dieter, Günter Franke with Hermann Henselmann
Engineers: W. Ahrendt with VEB Industrie-Projektmanagement I

Erected close to city hall and the Marienkirche in the city center, thus making it visible from every radial street, the 361-m-high mast meanwhile symbolizes the entire reunified Berlin. The tower's head – elevated as a pre-assembled construction onto a 250-m high reinforced concrete column – houses transmission-related, technical facilities as well as a restaurant, which makes a full turn on its own axis every hour. Among the exterior facilities are information and gastronomical services. The staggered, fountain and garden complexes include the newly restored "Neptunbrunnen" designed by Reinhold Begas in 1891.

106

Berolina-Haus / Alexander-Haus
1930–32
Mitte, Alexanderplatz, Dircksenstraße
Architect: Peter Behrens

The result of a 1927 competition: while following the urban planning guidelines of that time, two slab rows form a clearly defined, vertical, portal situation edged with two glazed elevators. The protruding, 1st floor is a base storey with a projected roof. Above this, six floors of offices rise up in the skeletal framework of a steel and concrete construction method in front of a grid of square and, at the same time, quartered double-windows. In 1952, the building was repaired and restored. It was renewed in 1993–95 by the office of Pysall und Stahrenberg. The connecting department store at the northern side received a new façade courtesy of the office of Kleihues + Kleihues in 2005/06. The overall area of Alexanderplatz is part of an expansive and not yet completed inner-city renewal, which reaches as far as the Jannowitz-Brücke and assumes the structural form of a "banana".

107

Stadtschloß competition 2008/09, 1st prize by Franco Stella

Karl-Liebknecht-Straße area
1968–73
Mitte, Karl-Liebknecht-Straße
Architect: Wolfgang Radke
Urban planning: Joachim Nähter

Opposite the Gothic-style Marienkirche from 1270, and parallel to the space-generating, red-brick, construction row located on the square of the "Rotes Rathaus" from 1861–1869, the complex has a metropolitan character, but also the power of the English "New Brutalism". With a strong horizontal orientation, its structures are subdivided by a colonnade, glazed band of stores on the 1st floor, and, above these, 3 x 3 m residential floors which develop a longitudinal passageway connected to both elevator shafts. Powerful, cast-in-place concrete and prefabricated construction elements complete the complex. The vast, open area formed here was spatially closed, directly on the Spree River (where the Stadtschloß once stood), by the "Palast der Republik", a GBR edifice now being demolished for rebuilding the Stadtschloß.

108

Block F north by Karl Souradny

Block B north by Richard Paulick

Karl-Marx-Allee
1952–58
Friedrichshain, from Strausberger Platz to Frankfurter Allee
Design: Egon Hartmann, Hermann Henselmann, Kurt W. Leucht, Richard Paulick, Karl Souradny and others

Parallel to West Berlin's "Interbau" **(416–435)** a counter-model was built here – the antithesis of Western-characterized urban concepts – in which a city street is determined by the flow of traffic without establishing a spatial relationship to the constructed surroundings. In any case, created here was a monumental, city square and street network with densely decorated 8- and 10-storey buildings (based on the Russian socialistic model), which consistently follow an axis and reflect in their entirety the axis of this 2-km long showpiece boulevard formerly known as "Stalin-Allee". The apartments were provided and refurbished with elevators and disposal systems.

109

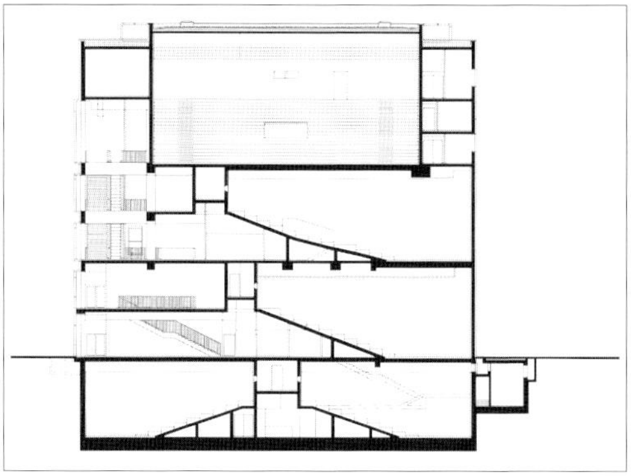

Cross section

CUBIX
2000/01
Mitte, Alexanderplatz / Rathausstraße 1
Architects: nps und partner (now: nps tchoban voss)
Client: TLG Treuhand Liegenschaftsgesellschaft

In *Berlin – Neue Architektur*, the author writes: "On a 37 x 46 m floor area and distributed over 4 levels, the multi-complex cinema offers seating for altogether 2,400 people in 9 newly built movie theaters. Surfaced with black granite slabs, the façade is interrupted by expansive, horizontally arranged strips of windows embracing the building's corners."

110

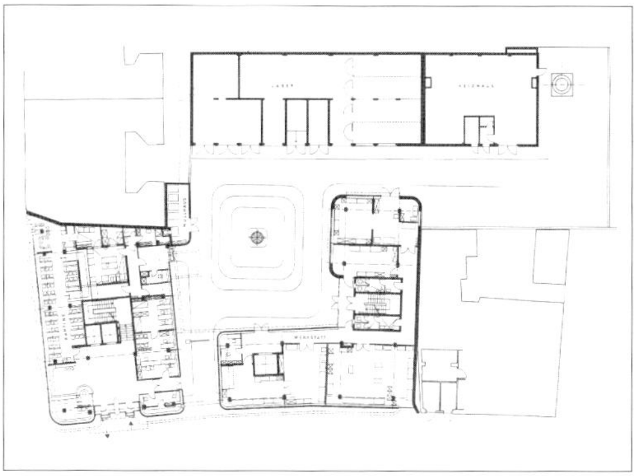

Plan of the 1st to the 5th floors

Administration building of the Wohnungsbaugesellschaft Berlin-Mitte
1984–87
Mitte, Dircksenstraße at the corner of Rochstraße
Architects: Jochen Jentsch, Bernhard Brabetz, Klaus Bendler
Client: Wohnungsbaugesellschaft Berlin-Mitte

This lift-slab construction visibly benefits from exposing its orthogonal, pre-cast concrete slabs: the movement on the street is further emphasized by the building's rounded corners. The glazed strips of clinker bricks are interrupted only once – to accommodate the entrance hall and give the building an astounding freshness. Some 50,000 of the district's communal apartments were managed and maintained from this spot since 1900.

111

Detail of the façade

Transformer station and commercial building
1930
Mitte, Dircksenstraße at the corner of Rosa-Luxemburg-Straße
Architect: Alfred Grenander

Built as a reinforced-concrete frame construction, today the commercial building houses part of the administrative facilities of the BVG (Berlin transportation authority). The building is located over a subway tunnel and encloses the transformer station in an angular arrangement in the courtyard. During this period, as director of the BVG construction department, Alfred Grenander gave many Berlin train stations and complexes their distinctive character.

112

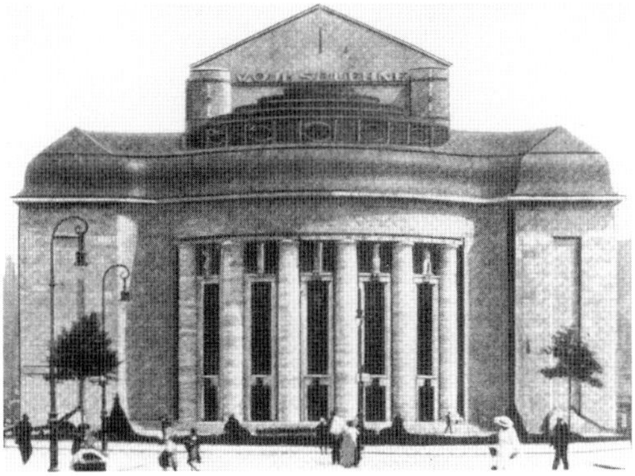

State preceding the destruction

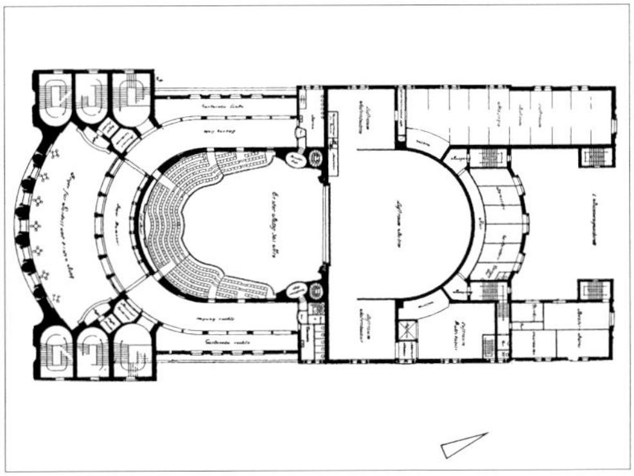

Gallery level

Volksbühne
People's theater
1913–15
Mitte, Rosa-Luxemburg-Platz
Architect: Oskar Kaufmann
Reconstruction: Hans Richter

Burned down during the war, the building was soon rebuilt in a somewhat altered form – without the visible roof over the auditorium and stage tower. During the renovation or clearing out of the historical city district Scheunenviertel, this building so extravagantly furnished for a people's theater, boasting revolving and lateral stages as well as a wealth of swung surfaces in its exterior design, was the first, new building to appear at this site. The development of the surrounding area first began 13 years later **(113)**. After its destruction during the war, the theater's 1950–54 reconstruction was carried out on a rather low budget, which unfortunately led to losing the distinctive roof silhouette and original interior space.

113

Design study

Lichtspiel-Theater Babylon
The Babylon movie theater
1928–30
Mitte, Rosa-Luxemburg-Straße 30
Architect: Hans Poelzig
Town planning with Richard Ermisch

The interior space of the "Lichtspiel-Theater" was completely redesigned to meet with today's standards. At the same time, the entire building was integrated in the east side of a city square development also designed by Poelzig. Instead of reacting to the asymmetric path of the traffic, the form assumed by the city square creates a highly distinctive space, symmetrically reflected around the centralized theater **(112)**. Large roof overhangs and horizontal cornices lend the square its modern appearance.

114

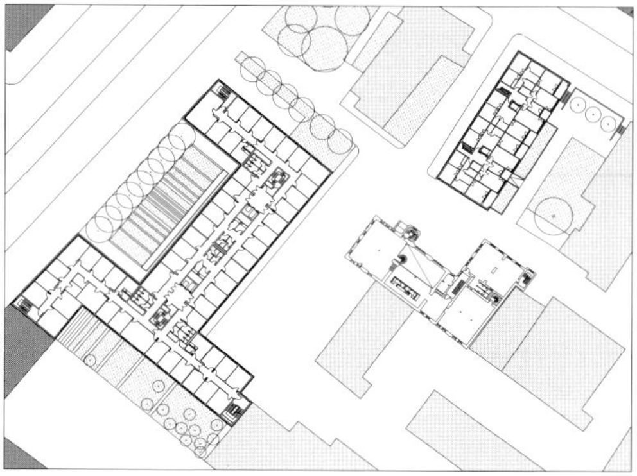

Site plan

Königstadt-Brauerei
1993–97
Prenzlauer Berg, Schönhauser Allee at the corner of Saarbrücker Straße
Architects: Thomas Müller, Ivan Reimann
Project manager: Regula Scheibler
Landscape planning: Kienast, Vogt und Partner
Client: Nürnberger Versicherung

The office and apartment building inserted in the brewery's former grounds at the south-facing slope of "Prenzlberg", the hill of this East Berlin district, transforms part of the malt-producing works into a series of lofts with office spaces. Here the outward-oriented spaces, together with internal passageways and streets, turn the building ensemble into a city within a city. Massive constructional forms, natural stone, and dark-hued sintered brick build bridges to the preserved building parts.

115

Floor-plan alternatives

ten in one
2004/05
Mitte, Anklamer Straße 52
Architects: Christoph Roedig, Ulrich Schop
Client: Bauherrengemeinschaft

While one part of the success was to find and bring together 10 congenial partners, the other was to have them all harmonize within a single design-related canon. The prerequisite for achieving this was the building's clear organization, conducive to individual design wishes; reserved façades with horizontal strips of metal; floor-high, asbestos cement paneling and wooden-framed windows; exposed concrete surfaces in the common-used ground floor, and a roof-top terrace with an apartment for guests.

116

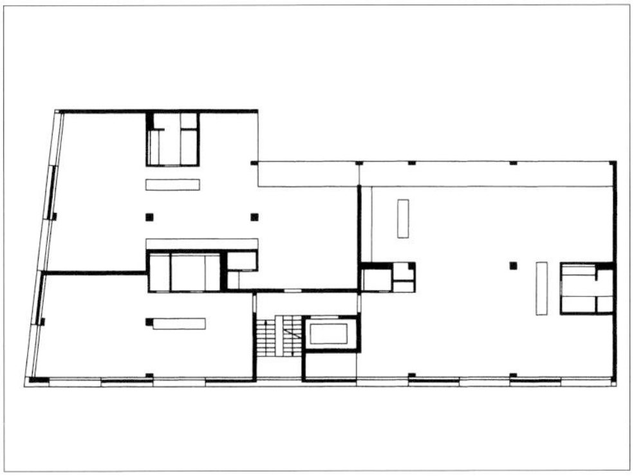

Loft house
2003–05
Mitte, Schröder-Straße at the corner of Bergstraße
Architects: Klaus Schlosser, Jean Lamborelle
Client: BLOG Berlin Loft

In this urban area made up almost entirely of well-preserved nineteenth-century housing (already offering hard to rent objects), the low ground floor of the building contributes to creating the tallest possible floor heights for apartments. Nevertheless this closed base was well-suited to accommodating an entranceway, 17 parking spaces, and storage areas for bicycles. The 5 floors and stepped floor are emphasized by vivid cement ledges, between which window panes and their encasements lie uniformly arranged in handsome rows, in keeping with the building's dignified character.

117

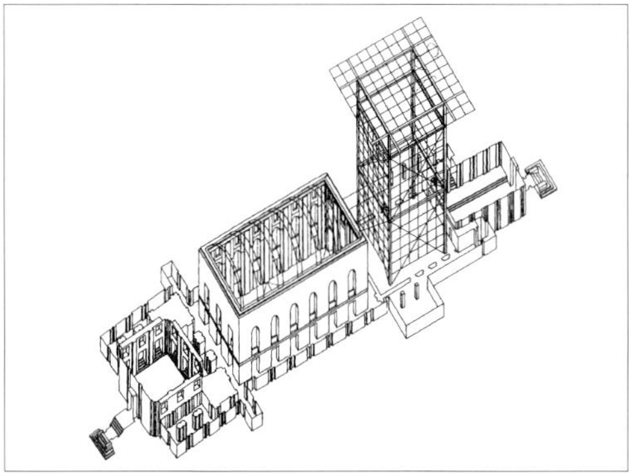

Axonometric drawing of the middle axis

Stadthaus
City hall
1911–14 / 1996–98
Mitte, Jüdenstraße at the corner of Stralauer Straße
Architect: Ludwig Hoffmann
Revitalization: Gerhard Spangenberg
Client: Senat von Berlin
Erected during the reign of Wilhelm II of Germany, this building designed by Ludwig Hoffmann was meant to supplement the "Rotes Rathaus" as a so-called technical city hall. After repairing its war-inflicted damages during the GDR period, it was given a substantially flatter roof. Today, following its well-conceived reconstruction and the addition of a glass tower, it serves as the Senate's department for the interior and sports, where representative summits and receptions are often held. The main auditorium, the so-called "Bärensaal", however lacks ideal lighting and acoustics.

118

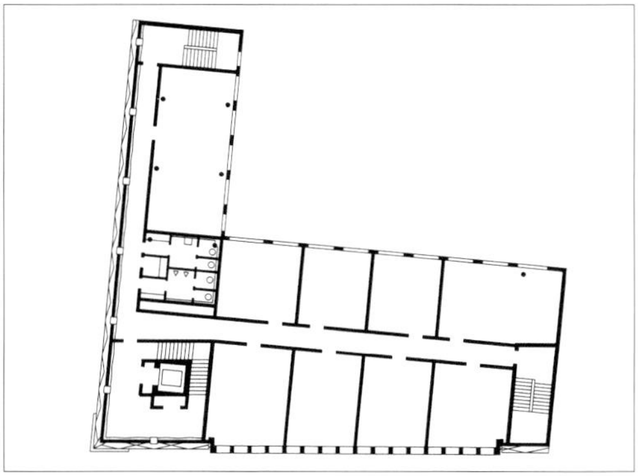

Plan of the ground floor

Office building
1998–2000
Mitte, Molkenmarkt at the corner of Mühlendamm
Architect: Christoph Langhof
Client: Deutsche Immobilien Leasing
The west-facing section of the three-part business headquarters is the seat of the Berlin waterworks "The chosen architectural language orients itself to the form-related canons of Expressionism and Cubism. While its self-sufficient language and the staging of the structural aesthetics establish a unique relationship to the urban surroundings, the resulting quality stimulates and strengthens the overall urban structure."

119

View of the entranceway court

Berliner Wasserbetriebe headquarters
1997–2000
Mitte, Neue Jüdenstraße 1
Architect: Joachim Ganz
Client: Berliner Wasserbetriebe

At the former central office grounds the existing building parts were preserved and expanded by newer ones. This led to creating the centralized, glass-roofed court at the entranceway as well as the lobby made of two sides of the old building and two entirely new sides. Their different levels connect here and combine all the publicly accessible locations – customer center, gastronomical services, press department, and bank. The theme of water and waves is repeatedly handled in a variety of ways, whether (as shown here) in the lobby's floor design or in the façade.

120

Niederländische Botschaft
Dutch Embassy
2000–04
Mitte, Klosterstraße 50
Architects: Rem Koolhaas / OMA with Ellen van Loon, Michelle Howard
Client: Dutch Foreign Ministry
Architekturpreis Berlin 2003

Engaged in part as a ramp placed alongside the outer wall, the building's spatial indenting and decentralized development culminate in an exciting route that travels over 8 levels. The solitary cube of office chambers "creates a structural manifesto in opposition to Berlin's prevailing architectural and urban planning schemes. Its enormously multifaceted architecture is further emphasized by the use of seemingly cool materials – in a building that leaves no one cold".

121

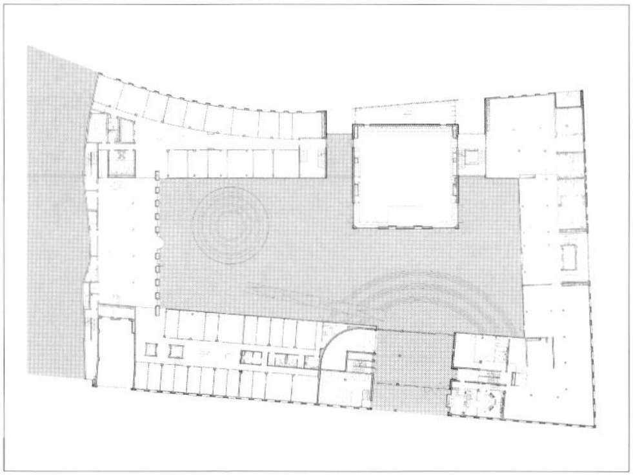

Plan of the ground floor

Haus der Deutschen Wirtschaft
1997–99
Mitte, Breite Straße 25–29
Architects: Schweger Assoziierte
Landscape Architect: Gustav Lange
General supervisor: Groth Gruppe
Client: DIHT, BDI, BDA

This project is the result of a 1994 competition focused on the headquarter for three, large business associations, and the sectioning of their façades by using either a lighter and more green sandstone surfacing or expansive glass surfaces along the Spree River – as with the conference tower and main entrance – together with a common, glazed courtyard. Floor area: 27,000 sqm; building costs: circa 100 million Euro. Schweger Assoziierte were also the architects of a great auditorium in the Bundesrat building near Leipziger Platz.

122

Conference hall

Office building of the Allgemeiner Deutscher Gewerkschaftsbund
1922/23
Mitte, Inselstraße, Wallstraße
Architects: Max Taut, Franz Hoffmann

This reinforced-concrete frame construction with filler walls made of masonry was one of the first concrete skeleton constructions to feature a "visible" façade subdivision. Not only the building's structural analysis is expressive; the same applies to its design – from the pilaster strips built over corner sections to the interior spaces and furnishings. This example of early 1920s architecture shows how the enduring influences of Expressionism, able to be traced back over the course of the entire Art Nouveau movement, were more inclined to promote the "new and heightened plasticity" of the "Neue Sachlichkeit" movement with Bauhaus aesthetics.

123

Art'otel Ermeler-Haus
1997
Mitte, Märkisches Ufer 10–12, Wallstraße 70–73
Architect: Johanne Nalbach
General artistic direction: Georg Baselitz
Clients: Sylvia Gädeke, Dirk Gädecke

An urban connection route is made possible through the block by linking the restaurant and banquet spaces of the Baroque-styled Ermeler building on the canal's north side to an austere, new building on its south side. This simultaneously creates a contrast between two worlds standing side by side. Following the hotel concept used for all the "Art'otels", the building also serves as a exhibition space for contemporary artists, showcasing many artworks by Georg Baselitz. In the Art'otel by the same architects on Joachimstaler Straße are works by the artist Wolf Vostell.

124

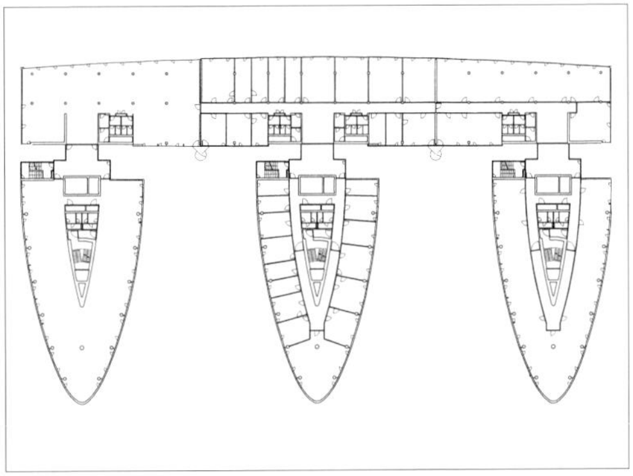

Plan of the 4h-floor

Trias office building
1994–96
Mitte, Holzmarktstraße 15–18
Architects: Lucia Beringer, Günther Wawrik
Client: DG Anlage

This unavoidable landmark in the commercial landscape and waterways of the Oberhavel area is a part of a development that stretches as far as Treptower Park "Mediaspree". Three identical, elegant, and ship-like forms, whose bows face the river, create a line of 13-storey office buildings. At their rear along the street, the Trias are connected by a linear building.

125

Aerial shot from the west

Sports stadium for cycling

Europa-Sportpark
1995–99
Prenzlauer Berg, Landesberger Allee 15–27
Architect: Dominique Perrault
Engineering: Arup
Landscape architects: Landschaft Planen und Bauen
Client: Olympia Sportstättenbauten

As part of the international competition for the 2000 Olympic Games, a well-configured sports stadium for the disciplines cycling and swimming was built at this site. Its axial alignment on the open block within a circle and rectangle, and having it well-embedded in the excavated property, allowed the western dimension of the open space to advance toward an undisturbed field of vision. The project planning and construction lasted 8 years. Floor area: 98,000 sqm; building costs: circa 280 million Euro.

126

"Sonnenhof" housing block
1926/27
Lichtenberg, Marie-Curie-Allee, Delbrückstraße
Architect: Erwin Gutkind
Client: Stadt- und Land-Siedlungsgesellschaft

This mid-1920s project concerns a closed peripheral development with various apartment types and shops arranged about the driveway to a courtyard. The roofs and slabs over the entranceways are finished in exposed concrete, and the parapets are given facings. Plastered surfaces extend beyond the consistently formated windows and join together in long bands, so that the building reveals a quality typical of Gutkind, namely, a certain heaviness with a marked stability at the same time; a quality that allowed the block to remain attractive over the following decades.

127

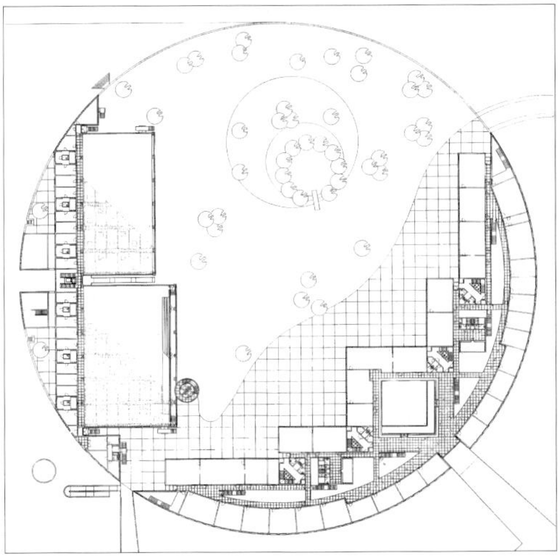

Plan of upper level

Barnim-Gymnasium
1995–98
Falkenberg, Ahrensfelder Chaussee 41
Architects: Bangert und Scholz
Project manager: Horst Krüger and Stefan Schlüleke
Client: Bezirksamt Hohenschönhausern

The building property's heterogeneous surroundings demanded an original solution powerful enough to set an order-giving accent. From this evolved the gymnasium's circular exterior form in which the two-leveled learning-and-sports area is inserted, allowing a north-oriented recreation court to develop between the levels' orthogonal interior lives at the same time. Two years later, close to the thoroughfare Hausvaterweg, Bangert designed a facility for housing animals, and its far-reaching garden complex also played with a circular motif. The office of Krafft + Wehberg took part in this project, with Joachim Hildebrandt as project manager.

128

View of the south façade

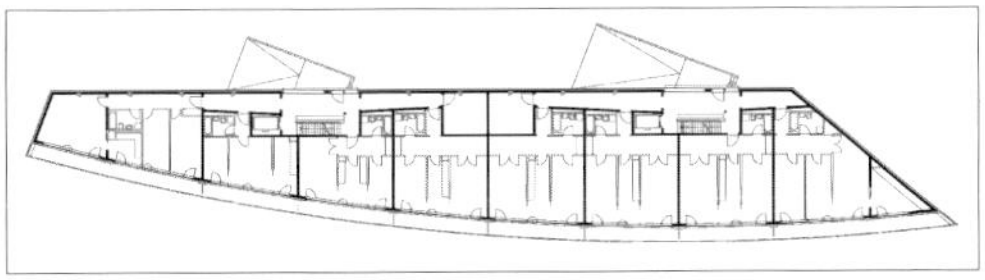

Plan of a standard floor

Low-energy house
1996/97
Marzahn, Niemeyer-Straße 2–4
Architects: Frank Assmann, Peter Salomon, Hermann Scheidt
Energy-saving concept: Arup
Client: WGB Marzahn

As the pilot project for energy-saving housing, the building form developed here uses a gently arched, convex southern façade with narrow continuous balconies to take advantage of the sun's lower position in the winter and to protect itself from the steeper angle of the sun's light in the summer months. Behind a scarcely opened northern façade lie public areas well-adapted to the advers weather side. The extravagant design of the building was meant to raise the property value of this district of concrete-slab constructions. Like elsewhere, here, too, the various necessary building measures resulted, in part, in surprising optical effects.

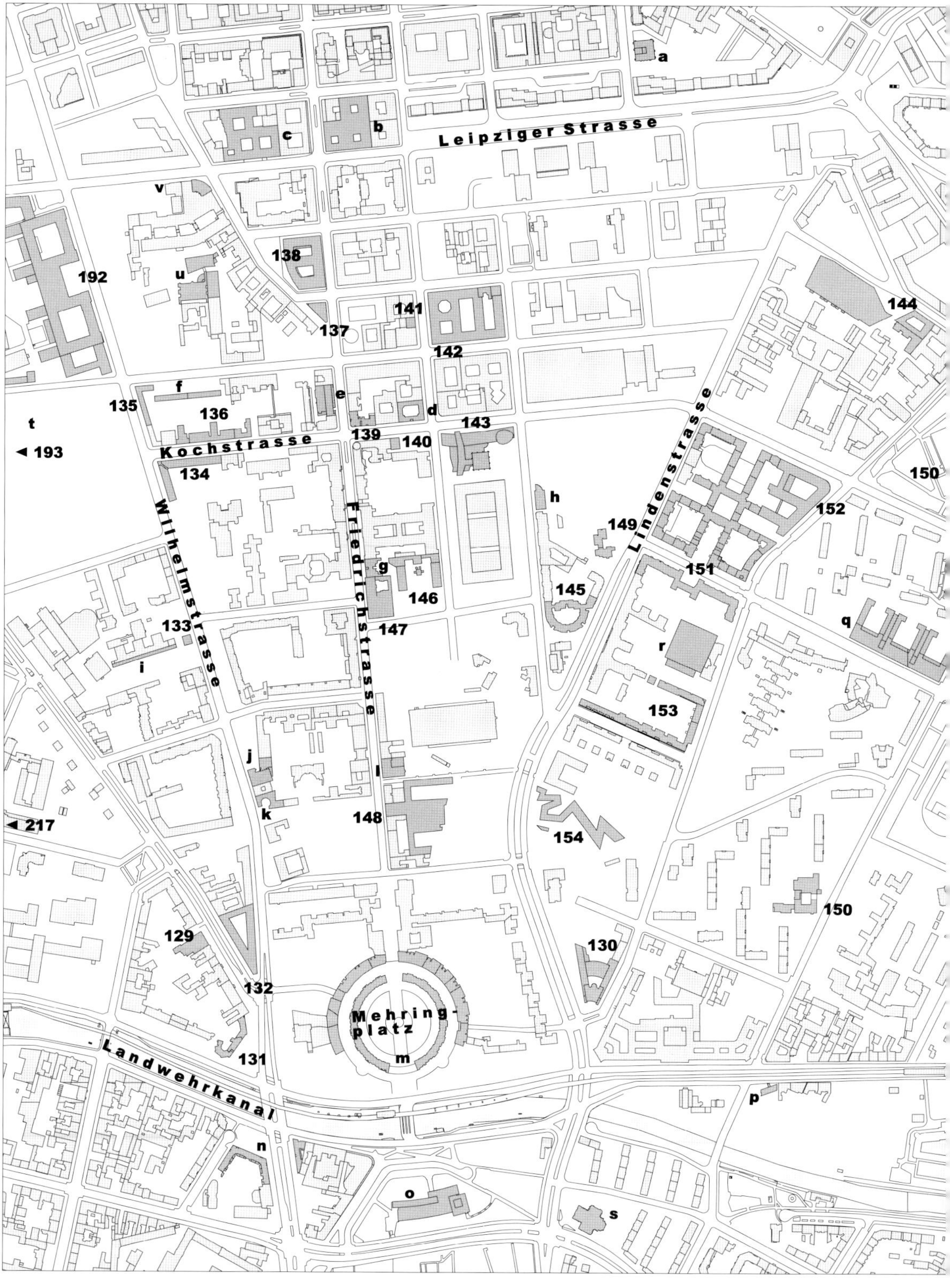
Leipziger Strasse
Kochstrasse
Wilhelmstrasse
Friedrichstrasse
Lindenstrasse
Mehring-
platz
Landwehrkanal
a
b
c
d
e
f
g
h
i
j
k
l
m
n
o
p
q
r
s
t
u
v
129
130
131
132
133
134
135
136
137
138
139
140
141
142
143
144
145
146
147
148
149
150
151
152
153
154
192
◄ 193
◄ 217

Mehringplatz SE

129	Hebbel-Theater	Oskar Kaufmann
130	Haus des Deutschen Metallarbeiter-Verbandes	Erich Mendelsohn, Rudolf W. Reichel
131	Apartment building and commercial spaces	Hermann Fehling, Daniel Gogel
132	Willy-Brand-Haus	Helge Bofinger
133	Apartment tower	Pietro Derossi
134	Apartment and business building	Aldo Rossi, Gianny Braghieri
135	Apartment building and courtyard with businesses	Joachim Schürmann
136	Southern corner development	Peter Faller, Christian Muschalek, Hermann Schröder; Martorell, Bohigas, Mackay;
137	Haus Triangel	Josef Paul Kleihues
138	Philip Johnson Building	Philip Johnson
139	Apartment and office building	Peter Eisenman, Jacqueline Robertson
140	Editorial offices of the taz newspaper	Gerhard Spangenberg
141	Apartment and commercial building	Johanne Nalbach
142	Quartier Schützenstraße	Aldo Rossi
143	GSW headquarters	Matthias Sauerbruch, Louisa Hutton
144	Bundesdruckerei	Bayerer, Hanson, Heidenreich, Schuster, Martinez, Stahlmann
145	LiMa apartment building	Herman Hertzberger, Laurens Cobben, Cor Kruter, Folker Stopsma
146	Apartment building with studio tower	John Hejduk
147	Hotel, office and commercial building	Max Dudler
148	Elementary school and special learning school	Gino Valle, Mario Broggi, Michael Burckhardt
149	"Alter Fritz" apartment and office building	Hans Müller, Georg Heinrichs
150	St.-Agnes-Kirche	Werner Düttmann
151	RIT apartment house	Rob Krier
152	Reichsschuldenverwaltung	German Bestelmeyer
153	Victoria housing development	Hans Kollhoff
154	Jüdisches Museum	Daniel Libeskind
192	Bundesministerium derFinanzen	Ernst Sagebiel
193	Abgeordnetenhaus von Berlin	Rolf Rave, Marina Stankovic, Jan Rave
217	District-court expansion	Oswald Mathias Ungers

a	Kindergarten	Volker Staab, Alfred Nieuwenhuizen, 2001/02
b	Atrium house	von Gerkan, Marg und Partner, 1995–97
c	Astron Hotel	Klaus Theo Brenner, 2000
d	Court house	Kammerer + Belz, Kucher und Partner, 1984/85
e	Checkpoint Charlie	Rem Koolhaas, 1987/88
f	Residential and commercial building	Fin Bartels, Christoph Schmidt-Ott, 1988–90
g	Residential and commercial building	Raimund Abraham, 1986/87
h	Haus der Presse	Jo Franzke, 1999–2000
i	Stepped building	Dietrich von Beulwitz, 1986–88
j	Residential building	Zeitler, Bier, Korn, 1990
k	House with a circular courtyard	Jan Rave, Rolf Rave, 1992–94
l	Ärztekammer Berlin	Hascher, Jehle Architektur 2001–03
m	Stadtquartier am Mehringplatz	Werner Düttmann, 1968–75
n	Residential and commercial building	Jan Rave, Rolf Rave, 1987–90
o	Amerika-Gedenkbibliothek	Bornemann, Jobst, Kreuer, Wille, 1952–58
p	Residential building	Plessow, Ehlers, 1992/93
q	Comb-like building	Andreas Brandt, Rudolf Böttcher, 1994
r	Berlinische Galerie	Jörg Fricke, 2002–04
s	Kirche zum Heiligen Kreuz	J. Otzen, 1884–88; v. Rosenberg, 1991–95
t	Topographie des Terrors	Ursula Wilms, Heinz Hallmann, 2008
u	Abspannwerk Buchhändlerhof/E-Werk	Hans Heinrich Müller, 1927/28; Hoyer, Schindele, 2004
v	Generalpostamt/Museum für Kommunikation	Carl Schwatto, 1872–74; Henze Vahjen, 1996–99

129

Hebbel-Theater
1907–09
Kreuzberg, Stresemannstraße 29
Architect: Oskar Kaufmann
This theater with seating for 676 guests on three levels was built using highly stylized forms and quaderstone surfaces to generate its monumental quality. The arrangement of the windows in the foyer's area and peripheral aisles is consolidated by larger forms and leads up to the swung pediment which typifies Kaufmann's designs. Another example of his couragous architecture is the Volksbühne **(112)** on Rosa-Luxemburg-Platz with four levels in former times. In the 1960s the modifications on the interior spaces were designed by Sigrid Kressmann-Zschach.

130

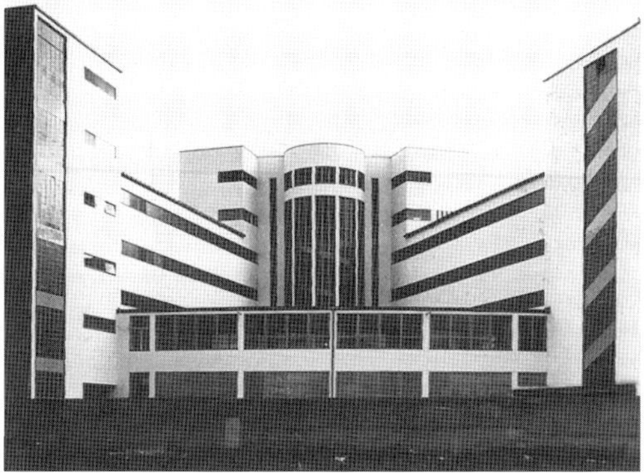

Rear view of the building

Haus des Deutschen Metallarbeiter-Verbandes
The German metal workers' union building
1929/30
Kreuzberg, Alte Jakobstraße 148–155
Architects: Erich Mendelsohn, Rudolf W. Reichel
In this reinforced concrete frame structure, the curve of the concave, head construction accommodates spaces for the board of directors and committee meeting rooms. Both lateral, 4-storey, office wings end at the printing works via the cross-connection. The round, glazed staircase located between the entrance hall and inner courtyard establishes a relationship to the bay windows at the front of the entrance, while the building's unique and consistent design concept is developed on all its sides.

131

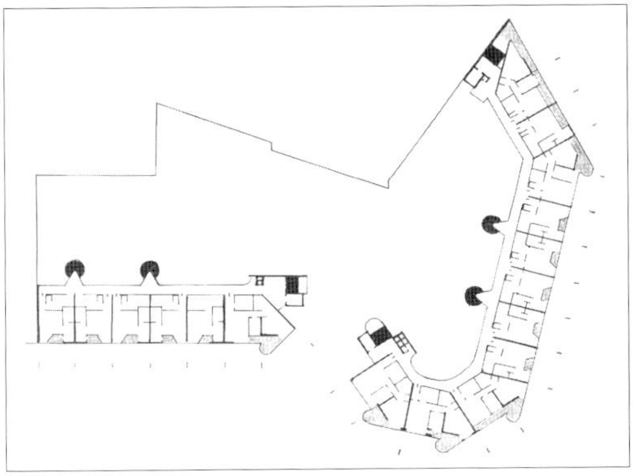

Plan of a standard floor

Apartment building and commercial spaces
1968
Kreuzberg, Hallesches Ufer 24–28 at the corner of Wilhelmstraße
Architects: Hermann Fehling, Daniel Gogel
Client: Heinz Mosch KG

At the conclusion of the street development along the Landwehrkanal, where the old playhouse of the Schaubühne stands even now, this strange building resembling a ship's bow, opposes the elevated train tracks and canal, and begins here a Scharoun-inspired interplay of open spaces and structural parts at the city square known as Mehringplatz. A prominent gap divides it into two parts which correspond with each other. In 1962, it was also Scharoun who conceived a newer, urban planning and traffic concept for the circular Belle-Alliance-Platz, where not even Werner Düttmann's massive, residential high-rises could compensate for the deserted streets.

132

Willy-Brandt-Haus
1993–96
Südliche Friedrichstadt, Stresemannstraße at the corner of Wilhelmstraße
Architect: Helge Bofinger
Statue of Willy Brandt: Rainer Fetting
Client: SPD

Moving the government's seat from Bonn to Berlin made it necessary for political parties to build new headquarters. An open passageway running through the ground floor and spacious glassed-over atrium make this building – with lecture hall, workspace for the press, and a gallery – a highly variable space for the government's administration. Multi-functionality is even part of the program. Both sides of the pointed triangular form, which resembles a ship's bow, are meticulously mirrored.

133

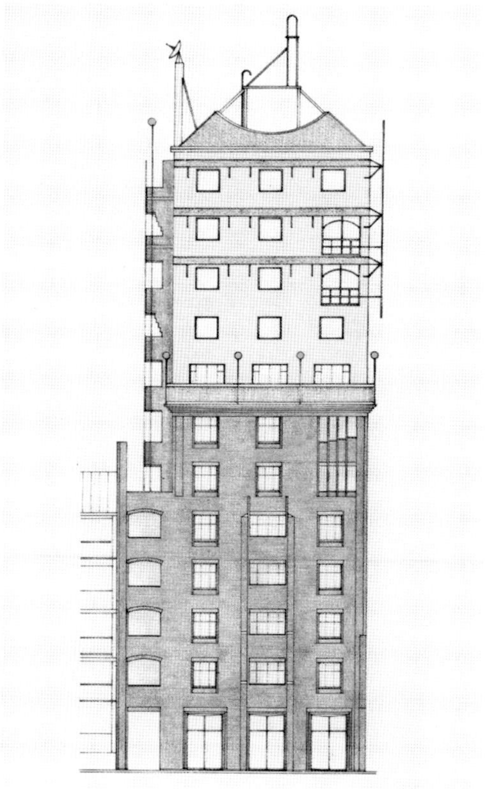

Elevation sketch

Apartment tower
1986–88
Südliche Friedrichstadt, Wilhelmstraße 119/120
Architect: Pietro Derossi
Contact architect: Klaus Kammann
Client: Klammt / IBA (InternationaBuilding Exhibition)

The public housing initiative subsidued by the city of Berlin and the Federal Government also made it possible to live in a tower – with 11 apartments, 11 storeys, elevator, trash disposal system, and staircases with escape balconies. This is more than a model living concept of the future. Thanks to its playful profile, cleverly conceived waistline section, and the broken open form of its tent roof, the apartment tower is also a visible landmark in the area of international constructing arts. Just behind is the terrassed self-made housing by Dietrich von Beulwitz.

134

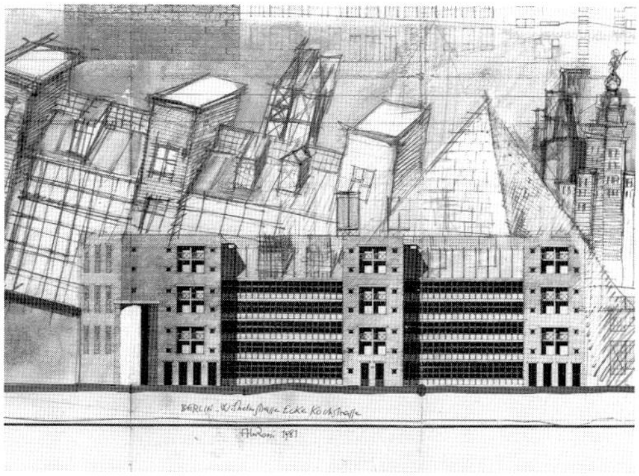

Drawing by Also Rossi

Apartment and business building
1986/87
Südliche Friedrichstadt, Wilhelmstraße at the corner of Kochstraße
Architects: Aldo Rossi, Gianni Braghieri
Contact architects: Grötzebach, Plessow, Ehlers
Client: Gebau / IBA (International Building Exhibition)

Following a 1980 IBA-sponsored competition, the design developed here was a clearly subdivided block corner supported by building materials with powerful colors: red and yellow bricks subdividing a façade perforated by small square windows and large 4-compartment windows; green-colored pitched-roofs capping staircase shafts, and a prominent white column, the pin of the hinge, as an icon of rational architectural thinking

135

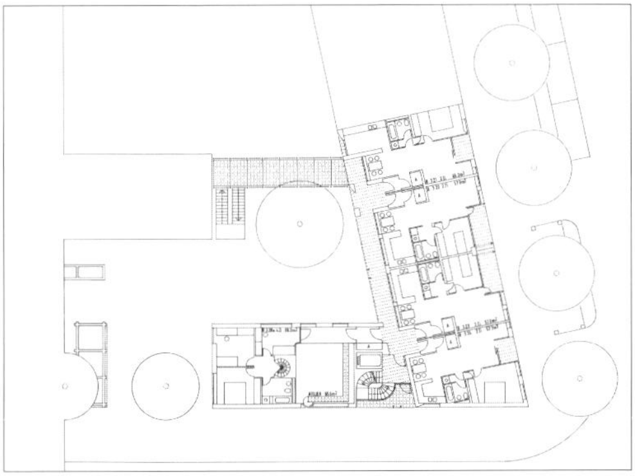

Plan of upper floors

Apartment building and courtyard with businesses
1988–90
Südliche Friedrichstadt, Wilhelmstraße at the corner of Zimmerstraße
Architect: Joachim Schürmann
Contact architects: Grötzebach, Plessow, Ehlers
Client: HKW / Konzepta / IBA (International Building Exhibiton)

The demonstrated goal of the International Building Exhibition had been to reproduce the almost entirely destroyed western part of the block while leaving undisturbed, on the northern border at Zimmerstraße, a sidewalk-width strip that runs along the city's border to the GDR and faces the Berlin Wall. So the well-balanced construction row by Bartels/Schmidt-Ott is somewhat recessed at this spot. The existing businesses integrated in the rebuilding concept included a large-scale commercial laundry.

136

Detailed view of the MBM part

Southern corner development
1987–89
Südliche Friedrichstadt, Kochstraße 69–75
Architects, longitudinal building: Peter Faller, Christian Muschalek, Hermann Schröder
Apartment courtyard and lateral buildings: Martorell, Bohigas, Mackay (MBM)
Clients: HKW / Konzepta / IBA (International Building Exhibiton)

Altogether both house types stand three times wall to wall, and hand in hand, as a corner construction on the edge of the street. One quickly recognizes the harmonizing of their cores here, produced by an impressive, well-devised urban row of building parts which contradict the prejudices – pathetically grey guidelines, for example – often voiced in connection with social housing.

137

Friedrichstraße view

Haus Triangel
1994–97
Südliche Friedrichstadt, Friedrichstraße 204
Architect: Josef Paul Kleihues with Norbert Heusel
Projekt manager: Peter Bastian
Client: Roland Ernst

Filling the entire corner, the building appears in the cityscape as a solitary structure and develops its own design principles as one: for the form of an unilateral triangle, it develops the theme of two like sides with a third side that remains unique. On Mauerstraße, the office and commercial building with its two attic floors emphasizes this theme to the same degree as it does its corner deviations.

138

Philip Johnson Building
1995–97
Mitte, Friedrichstraße at the corner of Mauerstraße
Architect: Philip Johnson
Contact architects: Pysall, Stahrenberg & Partner
Sculpture: Houseball by Claes Oldenburg

How often did the City of Berlin enlist the talents of famous, international architects who then found no access to this city? One of the contemporary giants is Philip Johnson, who unites here an alternating narrow and wide, stone tower using two horizontal bands, between which lie glass surfaces that casually assert themselves above the entranceways. At the rounded, west side of the building the pavement of a triangular area indicates the floor plan of the former so-called Böhmische Kirche to which the spherical sculpture, *Houseball*, also take reference.

139

Plan of a standard floor

Apartment and office building
1985/86
Südliche Friedrichstadt, Koch-/Friedrichstraße
Architects: Peter Eisenman, Jacqueline Robertson
Contact architects: Grötzebach, Plessow, Ehlers
Client: Hauert + Noack / IBA (International Building Exhibiton)

By way of the differentiating corner deviations and the motifs of its façade, the building reveals traces of an imaginary urban history and simultaneously releases the construction from the archetypal ending of a block. The fact that the building is used for social housing complicates the aspirations of the "release", but not regarding the so-called "Mauermuseum", who on the groundfloor commits itself to depicting the non-violent struggle, and does so here at the former "Checkpoint Charlie", once the border crossing between the East and West sectors. The apartment building integrated into the site in 1987 is strongly characterized by the design input of Rem Koolhaas together with Matthias Sauerbruch.

140

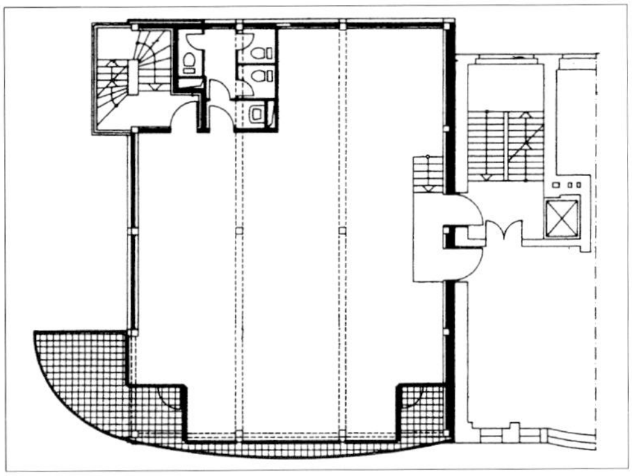

Plan of the 3rd floor of the addition

Editorial offices of the taz newspaper
1990/91
Südliche Friedrichstadt, Kochstraße 19
Architect: Gerhard Spangenberg
Construction manager: Felix Thoma
Client: taz

In today's urban planning schemes, the traffic produced by individuals alone is scarcely reflected in the overall concept. However, in the 1950s and 1960s, this was the top priority. The older office building at Kochstraße 19 barely escapes evolving from that period again: the bordering street was widened by an additional 21 m. Now the addition on the building's east side divulges the aligning of two property lines, and incorporates elements of the older building ..."without actually adapting itself to it".

141

Houses no. 78 and no. 77

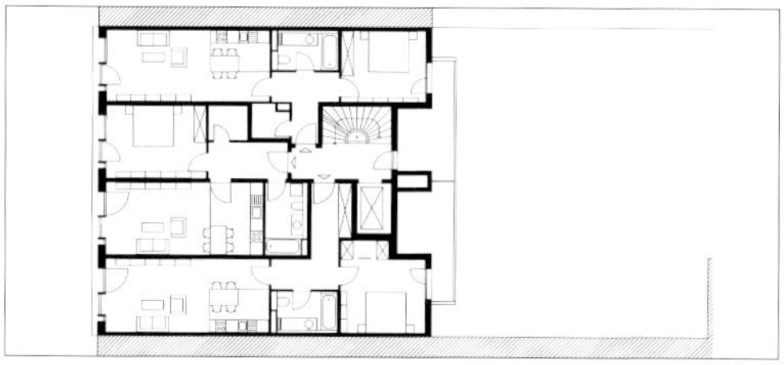

Apartment and commercial building
2000/01
Südliche Friedrichstadt, Charlottenstraße 78
Architect: Johanne Nalbach
Client: Winterthur Versicherungen

Beside the building renovated by the same architect (house no. 77), whose seemingly lightweight roof dormers compliment the façade's fine engraving, the façade of the new building stands in strong contrast to the other by virtue of its monolithic lava-stone facing, prominent floor slabs on each floor, powerful window encasements made of glazed pine wood, and its vivid structural elements. The building includes 5 storeys for apartments, each housing three 2-room apartments and two stepped floors. These rest on a ground floor whose shops are located above a 3-level underground parking facility.

142

Quartier Schützenstraße
1994–97
Südliche Friedrichstadt, Schützenstraße, Charlottenstraße
Architect: Aldo Rossi

Once again Aldo Rossi confirms his brilliance by questioning the basic principles of architecture and arriving at a perplexing result: the new block – at least a large portion of it – appears cleansed of all history. The alternating colors of history-generating façades, with a touch of the Palazzo Farnese in between, and office levels passing behind façades in perfect rows, tell us that the master builder can effortlessly break convention.

143

Southwest view

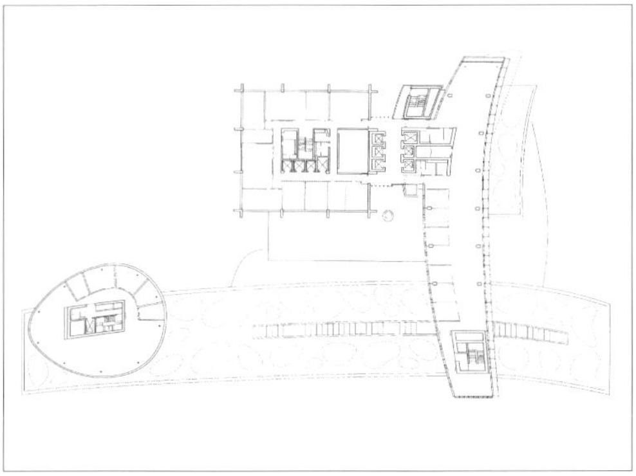

Plan of the 3rd floor

GSW headquarters
1995–99
Südliche Friedrichstadt, Kochstraße 22
Architects: Matthias Sauerbruch, Louisa Hutton
In-house technical facilities: Arup, Chris Trott
Façade: Emmer, Pfenniger und Partner
Architekturpreis Berlin 2000

Evolved from a 1991 competition, the structural ensemble conceptually encloses the existing building between two newer sections and produces a 3-storey, row construction with a cylindrical addition. The physiological concept, which explores the possibilities of two-shelled façades, makes the construction an energy-saving building. With its stores and surface coloring created by the façade's materials, the building becomes a complete work of art.

144

Mint and printing works

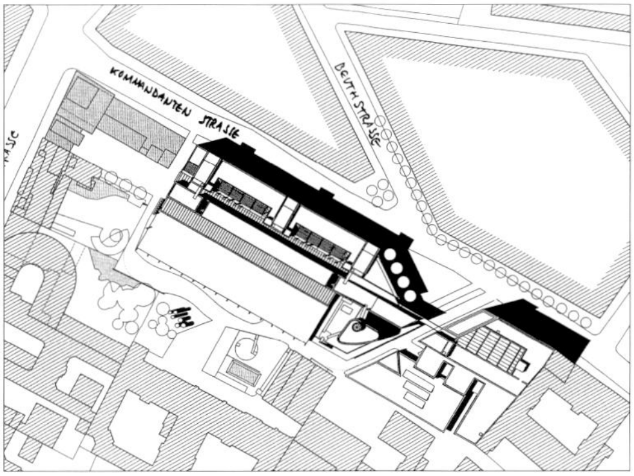

Site plan

Bundesdruckerei
National printing works
1993–2001
Kreuzberg, Kommandantenstraße 15
Architects: Peter Bayerer, Göran Hanson, Rainer Heidenreich, Wolfgang Schuster, Edmundo Martinez, Martin Stahlmann
Client: Bundesdruckerei

Both this building and the in-house facilities of the neighboring printing works no longer satisfied present-day standards, especially the so-called "mint" for manufacturing denominations of the Euro. The design of the new facility – including adjoining areas for production, development, administration, and security – developed from the results of an in-depth report. Carried out in two building phases, it extends from a forecourt to Beuthstraße. The undertaking was given to the English Apax in 2000.

145

Courtyard façade

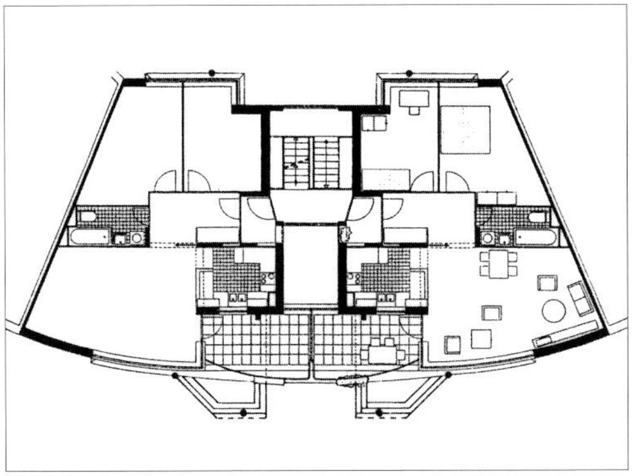

Floor plan

LiMa apartment building
1994–97
Südliche Friedrichstadt, Lindenstraße at the corner of Markgrafenstraße
Architects: Herman Hertzberger, Laurens Cobben, Cor Kruter, Folker Stopsma with Hinrich Baller and Inken Baller
Art: Akelei Hertzberger + Residents
Client: VEBA / IBA (International Building Exhibition)

The goal was to develop living standards at the corner of a traffic-congested street corner. This IBA contribution succeeds in addressing the subjects of urban living and the courtyard in a positive manner. In doing so, it stresses the importance of lighting and sunlight for open spaces, balconies, and terraces. The courtyard is made as publicly accessible as the staircase, which acts like a "vertical street".

146

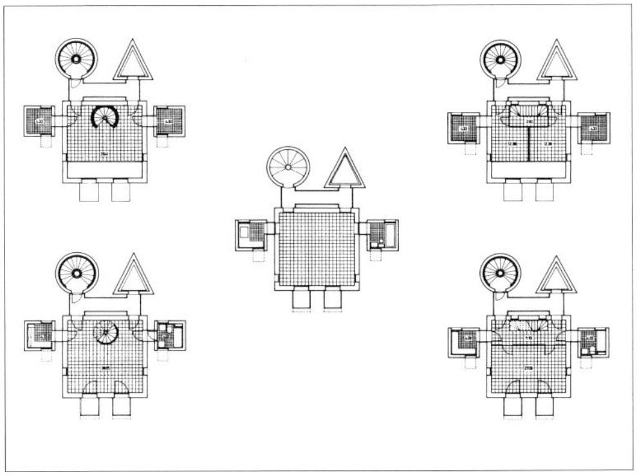

Plans of the studio tower

Apartment building with studio tower
1986–88
Südliche Friedrichstadt, Charlottenstraße 96–98
Architect: John Hejduk with Moritz Müller
Client: Katz KG / IBA (International Building Exhibition)

Outwardly, three incorporated pediment walls are lengthened by 5-storey structural rows containing apartments of different sizes, and generate an object-like presence. In front of the middle pediment stands a detached tower with seven 2-storey studio apartments; subdivided and connected, sanitary facility towers, and recurring small balconies and roof elements.

147

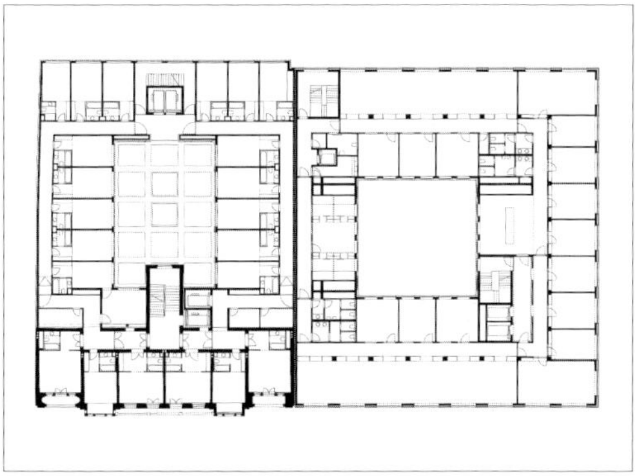

Plan of a standard floor

Hotel, office and commercial building
2001–03
Südliche Friedrichstadt, Friedrichstraße at the corner of Besselstraße
Architect: Max Dudler
Client: DGH / Berlinhaus

The sandstone façade of an old former commerce building was reconstructed, given additional side and rear wings, and re-utilized as a hotel. Built at the same time by the same architect was an office building lined with bright sandstone above a darker, 2-storey foundation made of green granite. The square window openings are provided with centrally and individually mechanized roller blinds. This building too, restructures an inner court with a dignified character.

148

Courtyard detail

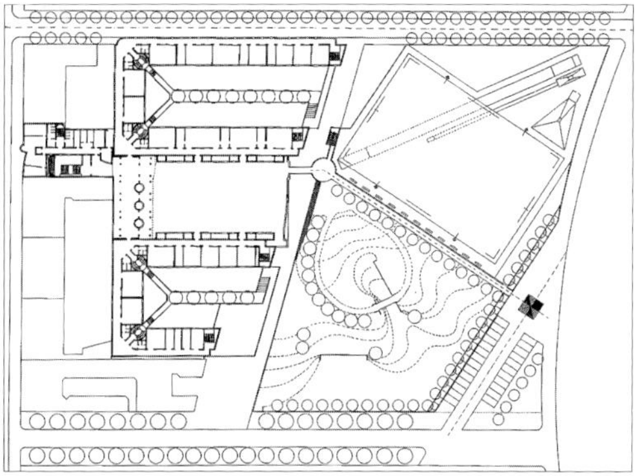

Plan of the main level

Elementary school and special learning school for the speech-impaired
1988–91
Südliche Friedrichstadt, Friedrichstraße 13
Architects: Gino Valle, Mario Broggi, Michael Burckhardt
Contact architect: Walter Hötzel
Client: Bezirksamt Kreuzberg / IBA (International Building Exhibition)

"As part of the IBA-erected school complex, the project consists of a 3-level elementary school for 550 children and special learning institution for 300 children. Its design evolves from the geometry of this historical district. The dividing in half of the corner between Lindenstraße and Friedrichstraße separates the volumes of the school complex from the park-like exterior facilities. The comb-like form of the complex, whose main development occurs at the head building on Friedrichstraße, reinterprets the typology of public schools of the Wilhelminian period."

149

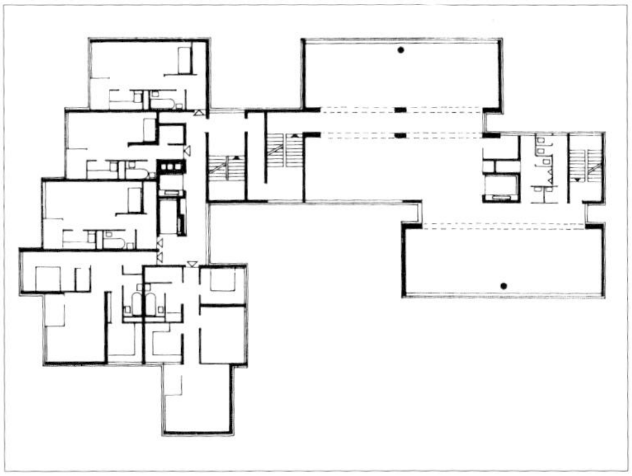

Plan of a standard floor

"Alter Fritz" apartment and office building
1966/67
Kreuzberg, Lindenstraße, Junkerstraße
Architects: Hans C. Müller and Georg Heinrichs with Siegwart Geiger
Client: Axel Springer

Erecting the Axel Springer publishing house made it necessary to demolish an old block development. The 70 newly devised apartments accommodate the relocated tenants and "Alter Fritz" restaurant as well as sections of the publishing house. The residential parts are oriented towards the south and the commercial spaces towards the east and west. The outer skin is made of white Hostalith-Z synthetic plating, but the contrasting dark-blue sections could only be achieved through the painted frames of the wooden windows.

150

View from the altar area

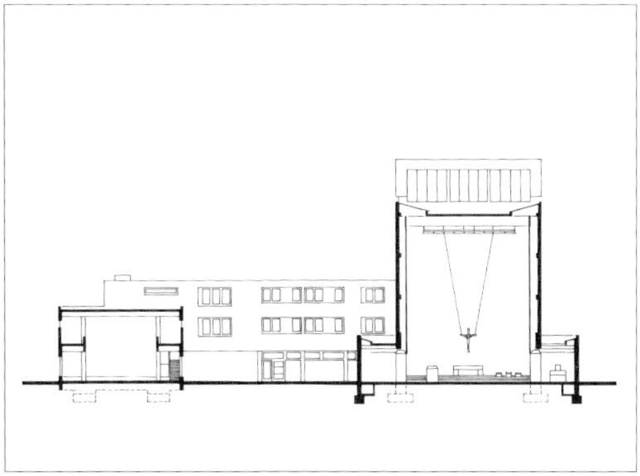

Cross section of the hall and the church

St.-Agnes-Kirche
1964/65
Kreuzberg, Alexandrinenstraße 21–23
Architect: Werner Düttmann

The principal element part of the church is a greatly stepped interior space, which utilizes a sophisticated lighting scheme. Aiding the overall spatial effect, the structural members are concealed behind an overhang of flashing made of mechanical plastering of the same type which appears on the exterior surfaces. The side entrance is located under a projecting roof and closes off the community center's inner courtyard with a kindergarten from the street. In 2012 architect Arno Brandlhuber converted the church into an art gallery for gallerist Johann König.

151

Ritterstraße, south view

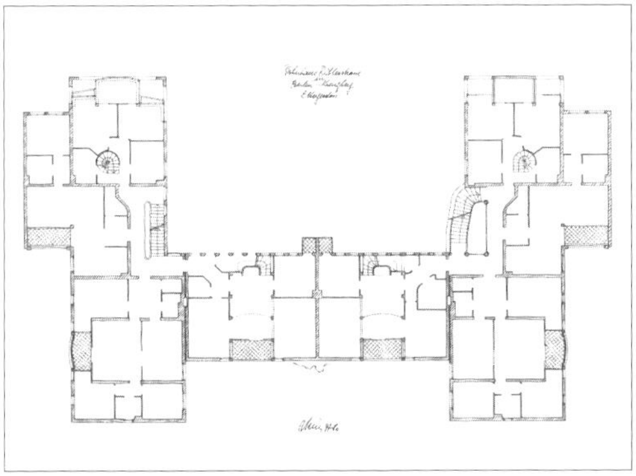

RIT apartment house
1979/80
Kreuzberg, Ritterstraße 63/64
Architect: Rob Krier with St. Böhm, L. Fromm, D. Henke, K. Müllner, U. Schauer, J. Wooding
Client: Konzepta Unternehmensgruppe / IBA (International Building Exhibiton)

The H-shaped building part, with access route to one of the Berlin Museum's planned internal passageways reaching as far as the garden, forms the axis of symmetry for a row of houses on Ritterstraße. The vivid, three-dimensional qualities of the homogeneous stucco building emerge from the persistent use of different means of perforations. Two four-way detached dwellings with 23 multi-floor and maisonnette apartments feature sculptural detail work in the façade by the same architect. Meanwhile the tenants have had a small stretch of fencing built, and now the axis develops only to the north. In this way, however, one arrives at a rectangular city square with a Schinkel-related design for the "Feilnerhaus".

152

Window detail and view of the project by Rogalla/Veit

Reichsschuldenverwaltung
State debt-management office
1919–24
Kreuzberg, Alte Jakobstraße at the corner of Feilnerstraße
Architect: German Bestelmeyer
Client: Deutsche Reichsbank

Neither the red brickwork nor variety of terracotta ornaments and pediment additions detract from the stringency of the starkly rhythmic façade with vertical pilaster strips and suspended wall surfaces. Developing to the south, the building façade at Ritterstraße incorporates the curve of the street. At Feilnerplatz, it concludes a quarter consisting of only 4 storeys. Besides the input of Rob Krier, ideas by Andreas Brandt, Thomas Heiß, Axel Liepe, Hartmut Steigelmann, Joachim Ganz, Walter Rolfes, Urs Müller, and Thomas Rohde characterize the site as well.

153

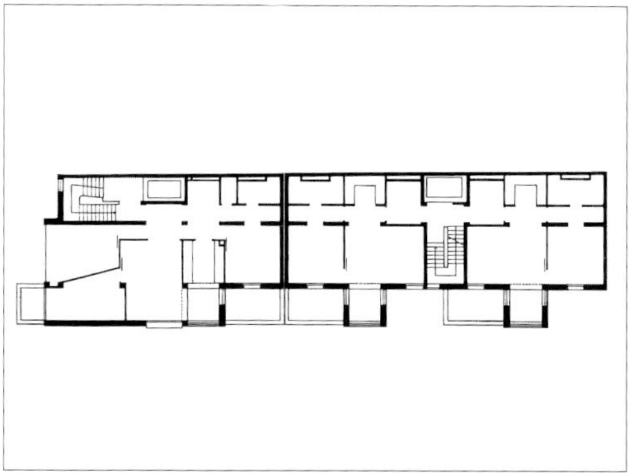

Plan of a standard floor

Victoria housing development
1980–86
Kreuzberg, Lindenstraße at the corner of Am Berlin Museum
Architect: Hans Kollhoff with Arthur Ovaska
Client: Stadt Berlin / IBA (International Building Exhibiton)

The building's placement and subdivisions "... lay claim to it being an apartment complex and not a segmented street-border development ..." The 9 buildings with unalike floor plans form a 180-m-long structural row. Apart from the white stucco of their surfaces, and brick shell sometimes running in front of them, what they also have in common are their proportions and subdivisions, which invite associations to life in a metropolis when compared to the "individual building" context. The entranceway to the courtyard leads directly to the Berlinische Galerie designed by Jörg Ricke, which now occupies one of the Berlin Senate's former glassworks depots.

154

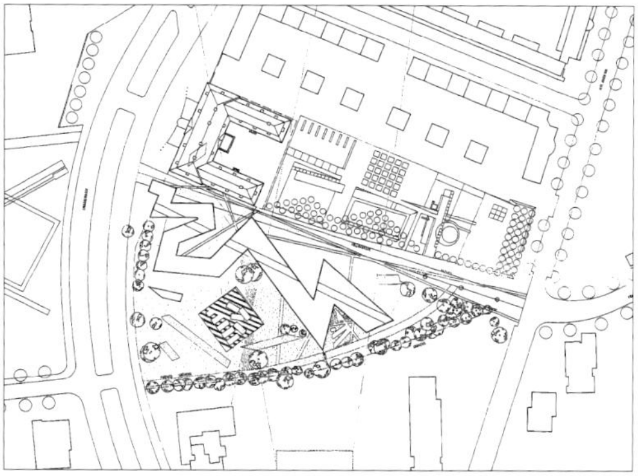

Site plan

Jüdisches Museum
1992–98
Kreuzberg, Lindenstraße 9–10
Architect: Daniel Libeskind with Marina Stanković, D. Bates, A. Terragni, M. Vido
E. T. A.-Hoffmann-Garten: Stefan Blach
Light design: Jan Dinnebier
Client: Senator für kulturelle Angelegenheiten

This 1988 competition winner was originally focused on creating an addition to the Berlin Museum in the old supreme court by Phillipp Gerlach (built 1734–1735), intended to house a new Jewish department. With its 12,000 sqm of exhibition space, the architectural language of the new museum develops as themes both the history of the Holocaust and the relationship between Berlin and its Jewish citizens. The frequently interrupted and/or incised axes of the museum's titanium-zinc skin suggest a broken star of David.

155

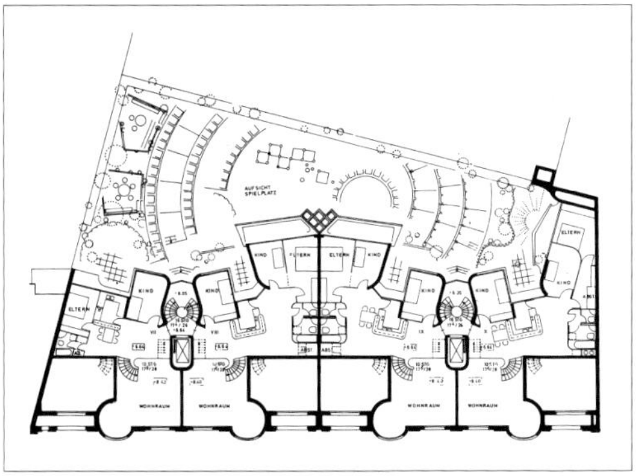

Apartment building with commercial spaces
1978–80
Kreuzberg, Kottbusser Damm 2/3
Architect: Bruno Taut
Architects of transformation: Inken Baller, Hinrich Baller
Client: Berax Immobilien

The project involves rehabilitating the façade of a semi-detached dwelling severely damaged during the war – an apartment house with movie theater, designed by Bruno Taut (1910/11). The building's 6 m deep front has the old floor height of circa 3,80 m, behind which attaches the circa 2,80 m floor height commonly used today. Each apartment receives a space with the traditional height and connects to the lower section through differentiating levels. Both new staircases are in the newer building part, whose floor plan freely develops around centralized areas for living, cooking, and eating. A second example of this period by Bruno Taut is near accross the street.

156

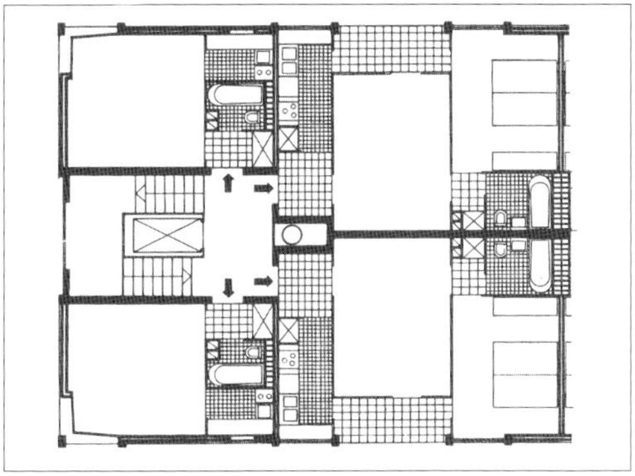

Plan of a standard floor in the high-rise building

Apartment buildings with stores
1956
Kreuzberg, Kottbusser Straße 2, Skalitzer Straße
Architects: Wassili Luckhardt, Hans Luckhardt

The difficult task of developing the tip of a block corner is solved by placing two 7-storey, single-loaded, winged constructions in front of the existing firewall wall, while an 11-storey building forms the tip of the site. By positioning the stores in the foreground, in unison the three building parts develop a narrow passageway. Ultimately the city block is resolved according to urban planning ideologies of the 1950s. In this time it was not possible to rebuild the old street profile.

157

Corner building

Fireproof-wall development

Corner building and fireproof-wall development 1983/84
Kreuzberg, Kottbusser Damm at the corner of Fraenkelufer
Architects: Hinrich Baller, Inken Baller
Client: GSW / IBA (International Building Exhibition)

What applied most in the less destroyed, southern part of the Kreuzberg district was directing the refurbishment or reutilization of buildings with the tenants, which made construction gaps or unused pediments rather exceptional here. The anthropological, free-form design principle of the two architects – a husband and wife team – gave a marked clarity of style to the corner and the firewall, and created the type of relationship to nature, garden, and landscape rarely attained in the inner city.

158

Hall with golden pillars

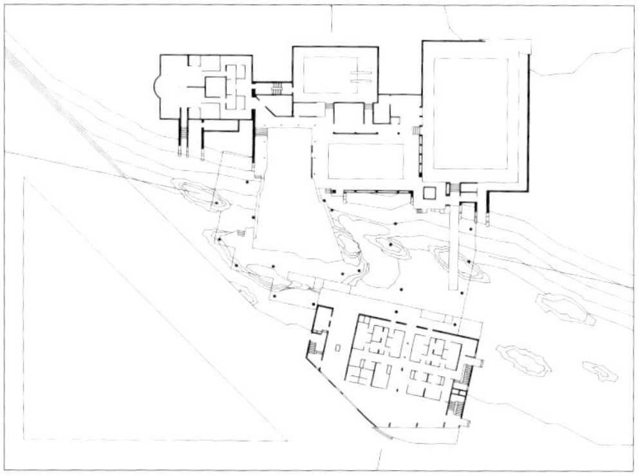

Plan of the ground floor

Sports and leisure pool at Spreewaldplatz 1984–87
Kreuzberg, Spreewaldplatz at the corner of Wiener Straße
Architects: Christoph Langhof, Thomas Hänni, Herbert Meerstein
Client: Bezirksamt Kreuzberg

A 1979 competition winner: after tearing down 5 terminus stations in Berlin's Kreuzberg district, it was possible to convert a portion of the resulting space into public green areas ideal for recreational activities. Four different pools, a sauna, and solarium are connected by ramps and passageway systems largely covered over by earth accumulations, thus preserving the green zones of the adjacient park. The facility's gold-colored load-bearing elements and supports, and black-and-white paneling, produce here a recreational atmosphere.

159

Elements of the former church as a wall decoration

St.-Michael-Kirche
1964/65
Kreuzberg, Waldemarstraße 4–10, Dresdener Straße 28–30 a
Architect: Hans Schaefers with Volker Theißen

The Berlin Wall dividing East from West also divided religious communities. Built for the West Berlin members of St.-Michael-Kirche was a temporary hall church whose expressive quality emerged directly from its technical simplicity: a visible reinforced-concrete skeleton filled with masonry made of calcareous sandstone, exposed insulation boards in the ceiling panels, and a parochial house with a kindergarten in the forecourt.

160

Staircase to roof terrace

Department store
1932
Kreuzberg, Oranienplatz 4–10
Architect: Max Taut

Originally planned as a department store, the building was also used as one for many years. Later, however, the alternating 5-, 7-, and 9-storey construction served as an office building. The reinforced-concrete skeleton is lined with limestone cladding, and some of its roof surfaces are used for gardens. The main staircase juts into the area of the street where it becomes an advertising element. After the war, the building required a great deal of repair.

161

Street side and corner building

Courtyard side

SKS housing on Reichenberger Straße
1981–85
Kreuzberg, Reichenberger Straße at the corner of Mariannenstraße
Architect: Wilhelm Holzbauer with Helmut Kirchhofer
Contact architects: Jan Rave, Rolf Rave
Client: GSW

During the last phase of the rehabilitation procedures in the southern part of Kreuzberg, the intervention of Senate housing-development director Hans C. Müller made possible the creation of a metropolitan yet highly sophisticated building form. This addressed the theme of a building's street and its courtyard side by providing a variety of development routes, small enclosures with ramps, and arbor passageways behind a green and greenery-bearing elongated metal façade. The terraces and loggia were thematically developed as well.

162

Senior citizens home
1983–87
Kreuzberg, Köpenicker Straße 191–193
Architect: Otto Steidle
Client: GVS / IBA (International Building Exhibition)
1998 architecture prize of the BDA

The result of a 1982 IBA-sponsored competition: "The neighboring, old building with small kitchenette apartments had to be incorporated in the overall plan of this senior citizens home. It also required to experience the functional connecting of the new and old building. So we positioned them 6 to 8 m away from each other, and the space between the two buildings allowed for a hall with pergola-like connecting platforms."

163

Sketch by Alvaro Siza

Corner building
1985–87
Kreuzberg, Schlesische Straße at the corner of Falckensteinstraße
Architect: Alvaro Siza
Contact architect: Peter Brinkert

Stylized as an icon, this contribution to the International Building Exhibition (IBA), which emerged from a 1980 competition, could only be conveyed by an architect possessing the greatest sensibility. Interacting with the crest of the wall, a slightly curved, grid façade makes gentle waves and sharply attaches to an angular, projecting roof. Pierluigi Nicolin comments on this by saying: "Siza firmly believes that he could never create all-conclusive solutions, and that his planning no longer adds new layers in the form of urban deposits."

164

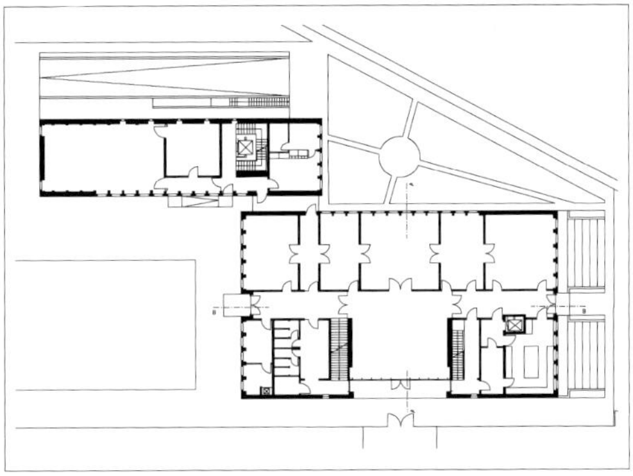

Plan of the ground floor

Apostolic nunciature
1999–2001
Neukölln, Lilienthalstraße 3a
Architect: Dieter G. Baumewerd
Landscape planner: Bernhard Korte
Glass window: Wilhelm Buschulte

Formerly located in Tiergarten's diplomatic quarter, the new building representing Germany's Holy See was built more by chance beside the Johannis-Basilika. Axially aligned with the basilica's cross section, on the ground floor the 2-storey entrance hall is three-sided, and surrounded by office spaces on the upper floor. Located above these are the archive and the sisters convent. An attached wing, forming a cour d'honneur, houses the chapel as well as living quarters of the nunciature and nuncio.

Station lobby

Ostbahnhof
1998–2000
Friedrichshain, Straße am Ostbahnhof
Architects: Becker, Gewers, Kühn Kühn
Project manager: Oliver Kühn
Client: Deutsche Bahn

"Radical reconstruction measures have given us the 'railway station of the future'. It gives modern transportation structures a clear, unrestricted language; generates positive curiosity, and allows us to see the railway in a new light. On every level, the old station parallel to the Spree River was hollowed out and deconstructed down to its support structure, and so the unobstructed view from the main hall could reach as far as the river again. At the same time the existing cubical structure of the station's entrance hall and elegantly curved gallery area were both incorporated and given new emphasis."

Canal side

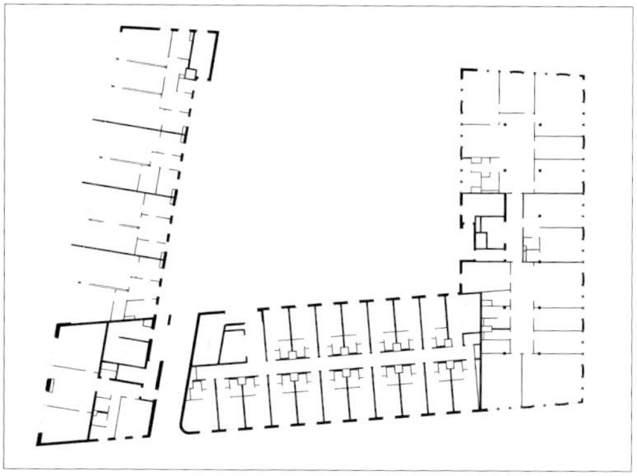

Plan of the 1st to the 3rd floors

Haus an der Schilling-Brücke
1999–2000
Friedrichshain, Holzmarktstraße 34
Architect: Gernot Nalbach
Clients: O. M. G. and F. Humplmair

With its three wings of different heights, used for different purposes; five storeys of residential spaces facing the Spree River; six storeys of office spaces facing noisy exit roads; and, rising from eight to ten storeys facing the Spree, a hotel, the building becomes an ensemble born of an ambitious, urban planning concept – homogenous yet formed of unalike structures. Hard to overlook, however, is a certain discrepancy between the wealth of ideas and financial means.

167

Aerial photo from the west with Oberbaum-Brücke

NARVA
1999–2000
Oberbaum City, Rotherstraße 8–26
Architects: Schweger Assoziierte
Clients: SIRIUS, Roland Ernst

Developed here at the upper reaches of the Spree River was part of an expansive commercial area with a largely well-preserved building substance – a good example being the NARVA factory for manufacturing electric light bulbs (1903–08). The tower building was heightened by 5 floors, and the new buildings not only harmonized with the older ones, but also with the part preserved, part renovated development. An entrée of the view over the Oberbaum-Brücke is Calatrava's cantilevered, suspended beam for the elevated railway.

168

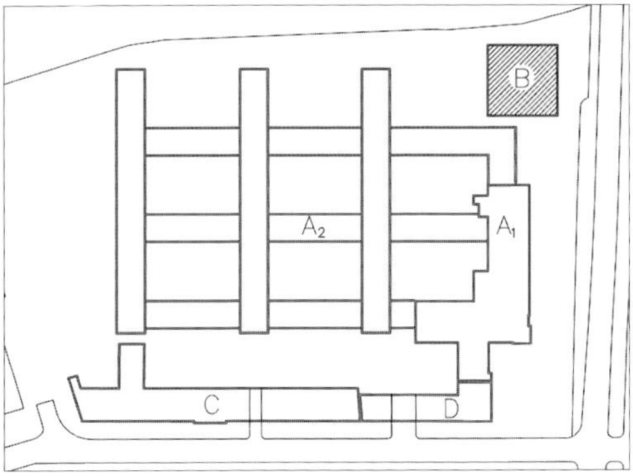

Site plan

Treptowers
1997/98
Alt Treptow, Elsenstraße at the corner of Hoffmannstraße
Architect of B and D: Gerhard Spangenberg
Architects of A and C: Schweger Assoziierte
Landscape architect: Gustav Lange
Molecule Man (sculpture): Jonathan Borofsky

The basis for the new office and service center complex on the banks of the Spree River "... evolved from a 1992 urban planning competition. In the immediate vicinity of the AEG administrative headquarters – protected by preservation laws, designed by Ernst Ziesel (1927/28), and erected together with the 1937 factory building – project client Allianz insurance company planned to build a dominating, high-rise and a courtyard development modeled after the nearby commercial courtyards in Kreuzberg."

Hufeisensiedlung, Britz

169

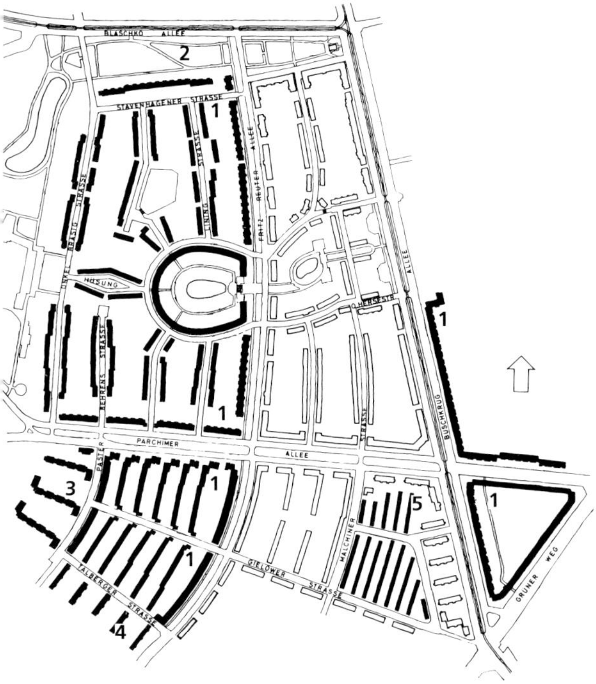

Louise-Reuter-Ring

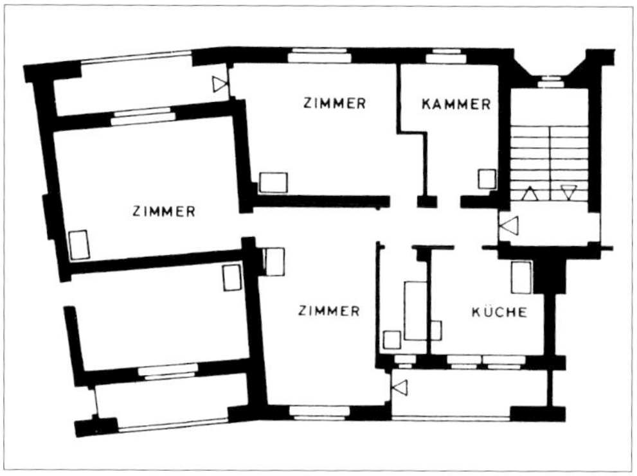

Plan of 3 1/2 room apartment

Key 1 Bruno Taut
2 Martin Wagner
3 Max Taut
4 Eduard Ludwig
5 Bruno Schneidereit

Hufeisensiedlung
1925–31
Britz, Fritz-Reuter-Allee, Blaschkoallee, Parchimer Allee
Architects: Bruno Taut, Martin Wagner
Landscape planning: Leberecht Migge
Client: Gehag

Wolfgang Schäche in *75 Years of GEHAG*: "With its more than 1,000 apartments, the housing colony erected from 1925 onward – far from what qualified in 1920 as the center of 'Groß-Berlin', while occupying part of the building property formerly the Britz manor – was the largest and likewise most ambitious housing-colony project of the young Gehag during the Weimar era. The already existing horseshoe-shaped pond in the heart of this 3-storey housing development gave the housing colony its name. Its construction followed the plans conceived by Bruno Taut and Martin Wagner. To a great extent, it was the first time that such work was ever carried out using industrial construction machinery (excavator, conveyer belts, revolving cranes) as well as cyclic work procedures. In the Hufeisensiedlung (horseshoe colony), Taut's characteristic subdividing of a structure through prominently placed stairwells and his engaging color as an architectural design element are effectively put to use here. This is one of the best known and best devised, large-scale housing colonies of the 1920s. Developed at a site with a small lake, the location is topologically defined by a glacial groove in the earth, and ultimately by the structural form from which it draws its name. The Hufeisensiedlung, all building considered, is Unesco World Heritage since 2008.

170

Fritz Reuter Allee

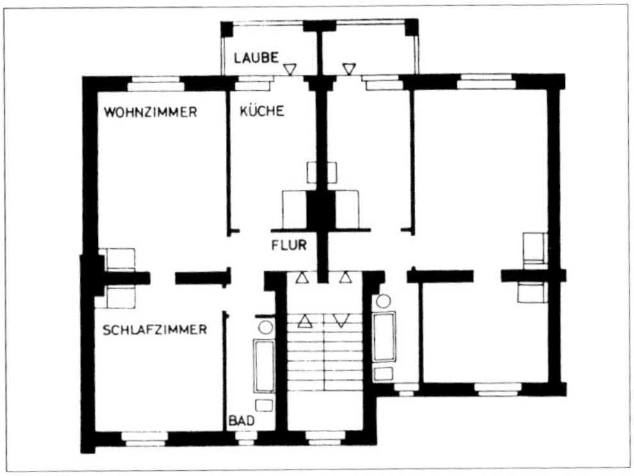

Plan of 2-room apartment

Hufeisensiedlung
1925–31
Britz, Fritz-Reuter-Allee, Blaschkoallee, Parchimer Allee
Architects: Bruno Taut, Martin Wagner
Client: Gehag

The first building phase (1925–27) occurred west of the Fritz-Reuter-Allee, north of the Parchimer Allee, and involved approximately 1,000 apartments. The 2- and 3-storey development at the colony's 4-storey core took on the form of a horseshoe and offered a sunken area with a lake which opened towards Fritz-Reuter-Allee. Stores and a café were located at this commonly used green area. In 1930/31 the housing colony was extended to the south by Bruno Taut, and to the east by Bruno Schneidereit.

171

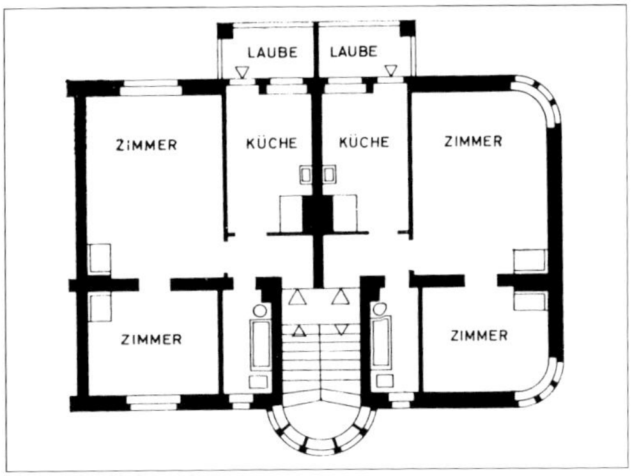

Partial plan of a standard floor

Hufeisensiedlung
1925–27
Britz, Stavenhagner Straße 4–32
Architect: Martin Wagner
Client: Gehag

Despite the similarity of concept from a social, urban planning, and design standpoint, when compared to buildings by Taut, the small windows and the roof overhang make these houses seem less lively and perhaps more lower middle-class. And the small 2-room apartments with coal-oven heating were in fact developed for classes of people with lower incomes.

172

173

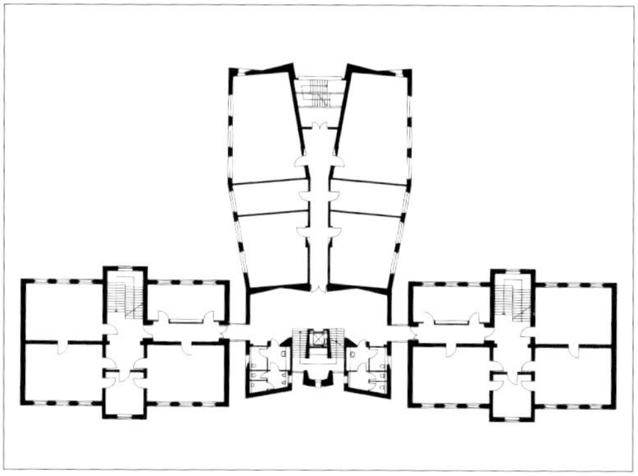

Plan of the 1st floor

Alexander-von-Humboldt-Schule (formerly the Dorotheen-Lyceum)
1928/29
Köpernick, Mentzel-, Oberspreestraße
Architect: Max Taut
Wall-relief: Rudolf Belling

The demand for "light, air, and sunlight" was meant to serve this two-winged construction especially well. In spirit it corresponded with the school's meanwhile stuccoed-over exterior walls made of yellow-hued ceramic plates, inlayed over a dark area in the foundation level. The classrooms arranged along Mentzelstraße, a peaceful street, face the courtyard. Arranged along Oberspreestraße is the gymnasium, whose roof was converted to a terrace. Both wings of the school join the curves of the reception hall and stairwell. The facility in Lichtenberg (on Schlichtallee at the corner of Firchestraße), built at the same time as this one and designed by the same architect, imparts a similar spirit and uses an identical formal language.

Levi-Strauss-Oberschule
1999–2002
Köpenick, Glienicker Straße 24–30
Architect: Christoph Mäckler
Project manager: Torsten Künzel
Client: Land Berlin

A 1994 competition winner: in place of the 1-storey connecting constructions, a new building appears – twice. It supplements both 19th-century school buildings with a multifunctional hall, assembly hall, and sports hall, and with impressively sculptural entranceways for specialized classes. Choosing brick as the material for the facing establishes a clear connection to school buildings from another century. Yet the construction's surface, color, and form leave no doubt in one's mind about the date of its creation – or the creator's guiding spirit.

174

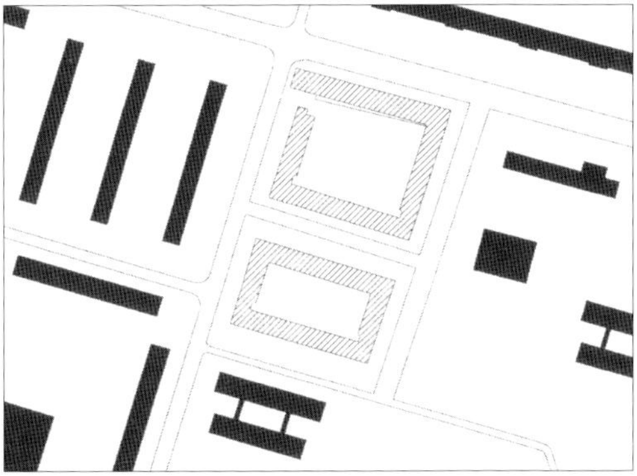

Site plan

Apartment blocks
1997
Friedrichsfelde, Dolgenseestraße, Sewanstraße
Architects: Georg Augustin, Ute Frank
Garden architect: Horst Schumacher

Two apartment blocks geared to accommodating local needs were built on a site formerly a courtyard service area. They emphasized the interplay between shops and commercial spaces, and differently sized apartments (either 1 1/2 or 2 rooms, but also as large as 5 rooms). On the other hand, because of the blue-colored plaster of their 4-, 5- to 8-storey building parts, they seemed to harmonize when seen among the surrounding slab-block buildings. Achieved here as well was an intense interacting of their inner and outer surfaces.

175

Wohnpark Stralau
Stralau residential park
1996/97
Friedrichshain, Alt-Stralau
Architect: Herman Hertzberger
Contact architect: Inken Baller
Landscape planner: Hans Loidl
Client: VEBA Immobilien

As the realized part of the1992 project of a general plan to develop the "water city" theme, namely a city on the water, the result was an abstract and idealized structure, resting on the factual remains of a former industrial landscape. In the event of spatial conflict, it interrupts itself or – as shown here – evades restriction with elegant arches. In this instance, no more than 72 of the planned 2,300 living units were actually completed. On top of the further consolidation of the area occurring with delays, it would have a difficult time functioning at all on the edge of the city.

176

Condolence hall

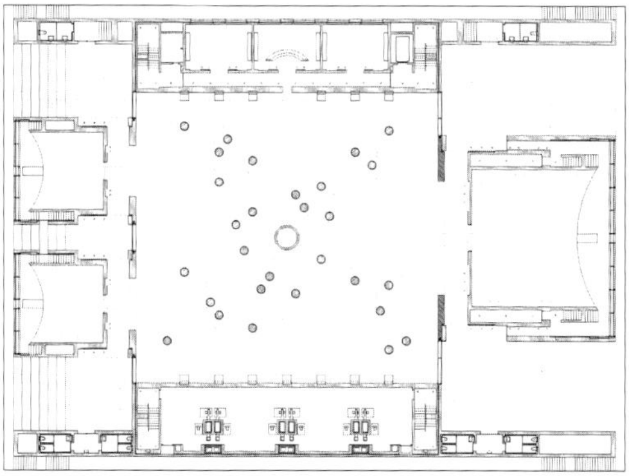

Plan of the ground floor

Krematorium Baumschulenweg
1996–98
Niederschöneweide, Kiefholzstraße 222
Architects: Axel Schultes, Charlotte Frank
Project management: Margret Kister, Christoph Witt
Landscape planner: Hannelore Kossel

After building the Ruhleben crematorium **(376)**, another was needed in the eastern part of the city, especially one with up-to-date, in-house technical services. This was made possible through a 1992 competition process. The architectural means, materials, details, lighting concept, and degree of differentiation between the large condolence hall and viewing rooms convincingly correspond with the crematorium's location and function.

177

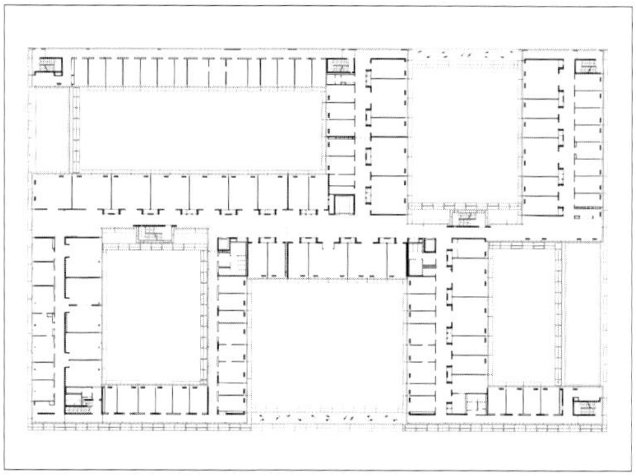

Plan of the 2nd floor

Institut für Physik of the Humboldt-Universität zu Berlin
2002
Adlershof, Newtonstraße 15
Architects: Georg Augustin, Ute Frank
Client: Senatsverwaltung für Stadtentwicklung

A 2003 Architekturpreis Berlin winner: the ashlar-walled structure with a 110 x 75 sqm floor area distinguishes between the different façades on its exterior side and 5 inner courts. But the four points of the compass, the corridors of vaulted wings, and urban planning orientation also play a role here. In this way, the northeast side, made of U-shaped (so-called "Profilit") glass sections, is interrupted by ventilation panels and built up to form large openings to courts and access areas.

178

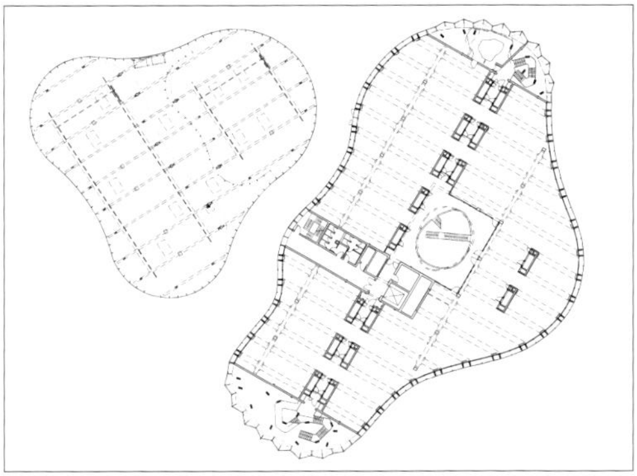

Plan of the upper floors

Photonikzentrum
1996–98
Adlershof, Rudower Chaussee 6
Architects: Matthias Sauerbruch, Louisa Hutton
Client: Wista management

A 1995 competition winner: two free-form pavilions – the smaller a 1-storey work space, the larger a 3-storey laboratory building with darkrooms – develop along a meridian line. The intensely colored, shading elements inserted between the two-shelled, full glazing of both buildings invite associations with the color spectrum of light "... and, with the swung outer form, produce a spatial tension one could see as an oscillating movement".

179

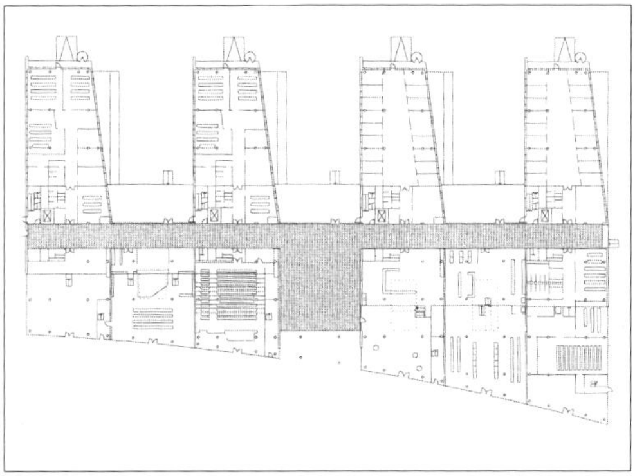

Plan of the ground floor

Institute of mathematics and information technology of the Humboldt-Universität zu Berlin
1996–98
Adlershof, Rudower Chaussee 25
Architects: Joachim Dörr, Axel Ludolf, Josef Wimmer
Project management: Drees + Sommer

The institute of mathematics and information technology of the Humboldt-Universität, part of the Wissenschafts- und Technologiezentrum Adlershof, is divided in 4 diagonal-to-the-street, building parts of different lengths and contents. These connect to a foundation zone, but also to a glass wall that borders the street and simultaneously shields the courtyard areas. The width of the constructional bar makes it ideal for housing combination offices, but also a lecture hall with seating for altogether 200 people.

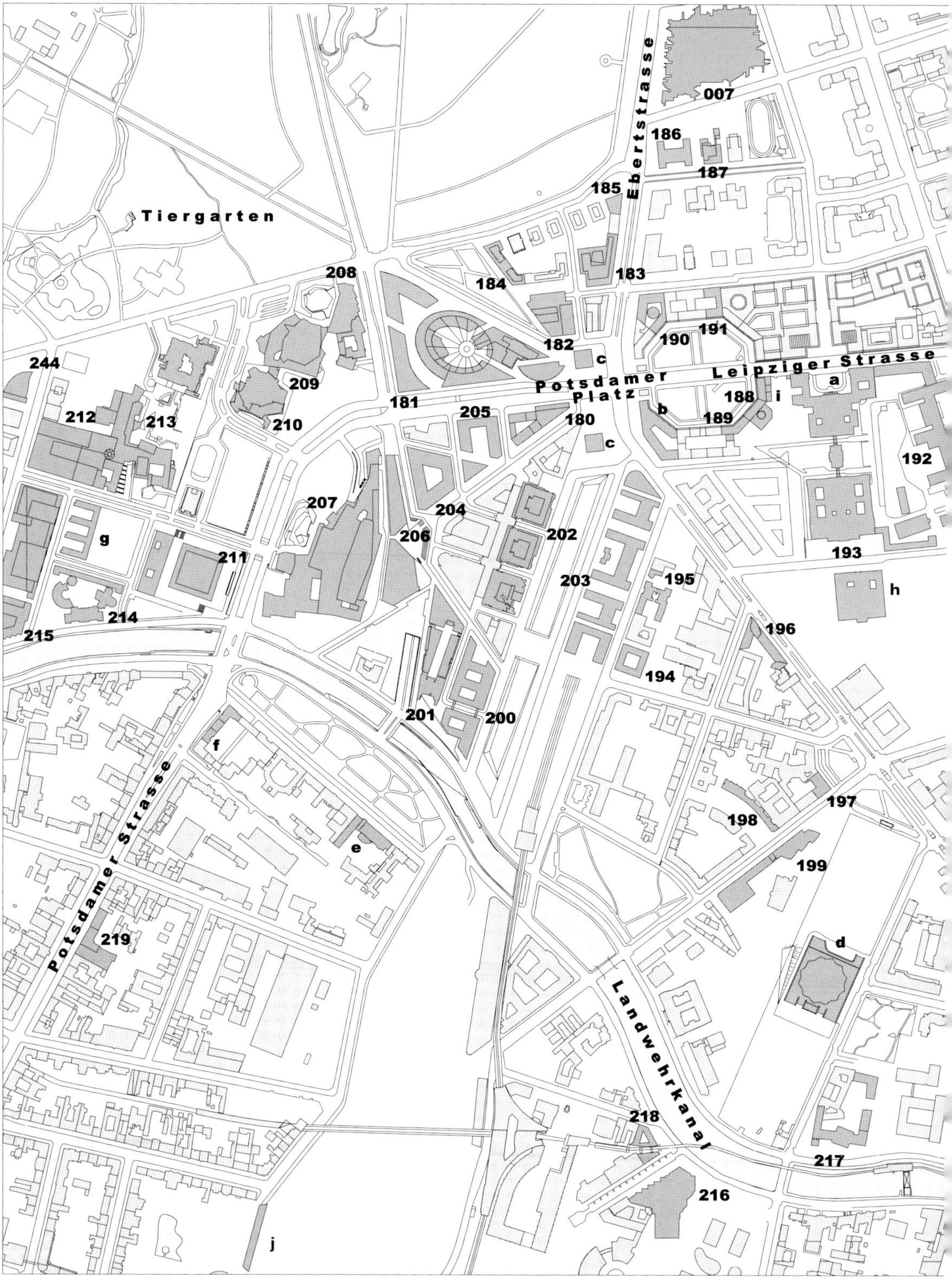

Tiergarten
Ebertstrasse
Potsdamer Platz
Leipziger Strasse
Potsdamer Strasse
Landwehrkanal
007
186
187
185
183
184
208
182
c
190
191
a
244
209
181
205
180
188
i
b
189
212
213
210
c
192
207
204
202
g
206
211
203
195
193
h
214
215
196
194
201
200
f
197
198
e
199
219
d
218
217
216
j

Potsdamer Platz S

007	Holocaust-Denkmal	Peter Eisenman, Richard Serra
180	High-rise office building	Hans Kollhoff, Helga Timmermann
181	Sony Center	Murphy/Jahn Architects
182	Ritz-Carlton Berlin	Heinz Hilmer, Christoph Sattler, Thomas Albrecht
183	Marriott Hotel Berlin	Bernd Albers
184	Parkside apartments	David Chipperfield Architects
185	Lenné 1	Petzinka Pink
186	Landesvertretung Niedersachsen/Schleswig-Holstein	Seelinger, Vogels, Cornelsen
187	Landesvertretung Rheinland-Pfalz	Heinle, Wischer und Partner
188	Haus Knauthe	Axel Schultes, Charlotte Frank
189	Classicon	Christoph Langhof
190	Kanada-Haus	Bruce Kuwabara/KPMB
191	Apartment and office buildin	Jan Kleihues
192	Bundesministerium der Finanzen	Ernst Sagebiel
193	Abgeordnetenhaus von Berlin	Jan Rave, Marina Stanković, Rolf Rave
194	Torhaus	Oswald Mathias Ungers
195	Residential development	Hans C. Müller, Moritz Müller
196	Wohnhof	Zaha Hadid
197	Apartment, office and commercial building	Hentrich-Petschnigg & Partner
198	Haus an der Brandwand	Josef Paul Kleihues
199	Fanny-Hensel-Grundschule	Wolfgang Scharlach, Rainer Wischhusen
200	Administrative headquarters of Volksbank	Arata Isozaki, Steffen Lehmann
201	debis-Haus	Renzo Piano Building Workshop, Kohlbecker
202	Blocks B4, B6, B8	Richard Rogers and Partners
203	A+T / Parkkolonnaden	Giorgio Grassi
204	Grand Hyatt Berlin	José Rafael Moneo
205	Blocks A2 and A3	Ulrike Lauber, Wolfram Wöhr
206	Musiktheater	Renzo Piano Building Workshop, Kohlbecker
207	Staatsbibliothek zu Berlin	Hans Scharoun
208	Musikinstrumenten-Museum	Edgar Wisniewski
209	Philharmonie	Hans Scharoun
210	Kammermusiksaal	Edgar Wisniewski
211	Neue Nationalgalerie	Ludwig Mies van der Rohe
212	Gemäldegalerie	Heinz Hilmer, Christoph Sattler, Thomas Albrecht
213	Kunstgewerbemuseum	Rolf Gutbrod
214	Wissenschaftszentrum Berlin	James Stirling, Michael Wilford
215	Shell-Haus	Emil Fahrenkamp
216	Deutsches Technikmuseum	Ulrich Wolff, Helge Pitz
217	District-court expansion	Oswald Mathias Ungers
218	BVG-Gebäude	Joachim Ganz
219	Der Tagesspiegel	Siegwart Geiger, Gerhard Spangenberg
244	Österreichische Botschaft	Hans Hollein

a	Bundesrat	Friedrich Schulze, 1901–04; Schweger Assoziierte, 1996–2000
b	Office and commercial building	Thomas Müller, Ivan Reimann, 2003–05
c	Bahnhof Potsdamer Platz	Heinz Hilmer, Christoph Sattler, Thomas Albrecht, 1996–2005
d	Tempodrom	von Gerkan, Marg und Partner, 1999–2001
e	Ingenieurzentrum	Maedebach, Redeleit & Partner, 1992–94
f	Residential and commercial building	Jürgen Sawade, Georg Heinrichs, 1984/85
g	Wohnen am Kulturforum	Kurt Ackermann, 1984–86
h	Martin-Gropius-Bau	Martin Gropius, Heino Schmieden, 1877–81; Winnetou Kampmann, 1981
i	Haus am Leipziger Platz	Walter A. Noebel, 1999–2001
j	Wohnen am Nelly-Körner-Park	Rainer Oefelein, 1995–97

180

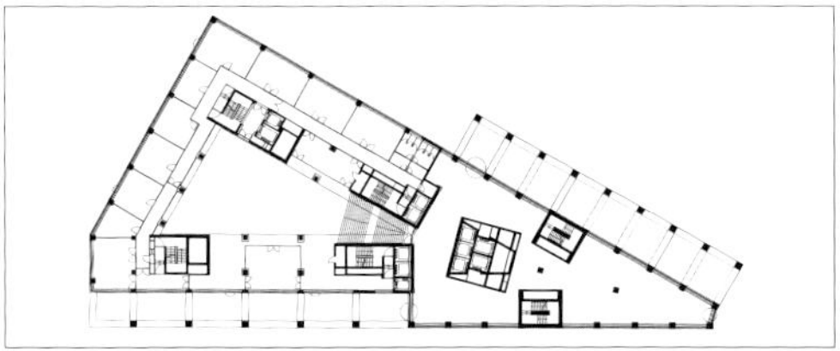

High-rise office building
1994–99
Tiergarten, Potsdamer Platz 1
Architects: Hans Kollhoff, Helga Timmermann, with Jasper Jochimsen
Client: Daimler Chrysler Immobilien

Erected at the tip of the new and old Potsdamer Straße, this 24-storey tower with red brick facing and crowned by golden crenelation has meanwhile become the focal point and emblem of Potsdamer Platz. The gastronomical services behind its grayish-green granite foundation, its representative entrée: Europe's fastest elevator, and incomparable view from the top of the tower contribute to making the office high-rise with rental spaces of different sizes so popular and accessible. 24-storey floor area: 29,000 sqm; building costs: circa 105 million Euro.

181

Bellevuestraße with the "Kaisersaal" (imperial hall)

View under the roof construction

Sony Center
1995–2000
Mitte, Potsdamer Platz at the corner of Bellevuestraße
Architects: Murphy/Jahn Architects
Client: Sony Deutschland

Focal point of the individual building parts is the inviting, roofed-over performance level – a private as well as public space with an atmosphere suited to relaxing here for a while. Apart from Sony's European center, located here as well are luxurious penthouse apartments, the multi-complex movie theater Deutsche Mediathek, and, threatened to be torn down, the so-called "Kaisersaal" (imperial hall) of the former Hotel Esplanade, literally rolled into place and installed under massive holding girders for festive events and receptions.

182

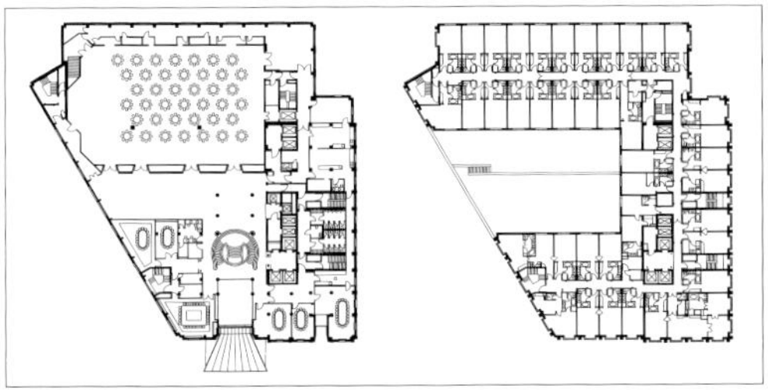

Plans of the 1st and a standard floor

Ritz-Carlton Berlin
2002–04
Mitte, Bellevuestraße at the corner of Auguste-Hausdener Straße
Architects: Heinz Hilmer, Christoph Sattler, Thomas Albrecht
Client: Otto Beisheim

This building is the winner of an urban planning competition whose guidelines took into account the entire area of Potsdamer Platz and Leipziger Platz, along with the area that Otto Beisheim, as project initiator, could acquire and name. The architects' contributions stand out on the strength of their distinctive formal vocabulary, and they satisfy all the demands of a 5-star hotel with suites in seven floors of a 19-storey tower.

183

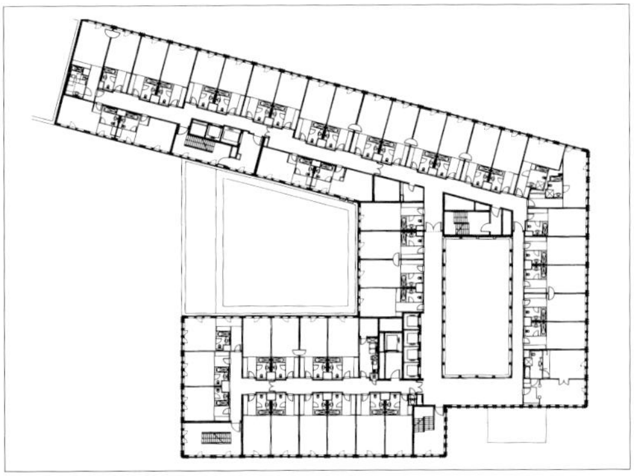

Plan of a standard floor

Marriott Hotel Berlin
2001–03
Mitte, Inge-Beisheim-Platz 1
Architect: Bernd Albers
Client: Immago

A year 2000 competition winner: 379 rooms on nine floors, above a 2-storey foundation. "With a finely subdivided and vertically aligned, façade structure made of expressive stone profiles as thick as 20 cm of Portuguese sandstone, the attempt was made here to have a large building appear elegant and light. The 'folded' design of the stone façade deliberately recalls a curtain. The play on this motif corresponds with the inner logic of a hotel in a metropolis: the façade stages the balancing of the public area's representative character with a hotel room's privacy."

184

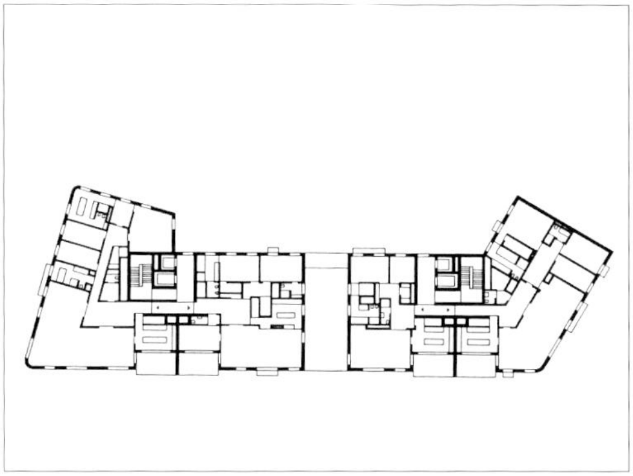

Plan of the 6th floor

Parkside apartments
2001–05
Tiergarten, Lennéstraße, Parkstraße
Architects: David Chipperfield Architects
Project management: Intertec
Client: IMMAGO

Located at the district's northern border, in the so-called Lenné-Dreieck, are six small residential blocks, whose 10-storey constructions largely accommodate apartments intended for highly discriminating tenants, offering a view of the Tiergarten city park. This particular block houses 34 apartments between 150 and 300 sqm in size. At the block's west end, the row is dominated by an homogenous sculpture – the cornected buildings made of a coarsely sanded, light-gray Bavarian limestone, with small balconies and large bands of loggia.

185

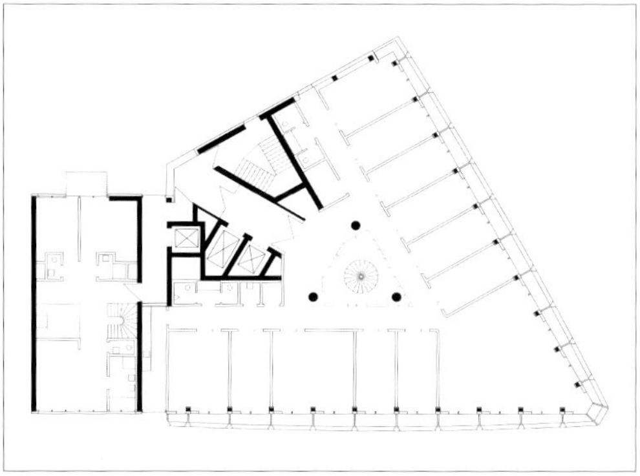

Plan of an office floor

Lenné 1
2002–04
Mitte, Lennéstraße at the corner of Ebertstraße
Architects: Petzinka Pink
Client: Karg'sche Familienstiftung

The east side of the 10-storey Beisheim Center ends at a pointed, northern corner in a glass prism resembling a ship's bow. Its slightly outward-swelling façade and roof surfaces, behind which lie a series of lights encased between two levels of shining glass, cause the structural levels to shine even more, when they beam a greenish color. A relatively short wing preserves the symmetry of the corner without the façade divulging the wing's function – do people live or work here?

186

Landesvertretungen Niedersachsen/Schleswig-Holstein

Representations of Lower Saxony and Schleswig-Holstein

1998–2000

Mitte, In den Ministergärten 8–10

Architects: Caspar Martin Seelinger, Maximilian Vogels, Birgit Cornelsen

Clients: Länder Niedersachsen and Schleswig-Holstein

Evolved from a 1997 European Union-wide competition, the representations of both German states now stand side by side, connected by a spacious glassed-over hall, in an "espace imaginaire" housing the function rooms and terrace café. The Italian, lava-colored sandstone is arranged in rows and separated by slender channel profiles. Planned in front of the hall's wall, housing the main entrance, is a structural framework for sun protection and cleaning purposes.

187

Landesvertretung Rheinland-Pfalz

Representation of Rhineland-Palatinate

1998–2000

Mitte, In den Ministergärten 6

Architects: Heinle, Wischer und Partner; responsible partner: Winfried Schmidbauer

Client: Staatshochbauamt Koblenz

The result of an 1997 European Union-wide competition: "A U-shaped building with side wings of different lengths was built on 3,150 sqm floor area. The guest house in the elongated east wing is reached by glazed passageways. Rebuilt to a roofed-over atrium, the courtyard of the complex opens out onto a garden. Developing from this central area are the administrative offices, function rooms, and – via a glazed elevator – the roof terrace."

188

Haus Knauthe
1998–2000
Mitte, Leipziger Platz 10
Architects: Axel Schultes, Charlotte Frank
Landscape architects: Cornelia Müller, Jan Wehberg
Client: Family Knauthe

The vividly structural façade is made of lacquered aluminum panels given their creator's distinctive Turkish-green accent. The paneling emphasizes the presence of sophisticated interior functions, rooms for receptions, conferences and offices, as well as 9 apartments. Toward the rear of the building is a cube of office spaces, whose center conceals a cylindrical conference room for 34 people.

189

Classicon
2002/03
Mitte, Leipziger Platz 9
Architect: Christoph Langhof
Client: IVG / Wert-Konzept

The self-contained basic form of Leipziger Platz had already revealed highly individual design concepts. Here a meandering band stretches over a 2-storey base with stores; pilaster strips characterize the 5-storey area of office spaces, and wall elements, similar to engravings, subdivide four recessed floors housing twelve large, representative apartments. Aluminum screens allowing windows without balconettes or railings to be opened also conceal the windows.

190

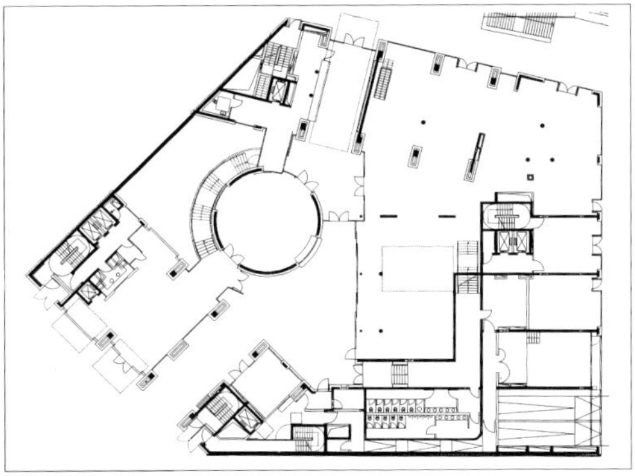

Plan of the ground floor

Kanada-Haus
2001–05
Mitte, Ebertstraße at the corner of Voßstraße
Architects: Bruce Kuwabara / KPMB with Gagnon, Marc Letellier
Implementation planning: Justus Pysall, Peter Ruge, Philipp von Matt
Client: Hannover Leasing

The building aspires to represent Canada, and it bundles together embassy-related and consular functions with office spaces for Canadian firms, stores, and gastronomical services. In this way, the building opens itself to a broader public. A passageway through the courtyard leads visitors to exhibition spaces, and to the Timber Hall, a centrally located and round construction lined with native Douglas firs – while the actual house is lined with typical perforation-riddled sandstone.

191

View of façade to Leipziger Platz

Apartment and office building
1999–2001
Mitte, Leipziger Platz 14
Architect: Jan Kleihues
Project manager: Johannes Kressner
Client: DG Immobilien

This might also be true in the future: despite the provocative placement of its entranceway in the façade, a building of only 9 storeys, and facing a city square, emits great peace and a well-proportioned dignity. What contribute to these qualities are the slightly beveled sections which widen the quadratic, skeletal grid of the window openings, and the generous width of the aforementioned entranceway. Such details pleasantly contrast the Mosse-Palais, whose extravagance commands as the central façade on the square.

192

Foyer in "Haus der Flieger"

Bundesministerium der Finanzen
1935–36
Mitte, Wilhelmstraße/Leipziger Straße
Architect: Ernst Sagebiel

At the same time as the neighboring Parliamentarians' offices **(193)** were rebuilt to the "Haus der Flieger", within only two years this steel-framed construction, lined with limestone and inspired by the architectural language of National Socialism, emerged in the full depth of the block as the Reichsluftfahrtministerium (national ministry of aviation). Hentrich-Petschnigg & Partner, the architects responsible for its structural conversion to the federal ministry of finance, preserved the representative spatial arrangement of the cour d'honneur, main entrance, pillared hall, and the staircase to the main assembly room. And Regina Poly oversaw the designing of the cour d'honneur in accordance with the current zeitgeist. Located south of Niederkirchner Straße are the former grounds of the arts and crafts school by Martin Gropius.

193

Assembly hall

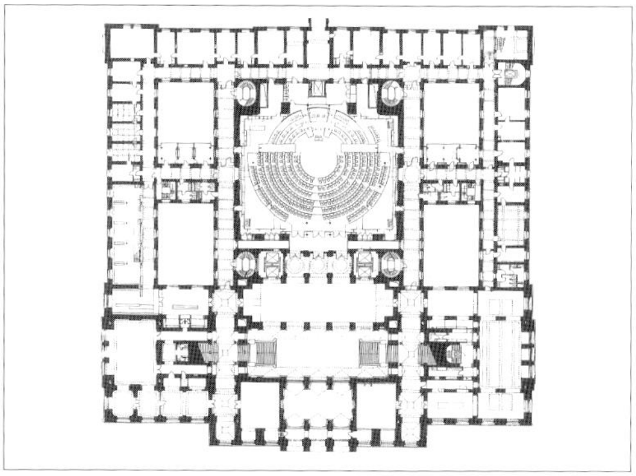

Floor plan of level 1

Abgeordnetenhaus von Berlin
Parliamentarians' house of Berlin
1990–93
Mitte, Niederkirchner Straße 5
Architects: Rolf Rave, Marina Stanković, Jan Rave
Project manager: Christian Huber, Heinz Jirout, Birgit Lenzen
Acoustics: Wolfgang Moll
Light installation: Jakob Mattner
Garden planning: Regina Poly
Client: Abgeordnetenhaus von Berlin

Designed by Friedrich Schultze and completed in 1899, the Prussian house of parliament was forced to undergo numerous changes. It was modified to the "Haus der Flieger" during the Nazi regime by Ernst Sagebiel, to the ministry of trade during the GDR period, and could finally be used by united Berlin's parliament after the political changeover. Besides the roof addition and a pair of new office towers, it was mainly the assembly room that had to be readapted to meet with today's standards.

194

Southeast view

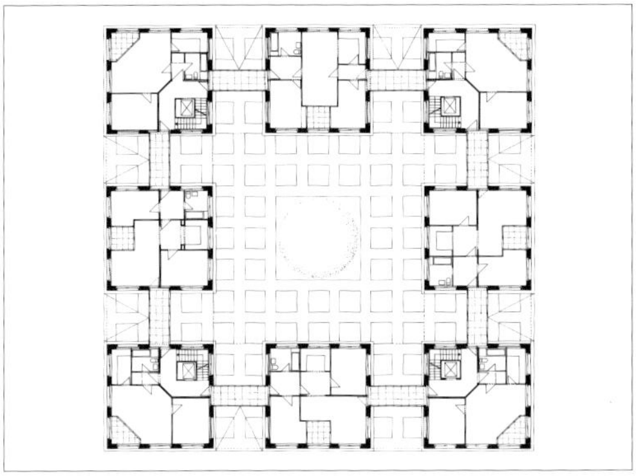

Plan of the 2nd floor

Torhaus
Gate house
1988/89
Südliche Friedrichstadt, Köthener Straße at the corner of Bernburger Straße
Architect: Oswald Mathias Ungers
Exterior facilities: Cornelia Müller, Jan Wehberg, Elmar Knippschild
Client: BOTAG / IBA (International Building Exhibiton)

While satisfying the general demands of apartment construction at that time, what actually occurs here in a single building filling the entire block with its clear geometric subdivisions and 8 large entranceway portals leading to a central inner court is a black-and-white play on the theme of a square, applied to 6 floors within a residential concept whose apartments have different sizes.

195

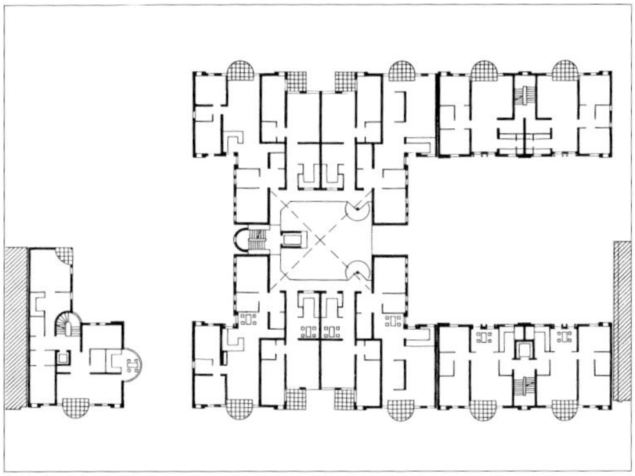

Plan of the 3rd to the 5th floors

Residential development
1983/84
Südliche Friedrichstadt, Köthener Straße 39–42
Architects: Hans C. Müller, Moritz Müller
Client: Braun + Co. / IBA (International Building Exhibiton)

Grouped around a central, connecting courtyard are 4 apartments whose eat-in kitchens all stand in clear view. Divided by only narrow slits, two more apartments connect to the left and right, another faces the street, and two more face the large courtyard further opened by the block's greenery. It's not hard to guess who was responsible for the reddish-brown brick and yellow plaster enhancing semicircular balconies hung in front of glazed areas.

196

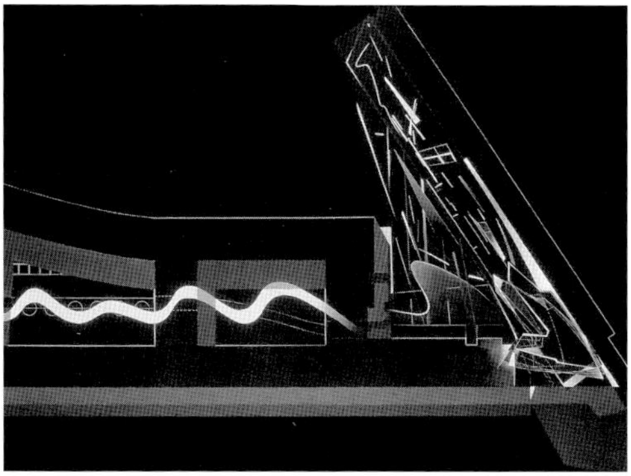

Floor-plan animation

Wohnhof
Apartment courtyard
1993/94
Kreuzberg, Stresemannstraße at the corner of Dessauer Straße
Architect: Zaha Hadid
Contact architect: Stefan Schroth
Client: DeGeWo / IBA (International Building Exhibiton)

After the completion of her first project, the fire station in Weil am Rhein, the buildability of the deconstructivist's bold, ambiguous drawings involving social apartment constructions, and their countless regularities, was put to the test. Yet her vivid constructions and colorful façades have long become the common property of the following generations of architects.

197

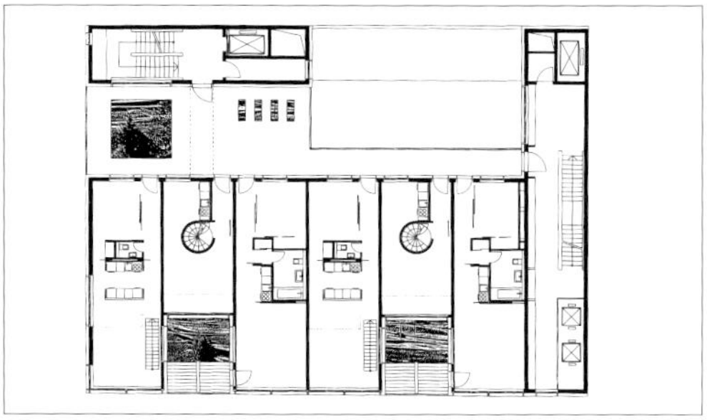

Plan of the 6th floor

Apartment, office and commercial building
1997/98
Kreuzberg, Askanischer Platz at the corner of Schöneberger Straße
Architects: Hentrich-Petschnigg & Partner with Wolfgang Keilholz
Client: HABERENT Grundstücks GmbH

Evolving from a 1993 expert opinion, the construction served as an important building block for repairing the former train station's forecourt. With stores on the ground-floor and basement levels, floors of offices on the 1st to 5th floors, and two attached floors for apartments, the wealth of functions is perfectly reflected in the building's well-structured façade, differentiating between the side facing the square and the other facing the street.

198

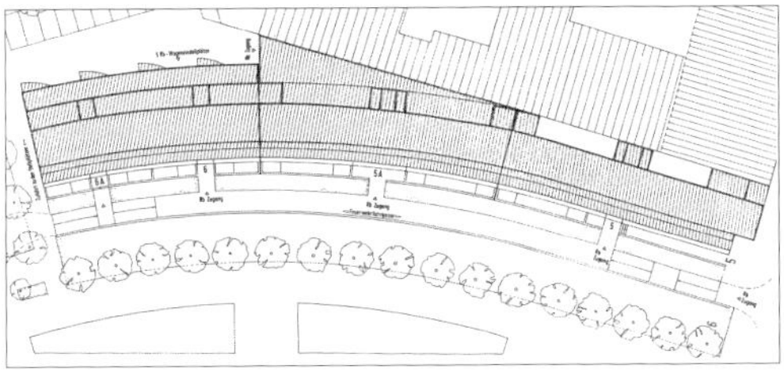

Haus an der Brandwand

House at the fireproofing wall

1988/89

Kreuzberg, Schöneberger Straße 5

Architect: Josef Paul Kleihues

Project manager: Stephan Gallant

Client: IBA (International Building Exhibition)

Thirty years after the 1957 Interbau **(416–435)**, the year 1987 was assigned to the second International Building Exhibition (IBA) after the war. This made the person responsible for the design of the exhibition's section for new buildings not only a latecomer, but also the forerunner of an architecture limited to essential design characteristics – an architecture which Kleihues himself calls a "critical reconstruction" of the city. The building is covering a large fire-wall and gives a new touch of elegance.

199

Courtyard side

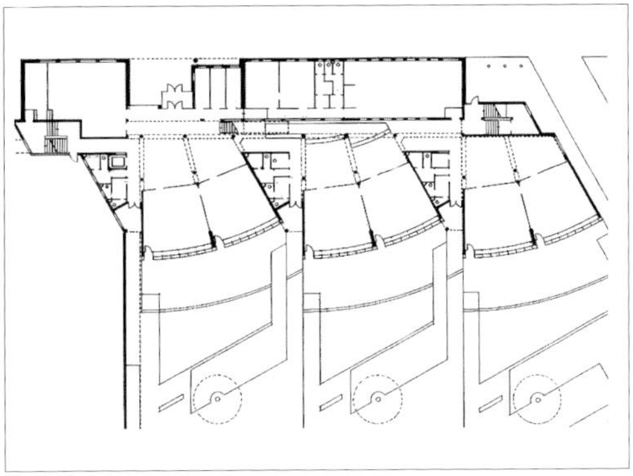

Fanny-Hensel-Grundschule

1988–91

Kreuzberg, Schöneberger Straße 21–23

Architects: Wolfgang Scharlach, Rainer Wischhusen

Client: Bezirksamt Kreuzberg / IBA (International Building Exhibiton)

The result of a 1984 competition, executed in stages: the 2-winged school building for 390 students, gymnasium for 3 athletic disciplines, covering for the exterior sports facility that stretches along the street, and the open field, orient themselves to the former railway station Anhalter Bahnhof – of which only the station's entranceway is preserved. Most striking is the form of the three 3-storey classroom sections in the receding arch: "The spatial disposition should also allow social and spatial activities to develop in the class and classroom."

200

Administrative headquarters of Volksbank
1993–1999
Tiergarten, Linkstraße 10–12, Schellingstraße 24
Architects: Arata Isozaki, Steffen Lehmann
Client: Daimler Chrysler Immobilien

By connecting altogether five 3-storey bridges, a double-loaded corridor construction was formed for the administrative headquarters of Volksbank and branches of the Raiffeisenbank at the southern tip of the entire Potsdamer Platz area. A bamboo garden and pond lie concealed between both building rows: "This building harbors a secret that it shows to whoever wants to see it", was printed in the brochure for the grand opening. The decorative façade is also characterized by unglazed ceramic slabs in two shades of pink, and sunken hinged windows that open outward.

201

Foyer

debis-Haus
1996–98
Tiergarten, Eichhornstraße at the corner of Schellingstraße
Architects: Renzo Piano Building Workshop, Christoph Kohlbecker
Client: Daimler Chrysler Immobilien

The 8-storey, elongated construction has a dignified foyer with an usual artwork by Jean Tinguely placed under towering arcs of light by François Morellet. The unchanging ceramic plates of the light-ochre façade end at the banks of the Reichpietschufer in a bundle of tower-like elements reaching a 21-storey height. The highest element, bearing the company's three-dimensional logo, is a ventilation shaft for the Tiergarten tunnel. Apart from this building and the storefront gallery, other constructions by Renzo Piano are in the immediate vicinity.

202

East side

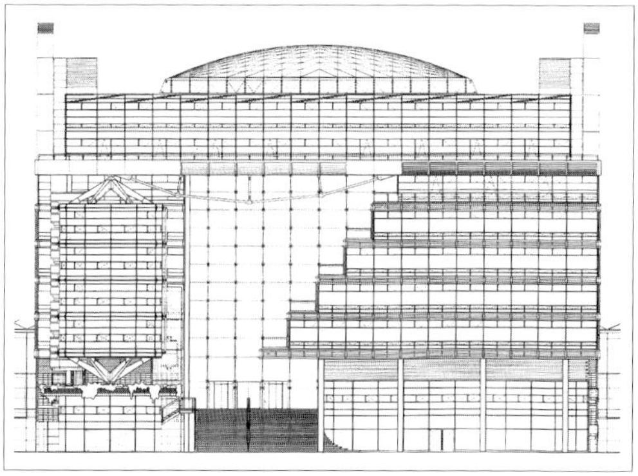

Section

Blocks B4, B6, B8
1996–99
Tiergarten, Linkstraße at the corner of Joseph-von-Eichendorff-Gasse
Architects: Richard Rogers and Partners
Client: Daimler Chrysler Immobilien

Facing the open field of the former railway station Potsdamer Bahnhof, the central span of the eastern development is made of three quadratic blocks of circa 50 x 50 m rising to a 9-storey height, and an atrium opening in a southwesterly direction towards the park. The 2,7 m grid of the vivid structural elements – echelons and cylinder – emphasizes the interplay of the building parts with colored panels, slats, red-colored clay slabs, metal bands, and glazed sections. Stores are located in the ground floor; office spaces occupy the 2nd to the 6th floors, and attic apartments are located above the atrium's glazing.

203

View from the west

Model

A+T / Parkkolonnaden
1998–2001
Tiergarten, Köthener Straße, Gabriele-Tergit-Promenade
Urban design: Giorgio Grassi
Coordination: Jürgen Sawade
Project development: Roland Ernst

Following a competition success by Giorgio Grassi, five building parts based on the principle of "the greatest possible uniformity" were developed along the Tilla Durieux installation by Bruno Doedens and Maike von Stiphout from Amsterdam, a grass-covered field at the same time an expansive sculptural work. From north to south appears the "head" by Schweger, with its enormous and glazed rounded front; two H-type constructions by Grassi, a third construction by Sawade, and finally the "tail" by Diener & Diener with Schweger Assoziierte, monolithically connected by the brownish-red color of its brick and identical eaves height.

204

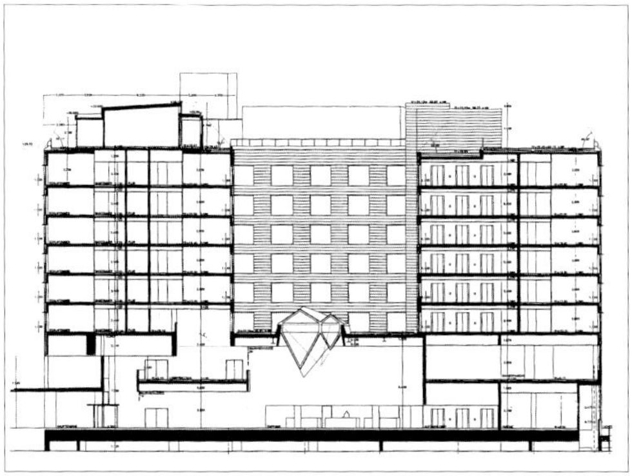

Cross section

Grand Hyatt Berlin
1996–98
Tiergarten, Marlene-Dietrich-Platz 2
Architect: José Rafael Moneo
Interior architecture: Hannes Wettstein
Contact architect: Jan Kleihues

Not only the hotel's size, clarity, and well-proportioned façade made of red sandstone, but also its interior with 342 clearly designed rooms, 3 restaurants, ballroom, library, and board rooms make it pleasantly stand out among the usual grand hotel. It also honors the surrounding contributions of great architects – Piano, Rogers, Kollhoff, Isozaki, and naturally Moneo – by including additional banquet rooms, each dedicated by name.

205

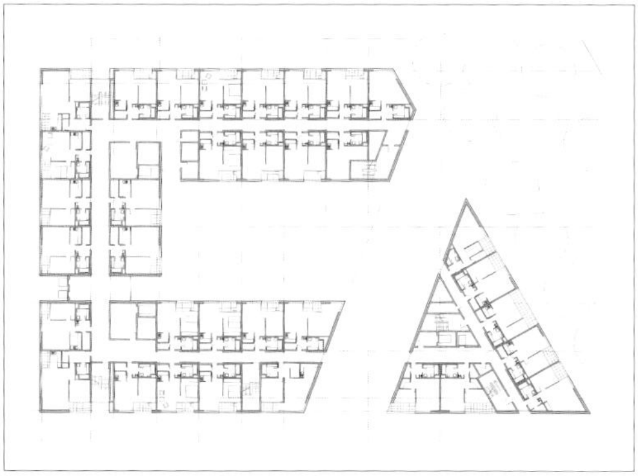

Plan of the 5th to the 8th floors

Blocks A2 and A3
1997–99
Tiergarten, Potsdamer Straße 3
Architects: Ulrike Lauber, Wolfram Wöhr
Client: DaimlerChrysler

Altogether 3 blocks resulted from the special prize awarded in conjunction with the "debis" competition, two of which stand side by side between the old and new Potsdamer Straße thoroughfare. While the smaller block accommodates apartments, the larger offers 19 movie theaters on three levels, the CinemaxX, the offices of the Internationale Filmfestspiele Berlin, and, from the 5th floor upward, the "Madison", an elegantly conceived boarding house with 166 suites, the restaurant "Facil" on the cinema's roof, and a highly aesthetic wellness area with a view of the city's skyline.

206

Stairwell

Musiktheater
1996–98
Tiergarten, Marlene Dietrich-Platz
Architects: Renzo Piano Building Workshop, Christoph Kohlbecker
Adagio Berlin: Moritz Müller, Martin Wallimann

As though receiving architectural signals from the architecture of the Staatsbibliothek, positioned back to back, the surfaces of the "Spieltheater" performing stage and "Spielbank" casino become interrupted here. On the other hand, the interruption forms the spacious entranceway hall with staircases and galleries as high as the passageway to the well-known Adagio Berlin, whose creepy architecture has nostalgic hints of the Middle Ages.

207

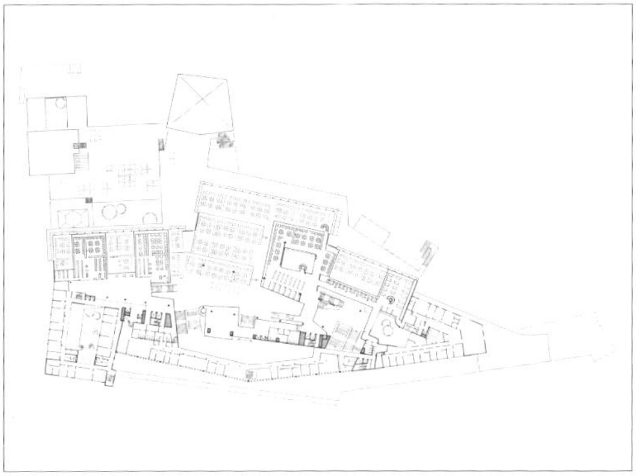

Plan of the 1st floor

Staatsbibliothek zu Berlin
State library
1967–76
Tiergarten, Potsdamer Straße 33
Architect: Hans Scharoun
Implementation planning: Edgar Wisniewski
Floor design: Erich F. Reuter
Glass-window design: Alexander Camaro
Client: Stiftung Preußischer Kulturbesitz

Greatly subdivided and staggered, the structures of the library stand alongside the Ibero-American Institute and form the southeastern conclusion of the cultural institutions at the Matthäuskirchplatz. The stacks in the higher building part shield quiet reading and users' areas, distributed over several levels, from a westerly tangent road still in the planning then, a six-lane highway from a time when cities were sympathetic to cars.

208

Musikinstrumenten-Museum and Staatliches Institut für Musikforschung
1979–84
Tiergarten, Potsdamer Straße 33
Architect: Edgar Wisniewski
Urban concept: Hans Scharoun
Glass-window design: Alexander Camaro
Client: Stiftung Preußischer Kulturbesitz

No differently than the planned chamber-music hall at the southeast end of the Philharmonie, the structural components of this building ensemble adopt the Philharmonie's design principles and expand them to a forum for music-related culture. The connecting 2-storey music hall is a right-angled institute construc- tion with an adjoining inner courtyard. A library forms the southern conclusion.

209

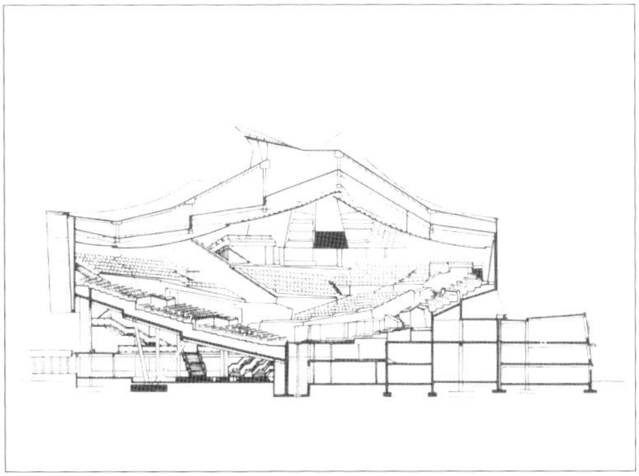

Philharmonie
1960–63
Tiergarten, Kemperplatz
Architect: Hans Scharoun
Implementation with Werner Weber
Roof-spire design: Hans Uhlmann
Floor mosaics: Erich F. Reuter

Even today this building – a first-prize competition winner marking the beginning of a center for the arts and sciences to be developed around the Matthäuskirche by Friedrich August Stüler (1844–1846) – remains the hub of all the other cultural buildings. The hall's 2,200 seats are grouped around the orchestra in an amphitheater-like and "vineyard" arrangement, above which is a folded, concrete roof reminiscent of a tent. Further design details include various secondary spaces and a foyer with cascading staircases leading off to different levels. The hall's synthetic, golden skin was applied at a later date and corresponds with Scharoun's idea to create a construction that would glow outwardly.

210

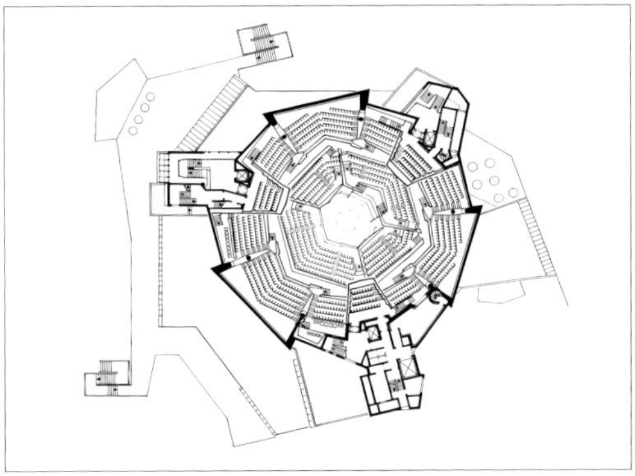

Kammermusiksaal
Chamber-music hall
1984–87
Tiergarten, Herbert-von-Karajan-Straße
Architect: Edgar Wisniewski
Urban concept: Hans Scharoun
Acoustics: Lothar Cremer
Structural engineers: Heinz Saar, Dieter Enseleit

After building the magnificent Philharmonie **(209)**, its structure was supplemented by those of the Staatsbibliothek **(207)** and Musikinstrumenten-Museum**(208)**. As an example of sound, urban planning and anthroposophic thinking, this multifaceted ensemble entered and rose up in the so-called "Kulturforum" cityscape and developed a convincing architectural dialog through its close proximity to the Potsdamer Platz quarter. But developing at the same time were plans for further changes, urbanization, and doubtful beneficial interventions.

211

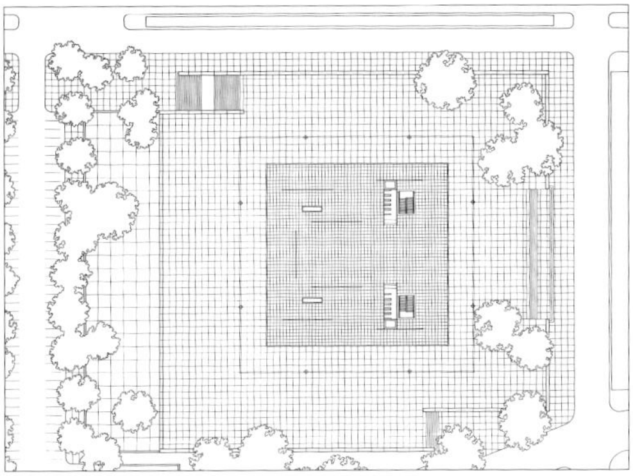

Floor plan of the main exhibition hall

Neue Nationalgalerie
1965–68
Tiergarten, Potsdamer Straße, Matthäikirchplatz
Architect: Ludwig Mies van der Rohe
Structural engineers: Dienst + Richter
Implementation: Senator für Bau- und Wohnungswesen
Overseeing firm: Krupp-Druckenmüller

A "universal space" with a square floor plan, freely dividable for changing exhibitions and opening on all sides to a terrace for displaying sculptures, lies below a steel waffle-roof elevated on eight pillars. On the foundation floor, one side of the museum spaces for showing works of nineteenth and twentieth century art opens out onto a sculpture garden. The grid module of 1,20 m determines all the other details, as well as both uncomfortable stairs. Meanwhile the gallery's exhibition hall has been used in so many ways that it could now be considered a multifunctional hall.

212

Main exhibition hall

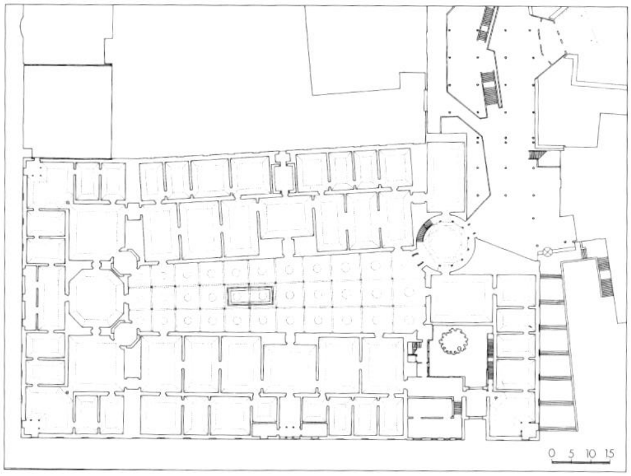

Plan of the main floor

Gemäldegalerie
1992–98
Tiergarten, Matthäikirchplatz, Sigismundstraße, Stauffenbergstraße
Architects: Heinz Hilmer, Christoph Sattler, Thomas Albrecht
Water pool: Walter De Maria
Client: Stiftung Preußischer Kulturbesitz

As an essential part of the "Kulturforum", planned and built since 1964, the fine arts gallery can probably be seen as the last building block, costing circa 127 million Euro. The architects linked this section to the incorporated and reworked, large staircase by Rolf Gutbrod still in its preliminary stages. In the process, the fine arts gallery received its own center – a pillared hall with overhead lighting, and a pool of water about which the pillars as well stand grouped and lit from above.

213

Kunstgewerbemuseum
Arts and crafts museum
1978–85
Tiergarten, Matthäikirchplatz
Architect: Rolf Gutbrod with Bernd Riede, Herbert Rebel, Dieter Dörschner
Client: Stiftung Preußischer Kulturbesitz

Developed from a design considered during a 1966 competition, the first building phase of this mammoth, construction project for completing a museum complex took into account the fine arts gallery, the sculpture department, the engraving collection, and the art library. Visible in the overall subdivisions and façades was the attempt to differentiate between building sizes according to their contents. Not realized here, however, was a wing meant to conclude the piazza, and the Gemäldegalerie **(212)** would later be completed in a greatly altered form.

214

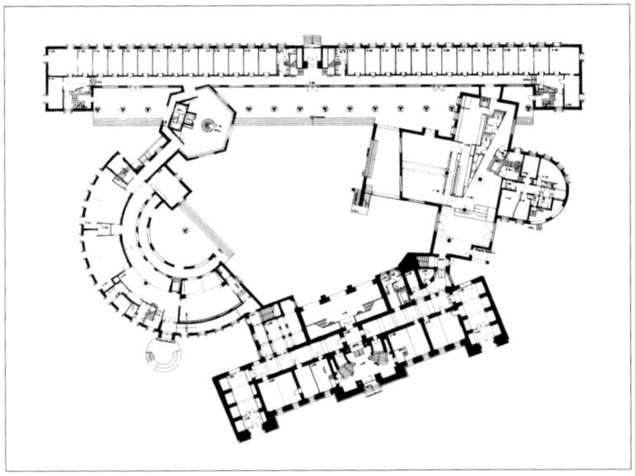

Plan of the ground floor

Wissenschaftszentrum Berlin für Sozialforschung
Social Science Research Center Berlin
1984–88
Tiergarten, Hitzigallee 23–29
Architects: James Stirling, Michael Wilford
Contact architect: Rudolf Schmitt
Incorporated here was the headquarters of the former Reichsversicherungsamt, designed 1894 by Alfred Busse, the four unlike, new buildings connect to it at their outermost corners. The courtyard's green space is boardered by wide stone staircases and a light-weight glass canopy. The alternating brick-red or blue-colored horizontal bands of the façades contrast with colored sandstone and dark-hued window surrounds.

215

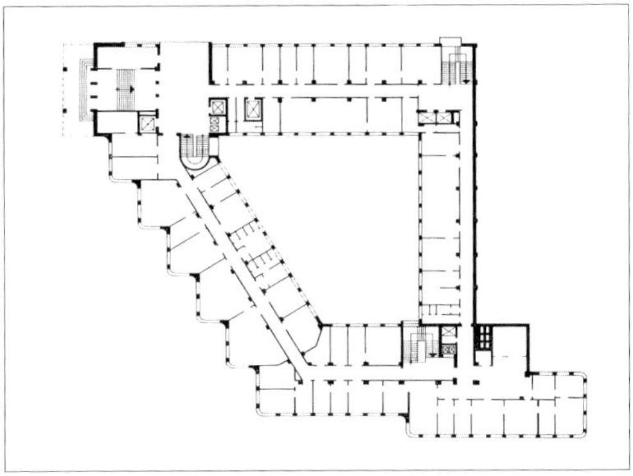

Plan of the ground floor

Shell-Haus
1931
Tiergarten, Reichpietschufer, Stauffenbergstraße
Architect: Emil Fahrenkamp
Structural engineer: Gerhard Mensch
In many discussions about Berlin and the Modern architecture many engaged people decided this example as the very best. This steel-frame construction, with gas concrete block infill, is clad with travertine slabs. The plan of the building's strongly staggered form, altering its height from 5 to 10 storeys, as well as its outer skin, make it one of Berlin's most elegant office buildings. Since 1952, it serves as the administration building of the BEWAG electric company. A large portion of the building's subsequent reconstruction, designed by Paul G. R. Baumgarten, was torn down in order to make room for a hotel whose façade was designed by Jan Kleihues.

216

Deutsches Technikmuseum
German museum of technology
1995–2001
Kreuzberg, Tempelhofer Ufer at the corner of Trebbiner Straße
Architects: Ulrich Wolff, Helge Pitz
Client: Senatsverwaltung für Stadtentwicklung

Together with part of the former Anhalter Bahnhof's depot, the old and the new building – the latter boasts the museum's innovative in-house technology – form a structural ensemble, which includes old locomotive sheds and coach hangars, lacking neither drama nor a wealth of information. The building visibly advertises itself with a vintage Dakota, the so-called "raisin bomber" of the cold war blockade period. The collection contains a model of the first computer developed and built in 1936 by Konrad Zuse.

217

Court room

District-court expansion
1992–95
Kreuzberg, Hallesches Ufer at the corner of Möckernstraße
Architect: Oswald Mathias Ungers with Karl-Heinz Winkens
Client: Senat von Berlin

"To avoid presenting a false representation, the outward appearance of the state's third power was meant to be inconspicuous. Its uniformly orientated structures led to the new family division appearing as a solitary construction. A 'Kinderhaus' or children's home was built in the green of the 'Robinienwäldchen' at the property's southwest corner."

218

Canal side

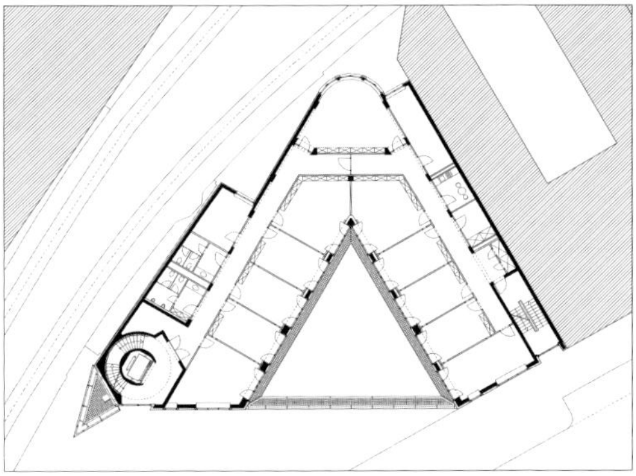

Plan of the 2nd to the 5th floors

BVG-Gebäude
Offices of the Berlin transportation authority
1998 – 2000
Kreuzberg, Tempelhofer Ufer 30/31
Architect: Joachim Ganz
Client: BVG

Erected on an extremely small triangular plot, where it endures traffic routes on four levels – elevated railway, street, canal, underground railway – the building of the Berlin transit society (BVG) is nevertheless sophisticated commercially effective, and makes a clearly defined architectural statement born of both its functions and complications. It showcases two entranceway portals – one extroverted, back-lit, and functioning as a glowing gateway for the elevated railway; the other introverted and placed at an atrium with subdued lighting.

219

Der Tagesspiegel
Main offices of the *Tagesspiegel* newspaper
1989–91
Tiergarten, Potsdamer Straße 87
Architects: Siegwart Geiger, Gerhard Spangenberg
Client: Merkator Druckerei

The refurbishment measures originally meant to improve only the soundproofing and heat insulation not only gave the editorial building a totally new appearance, but also the 7-storey building part from 1956, and the 12-story tower construction from 1974, which pushes the lettering of the newspaper's masthead into the sky over the street in the style of revolutionary Russian architecture. All the façade elements come into play at a depth of 40 cm in the remaining space between the main building and edge of the street.

220

Connection to existing development

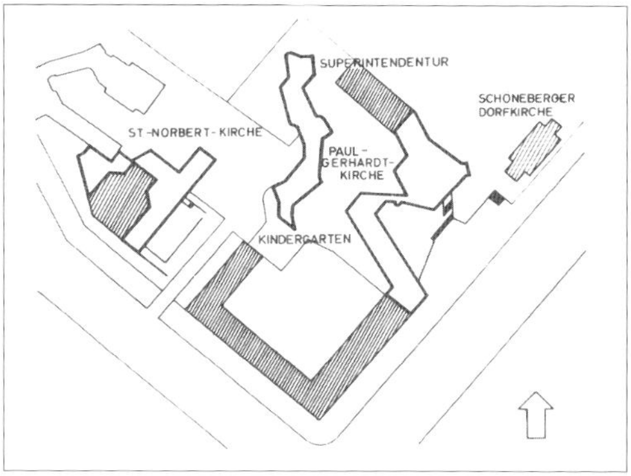

Site plan

St.-Norbert-Kirche
1961/62
Schöneberg, Dominicusstraße
Architects: Hermann Fehling, Daniel Gogel

Apart from the side of the church on Dominicusstraße, the existing domed construction is surrounded by new building parts whose roofs, at the eave of the slanted main roof, assume the same inclination and are at times carried down flat to the ground. At the lowest points, rainwater is directed through spouts into open containers. The structural additions include an entrance hall, priests' chambers, and a kindergarten.

221

Paul-Gerhardt-Kirche
1961/62
Schöneberg, Hauptstraße 47–48
Architects: Hermann Fehling, Daniel Gogel

This new construction takes the place of the destroyed church beside the old Schöneberg village church and, together with it, forms an extension of Hauptstraße resembling a city square. Its structural form and building materials establish a relationship to the neighboring St.-Norbert-Kirche. The functional spaces of the church, priest's apartment, and parochial house connect it to the existing development. Gray shotcrete plaster creates the structural vividness of the walls, and the overall construction is roofed over with slate cladding.

222

Swimming hall after 1999

Stadtbad Schöneberg
Schöneberg municipal swimming pool
1930
Schöneberg, Hauptstraße 39
Architect: Heinz Lassen
Modernization: Peter Arnke, Brigitte Häntsch
Client: Bezirksamt Schöneberg

This well-proportioned, functional building was modestly built. The floor and staircases are made of artificial stone, and the outer skin of clinker brick. Located in the front building are apartments, administrative offices, and the showering and bathing facilities. The swimming-pool area is encircled by dressing rooms. In 1964/65, the construction department of Schöneberg carried out some technical renovations to the building. The complete modernization of the swimming pool, which followed in 1995–99, raised its competitive standards to those of other district-run municipal swimming pools.

223

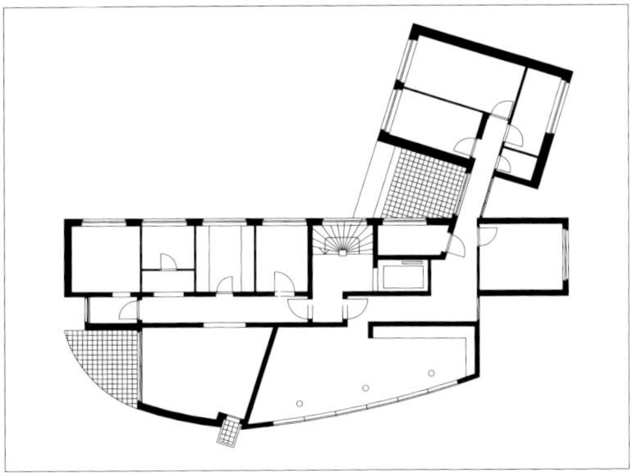

Apartment and commercial building
1995–96
Schöneberg, Kolonnenstraße at the corner of Feurigstraße
Architects: Georg Eyl, Werner Weitz, Joachim Würmle with Laura Wendt-Mieser
Client: Stadt and Land Wohnbauten-Gesellschaft mbH

The structure represents a synthesis between the closing of an edge of a block and a detached solitary construction, drawing from this an aesthetic tension in the urban planning context. Propping the 5-storey building part for the apartments atop "three" storeys with businesses qualifies as yet another tension-filled nuance: the classical base height is usually made of only two floors.

224

Kathreiner-Hochhaus
Kathreiner high-rise building
1929/30
Schöneberg, Potsdamer Straße, Kleistpark
Architect: Bruno Paul
The administration building of Kathreiner Inc. rises up alongside Carl von Gontard's Königskolonnaden, built 1777–1780 and transferred to this spot in 1910. A 12-storey central building stands between two 6-storey wings, and the steel-framed construction, window piers, and foundation are lined with German and Roman travertine. The building's structure as well as its horizontal and vertical subdivisions assume here a classical balance.

225

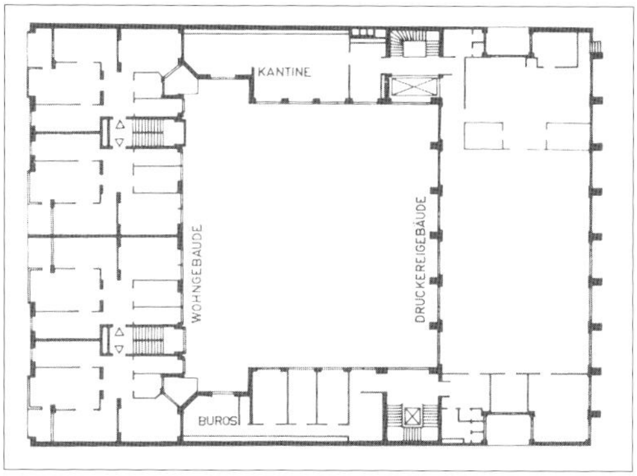

Plan of a standard floor

Verbandshaus der Deutschen Buchdrucker
German book-printers association building
1925/26
Tempelhof, Dudenstraße 10
Architects: Max Taut, Franz Hoffmann
Client: Buchdruckerverband
Though built with utter clarity at a middle axis of the street, a few of the building's façade details playfully reveal variations of the loggia, solarium, and wall facings. What stand out are the yellow ceramic plates, but also the lettering over the ground floor, and, in addition to these, the ceramics in the staircases. By comparison, the courtyard building with two side wings connecting to offices and function rooms is a rigid, concrete frame construction spanning over 13,50 m, and can therefore offer the space needed for printing presses and other machinery. The connected houses on the left side are designed by the same architect in the 1950s, an example of the very gingerly beginning after the war.

226

Main entrance

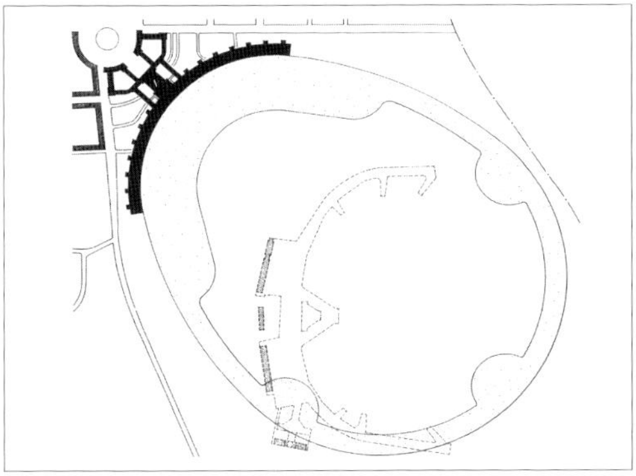

Site plan of the former situation

Zentralflughafen Tempelhof
Tempelhof central airport
1939
Tempelhof, Platz der Luftbrücke
Architect: Ernst Sagebiel

This structural manifesto derives its fascistic emotionalism from the Nazi regime. The connecting member of both directionally opposed and curved building parts (gate and administration building) is a 100-m long and 50-m wide check-in area roofed over by 32-m long truss girders made of reinforced concrete. The support-free gates are located at the side of the building reserved for departures. The back ends of the far-reaching, projecting steel trusses are secured by tie bars, between which are tall glass windows. Though protected by preservation laws, the building's existence is threatened by the renovations and improvements on the new Schönefeld Airport. Opposite the airlift memorial, design by the architect Eduard Ludwig in 1951.

227

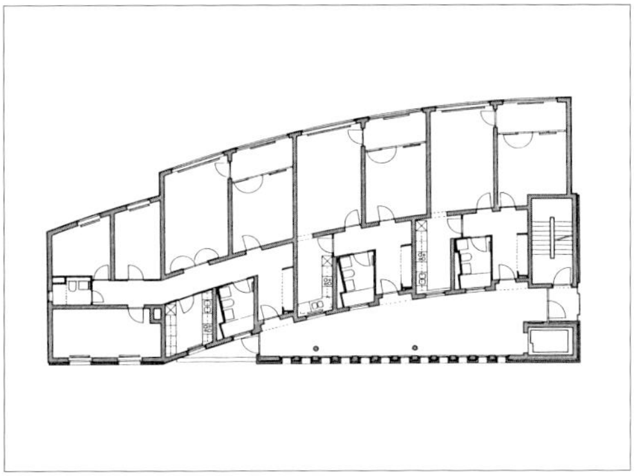

Plan of the ground floor

Two apartment buildings
1990–92
Tempelhof, Tempelhofer Damm 44–46
Architects: Rebeca Chestnutt, Robert Niess with Bendoraitis, Gurt, Meißner, Glass
Client: Tempelhofer Feld AG

The result of a competition, two buildings form a gate-like situation marking the access to a "garden city" in the Neu-Tempelhof district. The undertaking was originally conceived by Hermann Jansen in 1911 and later reworked by Fritz Bräuning, who expanded it with 2- to 3-storey duplexes and row houses. The both new buildings are oriented away from the street, the apartments are protected by a pair of screens as perforated walls. 53 apartments exist in this public housing construction covering 4,067 sqm of floor area. Building costs: circa 6,5 million Euro.

228

Central animal research laboratories of the Freie Universität Berlin
1962–75, 1978–80
Lichterfelde, Krahmerstraße 6–12
Architect: Gerd Hänska with Kurt Schmersow
Client: Senator für Bau- und Wohnungswesen for Freie Universität Berlin

Divided into different germ-free work areas, the entire building is cut off from environmental or climatic influences, as well as from insects. The air-suction piping protrudes so far from the outer wall that, outside of the incurring heat congestion, decentralized fresh air can be drawn in. Only a few spaces in the corner regions have orientation windows with north-facing gabled dormers. The façade is made of two-shelled, prefabricated concrete components.

229

Institute of hygiene and medical microbiology of the Freie Universität Berlin
1971–74
Lichterfelde, Hindenburgdamm 27
Architects: Hermann Fehling, Daniel Gogel with Jürgen Kümmel, Manfred Walz
Client: Senator für Bau- und Wohnungswesen for Freie Universität Berlin

The subdividing of the laboratory building was carried out according to a functional ordering. This resulted in placing different building parts beside one another, with each part revealing its own distinguishing characteristics. The architects especially focussed on the task of creating from a "beside one another a with one another" able to unify the entire complex.

230

General view with the new commercial center

Ullstein publishing house
1923–30
Tempelhof, Mariendorfer Damm 1–3
Architect: Eugen Schmohl
Commercial center 1994/95
Architect: Gernot Nalbach
Project manager: Thomas Stahl

Developed along the Teltowkanal, in the extension of the publishing house and printing works, was a 3-storey commercial strip to which three 10-storey square towers built as steel-frame constructions were connected. The 70,000 sqm floor area could also be used to accommodate Berlin's fashion center. The original construction ranks as Berlin's first high-rise to be built using a reinforced-concrete construction method for bearing floor loads up to 2 tons/sqm. The brick lining of the tower housing the printing works and administrative building is subdivided in vertically accentuated sections of decorative stonework, which visually correspond with the representative demands of the firm's main office in Berlin.

231

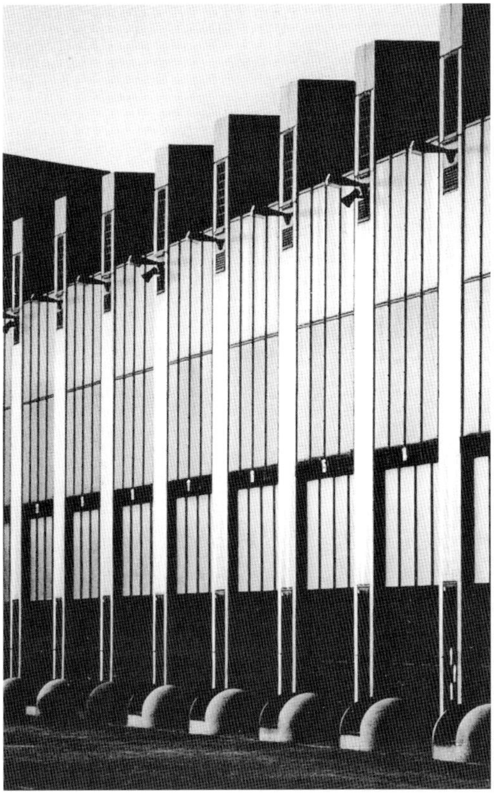

Central workshop of Berliner Stadtreinigung
1975–78
Tempelhof, Ringbahnstraße 88–124
Architect: Josef Paul Kleihues with Axel Schultes, Walther Stepp
Client: Berliner Stadtreinigung

On a miniscreen of 12.5 x 12.5 cm in highest discipline and order designed as a shining example not only for architects and engineers, but for the people who work in here and have to take care for keeping order and cleanness in the city. Between the prefabricated concrete towerlike pillars the gateways open the carports for the garbage trucks on both sides. In the middle – like a backbone – is a supply service line sited and gives the junction to the upper storeys for storage or staff rooms. The western end of the 213 m large building connects both sides by a impressive semicircle.

232

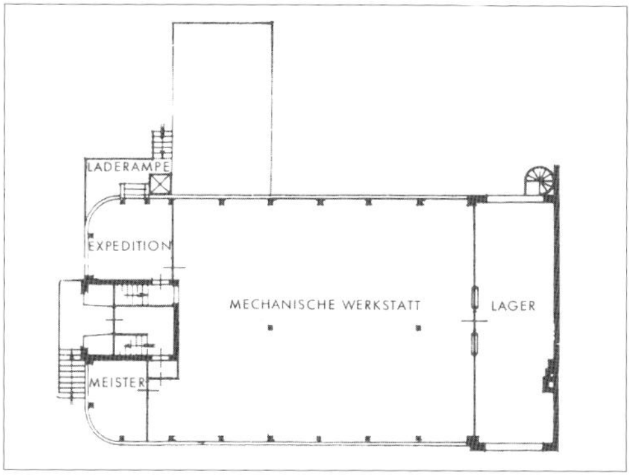

Plan of the ground floor

Factory for electromechanical devices
1928
Lankwitz, Nicolaistraße 7
Architect: Martin Punitzer
Client: Abrahamson

The building was erected as a factory for manufacturing electronic measuring devices. On the well-lit ground floor, the light provided by encircling bands of windows reaches to the middle of the technical workshop's space. On the upper floors are offices as well as weighing and testing zones. In the basement storey are social rooms and spaces for massive, punching machines. The building's depth is 13,50 m. Every parapet wall is lined with lime-green tiles. The overall structure is slightly damaged from the war. As early as 1913, the Deutscher Werkbund confronted the issue of an aesthetic for industrial constructions from which a new architectural language was meant to develop. Well known is the Roxy cinema by Punitzer in Steglitz, Hauptstraße 78, one year later.

233

The hall

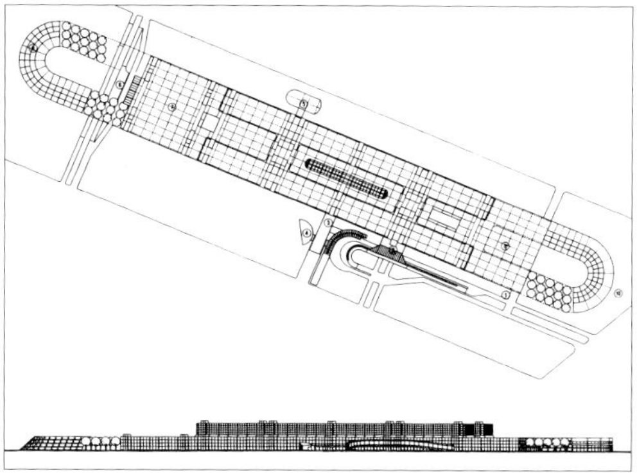

Site plan and elevation

Krankenhaus Neukölln
1977/78
Buckow, Rudower Straße 56, Kormoranweg
Architect: Josef Paul Kleihues
Project manager: Jürgen König
Wall paintings: Markus Lüpertz
Client: Bezirksamt Neukölln for Land Berlin

Recognizable here is the wealth of form and precise detailing which typifies a "JPK" design. "This involves the first construction of a still-operating hospital cited to be preserved and completed as a pavilion system. The new building with 700 beds connects with facilities for examinations, specialized treatment, and general health care, which accommodate altogether 1,200 beds. The steel-frame construction has a lightweight, curtain wall, aluminum façade; a white fired-on coat; black screwed-on joints, and electronically-operated shading elements. Its urban planning measures provide for apartments and stores."

234

View of the living area and the studio from the garden

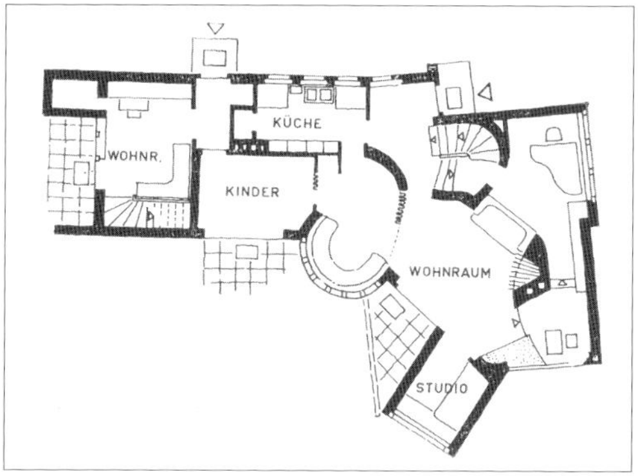

Plan of the ground floor

Haus Mohrmann
1939
Lichtenrade, Falkensteinstraße 10
Architect: Hans Scharoun

Only an intimate knowledge of the future inhabitants could have led to such an individualized design for living. Using the simplest of means, the house was conceived to satisfy only its living comfort, interplay of rooms, and garden. Spaces of varying heights, platforms, walls in some cases movable walls, as well as a great many small light sources concealed at different locations, make the house unusually lively for its inhabitants.

235

Photo from 1913

Grandstands of Trabrennbahn Mariendorf
1913
Mariendorf, Mariendorfer Damm 222–298
Architect: August Endell

With ease the grandstands combine lightness with elegance in this visible, latticed girder construction made of steel. The original development consisted of two grandstand boxes, the racetrack's tower, and a café. But only the racetrack tower and southern grandstand were preserved. Atop the grandstand's massive foundation stands an open roof construction of riveted and latticed steel girders. Meanwhile the northern grandstand has been replaced by a fully-glazed new building. In 1961, a café designed by Werner Weber was built on the southern part of the facility.

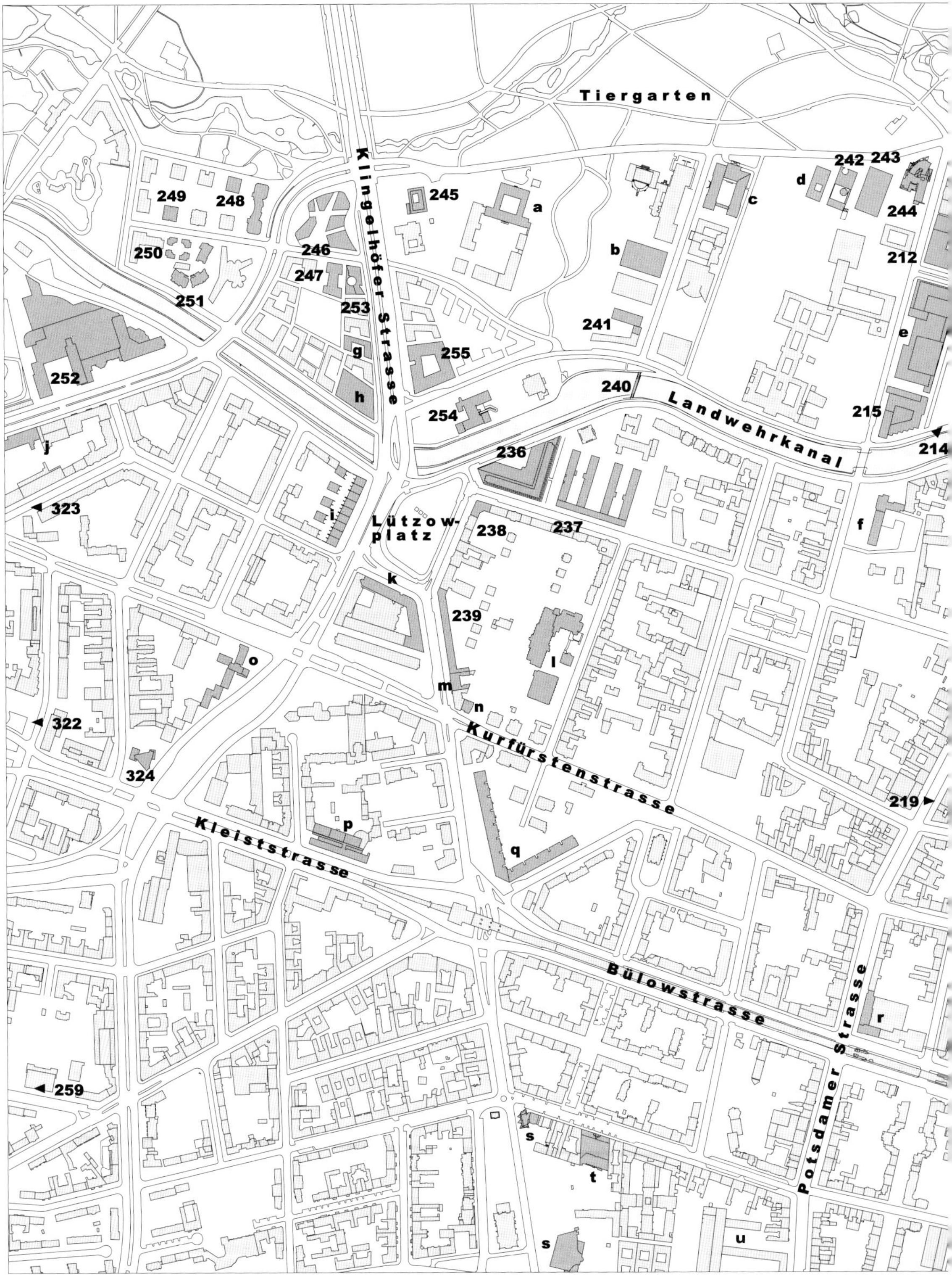

Tiergarten
Klingelhöfer Strasse
Landwehrkanal
Lützowplatz
Kurfürstenstrasse
Kleiststrasse
Bülowstrasse
Potsdamer Strasse
a
b
c
d
e
f
g
h
i
j
k
l
m
n
o
p
q
r
s
t
s
u
212
214
215
219
236
237
238
239
240
241
242
243
244
245
246
247
248
249
250
251
252
253
254
255
259
322
323
324

Lützowplatz SW

212	Gemäldegalerie	Heinz Hilmer, Christoph Sattler, Thomas Albrecht
214	Wissenschaftszentrum	James Stirling, Michael Wilford
215	Shell-Haus	Emil Fahrenkamp
219	Der Tagesspiegel	Siegwart Geiger, Gerhard Spangenberg
236	Grand Hotel Esplanade	Jürgen Sawade
237	Torhäuser	Vittorio Gregotti
238	Apartment and commercial building	Mario Botta
239	Office building	Heinz Hilmer, Christoph Sattler
240	Hiroshima-Steg	Klaus Theo Brenner, Benedict Tonon
241	Landesvertretung der Freien Hansestadt Bremen	Hilde Léon, Konrad Wohlhage, Siegfried Wernik
242	Botschaft der Republik Indien	Hilde Léon, Konrad Wohlhage, Siegfried Wernik
243	Landesvertretung Baden-Württemberg	Dietrich Bangert
244	Österreichische Botschaft	Hans Hollein
245	Konrad-Adenauer-Stiftung	Thomas van den Valentyn
246	Botschaften der Nordischen Länder	Alfred Berger, Tiina Parkkinen
247	Wirtschaftsprüferhaus	Heike Büttner, Claus Neumann, Georg Braun
248	Apartment house	Klaus Theo Brenner, Benedict Tonon
249	Apartment house	Rob Krier
250	Vier Stadtvillen	Bangert, Jansen, Scholz, Schultes
251	Öko-Haus	Frei Otto, Hermann Kendel
252	Berlin Hilton/Hotel Intercontinental	Pereira & Luckman; Jan Bassenge, Kay Puhan-Schulz, Johannes Heinrich, Walter Schreiber
253	Botschaft der Vereinigten Staaten von Mexiko	Teodore González de León, Francisco Serrano
254	Bauhaus-Archiv	Walter Gropius TAC
255	National office of KPMG International	Nicolas Grimshaw
259	Prager-Platz-Ensemble	Karl Pächter; Jan Bassenge, Johannes Heinrich, Kay Puhan-Schulz
322	Wittenbergplatz U-Bahn station	Alfred Grenander
323	Lenzhaus	Heinrich Straumer
324	Haus der Werbung	Rolf Gutbrod, Horst Schwaderer, Hermann Kiess

a	Krupp headquarters /Canisius-Kolleg	Mebes & Emmerich, 1936; Pankrath, 1979
b	Landesvertretung Nordrhein-Westfalen	Petzinka Pink, 2000–02
c	Italienische Botschaft	Friedrich Hetzelt, 1938; Vittorio de Feo, 2003
d	Botschaft der Republik Südafrika	Movojele, Mpahlwa, Samuels, 2003
e	Maritim-Kongresshotel	Jan Kleihues, 2003–05
f	Youth hostel	Hans Müller & Georg Heinrichs, 1963–65
g	Botschaft der Republik Malaysia	Pysal, Stahrenberg, 1999–2000
h	CDU party headquarters	Petzinka Pink, 1999–2000
i	Peripheral development	Oswald Mathias Ungers, 1982/83
j	Hotel Schweizer Hof	Jan Bassenge, Kay Puhan-Schulz, 1997–99
k	Hotel Berlin	Schwebes + Schoszberger, Brenner & Tonon, 1987
l	Französisches Gymnasium	Pysall, Rollenhagen, 1971–74
m	Transformer station	Max Dudler, Karl Dudler, 1986–89
n	Residential building	Heinz Hilmer, Christoph Sattler, Thomas Albrecht, 1998
o	Bürohaus an der Urania	Werner Düttmann, Fischer, 1966/67
p	Apartment and commerccial building	Fridtjof Schliephacke, 1970/71
q	Dreieck am Nollendorfplatz	Gerhard Krebs, Josef Paul Kleihues, 1970–73
r	Commerzbank Berlin headquarters	Heidenreich, Polensky, Vogel, Zeumer, 1989–91
s	Winterfeld-Platz-Ensemble	Hinrich Baller, Inken Baller, 1995–2002
t	Zentrale Vermittlungsstelle	Jan Bassenge, Kay Puhan-Schulz, 1984/85
u	Wohnen am Kleistpark	Grötzebach, Plessow, Sawade, Frowein, 1974 to 1977

236

View from the south-east

Grand Hotel Esplanade
1986–88
Tiergarten, Lützowufer 15
Architect: Jürgen Sawade
Interior design: Gernot Nalbach, Johanne Nalbach
Client: Grundstücksgesellschaft am Lützowufer

"The new building type developed from this site ... conceptually draws from the image of a Berlin block with courtyard segmented to a block fragment by the blending in of the existing triangular plot ..." The roofed-over courtyard, facing the street but detached from it by a shielding wall, serves as a generously proportioned yet intimate American-style, drive-in entranceway. The hotel's function rooms and restaurant orient themselves towards a glazed gallery that borders this courtyard.

237

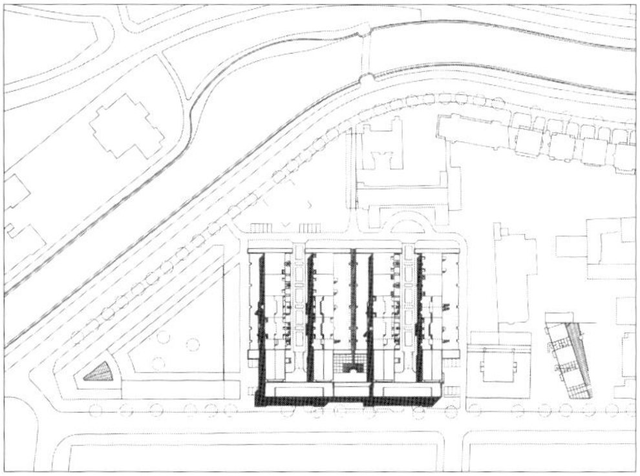

Site plan

Torhäuser
Gateway buildings
1980–86
Tiergarten, Lützowstraße 43–51
Architect: Vittorio Gregotti
Contact architect: Walter Noebel
Client: Deutschbau / IBA (International Building Exhibition)

The red and yellow brick façade as well as dark-hued bridged floors made of steel form two gateways to intimate rows of residential spaces within the block. The interior spaces are flanked by apartment floors developing to so-called 3-storey "town houses" on which five different architect's offices collaborated: Brandt, Heiß, Liepe, Steigelmann, and Oefelein + Freund, as well as Manfred Schiedhelm. Planned here in the IBA's block competition were mirrored courtyards on whose surfaces the striking corner constructions would each appear four times.

238

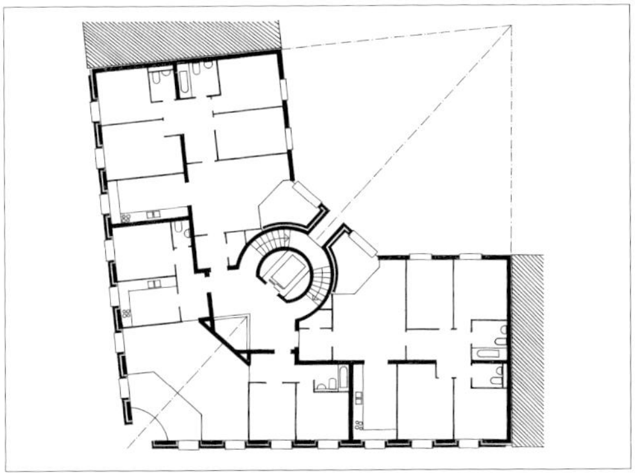

Plan of the 2nd to the 5th floors

Apartment and commercial building
1989–91
Tiergarten, Lützowplatz at the corner of Lützowstraße
Architect: Mario Botta
Client: DIIAG / IBA (International Building Exhibition)

The brick rows of the façade simultaneously form equally large windows within a stringent grid, and produce the strong rhythms of affectionately applied detail work. The loggia at the outer corner allows light to penetrate into the depths of the building's diagonals. On this city square, the building stands for the development of the eastern edge of a former block of upper-class housing, and it incorporates the IBA-sponsored design contributions by Peter Cook and Christian de Portzamparc.

239

Street side

Office building
1986–88
Tiergarten, Einemstraße 20–22
Architects: Heinz Hilmer, Christoph Sattler
Light elements: Jan Roth
Client: Dr. Hecker / IBA (International Building Exhibition)

"The ceramic surfacing of Hotel Stadt Berlin on the opposite side of the street prompted us to line the façade of this concrete-frame construction with terracotta produced from different firing processes, thus revealing varying color nuances and visual effects on the building's surfaces. In order to avoid handling the construction with concrete at its longer side, the terracotta supports were profiled vertically. The resulting effect functions best when seen in perspective."

240

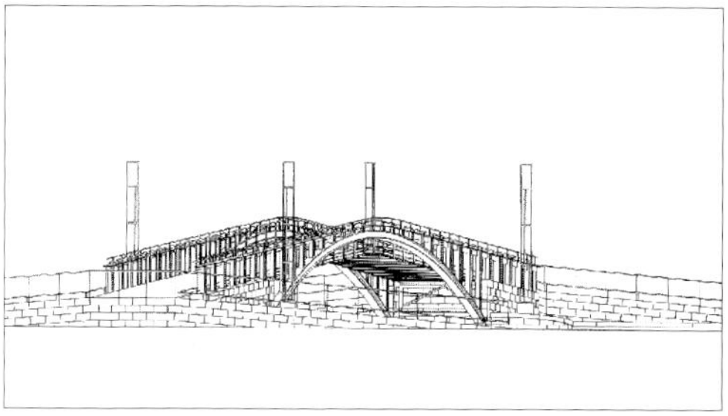

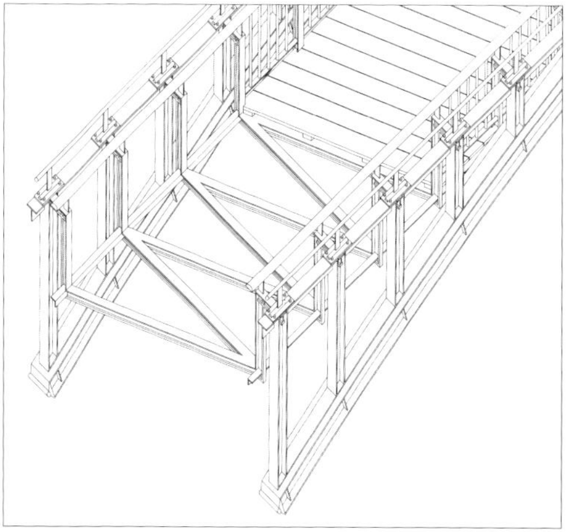

Construction detail

Hiroshima-Steg
1987
Tiergarten, Lützowufer, Reichpietschufer
Architects: Klaus Theo Brenner, Benedict Tonon
Structural engineer: Franz-Joseph Hilbers
Client: Senat von Berlin

One of the first bridges to be reworked by architects after World War II was naturally a footbridge. This particular bridge spans the Landwehrkanal. In order to achieve a sufficient clearance height, both supporting arches surpassing the footpath area form a fragile, black-and-red steel construction with their four candelabras.

241

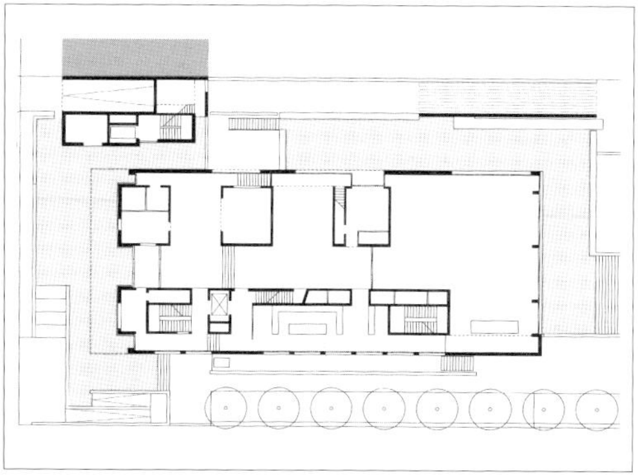

Plan of the ground floor

Landesvertretung der Freien Hansestadt Bremen
Representation of the Free Hanseatic City of Bremen
1998/99
Tiergarten, Hiroshimastraße 22–26
Architects: Hilde Léon, Konrad Wohlhage, Siegfried Wernik
Lighting plan: Licht-Kunst-Licht
Landscape planning: Karl Thomanek, Hiltrud Duquesnoy

This two-part building with a powerful brick-red stucco and monolithic aura stands as a solitary structure in the surrounding greenery. Yet the 1996 competition winner considers itself a part of the block exposing the windowless firewall of the guest house. The 4-storey administration building orients its representative spaces – "Bremer Club", foyer, and grand hall – towards the garden as a spatial continuum.

242

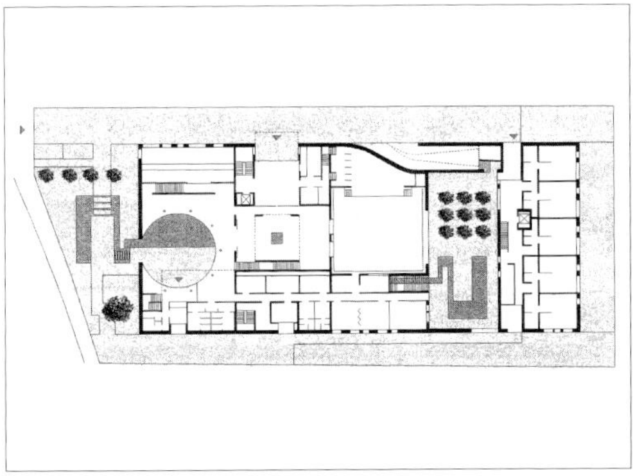

Plan of the ground floor

Botschaft der Republik Indien
Indian Embassy
1999–2000
Tiergarten, Tiergartenstraße 16–17
Architects: Hilde Léon, Konrad Wohlhage, Siegfried Wernik
Open-space planning: S.A.L.
Client: Republic of India

On a small plot, the Indian Embassy completes the row of foreign representations along the southern edge of Tiergarten's historic, diplomatic quarter. The cubical building's outer surface made of raw broken sandstone conceals a complex series of rooms and open spaces, among them the cylinder of the entranceway courtyard visible from the street, and the rectangular garden court behind a grand hall with a stage.

243

Central reception hall

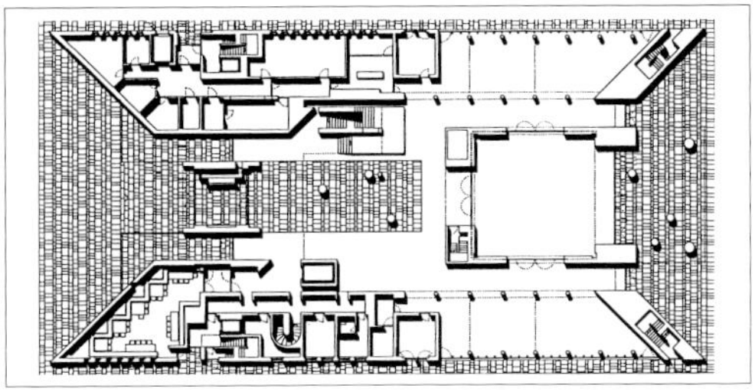

Plan of the ground floor

Landesvertretung Baden-Württemberg
Representation of Baden-Württemberg
1998–2000
Tiergarten, Tiergartenstraße 15
Architect: Dietrich Bangert
Project manager: Birgit Decker
Open-space planning: Cornelia Müller, Jan Wehberg
Client: Land Baden-Württemberg

The spatial ordering is greatly accentuated by a wide opened portico, foyer, and reception hall, and extends as far as the loggia facing the garden terrace along the middle axis, around which the remaining functional and office areas are arranged – optically connecting the building with the greenery of Tiergarten's city park. In the massive roof decking covering the sculptural cavity of the portico are the apartments provided by the representation.

244

Residential part

Österreichische Botschaft
Austrian Embassy
1999–2001
Tiergarten, Tiergartenstraße at the corner of Stauffenbergstraße
Architect: Hans Hollein
Client: Republik Österreich / Bundesministerium für auswärtige Angelegenheiten
In *Die neuen Architekturführer*, no. 41, Lars Klaaßen writes: "The complex consists of three unlike structures. Both their relationship to one another and their inner subdivision reflect the embassy's various functional areas. On one hand, the building houses administrative and office spaces, as well as an embassy and consulate in a lengthy 4-storey construction; on the other, the ambassador's residence is located at the back side of the wing of office spaces – a villa-like structure placed in a peaceful setting and surrounded by greenery as though it were a garden house."

245

Lecture hall

Konrad-Adenauer-Stiftung
Konrad Adenauer foundation
1995–98
Tiergarten, Klingelhöferstraße at the corner of Tiergartenstraße
Architect: Thomas van den Valentyn
Project management: Gernot Schulz, Anja Hupperich
Client: Konrad-Adenauer-Stiftung
As one of Berlin's noblest addresses for political activities, lectures, exhibitions, and receptions, instead of by a wealth of architectural nuances, the building's unique atmosphere is produced by a reduction of nuances – to simple minimalist forms, and to "simple" dignified materials such as the Roman travertine, etiolated maple wood, and red upholstery.

246

Aerial view

Botschaften der Nordischen Länder
The Nordic Embassies
1997–99
Tiergarten, Rauchstraße 1
Architects: Alfred Berger, Tiina Parkkinen
Contact architect: Justus Pysall

Respecting a 1995 competition decision, the five embassies of Denmark (Nielsen), Finland (VIIVA), Iceland (Kristmundsson and Palmar), Norway (Snoehetta), and Sweden (Wingardh) were joined together in an urban planning design similar to that for a gardening concept, and surrounded by a Turkish-green wall – the "Kupferband" (copper band). The "Faelleshues" – a congress hall and exhibition space in one – stands as the sixth pavilion near the entranceway and outside the security area.

247

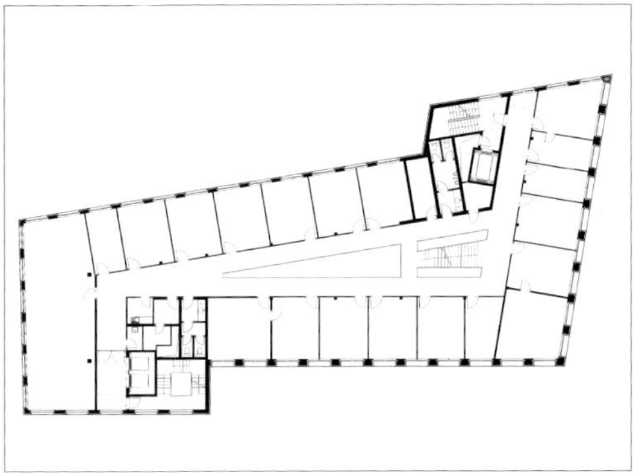

Plan of a standard floor

Wirtschaftsprüferhaus
Economic auditors' building
2000/01
Tiergarten, Rauchstraße 26
Architects: Heike Büttner, Claus Neumann, Georg Braun
Client: Groth Gruppe

Based on an excellent, urban planning concept by Hille Machleidt and Walther Stepp, the design's clear forms defend themselves against the prominent competition. In what seems more like a sienna-colored and nostalgic city square, the building's bright Portuguese lime sandstone makes it practically glow. Twice, the stipulated double-T is converted to a Z, and calms the smaller subdividing and beveling of the structural guidelines. The skylight lends the central corridor a quality that invites relaxation.

248

South-east view

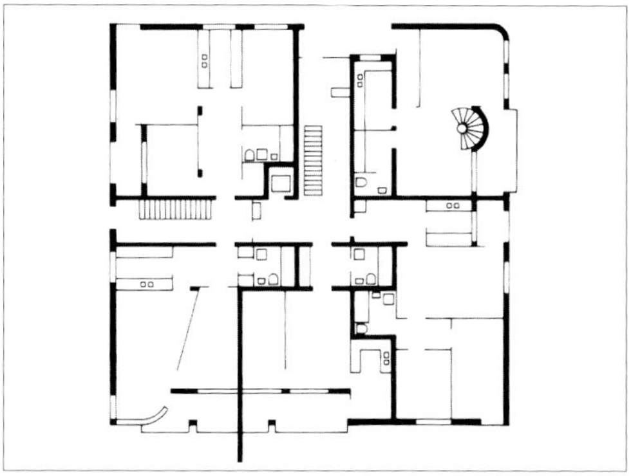

Plan of the ground floor

Apartment house
1985
Tiergarten, Rauchstraße
Architects: Klaus Theo Brenner, Benedict Tonon
Client: Groth + Graalfs

Developed after the first construction on Rauchstraße **(250)** was a diverse series of designs arranged around a common, green area and based on the "city villa" construction type, as with this contribution. While assuming a counter-position to Postmodern tendencies, despite the different structural interplay it still holds to a cubical building form. Additional examples are recognizable in works by Aldo Rossi, Henry Nielebock, Giorgio Grassi, Valentiny + Hermann, and Hans Hollein.

249

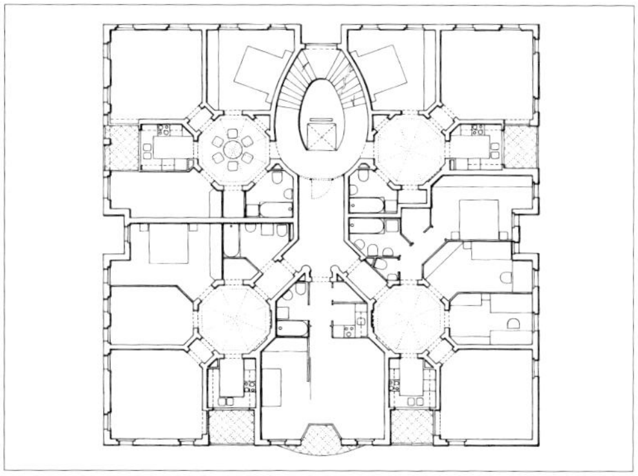

Plan of the 1st to the 3rd floors

Apartment house
1983/84
Tiergarten, Rauchstraße 6
Architect: Rob Krier
Contact architect: Klaus Kammann
Client: Groth + Graalfs / IBA (International Building Exhibiton)

Krier is especially important where he involves in developing the "city villa" building type. His quoting of historic and, most of all, Classical elements weakens the grip of functionalists, and creates a new way of seeing at the same time. By connecting two buildings with a wide arch, similar to his building on Ritterstraße **(151)**, he develops as his theme the entrance, passageway, and entranceway portal. Here Krier develops the connecting of the spatial ordering and axial alignment.

250

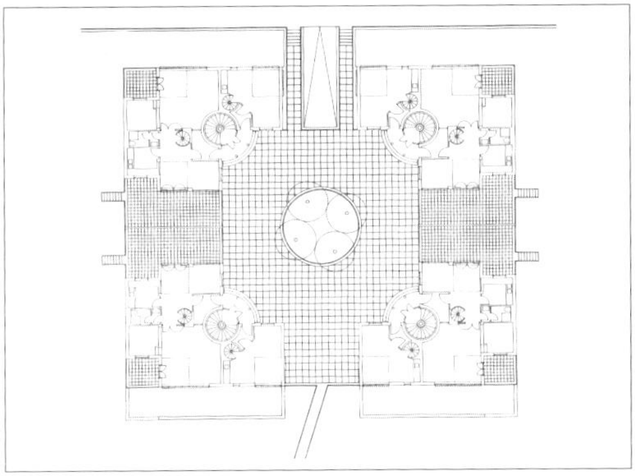

Plan of the ground floor

Vier Stadtvillen
Four city villas
1980/81
Tiergarten, Rauchstraße 19/20
Architects: Bangert, Jansen, Scholz, Schultes
Client: Neue Heimat Berlin

Following the "grand villa" building type once found in the former diplomatic quarter, the staggered, maisonnette apartments of this ensemble consisting of four, 4-storey city villas were meant to combine all the advantages of a house for several families with those of a house which accommodates single parties. The villas develop mutually on all four sides via an entranceway courtyard and external reference.

251

Southwest building

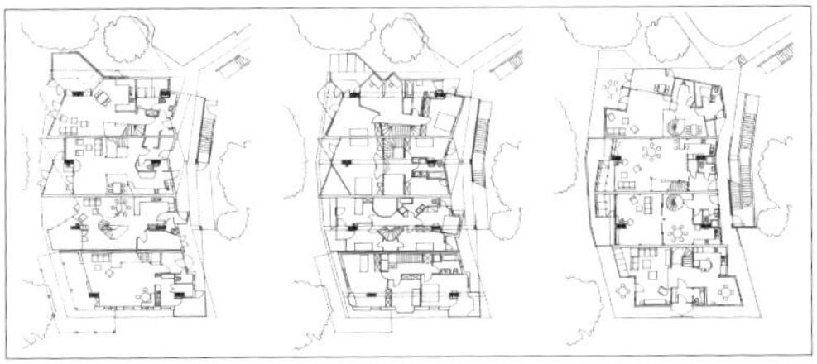

Plans of ground, 1st and 2nd floors

Öko-Haus
1986–89
Tiergarten, Rauchstraße 21, Corneliusstraße 11/12
Architects: Frei Otto, Hermann Kendel
Client: BOTAG / Eigentümergemeinschaft / Berliner Eigenheimbau

Erected in accordance with architectural-ecological design concepts, in 3 buildings 26 "private homes on different floors" were developed under scientific supervision. In many respects, the homes make use of alternative forms of group-dynamic processes, financing, and energy-saving measures. Their expanded functions culminate in a somewhat naive, romantically daring, but hardly unappealing overall appearance. For several years now, the undertaking is overseen by experts of the Freie Universität Berlin.

252

Expansions 1979, 2002

Berlin Hilton / Hotel Intercontinental
1957/58
Tiergarten, Budapester Straße 2
Architects: Pereira & Luckman
Contact architects: Paul Schwebes, Hans Schoszberger
Reconstruction and expansion: Jan Bassenge, Kay Puhan-Schulz, Johannes Heinrich, Walter Schreiber
Client: Hotelbaugesellschaft

The hotel forms the conclusion of a colonnade of stores which border the street and, below the guest rooms, ultimately develops to a foundation with entranceway, hall, and business rooms. Greatly altered by interventions and expansions, this area now includes a structurally significant, glass pyramid. What remained unchanged was the clever interplay of windows over 11 standard floors, concluded by an attic floor with garden. Since 2002, the recessed 8 storeys of an additional wing of guest rooms extend along the street as well.

253

Customer-service hall

Botschaft der Vereinigten Staaten von Mexico
Mexican Embassy
1999–2000
Tiergarten, Klingelhöferstraße 3
Architects: Teodore González de León, Francisco Serrano
Client: Republic of Mexico

With an aura not exactly Berlin-like or European, this building refers to a distant embassy. The slanted positioning of the façade's heavy, 18 m concrete slats with coarse marble aggregates in their powerful framework produces here the effect of a lightweight curtain parting at the building's entranceway, while protecting a rather fragile, glazed structure directly behind the slats.

254

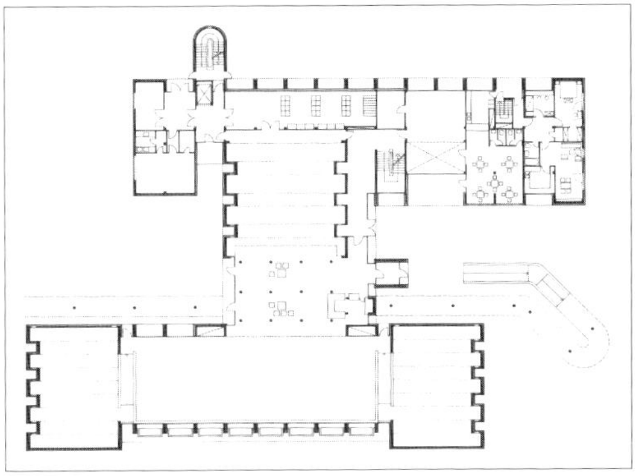

Plan of the ground floor

Bauhaus-Archiv
1976–78
Tiergarten, Klingelhöferstraße 13/14
Architects: Walter Gropius TAC (design), Alexander Cvijanovič (remodeling), Hans Bandel (implementation planning)
Client: Senator für Bau- und Wohnngswesen für Land Berlin

The design by Gropius, originally intended for a site located on an elevation in the Rosenhöhe district of Darmstadt, was reworked to function on the Landwehrkanal after the Bauhaus-Archiv was moved to Berlin. In the process, a rotation of the development plan created a long ramp. Included here are a variety of naturally-lit forms and, most of all, a series of rounded shed roofs. The overall design is equally determined by the exhibition spaces and the expansive, white concrete panels.

255

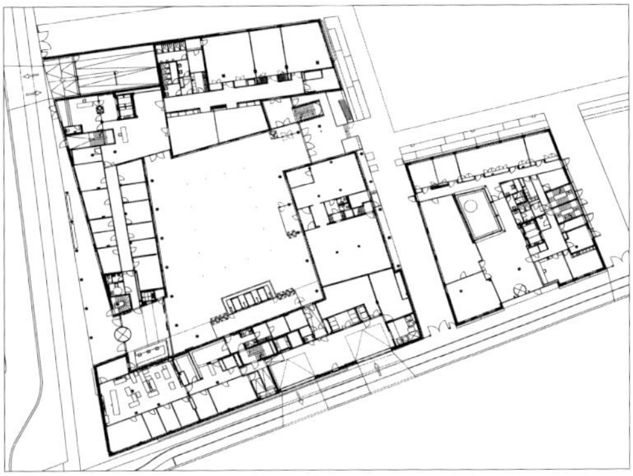

Plan of the ground floor

National office of KPMG International
2004/05
Tiergarten, Klingelhöferstraße / Von-der-Heydt-Straße
Architect: Nicholas Grimshaw
Contact architect and interior design: Claus Neumann

Located at the corner, the main building faces the party headquarters of the Christian Democratic Union (CDU) conceived by Petzinka Pink; and no differently than an additional building, the Konrad-Adenauer-Stiftung conceived by Claus Neumann and located at the site's northwest corner, these are just as much structural parts surrounding a centralized pocket park. The 7-storey main building and the subsidiary building are connected by a two-level underground garage, with the main building independently forming a large, roofed-over interior court and entrance. The four wings generously subdivided by different building materials and the rows of windows capable of being drawn together using sun-shielding slats strongly convey the feeling of a commanding architectural language.

256

Plan of an apartment floor

ADAC-Gauhaus
ADAC administrative-district building
1959/60
Wilmersdorf, Bundesalle 29–30
Architect: Willy Kreuer with Herbert Stranz
Client: ADAC

Built along a firewall and facing south in order to receive ample sunlight, the apartment and office building forms a corner situation, while its office floor protrudes far over the customer's lobby. One to 2-room apartments are located on 5 apartment floors. The building's masonry-hewn ballast rests on reinforced concrete supports, and its outer skin made of anodized aluminum plating is further enhanced by wooden windows. With such a lively construction form, the block's corner could even be closed if desired.

257

Former situation

Plan of a standard floor

Art'otel Andy Warhol
1999–2002
Wilmersdorf, Lietzenburger Straße at the corner of Pfalzburger Straße
Architect: Helge Sypereck
General artwork: Andy Warhol
Interior design: Beate Weller
Client: The Royalton Hotel

A corner solution also a joint, which reacts to the varying heights of neighboring buildings: what was originally an office building was transformed to the "Art'otel Andy Warhol", erected on an extremely small floor area (750 sqm) and offers 91 rooms, gastronomical services, conference rooms, and 10 parking spaces – while it also aids the street running parallel to the traffic-devastated Ku'damm thoroughfare.

258

South side

Domed glass-roofed patio

Apartment building
1982
Wilmersdorf, Fasanenplatz
Architect: Gottfried Böhm
Project manager: Hans Linder
Client: Klingbeil

The building closes the southern tip of a block where, on Fasanenstraße, traces of a planned expressway were recognizable for a long period of time. Rounded corner towers, French windows, and a glass-roofed connecting courtyard turn the building and adjoining city square into an unmistakable location. At a later date, the small units of business spaces located in the ground-floor area had to be converted into maisonnette apartments. Opposite the building, on Schaperstraße, is the former Freie Volksbühne, now Haus der Berliner Festspiele, designed by Fritz Bornemann.

259

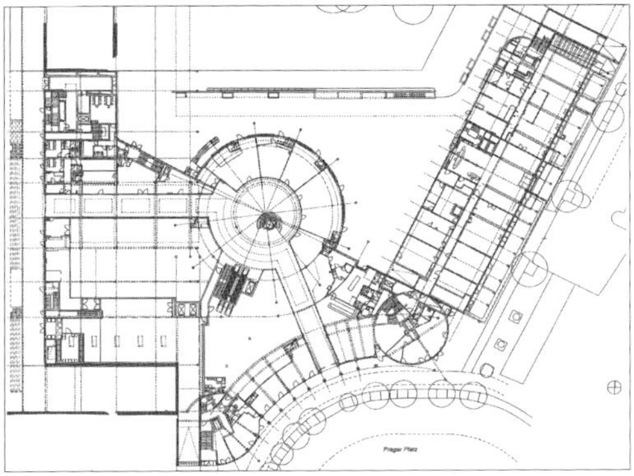

Plan of the ground floor

Prager-Platz-Ensemble
1996–2002
Urban planning concept 1987
Wilmersdorf, Prager Platz
Senior citizens residence architect: Karl Pächter
Hotel reconstruction and courtyard development: Jan Bassenge, Johannes Heinrich, Kay Puhan-Schulz
Client: VGH

Similar to his work completed at Fasanenplatz, here too, Gottfried Böhm added an accent to a showpiece upper-class city square by designing a solitary construction – in this case, an octagon in contrast with the square's swung northern wall: built over 2 arcade floors are 5 to 7 floors of dignified living spaces, behind a displayed and white-plaster sandstone skin. The senior citizens residence, rebuilt to the Ramada Plaza Hotel, features a large fitness area in the courtyard.

260

Church at Hohenzollerndamm
1931–33
Wilmersdorf, Hohenzollernplatz
Architect: Fritz Höger
Glass window from 1962 by Sigmund Hahn

The construction consists of a church, a congregation hall, and a residence for priests with four apartments. In 1933, in *Bauwelt* magazine, Fritz Höger, best known for his Chilehaus in Hamburg, refers to the church on Hohenzollerndamm as exemplary proof "that even in the case of modern constructions, geared purely to their functionality and application, one can produce a sacred effect on a spiritually high level and an enormous spatiality. My building was meant to address a Gothic spirit, no differently than all my constructions bear such an inner stamp." The nave of the church rests on a congregation hall of almost the same size.

261

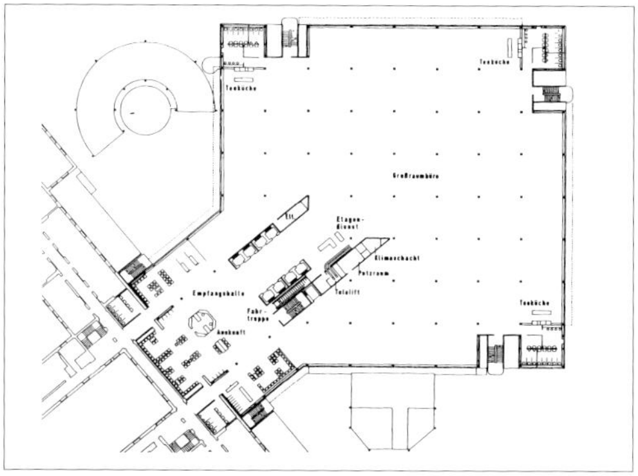

Plan of the 1st floor

Office building of the Bundesversicherungsanstalt für Angestellte (BfA)
1970–73
Wilmersdorf, Fehrbelliner Platz 5
Architects: Jan Rave, Rolf Rave with Hans J. Knöfel, Dieter Meisl
Light sculpture: Dieter Finke
Lighting system: Christian Bartenbach

The annex of the national pensions center for salaried employees features a ground-floor passageway with shops, a support-free 6th floor for the accounting center, and a 5th floor for heating and cooling facilities. Located between these floors, in a steel-framed column grid of 8 x 8 m units, are large office spaces, the prototype of a combination climate-control and light-giving ceiling, and the collected prefabricated, concrete components used with a profiling developed especially for this project. The building concludes the city square with respect to a concept developed in the 1930s by Otto Firle, while employing other design considerations here.

262

Glass-roofed inner courtyard with staircase

Apartment building
1929/30
Wilmersdorf, Hohenzollerndamm 35/36, Mansfelder Straße 29
Architect: Hans Scharoun

This building utilizes the collected experiences acquired while constructing the apartment building on the Kaiserdamm thoroughfare **(350)**: two-bed apartments, sleeping niches, and living rooms of different sizes. It consists of two structural wings, arranged parallel to one another, connected by circular staircases, and staggered by a half floor. Studio apartments are found in the attic floor, and garages are available in the courtyard's basement area.

263

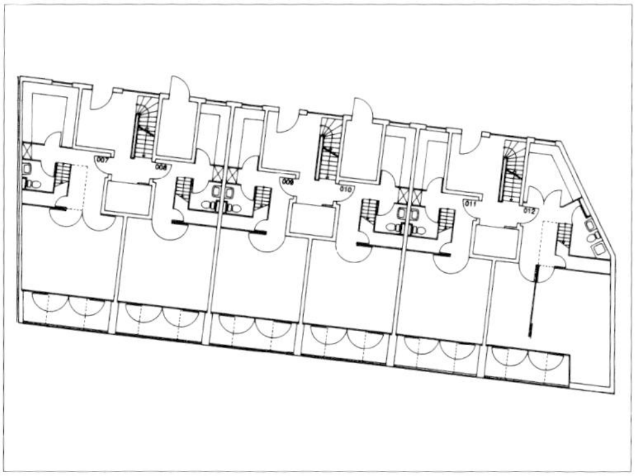

Plan of building's right half

Residential block
1992–94
Wilmersdorf, Seesener Straße 70 a–f
Architects: Hans Kollhoff, Helga Timmermann with Ingemar Vollenweider
Client: Onnasch

On the remains of a small plot, and built directly on the urban railroad's circle line behind a 5-storey roadside development from the 1930s, the building reacts to the exterior forces through the continuous, folded façade of its solarium; its shell of reddish-brown brick, and glassed-over atriums in the attic floor. But it also reacts to its unfavorable location through sophisticated detail work for its entranceways and staircases, similar to his apartments block built at that time near Amsterdam.

264

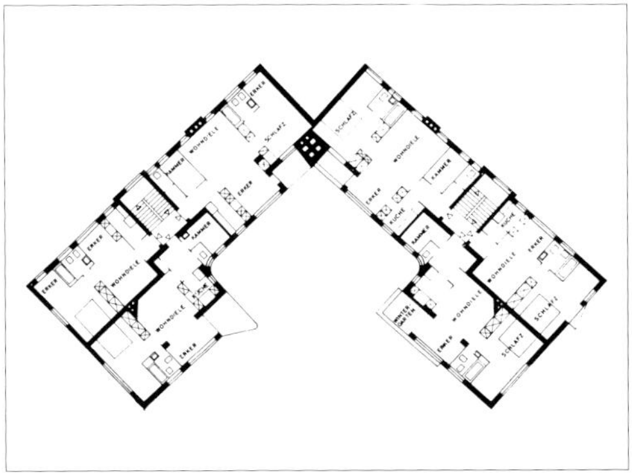

Plan of the 1st floor

Apartment block
1931
Schmargendorf, Flinsberger Platz 3
Architect: Hans Scharoun

The residential side facing southwest is developed by a street corner. This causes the angular building to stand back from the property's rear boundary line and form a peaceful garden courtyard. The apartment house has two staircases, 3-part detached structures housing 2 to $2^1/_2$-room apartments, and bedrooms with bathrooms installed behind living spaces. So-called oriels with flower windows form the connecting link between the interior and exterior.

265

Entrance

Kreuzkirche
1930
Schmargendorf, Hohenzollerndamm, Forkenbeckstraße
Architects: Ernst and Günther Paulus

The wide, closed tower with bridal hall in its groundfloor projects forward into the immediate area of the Hohenzollerndamm thoroughfare, with a long gangway connecting it to a recessed, eight-cornered church construction arrowed with a two-shelled dome. Chosen areas along the smooth wall surfaces are accentuated by decorative brickwork or – as in the entrance hall – by multicolored, glazed ceramic files. In 2004, during the building's interior restoration, the prevailing dark tones were exchanged with lighter tones. Opposite that church Paul G. R. Baumgarten created 1935/36 his first projekt of a large overall 200-m 4-storey apartment house, simple and clear.

266

Stairs on the courtyard side

Internationales Begegnungszentrum der Wissenschaften

Center for international academic meetings

1979–83

Wilmersdorf, Wiesbadener / Ahrweiler Straße

Architect: Otto Steidle with Siegwart Geiger, and Alexander Lux; competition project with Hans Kohl and Roland Sommerer

Energy concept: Vladimir Nicolic

Client: Senator für Bau- und Wohnungswesen

The result of a limited 1977 competition. A diagonally aligned staircase running through five apartment houses leads to an additional communication space, as well as to a rooftop greenhouse with garden surfaces. Heat pumps utilize the summer temperatures. Included here are bay windows with solarium. Both the building height and slanted roof integrate the construction into the so-called Rheinviertel by Paul Jatzow (1911–15), based on a freely interpreted version of English country houses.

267

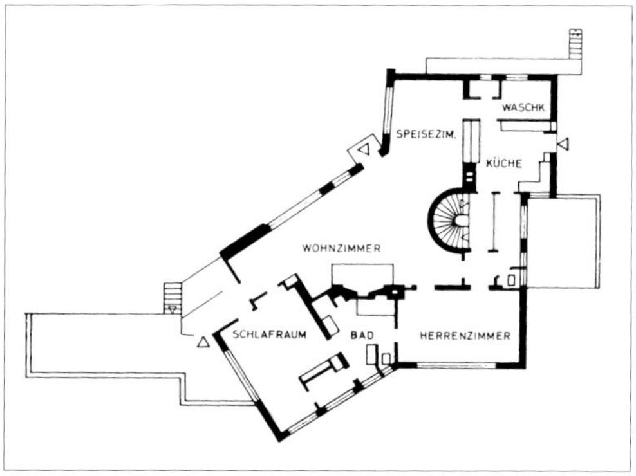

Plan of the entrance level

Haus Ziegler

1936

Steglitz, Lepsiusstraße 112

Architect: Hugo Häring

This involves two orthogonal systems rotated one against the other. The house develops upward from the exposed concrete foundation of the basement storey and southern enclosure of the "Fichteberg", a natural elevation with spruce trees. The walls are uniformly lined with the arranged, pairs of bricks also used by Häring as an economical material for building the "Prüßverband", and for other objects in the Wedding and Siemensstadt districts **(385)**. The slate roof reveals projected areas. A solarium was later built in front of the living room.

268

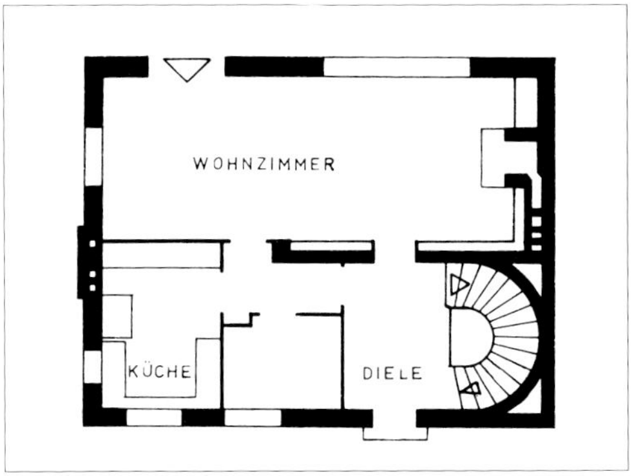

Plan of the main floor

The architect's private residence
1932
Steglitz, Schmidt-Ott-Straße 17
Architect: Erich Richter

The property's varying heights make it possible to accommodate two terraces. The apartment terrace stands 3 m higher than the terrace in front of the garden, where, on the same level, one finds the entrance, studio, kitchen with washing facilities, and heating system. Above these, on the main floor, are the master kitchen and the living areas, with bedrooms on the upper floors. The whitewashed, brick construction has contrasting window frames painted black. In the meantime a second house was added on the right side.

269

Entrance hall

Max-Planck-Institut für Bildungsforschung
1965–74
Schmargendorf, Lentzeallee 94
Architects: Hermann Fehling, Daniel Gogel

From the outset, the dark, strongly articulated cubes, with a white cylinder, the sky light for the central stairwell, towering over them, suggest that here the institute's requirement are being met by organizing space in a very special way. Small, cell-like work-spaces as well as lavish communication areas extend from this hall like fingers. The architects have developed their formal idiom further since the 1950s and so have produced a style that is entirely their own. An astrophysics institute using similar formal language was built in Garching near Munich in 1978.

270

Detail of staircase

Reichsknappschaftshaus
German miners' guild building
1929/30
Schmargendorf, Breitenbachplatz
Architects: Max Taut, Franz Hoffmann

In this 3-storey, steel-framed construction, the ceramic plating follows the structural lines of the building's framework. The masonry-filled parapets and walls are surfaced with clinker brick. The staircase and conference room were greatly altered following the war. Today the building serves as an institute building of the Freie Universität Berlin.

271

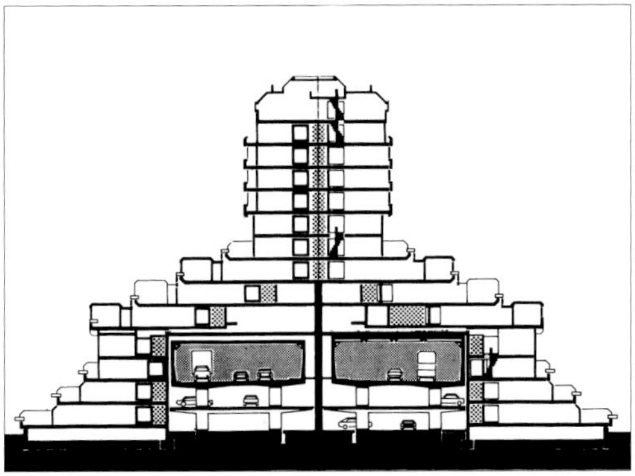

Cross section

Expressway superstructure
1971–82
Wilmersdorf, Schlangenbader Straße
Architect: Georg Heinrichs with Gerhard and Klaus Krebs
Project manager: Wolf Bertelsmann
Site management: Rolf Niedballa
Client: DEGEWO, Senator für Bau- und Wohnungswesen

This construction served as the prototype for testing the feasibility of a large-scale expressway superstructure intended to compensate for the scarcity of West Berlin building plots due to the amount of space devoted to accommodating traffic. After passing through a pair of hollow, box-like forms, whose acoustics and construction are indepent from the rest of the building, the urban expressway continues through an entire complex of over 2,000 apartments. Divided in seven construction areas, the 14-storey "apartment snake" consists of a hill-shaped terrace house with a centrally located building transom.

272

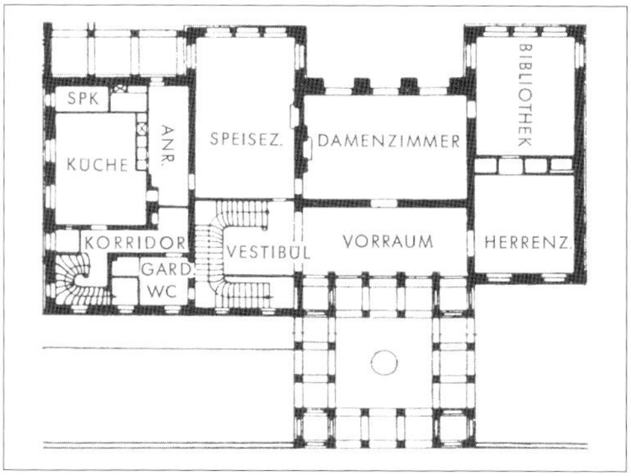

Plan of the ground floor

Haus Dr. Wiegand
1911/12
Dahlem, Peter-Lenné-Straße 28–30
Architect: Peter Behrens

This powerful, hewn stone construction made of limestone and its rows of contracted wooden windows follow a Neoclassical basic approach also visible in industrial constructions by Behrens. The house aligns with an axis – on which an entrance hall, vestibule, and salon stand arranged in a row along the street – continued in the garden through a wide terrace. The building currently houses the German archaeological institute.

273

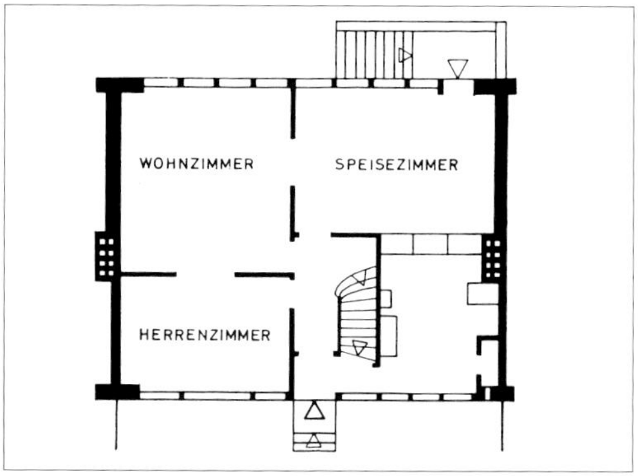

Partial plan of the ground floor

Row houses
1928
Dahlem, Schorlemerallee 12–12 c
Architects: Wassili Luckhardt, Hans Luckhardt, Alfons Anker

These 2-storey row houses are concrete-frame constructions. By contracting the opening of each house in the width of their window bands, and adding the perpendicular panes of glass blocks which project forward at the access front, on the street-facing side the series of houses becomes divided into single homes without denying its arrangement in a row.

274

Single-family houses
1927
Dahlem, Schorlemerallee 7–11, Spilstraße 9
Architects: Wassili Luckhardt, Hans Luckhardt, Alfons Anker

These four, single-family homes are steel-framed constructions with staggered floor levels. Facing north, they feature 3 storeys – with the kitchen at the bottom, dining space above it, and bedrooms in the top floor. The building part below the half-storey-tall living area facing the street has a cellar. On the same level as the living area is a spacious apartment terrace.

275

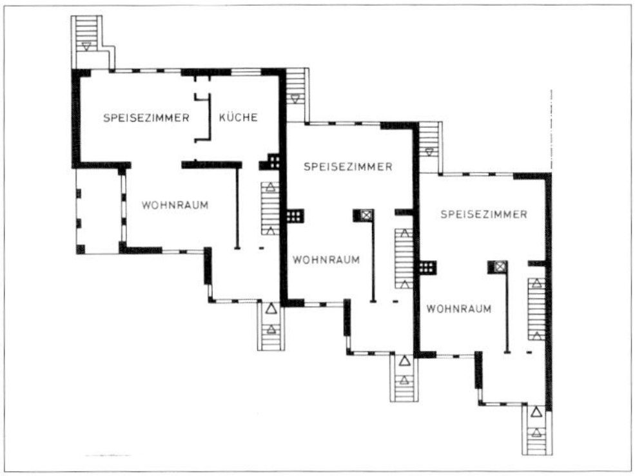

Plan of a row

Staggered houses
1925
Dahlem, Schorlemerallee 13–23
Architects: Wassili Luckhardt, Hans Luckhardt, Alfons Anker

Two rows of each of the six houses are staggered and shift their centers away from the street. To a certain extent, the rows' symmetry retrieves the effect of a interrupted view. The houses were severely damaged during the war. The architects' studio space stands at a recessed spot between both rows of houses.

276

Interior of the former movie theater

Titania-Palast
1927/28
Steglitz, Schloßstraße 5
Architects: Ernst Schöffler, Carlo Schloenbach, Carl Jacobi

After the war, this large-scale movie theater typical of the 1920s, with seating for altogether 2000 moviegoers, replaced the destroyed "Philharmonic" concert hall, whose orchestra moved into the building on May 26, 1945, with Leo Borchard as its conductor. Despite the concert hall's faulty acoustics, musical celebrities such as Wilhelm Furtwängler later conducted here. On December 4, 1948, the founders' conference of the Freie Universität Berlin was held here. While numerous details were lost to modifications and additions, the enduring splendor of the 1920s' lighting design is still discernible.

277

Galleria
1993/94
Steglitz, Schloßstraße 101
Architects: Klaus Quick, Michael Bäckmann, Susanne Quick
Client: Peter Fritz

Without separating itself from the urban planning context, as an attractive and welcoming "shop in shop" construction, the structure presents itself to the street with a convex, glass shell made of 5 commercial floors over its foundation, and the theme of the corner is developed here in a clearly conceived manner. Floor area of shopping spaces: 3,625 sqm; building costs: circa 10 million Euro. What the architecture can't afford, the doubled "ll" of Galleria certainly can!

278

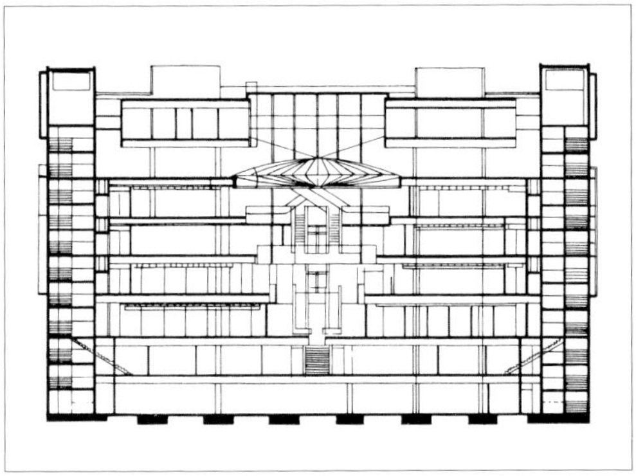

Cross section

Forum Steglitz
1967–70
Steglitz, Schloßstraße 1/2
Architect: Georg Heinrichs
Project manager: Wolf Bertelsmann
Site management: Walter Hötzel
Clients: Dr. Herbert Jovy, Gerhard Marcks

Designed according to the "shop in shop" principle, the shopping center develops the entire building block of a piece of property located in attractive surroundings. A multi-storey, intermediate hall with moving walkways and escalators provides the central access to 4 shopping levels. With its simple, unifying, yet highly sophisticated design details and choice of materials, the architecture of this seemingly timeless complex creates a pleasant atmosphere that stands in contrast to the bustling and "visually noisy" shopping center as we know it today. The building's interior and exterior are currently being renovated.

279

North view

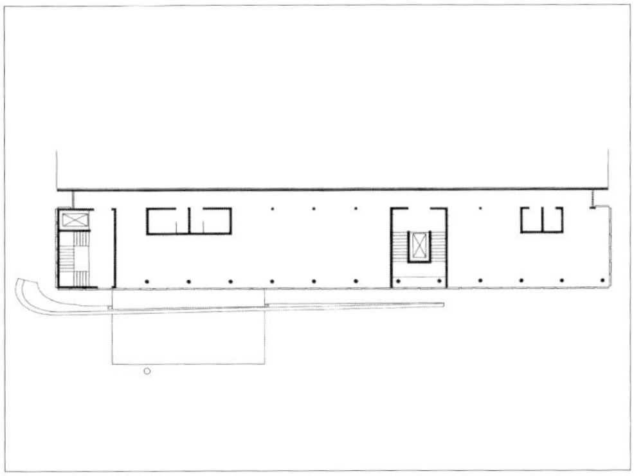

Plan of the 6th floor

Office and commercial building
1991/92
Steglitz, Schloßstraße 40
Architects: Frank Assmann, Peter Salomon, Hermann Scheidt
Client: HABERENT

The full length of this single-loaded building, planned in 1987, attaches to a large fireproof wall. Since the sectioning of its façade includes the existing dimensions of a Volkswagen dealer's pavilion and the Schwartz villa, a self-contained ensemble is created here. The incorporated remains of what was formerly a protective firewall transform to a concrete wall further developed as a counterpoint and visual sign.

280

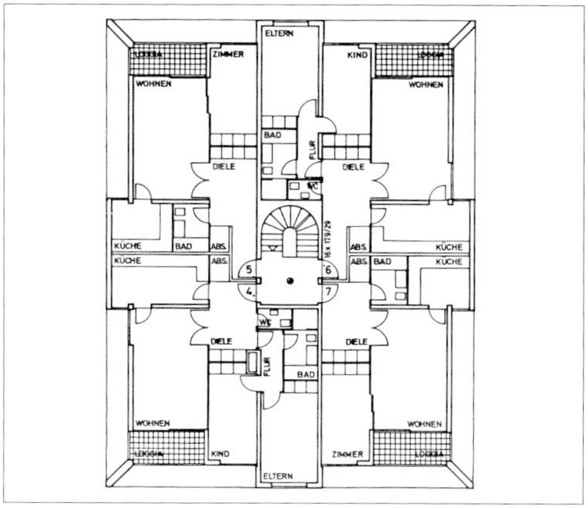

Plan of the attic-floor

Apartment house
1982/83
Grunewald, Hubertusallee 7
Architects: Fin Bartels, Christoph Schmidt-Ott

With its 12 apartments, large copper roof over a structural framework made of diagonal pillars, and massive attic floor above a low foundation, the house assumes the dimensions and dignity of an older villa in the Grunewald district. In doing so, it adapts to a trend of the times, which takes into account the morphology of the district on the one hand, while counting the number of allowed floors with an embarrassing precision on the other. Through urban-planning director Richard Röhrbein, and instating section no. 34 of the construction regulations, building codes were first given top priority, thus making it possible to create proportions similar to those of the existing structures in Grunewald.

281

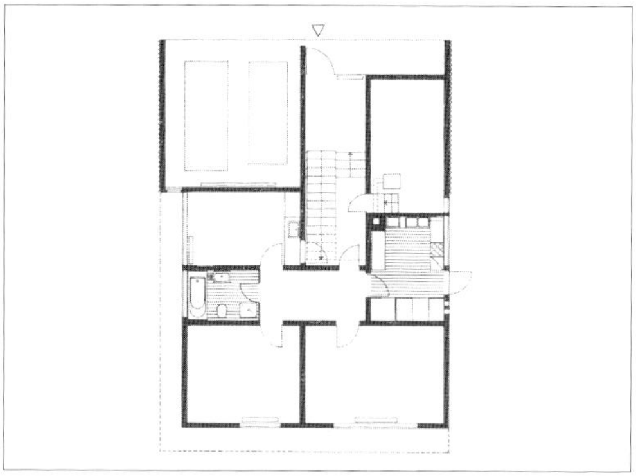

Plan of the ground floor

Eternit guesthouse
1955
Grunewald, Wißmannstraße 12 a
Architect: Paul G. R. Baumgarten

The building offers a guest apartment, caretaker's quarters, and two garages. The guesthouse is located directly on the street, farther up from an older apartment house, with two floors opening out towards Königssee. Its roof and wall coverings are made of a fiber cement commercially known as "Eternit'. The design of the building includes a steel staircase with ready-mixed concrete flooring and Eternit overlays.

282

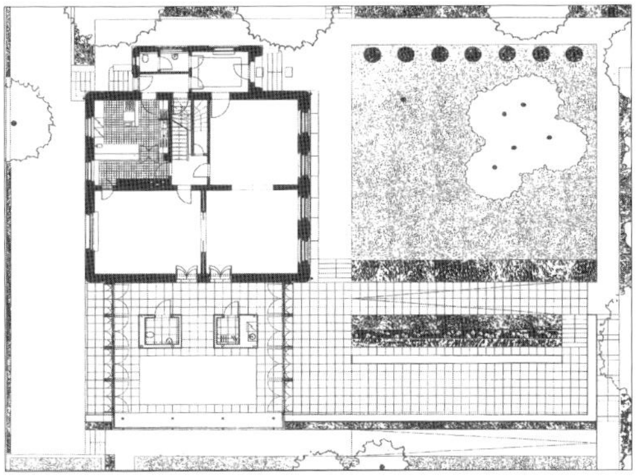

Plan of the ground floor

Residence of the ambassador of the Czech Republic
1998/99
Grunewald, Gustav-Freytag-Straße at the corner of Oberhardter Weg
Architects: Thomas Müller, Ivan Reimann
Client: Foreign ministry of the Czech Republic

The addition to the Grunewald villa resembles a solarium, and the long supporting wall under its front edge refers to Haus Riehl by Mies van der Rohe in Babelsberg – a reference which not only seems obligatory in the floor plan, but also plays a role in the carefully handled detail work of the steel and glass construction. With great care, the interior of the villa was adapted to the demands of an ambassador's residence.

283

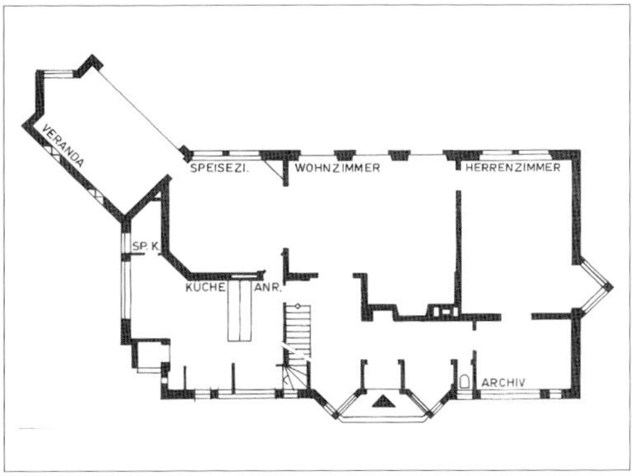

Plan of the ground floor

Haus Auerbach
1923–25
Dahlem, Clayallee 34–38
Architect: Bruno Paul

Bruno Paul, who for many people was best known for his illustrations in the magazine *Simplicissimus* alone, was also an architect who designed comfortable houses. Here he not only combines the classical villa-type house with elements of the country house facing a garden, but also an Expressionistic decor with a modern austerity and elegance. In this time the architect was not only designing the house, floor plan, section and the façade, just so he made the interior design, banisters, doors, the ceilings and furnitures as well. Paul did that many times for big passenger liners. In 1973 Georg Heinrichs acquired the house and renovated it completely. His rich collection of minimal-art objects created the atmosphere of a very special art cabinet throughout the house.

284

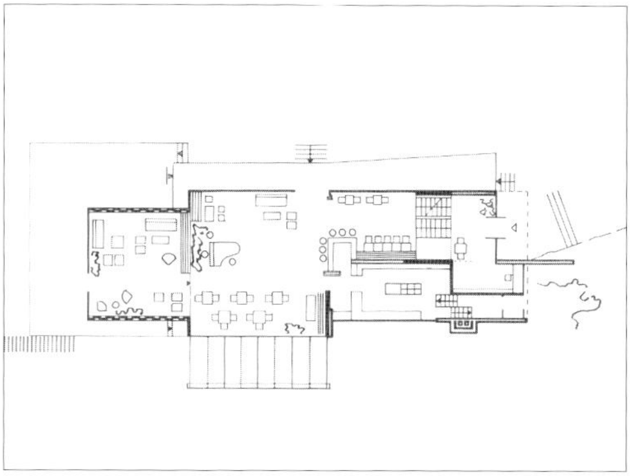

Clubhouse of the Lawn-Turnier-Tennis-Club Rot-Weiß
1958
Grunewald, Gottfried-von-Cramm-Straße 47–55
Architect: Paul G. R. Baumgarten
Client: Lawn-Turnier-Tennis-Club Rot-Weiß

The "Rot-Weiß" is Berlin's most renowned tennis club hands down, and a great many international matches are played on its courts. Yet the facility lies somewhat fenced in between the highway and the sloped property leading to the Hundekehlesee. Another spatial infringement on the small clubhouse is the newly constructed, hydraulic grandstand. The oblong structure conceals clubhouse spaces of different sizes arranged under three extremely lightweight interconnected roofs, with glass walls leading to its terraces. The basement storey accommodates a cloakroom and an apartment.

285

Guest cloakroom

Tennis-Club 1899 Blau-Weiß
1927
Grunewald, Waldmeisterstraße at the corner of Wildpfad
Architect: Paul Karchow
Client: Tennis-Club 1899 Blau-Weiß

By subdividing the building mass into two, identical, and 4-axial building parts, Karchow succeeded in producing the artful columns and landscaping decor which correspond with the flat and projecting roof of the garden plan's pavilion. This club dating from 1899, so rich in tradition, and considered one of Berlin's noblest addresses, is enhanced 2002 by a new building designed by Roosje Rave. The addition was required to respect the standards of a building ensemble already protected by preservation laws, as well as the hierarchy of the buildings. The new building's outer skin is a sanded wall made of Dutch, frost-resistant brick.

286

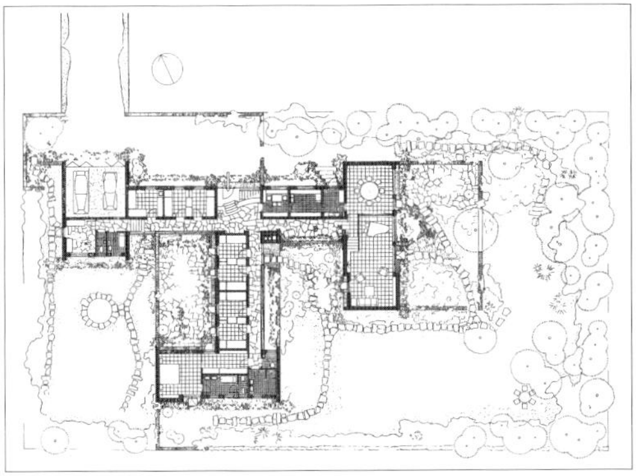

Haus Vollberg
1938/39
Grunewald, Delbrückstraße 29
Architect: Egon Eiermann

The 1-storey clinker brick construction has a flat, Eternit-surfaced, saddle-back roof. The entrance is located at the pivotal point of the wings for its living, sleeping, and socializing areas. The various open spaces created by the slenderness of the building's design become at times separated by walls of differ-ent heights for its various parts: the entranceway courtyard, playing area, regions arranged in front of the bedrooms, and the spacious apartment terrace.

287

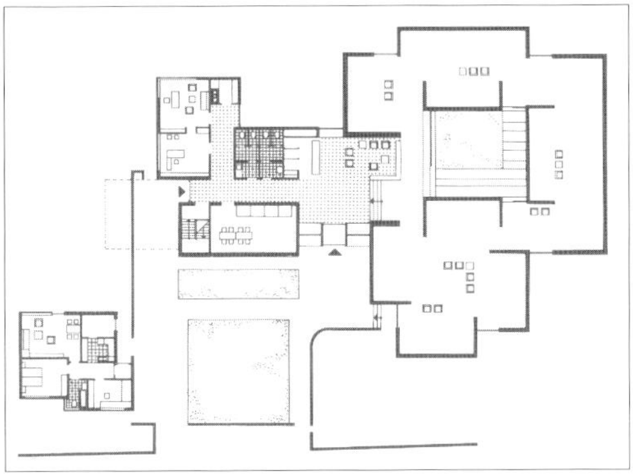

Brücke-Museum
1966/67
Dahlem, Bussardsteig 9
Architect: Werner Düttmann with Hans-Joachim Lorenz and Barbara Simon
Client: Senator für Bau- und Wohnungswesen

"The small-scaled museum founded in 1905, in Dresden, stands on the edge of Grunewald forest in the shade of pine and birch trees. Named 'Die Brücke', the museum dedicates itself to an art movement of the same name and consists of three 1-storey, white-washed, cubical building structures, which house exhibition spaces, a wing for the administration, and an archive, behind which are the caretaker's quarters. Striking about the museum is the pleasant and intimate arrangement of its spaces, and a lighting which accentuates the wall surfaces."

288

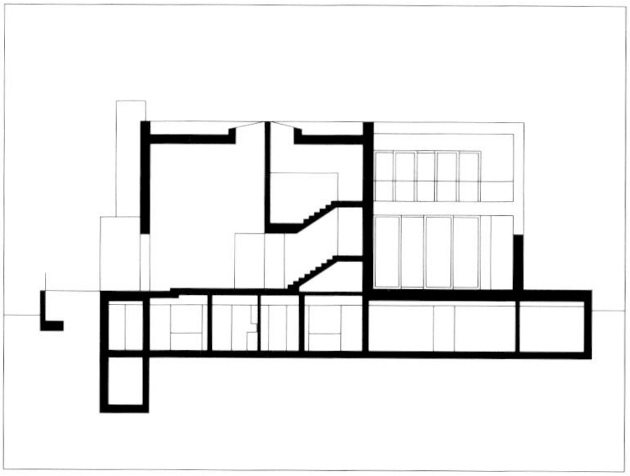

Section

Haus Dahlem
1997
Dahlem, Im Schwarzen Grund
Architect: David Chipperfield Architects

The Haus Dahlem is a declaration of the Modern. Connected by an homogenous brick skin, the differently dimensioned cubes of the respective spaces are interrupted by no more than expansive groups of windows, supporting walls, and enclosures for open spaces, while the house orients itself mainly towards its garden side and closes itself off from the gaze of onlookers.

289

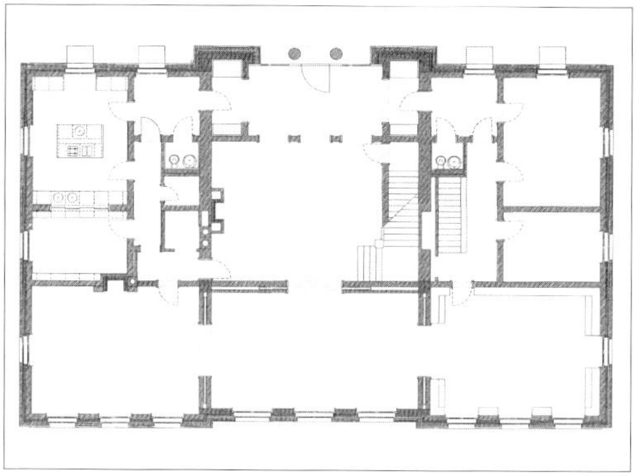

Plan of the the main level

Villa Gerl
2000
Dahlem, Im Schwarzen Grund 20
Architect: Hans Kollhoff
Client: Dr. Andreas Gerl

Following the destruction caused by war and Berlin's social impoverishment, "the villa", of which so many fine examples exist in Berlin, came to be considered a relic of bygone and better times. The Villa Gerl can be seen as exemplifying a new Classicism. It seems less like a country house and far more obliged to the structure-giving axes and symmetries of representative city villas. The 4 corner pavilions, intended for children, establish a direct relationship to Schinkel's small castle built in the Tegel district.

290

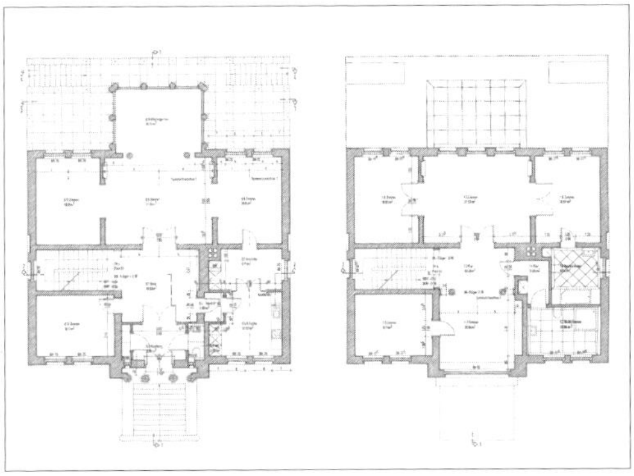

Plan of the main and the upper floors

Haus B.
1994
Dahlem, Max-Eyth-Straße 29
Architects: Paul Kahlfeldt, Petra Kahlfeldt

Is it our deep-rooted longing for antique beauty that makes this house so fascinating? Based precisely on such Classical models, and employing a high degree of design sophistication in the exterior and interior areas, the type of villa built here has an authentic Dahlem-district provenance, also suggested in the structure's plinth-like basement floor. Apart from its more conspicuous aspects, the house nevertheless harbors a grandly reserved and dignified quality.

291

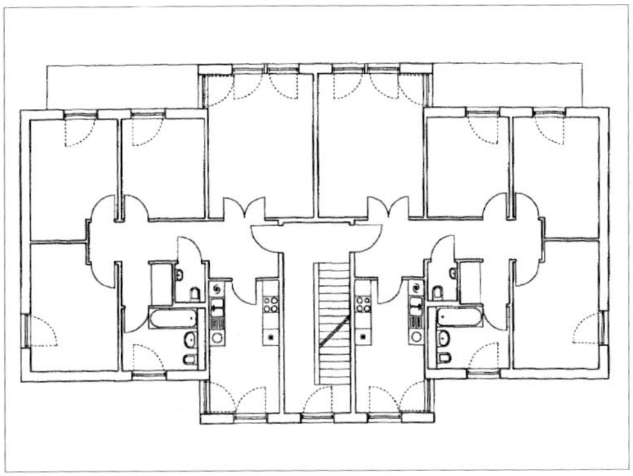

Plan of a standard floor

Town houses
2000
Zehlendorf, Hüttenweg, Am Petersberg 2–30
Architect: Klaus Theo Brenner
Client: Gehag

The withdrawal of the Allied Forces left behind many abandoned barracks and training installations on the outskirts of Berlin. Here, in place of American tanks, lined up in formation now are fifteen 4-storey housing units, alternating in pairs their construction type, and offering a total of 105 apartments with precast concrete components and wooden-framed windows constructed with dark, glazed spruce – in front of an underground garage. Like elsewhere, the single flight of stairs makes realigning the height of the staircase window unnecessary.

292

Former main entrance in the Arnimallee

Building housing the studies collection

Völkerkundemuseum
Ethnological museum
1914
Dahlem, Lansstraße, Fabeckstraße, Arnim-Allee
Architect: Bruno Paul
1964/65 structural expansion: Wils Ebert with Fritz Bornemann
Client of expansion: Stiftung Preußischer Kulturbesitz

The expansion of the ethnological museum was originally conceived as the second, museum complex after the "museum island" in East Berlin. But only a portion of it was completed at the boulevard Arnimallee, and used as a stockroom. Later, after the war and the dividing of Berlin, it served as a fine-arts gallery. The building structures added by Wils Ebert during the expansion imply the new entrance on the museum's north side. Exhibition design partly by Helge Sypereck.

293

Auditorium Maximum

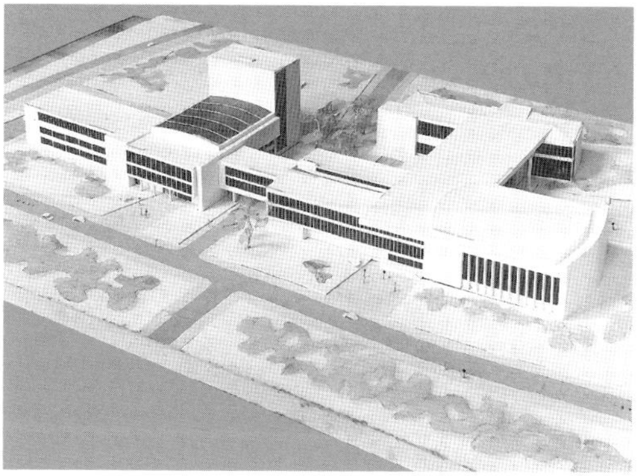

Model

Henry-Ford-Gebäude, Freie Universität Berlin
1952–54
Dahlem, Garystraße/Boltzmannstraße
Architects: Franz Heinrich Sobotka, Gustav Müller
Client: Senator für Volksbildung

As early as 1948, the increasing division of Berlin led to founding in the Western sector a so-called "Freie Universität" intended to satisfy every significant area of study. While single buildings and existing villas often housed the university's various departments, the building – with auditorium maximum, additional spaces for lecture halls, and a central library with an extensive, archive building for the Dahlem district – was meant to serve primarily as the center of the campus. Its strongly subdivided structure, powerful ledges, and natural crushed stone represent the standards of a second university which upholds a democratic outlook.

294

Institute of chemistry and biochemistry of the Freie Universität Berlin
1975–78
Dahlem, Takustraße 3
Architects: Kiemle, Kreidt + Partner with Garski, Dybe, Herrenkind
Project management: Bernhard Kühn, Reinhard Steinweg
Kinetic sculpture, court design: Henner Kuckuck
Client: Senator für Bau- und Wohnungswesen for Freie Universität Berlin

The building structure proposed by Candilis, Josic, and Woods **(296)** to satisfy the needs of a natural sciences institute (high degree of integration, low degree of constructional variability) while respecting the general plan's guidelines (minimum of height development, sensible networking principle) had to be modified. At that time, all the development areas of the new campus and university were agricultural plots or fruit plantations in the domain of Dahlem.

295

Department of physics of the Freie Universität Berlin
1976–81
Dahlem, Takustraße 3
Architect: Henning Larsen
Project management: D. Bretton-Meyer, C. Schaberg-Dollmann
Client: Senator für Bau- und Wohnungswesen for Freie Universität Berlin

"The first of three building phases originally planned for the physics department: on two to three storeys, the functional zones located between inner courtyards are arranged along an inner and outer, directional structure with a large-scale grid measuring some 36 to 72 m. According to Larsen's general plan, this uses the triangle of the Königin-Luise-, Altenstein-, and Takusstraße complex for the further development of the natural sciences institute."

296

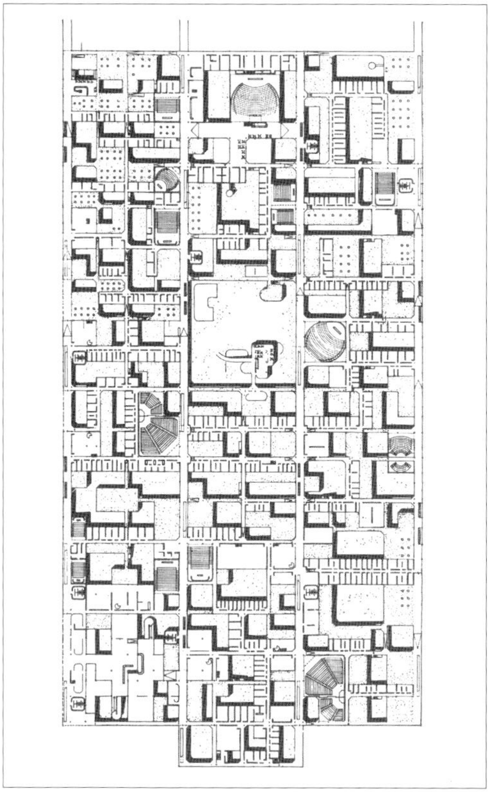

Site plan of the competition project

Campus buildings of the Freie Universität Berlin
1963–79
Dahlem, Thielallee, Fabeckstraße
Architects: Georges Candilis, Alexis Josic, Shadrach Woods with Manfred Schiedhelm
Client: Senator für Kunst und Wissenschaft
Implementation: Arge Friedrich Krupp, Universal-bau

A 1962 competition result: the conceptual framework of the plan's overall approach calls itself a "manière de penser" universally, a form of spatial organization, and a way to inspire growth and change. The basic principle of the montage system, stipulated by the competition, was to apply a technical language to a 7,20 m grid. During the general rehabilitation process, the wall elements originally made of Corten steel were replaced with bronzed plates.

297

Cafeteria of the Freie Universität Berlin
1952/1975
Dahlem, Van't-Hoff-Straße 6
Architects: Hermann Fehling, Daniel Gogel
Project manager: Thomas Tafel
Client: Senator für Bau- und Wohunungswesen for Freie Universität Berlin

In the case of this annex of the old cafeteria, designed by Hermann Fehling and Peter Pfankuch in 1952, the architects were given an exciting task: to expand – for a growing number of students – their own building, to confront it with a meanwhile further developed sense of architectural perception, and to create here a new unity.

298

Educational studies library of the Freie Universität Berlin
1981/82
Dahlem, Kiebitzweg
Architects: Manfred Schiedhelm, Justus Burtin
Client: Senator für Bau- und Wohunungswesen for Freie Universität Berlin

"This compact building with spacious interiors on all its floors is lit from above by a glass roof. On the ground floor and roof terraces, vines of tendril plants cover the outer walls made of masonry. All the roof surfaces are given greenery. For this project, solving energy-related and technological problems as well as integrating vegetation were the main concerns."

299

Philological library of the Freie Universität Berlin
2004/05
Dahlem, Thielplatz at the corner of Habelschwerdter Allee
Architects: Foster + Partners
Structural support planning: Pichler Ingenieure
In-house technical planning: Schmidt Reuter
Client: Senatsverwaltung für Stadtentwicklung

The department's new library, reached through the building known as the "Rostlaube" (rusted pergola) **(296)**, emerged from an elaborate development series focussed on optimizing the relationship of an outer skin to a functional surface: a consideration the catalyst for an astounding number of diverse building types since the year 1997. In conclusion, the chosen 2001 development concept involved imposing the basic form of a drop of water on a horizontal surface of 4 structural levels, whose greatly swung edges reach out for sunlight while filtering it at the same time.

Siedlung Onkel-Toms-Hütte 300

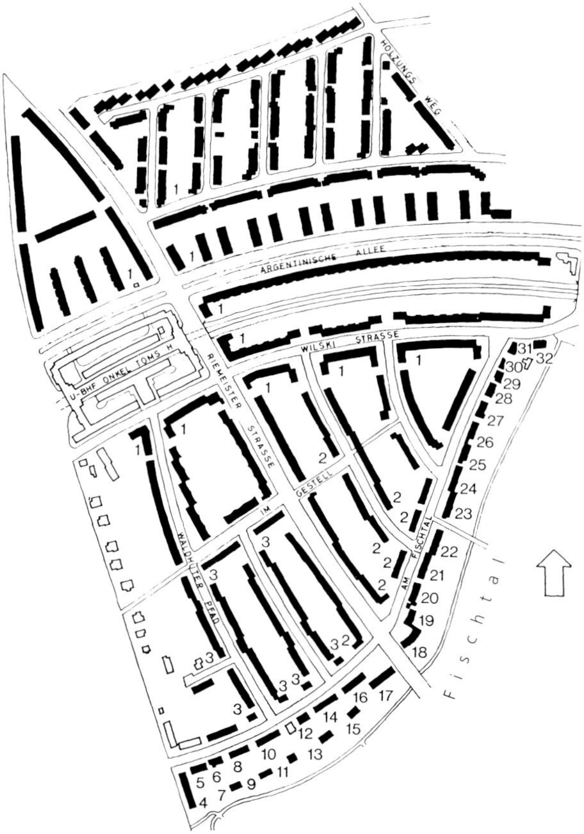

1 Bruno Taut (300)
2 Hugo Häring (301)
3 Otto Rudolf Salvisberg (301)
4/5/6 Alexander Klein (302)
7/10 Hans Gerlach
9/18/19 Mebes, Emmerich
11/12 Hans Poelzig
15/29 Paul Schmitthenner (304)
16/17/30/31 Heinrich Tessenow (303)
21 Ernst Grabbe
22 Gustav Wolf
23 Fritz Keller
24 Fritz Schopohl
25 Wilhelm Jost
26 Emil Rüster
27 Karl Weishaupt
28 Georg Steinmetz
32 Arnold Knoblauch

Houses on Waldhüterpfad

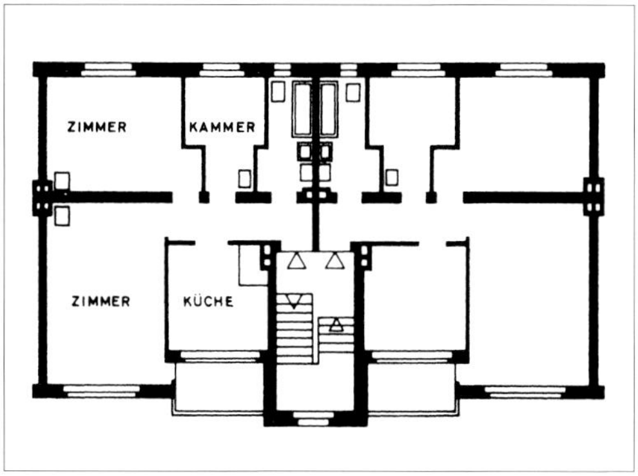

Plan of a standard floor

Großsiedlung Onkel-Toms-Hütte
1926–31
Zehlendorf, Argentinische Allee
Architect: Bruno Taut
Client: Gehag

The notion of a modern, flat-roofed, and large-scaled housing colony asserts itself in the villa-laden suburb of Zehlendorf as well – here under the name of "Waldsiedlung" (forest colony). At the U-Bahn subway stop Onkel-Toms-Hütte, a series of two to 3-storey buildings and apartment houses are developed here as long, 4-storey building rows incorporating the arcs of the train and street. Otto R. Salvisberg restructured the U-Bahn station stop to a highly attractive, commercial center with two streets accommodating stores. Additional stores appear at the end of the individual rows. Strong colors are used here. The attic storeys are recessed for the most part. In the case of houses still the private property of building associations, over recent years their vivid colors in particular have been carefully restored during the needed repair work.

301

Building part by Häring

Building part by Häring

Großsiedlung Onkel-Toms-Hütte
1926–31
Zehlendorf, Eisvogelweg, Riemeisterstraße, Am Fischtal, Reiherbeize, Waldhüterpfad, Im Gestell
Architects: Hugo Häring, Otto Rudolf Salvisberg

In the southeast sector of the housing colony, the building parts by Häring and Salvisberg are developed from the same floor plan for a row-house type. The staggering and blending of the rows form street spaces with lawns at the entrances, while the side of the house facing the garden is parceled out and only connected by way of a narrow footpath. After the majority of these houses were sold in the 1970s, they underwent many small changes.

302

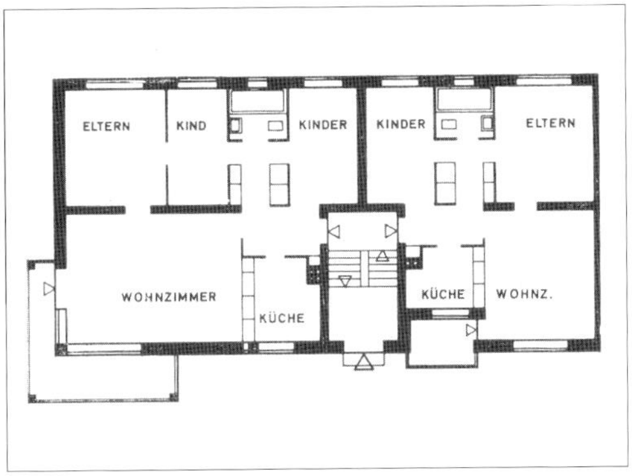

Siedlung Fischtalgrund
1929
Zehlendorf, Onkel-Tom-Straße 63–67
Architect: Alexander Klein
Client: Gagfah

The goal of this housing colony experiment was to develop a variety of house types for middle-class inhabitants near the low-building constructions of the "Onkel-Toms-Hütte" housing colony. Under the leadership of Heinrich Tessenow, 17 participating architects contributed one, two, or three houses. Facing the houses by Klein, on Onkel-Tom-Straße, Gropius erected an exhibition pavilion as a wooden construction, which no longer exists.

303

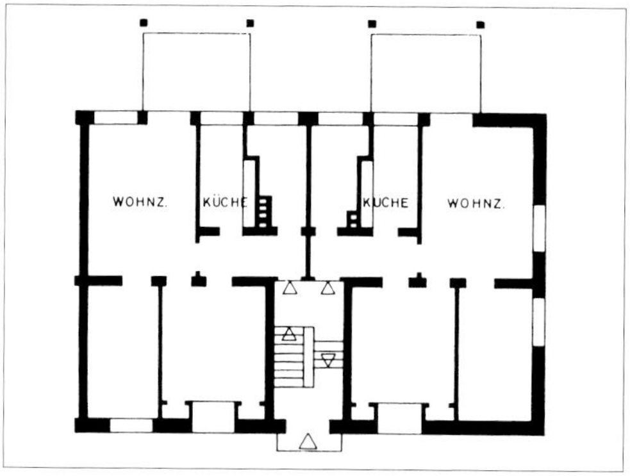

Partial plan of the ground floor with 3-room apartment

Siedlung Fischtalgrund
1929
Zehlendorf, Am Fischtal 58–60
Architect: Heinrich Tessenow
Client: Gagfah

On each staircase are four 3-room apartments. The dimensions of their hallways, bathrooms, and kitchens are greatly minimized in order to fit the living room and bedrooms for the parents and children into a very tight floor area. On the building's south side, each ground-floor apartment has a terrace in front of it. The building on Riemeisterstraße features four bachelor's apartments with a combination living-and-sleeping area. The so-called "fish-valley", a groove ot the glacial period, is designed in 1930 as a park by Leberecht Migge.

304

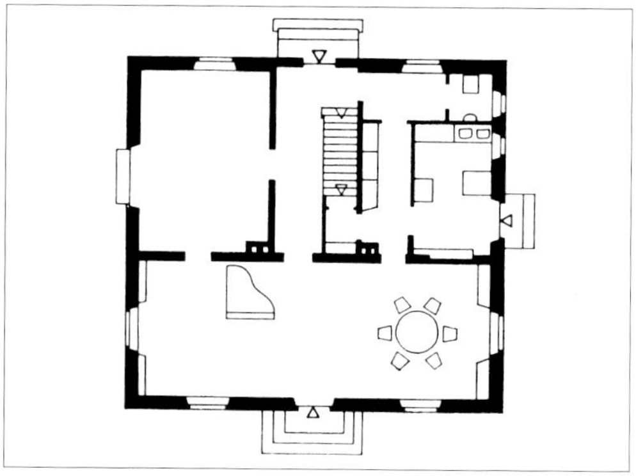

Plan of the ground floor

Siedlung Fischtalgrund
1929
Zehlendorf, Am Fischtal 4
Architect: Paul Schmitthenner
Client: Gagfah

Intended as a contribution to the detached single-family house concept and built especially for middle-class inhabitants, this design quickly developed to a dollhouse. In 1928, in *Bauwelt* magazine, Schmitthenner commented: "When designing a small house, what seems important to me is creating a great lightness of space through the sensible wasting of space. The 2,50-m wide staircase is meant to verify this idea. The decisive factor, however, is the spacious living room, which connects the house to the garden."

305

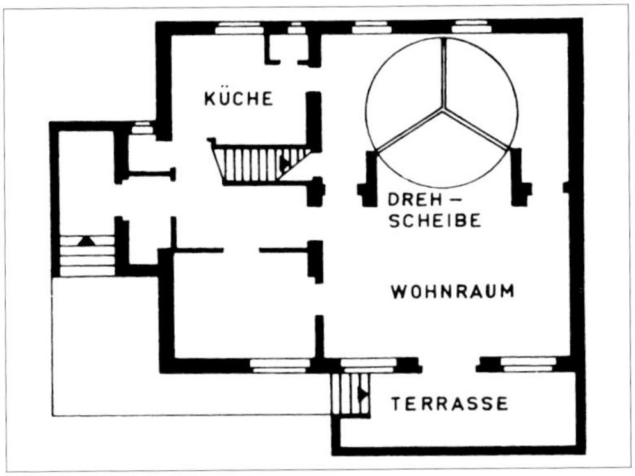

Plan of the ground floor with revolving stage

Four one-family houses
1923
Zehlendorf, Onkel-Tom-Straße 85–91
Architects: Richard Neutra, Erich Mendelsohn

These are 2-storey constructions with flat roofs. In two of the houses, the living room has a revolving stage, the attempt here being to give the space a greater variability by having it turn, when desired, towards the decked dining-room table, piano, or sitting area – a feature that was meant to increase the space while also saving on building costs

306

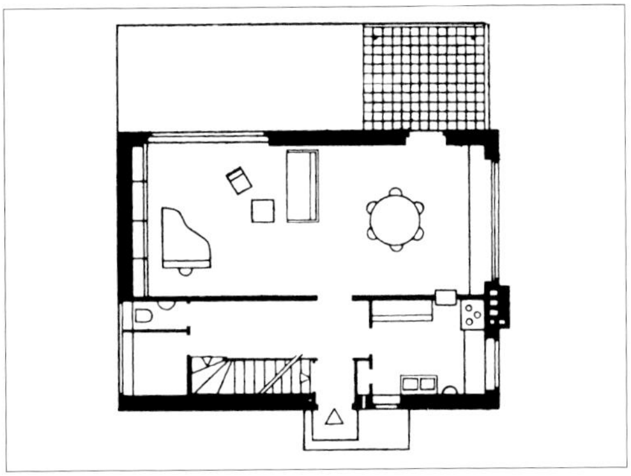

Plan of the ground floor

Haus Dr. Blumenthal
1932
Zehlendorf, Wilskistraße 66
Architect: Ludwig Hilberseimer

All the living and sleeping areas open towards the garden, while the street-facing side of the building remains sealed. From here the pitched roof is slightly lowered. In contrast to the rigid cube, the projecting balcony seems graceful and light. A subsequent addition accommodated a garage. Minimizing a one-family house without the use of emotionalism or any representative detailing permits the question: Is this a house or a residential cube?

307

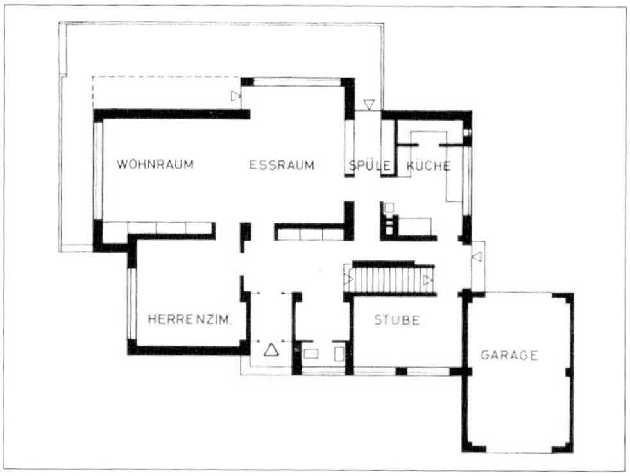

Plan of the ground floor

Haus Lewin
1928
Zehlendorf, Fischerhüttenstraße 106
Architect: Walter Gropius

The uniformed grid in the steel-framed windows and limiting all the wall components to the color white hold together a building structure that develops directly from the style of living expressed by the house. The north-facing side of the house with the entranceway is practically void of windows. The living room and bedroom open to the south. Later, a second garage was built here, but unfortunately the same color as the house.

308

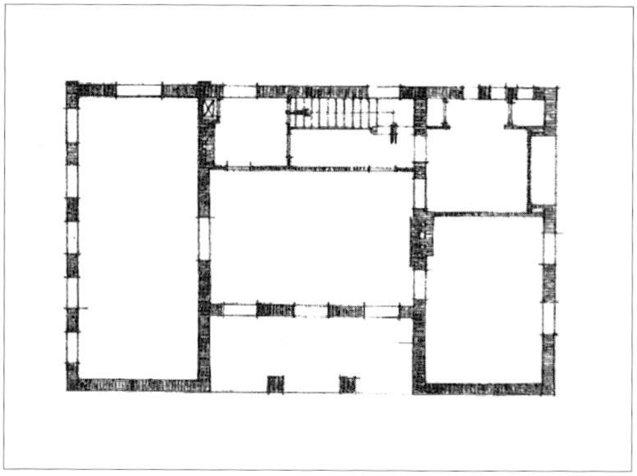

Plan of the ground floor

Haus Perls
1911
Addition, 1928/29
Zehlendorf, Hermannstraße 14
Architect: Ludwig Mies van der Rohe
Client: Perls family

After Haus Riehl in Babelsberg, two years later, came the second house to be designed with a classical clarity by the architect working at that time under Peter Behrens. This was clearly a modern addition, created for one of the new tenant's Oriental-art collection. The building's 1980 renovation effected only the façade and not the artfully constructed window sills or the wall paintings such as the figure study by Max Pechstein. Worth visiting is the garden of the neighboring villa behind the house – also a "Mies" design.

309

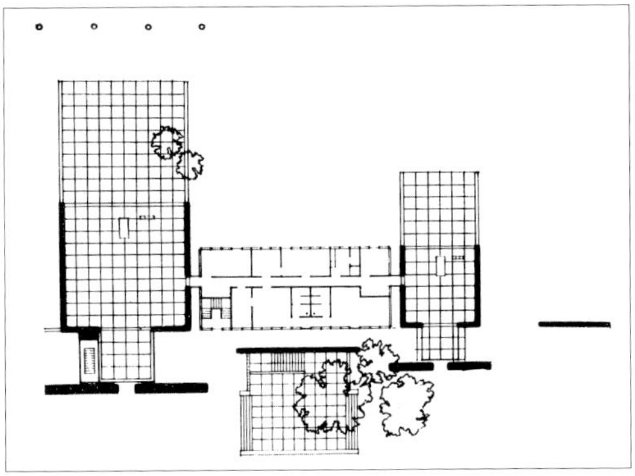

Memorial hall of Waldfriedhof Zehlendorf
1956/57
Nikolassee, Potsdamer Chaussee
Architects: Sergius Ruegenberg, Wolf von Möllendorf

A larger and a smaller hall for conducting memorial services form two construction cubes of different sizes. These are connected by a wing of administrative spaces. A pair of high, free-standing walls lined with travertine slabs stand in front of the metal doors of each hall. Because of the narrow, slit-like space between the walls, they form a gate to the burial grounds. The masonry-filled concrete skeleton construction is painted white.

Just now is decided that the student campus across on the Potsdamer Chaussee, a brilliant complex, typical for the late 1950's and built with modest means by the architects Hermann Fehling, Daniel Gogel, Peter Pfankuch together with the landscape gardener Hermann Mattern will be protected as a national monument.

310

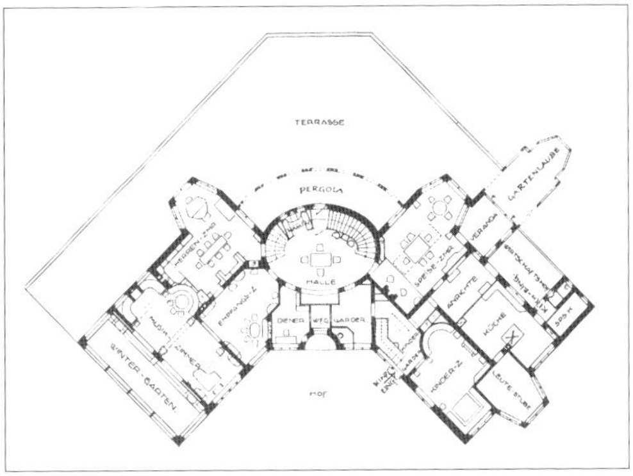

Plan of the ground floor

Haus Freudenberg
1907/08
Nikolassee, Potsdamer Chaussee 48
Architect: Hermann Muthesius

Muthesius built a dozen or more private houses in southwest Berlin. This house is strongly influenced by English country houses, not unlike the one circa 200 m west of it: the rooms are arranged on a common level in close proximity to the house-neighboring garden area, and they develop directly into nature – as shown here along the south side of the so-called "Rehwiese". In these structural examples, notions of representation and symmetry play a lesser role, emphasized even more in the house that the architect built for himself, which also connects with his office.

311

Stairway to the terrace

Strandbad Wannsee
Wannsee beach resort
1930
Nikolassee, Wannseebadweg
Architects: Martin Wagner, Richard Ermisch

Arranged along an artificial beach, the resort's 2-storey halls housing the changing rooms and showers nestle against the facilities as well as a neighboring pine forest. The halls' roof terraces offer 430 sqm of surface space. All the floors, stairs, and parapet walls are uniformly lined with yellow brick. A planned, axial expansion of the beach restaurant meant to connect it to a main restaurant and additional halls were never carried out. The bridge leading from the Nikolassee S-Bahn station stop across the highway was built especially for reaching this beach resort – and with it the general public reached a new love of nudism.

312

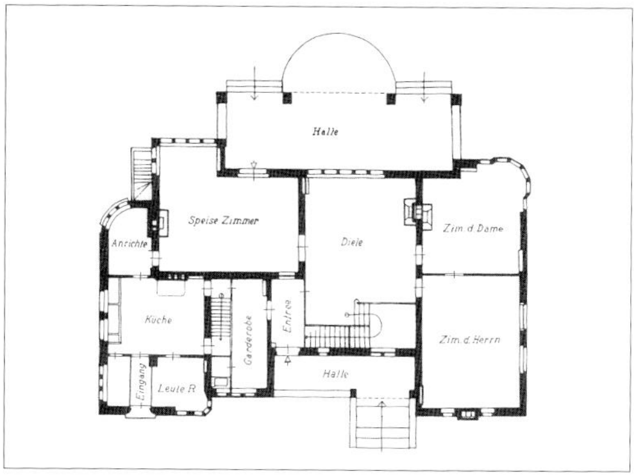

Plan of the ground floor

Haus Springer
1901–03
Wannsee, Am Großen Wannsee 39
Architect:: Alfred Messel
Client: Ferdinand Springer

This building, one of the few preserved villas of the "Colonie Alsen", is part of the stretch of property to emerge along the Havelkanal with the building of the Potsdam–Berlin railway line. In unison, World War II, Nazi-instigated expulsions, and colony politics blindly applied after the war led to the destruction of this El Dorado. The villa follows the concept of the English country house. Owing to its chiseled stone, gables surfaced with wooden shingles, roofed-over garden terrace, and bay windows, it literally assumes a fairytale-like quality. Of course the small English garden fell prey to the building of a parking lot at this spot. For the most part well-preserved, the interior spaces are presently inhabited by three different parties. Somewhat behind this villa, designed by the same architect, lies the Villa Oppenheim.

313

Garden side

Entrance side

Haus Liebermann
1909/10
Wannsee, Am Großen Wannsee 42
Architect: Paul Baumgarten
Client: Max Liebermann

As a successful painter and teacher, also the president of the Preußische Akademie der Künste, alongside his city residence **(001)**, Liebermann also had a country residence built in accordance with his own wishes. This was intended to directly correspond with the multipurpose garden with flower beds at its front, and the natural garden at its rear. A helpful, overall influence here was the historian Alfred Lichtwark: the pleasantly proportioned rooms never resort to any representative measures in their design, and both garden sides are neatly integrated by the window axes. The artist captured this in numerous paintings. After the owner took flight and left the country, and following his death, his residence was given to the city of Berlin. Since 2005, the house devotes itself to presenting Liebermann's work and is open to the general public.

314

Plan of the 3 levels

Apartment houses
2002/03
Wannsee, Am Großen Wannsee, Kaiserstraße
Architects: Susanne Quick, Michael Bäckmann, Klaus Quick, Henner Rolvien
Landscape architect: Hannelore Kossel
Client: Petruswerke

After founding the "Colonie Alsen" with a house occupied by the von der Heydt family, in 1960 came the option to use a "clinic in the Wannsee district", which from 1997 onwards led to new ideas for the park-like property: 26 houses, as duplex houses or lined up in rows, built in ecology-friendly settings along the edges of lush greenery, trees, and open areas, with the middle part of the 3 levels closed and oriented towards the waters of the Havel – and so, in stages, the small cubes with large, glazed sections and peat-brown colored brick soon developed into a well-balanced unity.

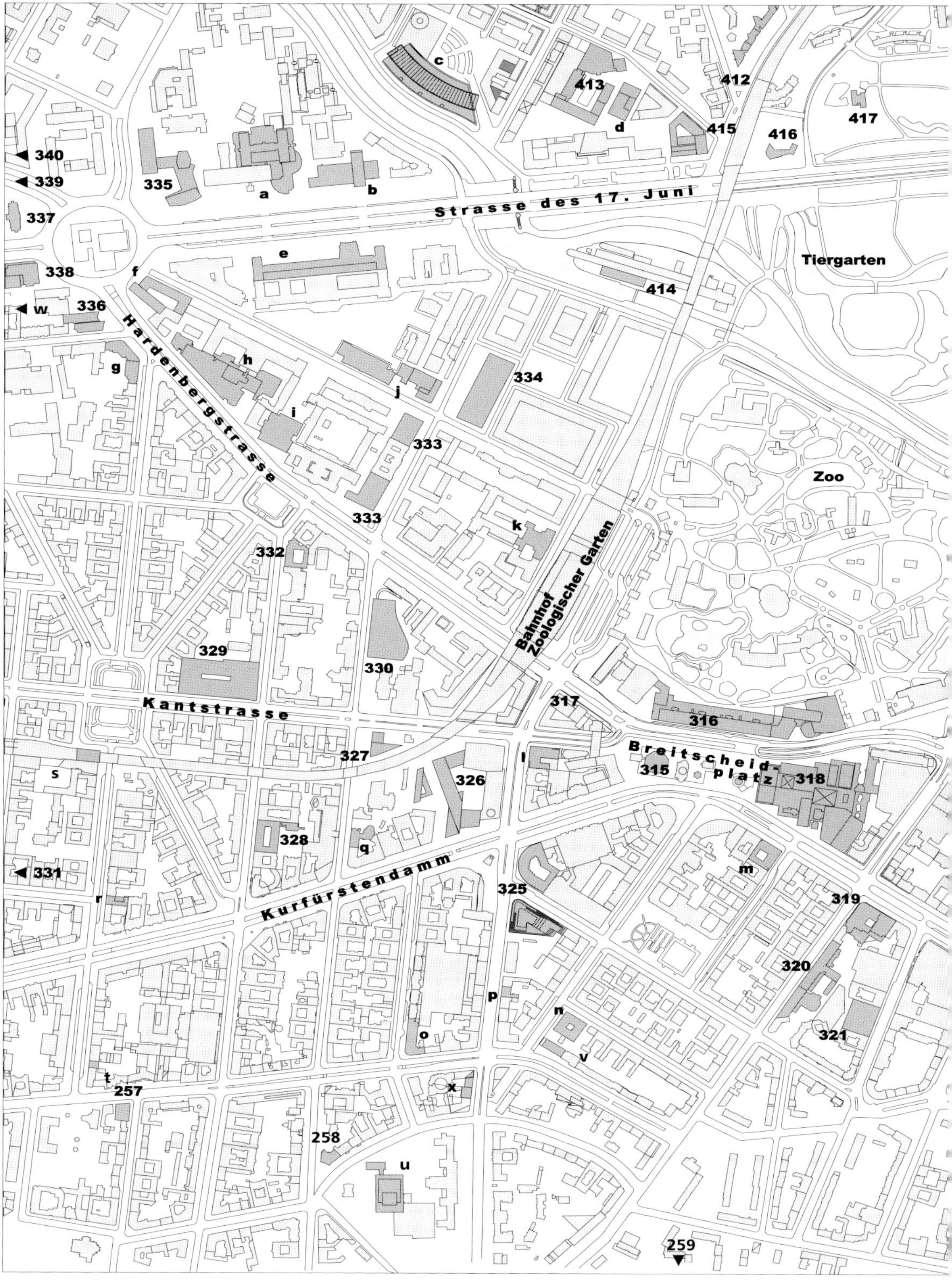

Strasse des 17. Juni
Tiergarten
Zoo
Hardenbergstrasse
Kantstrasse
Bahnhof Zoologischer Garten
Breitscheidplatz
Kurfürstendamm
340
339
337
338
336
335
a
b
c
d
e
f
g
h
i
j
k
l
m
n
o
p
q
r
s
t
u
v
w
x
z
412
413
414
415
416
417
334
333
333
332
329
330
317
316
327
326
315
318
328
331
325
319
320
321
257
258
259

Breitscheidplatz W

No.	Building	Architect
257	Art'otel Andy Warhol	Helge Sypereck
315	Kaiser-Wilhelm-Gedächtniskirche	Egon Eiermann
316	Zentrum am Zoo	Paul Schwebes, Hans Schoszberger
317	Zoofenster	Christoph Mäckler, Inter-Art Études
318	Europa-Center	Helmut Hentrich, Hubert Petschnigg
319	Peek & Cloppenburg	Gottfried Böhm, Peter Böhm
320	Femina-Palast	Hans Bielenberg, Josef Moser
324	Haus der Werbung	Rolf Gutbrod, Horst Schwaderer, Hermann Kiess
325	Concorde Hotel	Jan Kleihues
326	Kranzler Eck	Murphy/Jahn Architects
327	Office high-rise Kantdreieck	Josef Paul Kleihues
328	Kempinski Plaza	Jan Rave, Rolf Rave
329	stilwerk	Novotny Mähner Assoziierte
330	Ludwig-Erhard-Haus	Nicholas Grimshaw & Partners
331	Apartment house	Alfred Geßner
332	Haus Steinplatz	August Endell
333	Concert hall of the Hochschule für Musik	Paul G. R. Baumgarten
334	Volkswagen Universitätsbibliothek	Walter A. Noebel
335	Architecture department of TU Berlin	Bernhard Hermkes
336	IBM office building	Rolf Gutbrod, Bernhard Binder
337	Telefunken skyscraper	Paul Schwebes, Hans Schoszberger
338	Ruhrkohle-Haus	Paul G. R. Baumgarten
339	Deutsche Oper Berlin	Fritz Bornemann
340	Opernviertel	Hans C. Müller, Georg Heinrichs
412	Residential development	Hans C. Müller, Moritz Müller
413	Königliche Porzellan-Manufaktur Berlin	von Gerkan, Marg und Partner
414	Canal-circulation facility of TU Berlin	Ludwig Leo
415	Dorint Novotel	Laurids Ortner, Manfred Ortner
416	Berlin-Pavillon	Hermann Fehling, Daniel Gogel, Peter Pfankuch
417	Interbau, object 2	Klaus Müller-Rehm, Gerhard Siegmann

	Building	Architect
a	Institut für Mathematik, TU Berlin	Barna von Sartory, Georg Kohlmaier, 1976–80
b	Institut für Technische Chemie, TU Berlin	Willy Kreuer, 1965–68
c	Mercedes Autowelt	Lamm, Weber, Donath & Partner, 1998–2000
d	Bundesärztekammer	Heinle, Wischer und Partner
e	Main building of TU Berlin	Hitzig, Raschdorff, Lucae, 1878–84; Dübbers, Schwennicke, 1961–65
f	Institut für Bergbau- und Hüttenwesen, TU Berlin	Willy Kreuer, 1955–59
g	Geschäftshaus Hardenberg (Kieperthaus)	Paul Schwebes, 1955/56; K.H. Winkens, 2003–05
h	Physikalische Institute, TU Berlin	Hundertmark, Lambart, 1980–83
i	Mensa am Steinplatz	Werner Düttmann, 1965–67/2002
j	Institut für Umwelttechnik, TU Berlin	Planungskollektiv Nr.1
k	Museum für Fotografie, Helmut Newton Stiftung	H. Schmieden, J. Boethke, 1908; Kahlfeld, 2004
l	city light house	Collignon, Fischötter, 2002–04
m	Salamander-Haus	von Gerkan, Marg und Partner, 1990–92
n	Bürohaus Ranke	Georg Heinrichs, 1991–93
o	Mark Hotel	Grötzebach, Plessow, Ehlers, 1985/86
p	Art'otel Wolf Vostell	Gernot Nalbach, Johanne Nalbach, 1984
q	Bankhaus Löbecke	Stefan Schroth,
r	Hotel Q	graft, 2002–04
s	Bücherbogen, Galerie Aedes West	Gerhard Spangenberg, 1980
t	Galerie 2000	Wolfgang Chrobok, 1970
u	Freie Volksbühne	Fritz Bornemann, 1960–63
v	Office building of Volkshilfe	Hans Schaefers, 1956
w	Schiller-Theater	Heinz Völker, Rudolf Grosse, 1950/51
x	Volkswohlbund	Hüffer, Ramin, 2004/05

315

Kaiser-Wilhelm-Gedächtniskirche
1960/61
Charlottenburg, Breitscheidplatz
Architect: Egon Eiermann

In this design emerging from a competition, a terrace connects all the building parts: the octogonal church construction, the old spire (a war-scored remnant of the former church designed by Franz Schwechten in 1891), the new tower, the chapel, and other architectural expressions of sacristy. The collected parts create a small ensemble of the old and the new, positioned where the nave of the former church stood. The entrance is located between the old tower and the new, octagonal structure. The steel-framed construction, bearing two-shelled inlays of honeycomb elements, is sealed at the bottom. Otherwise the building is largely glazed with segments of blue glass, but the pronounced darkness of the interior space hinders the full effect of the segments' blue light.

316

Photographed shortly after its completion

The end to the west with the cinema "Zoo-Palast"

Zentrum am Zoo
1956/57
Charlottenburg and Tiergarten, Hardenbergstraße 29, Budapester Straße 38–50
Architects: Paul Schwebes, Hans Schoszberger

This uniform, block perimeter development between Breitscheidplatz and Berlin's city zoological garden took the place of the war-destroyed "Haus Gourmenia" by Leo Nachtlicht and "Capitol" movie theater by Hans Poelzig. The high-rise and long structure in one houses a movie theater with two auditoriums: one with seating for 1,200 guests, and another for 550. To the east, the building's conclusion is formed by a public parking facility that accommodates 350 vehicles. The 3rd floor was left open to have a good air circulation for the animals in the zoological garden behind the building.

317

Zoofenster

1999–2012
Charlottenburg, Hardenbergstraße 28
Architect: Christoph Mäckler
Interior designers of the hotel: Inter-Art Études
Client: Svan Operations

While the eastern part of the city around Alexanderplatz began to draw attention to itself with the Television Tower (105) and a group of high-rise buildings, the western section held back discreetly for a time. But after everything had been pulled down in the triangle between Hardenbergstrasse, Joachimstaler Strasse, and Kantstrasse, a new and highly conspicuous landmark emerged in this area of Berlin as well. A tower up to 118 m high, housing a five-star hotel with 232 rooms, the Waldorf Astoria Berlin, grows out of a base storey that deliberately takes up the height of the six-storey buildings around it.

318

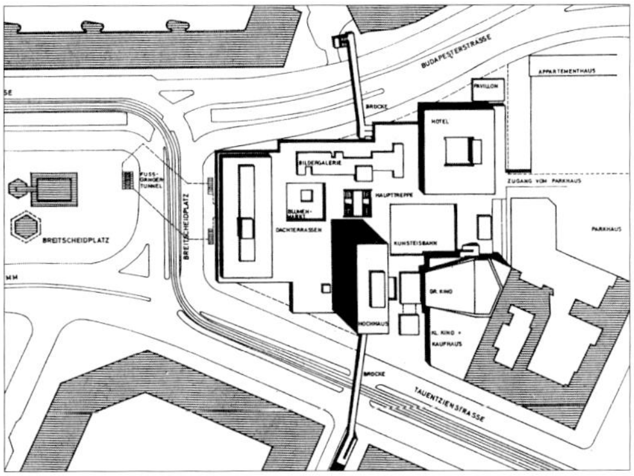

Site plan, 1963

Europa-Center

1963–65
Charlottenburg, Tauentzienstraße, Budapester Straße
Architects: Helmut Hentrich, Hubert Petschnigg
Creative advisors: Werner Düttmann, Egon Eiermann
Client: Europahaus Grundstücksgesellschaft, Karl H. Pepper

Thanks to its 22-storey office high-rise, this commercial focal point in the west of the city remains visible even today. A 2-storey base fills all the surface area of the property. Stores are located on every building level, including the basement. Lighting is also supplied by the courtyard areas which develop in more of a railroad effect through the construction. A department store, hotel, public parking facility, and "Haus der Nationen" movie theater connect to the complex as well. The former routing of the street, requiring two pedestrian bridges, was radically altered in favor of an unbroken pedestrian zone.

319

Peek & Cloppenburg
1994/95
Charlottenburg, Tauentzienstraße at the corner of Nürnberger Straße
Architects: Gottfried Böhm, Peter Böhm
Project management: Elmar Wolf, M. Rachfahl, Ch. Seichter
Painting: Markus Böhm

The 7-storey department store for apparel has an overall floor area of 24,700 sqm. With respect to its dimensions, the building orients itself more to the standards of the new Tauentzienstraße than it does to the former Femina-Palast on Nürnberger Straße (**320**), with its "glass dress" creating a reference to the merchandise sold here: the rippled-glass elements serve as both an environmental covering and protection from rain, but also as a lively "garment" hung between the ribs of the massive, concrete skeleton.

320

Femina-Palast
1928
Schöneberg, Nürnberger Straße 50–55
Architects: Hans Bielenberg, Josef Moser

Four upper storeys rest on the ground floor which accommodates businesses. Included here are office spaces, restaurants, and an auditorium. Currently known as the Tauentzien-Palast, the building formerly housed the "Berliner Theater" and popular dance clubs. Running laterally across the façade, inconspicuously aligned with an axis of symmetry, rounded parapet bands lined with travertine stone and brick frame the assorted bay windows. The building's landmark status saved it from being torn down.

321

Atrium

Senior citizens residence
1999–2000
Schöneberg, Passauer Straße 5–7
Architects: Heinz Hilmer, Christoph Sattler with Thomas Albrecht
Garden planning: Regina Poly
Client: Tertianum Besitzgesellschaft

The concept's commanding, outward-oriented wave-like bay windows subscribe to the trend of making the design of inner-city districts near the Tauentzien thoroughfare and KaDeWe department store attractive for older citizens. The offer is completed by a peaceful, spacious, and bright development hall with maritime accents, a swimming pool, a restaurant, and an underground garage with car-lift. The "front building" and "garden house" incorporate the entire building depth common to Berlin structures. Opposite a typical courtyard house of Hans C. Müller.

322

Entrence hall

Wittenbergplatz U-Bahn station
1913
Schöneberg, Tauentzienstraße
Architect: Alfred Grenander

As one of the most successful designs by Grenander, who was responsible for many subway (U-Bahn) stations in Berlin, including the clearly more Modern Krumme Lanke station as a circular building (1929), the cruciform shape of this particular station helps make it a highly sophisticated centralized building. Its extravagant design allows it to serve as a showpiece of both that period and the refined district surrounding it, together with the KaDeWe department store designed by Johann Emil Schaudt (1907). The station's entrance and hall are masterfully separated from the platforms and further defined by a surmounted tent-shaped roof.

323

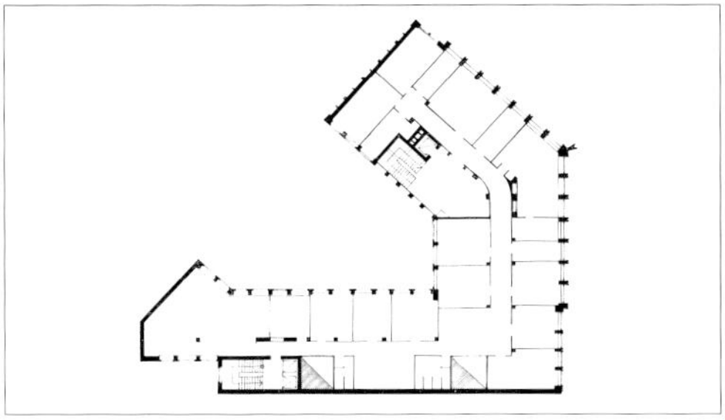

Plan of the 3rd floor

Lenzhaus
1928
Tiergarten, Kurfürstenstraße 87
Architect: Heinrich Straumer

The office spaces of this steel-frame construction, an 8-storey office building, were built to be freely subdivided as needed. The limestone façade has powerful vertically arranged subdivisions with an ashlar facing. Repaired after being destroyed by fire, the building remains an example of the global Expressionistic architecture of its time period.

324

Haus der Werbung
Advertising center
1964–66
Schöneberg, An der Urania 20–22
Architects: Rolf Gutbrod, Horst Schwaderer, Hermann Kiess

The 15-storey office building was intended as the counterpoint of what was decisively executed at that time as the south-oriented tangent with a triangular building plan. The high-grade steel façade combines the decorative and clear design. Reception and exhibition spaces are freely inserted behind elaborately secured, pediment cladding on the ground-floor level. The work areas can be divided as needed into individual or large-scale office spaces. Striking about the building are the well-conceived interior details which nearly correspond with today's standards.

325

Guest room

Concorde-Hotel
2002–05
Charlottenburg, Joachimstaler Straße at the corner of Augsburger Straße
Architect: Jan Kleihues
Project manager: Johannes Kressner
Client: Grothe Immobilien Projektgruppe

Directly behind the Swiss Hotel by von Gerkan, Marg und Partner, replacing at this spot the old "Kudamm Eck" construction built in 1998 and featuring allegorical figures by Markus Lüpertz on its wall projections, another towering and vertically aligned structure was built at this site. The newer hotel, which tops the first one by 6 storeys, is lined with Kirchheimer limestone and houses 311 rooms and suites above its congress and banquet floors. Two apartments are on the 12th floor, and offices as well as fitness and wellness areas are at the top. The step-back form was the result of having to maintain the stipulated minimum distance from the neighboring properties.

326

The new Kranzler Eck

View of pedestrian passageway

Kranzler Eck
1998–2001
Charlottenburg, Kurfürstendamm at the corner of Joachimstaler Straße
Architects: Murphy/Jahn Architects
Construction supervisor: Gerkan, Marg und Partner
Client: DiFA Fonds

The 2-storey development from the 1950s, crowned with a round pavilion, is an enduring symbol of the reconstruction era and prosperity following World War II. For that reason too, the glazed form of the pedestrian passageway, which reaches as far as Kantstraße (with a 71,300 sqm floor area for rental spaces and costing circa 360 million Euro), respects the historic preservation laws, and, while in a dialog with the "Kranzler Eck", creates a metropolitan space and an attractive passage to Kantstraße – after the Victoria insurance company abandoned its construction plans for this site.

327

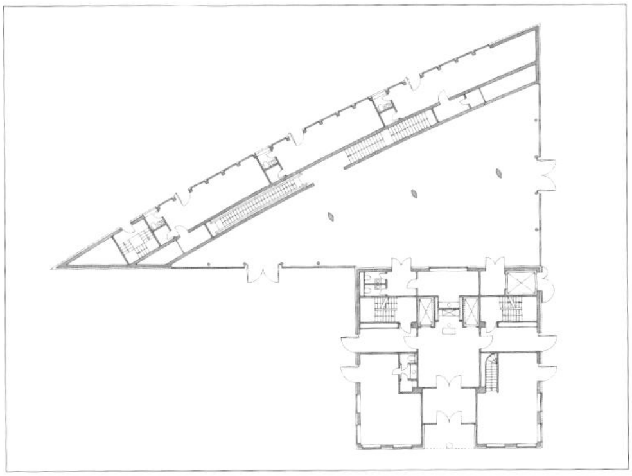

Plan of the ground floor

Office high-rise Kantdreieck
1992–94
Charlottenburg, Fasanenstraße at the corner of Kantstraße
Architect: Josef Paul Kleihues
Project manager: Frank Strobel
Client: KapHag
Architekturpreis Berlin 1994

The long history of its planning was burdened by having to decide on the building's appearance, and by high-rise polemics in particular. In 1986, this began with a tower rising from a cubical foundation, and three attached cubes with diagonal wind braces. Over the next five years, though, two of the cubes were discussed out of existence. What remains of the original plan, as a roof spire, is a large, movable flagstaff on which often hangs a gondola made of façade plaster. The attractive foundation level is meanwhile occupied by the Raab Galerie.

328

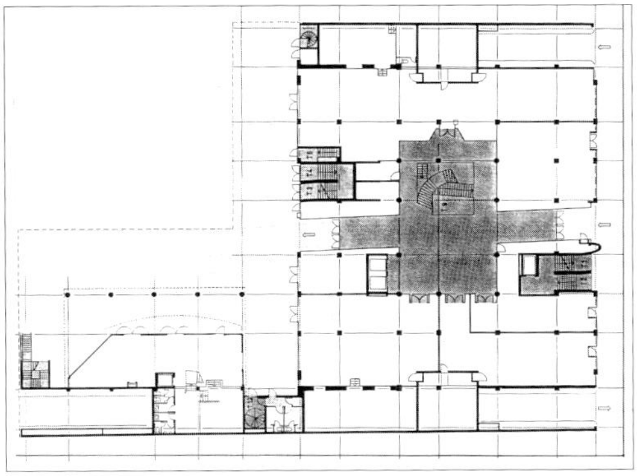

Plan of the ground floor

Kempinski Plaza
1988–92
Charlottenburg, Uhlandstraße 183–187
Architects: Jan Rave, Rolf Rave with Dieter Meisl and Roosje Rave
Clients: Gädeke & Landsberg

The centralized development of this apartment, office- and commercial building is the passageway through a glass-roofed atrium leading to the Hotel Kempinski. The entrance with columns surfaced with gold leafing, and the operating balcony, divide and connect the two building parts whose old structural division becomes accentuated through the use of light and dark-hued stone slabs. In the courtyard, a 2-storey pavilion is suspended over an underground garage. In 2001, a third of the atrium was remodeled and thoroughly enriched by the surface polishing conceived by Frank Oehring.

329

View into the mall

stilwerk
1998/99
Charlottenburg, Kantstraße at the corner of Uhlandstraße
Architects: Novotny Mähner Assoziierte with Dieter Schweinlin and Manfred Elter
Client: DEGI

Focussed on design and better living, this "theme" department store with 60 individual shops and firm representations was built around a mall area on 5 levels. Located at the western end is a restaurant with parking facilities available directly below the building. The façade part that spreads open at the street corner draws its unmistakable charisma from the color of the Brazilian quartzite; floor-high, darkened brass panels, and an mobile designed object (covered with gold leafing), which can be entered and serves as a façade-cleaning device on tracks.

330

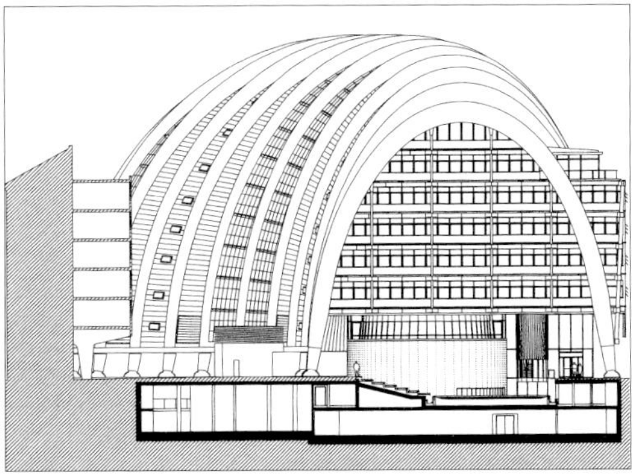

Cross section

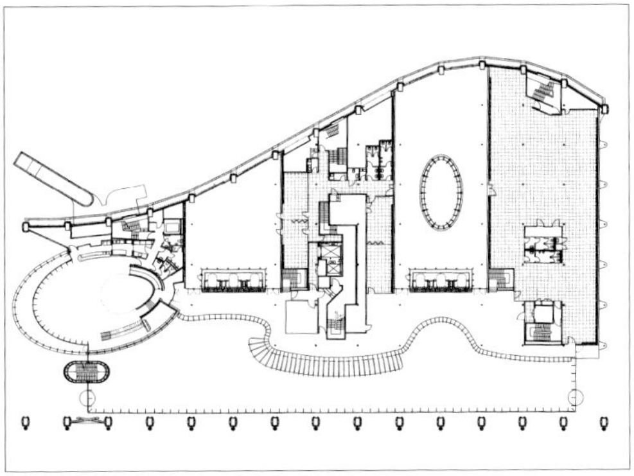

Plan of the 1st floor

Ludwig-Erhard-Haus
1994–98
Charlottenburg, Fasanenstraße at the corner of Hardenbergstraße
Architects: Nicholas Grimshaw & Partners
Building construction: Krupp Stahlbau/Züblin AG
Client: Industrie- und Handelskammer zu Berlin

The middle section of the communications and service center, a 1991 competition winner, houses Berlin's stock exchange. Its 15 rib-like arches of different sizes create a staggering volume. Six ascending office floors stand detached from the arches in way that forms the large, support-free foyer from which all the functional spaces in the 22,000 sqm of floor area develop. Building costs: circa 154 million Euro. What had to disappear was the landmark businessman's lounge from the 1950s.

331

Mommsenstraße 4–5

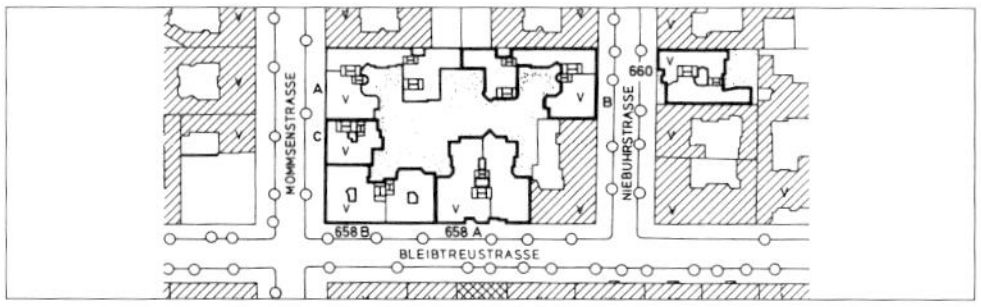

Site plan

Apartment house
1906/07
Charlottenburg, Mommensenstraße at the corner of Bleibtreustraße
Architect: Alfred Geßner

In this case, the rigid grid of the Berlin apartment house – encircling a courtyard with two side-wings, and a so-called "garden house" – is broken open to create totally new and freer apartment forms. The restricting symmetry dissolves altogether. The open spaces, interacting via "small" naturally-lit hallways, develop the living and sleeping quarters, and replace the dark corridors. This concept was later used by Rob Krier in Kreuzberg **(151)** and Tiergarten **(249)**. Geßner too, applied his early reforms only in the urban planning context, and completed them in the corners of several parks.

332

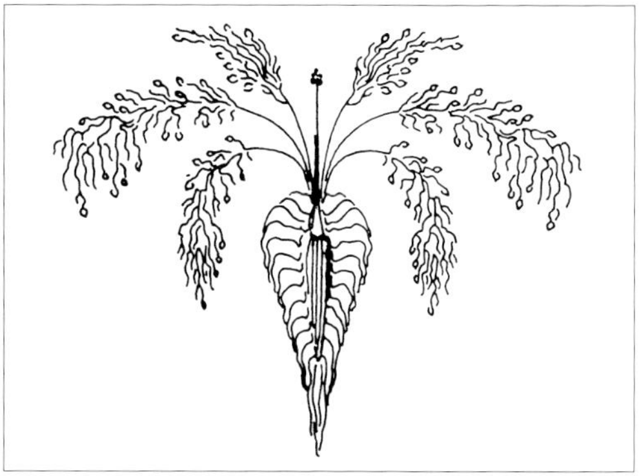

Sample of the ceiling ornamentation

Haus Steinplatz
1906/07
Charlottenburg, Uhlandstraße 197
Architect: August Endell

The type of plot development typical for Berlin was used here: a front building with a rear building encircling a courtyard. The subdivisions, which occur through various structural elements, rely on vertical accents as basic components. In both the exterior and interior areas, these so-called components also utilize a plantlike ornamentation. Until now, the building has been able to withstand the modernizing of its old and well-preserved façades while ennobling itself with a small piece of green property in front of the Universität der Künste at the same time.

333

Concert hall of the Hochschule für Musik

1955

Charlottenburg, Hardenbergstraße 32

Architect: Paul G. R. Baumgarten

Mural: Theodor Werner

The prize-winning submission of a 1949 competition, this building offers seating for 1,360 guests. The elongated form is caused by the narrowness of the building property. On the foyer level are two artworks: a sculpture by Hans Uhlmann and a mural by Theodor Werner, which, by night, can be viewed without obstruction from the bordering street area. The concert hall's ash-wood ceiling, hung in sections between the longitudinal ribs, forms a pronounced vertical alignment directed towards the orchestra's podium. On the north side of the old college building from 1902 is a studio hall by the same architect in 1975.

334

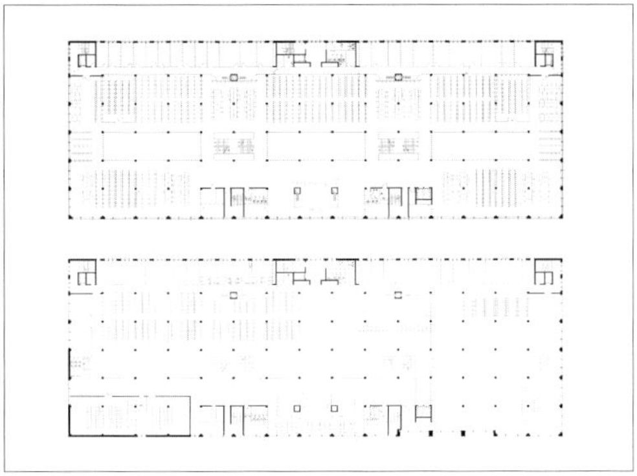

Plan of the ground and the upper floors

Volkswagen Universitätsbibliothek

Volkswagen university library

2002–04

Charlottenburg, Fasanenstraße at the corner of Hertzallee

Architect: Walter A. Noebel

Light stelae: Raoul Hesse

Client: Senator für Stadtentwicklung

Its first architect was the 1988 competition winner Lothar Jeromin. But only through funding from Volkswagen, and a cost-optimizing plan, could the library be erected at all. Saving 8 million Euro led to a rational construction form whose qualitative details included 715 data-processing banks for users, and satisfied the academic needs of both the central library of the Technische Universität Berlin and the Universität der Künste.

335

Architecture department of the Technische Universität Berlin
1966–68
Charlottenburg, Straße des 17. Juni
Architect: Bernhard Hermkes

Chronologically, the architecture department was the last building part of the Technische Universität Berlin completed at Ernst-Reuter-Platz, following an urban planning concept by the same architect. This building for seminars has two, spacious lecture rooms with cleverly staggered levels and galleries in an exposed reinforced concrete construction. While completing the northern development, it hardly multiplies the spatial value of the "square". Connecting in an easterly direction is the city-planning institute and the Architekturmuseum by Hans Scharoun, and a bronze sculpture, *The Flame*, by Bernhard Heiliger.

336

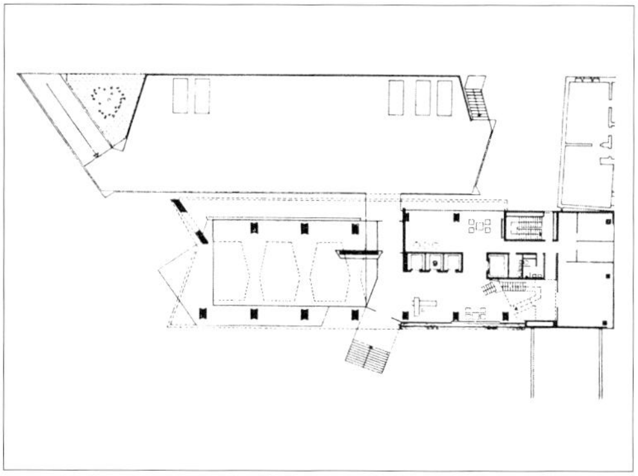

Floor plan of the entrance level

IBM office building
1961
Charlottenburg, Ernst-Reuter-Platz
Architects: Rolf Gutbrod, Bernhard Binder
Contact architect: Hansrudolf Plarre

The 9-storey office building has a bent pediment wall, which emphasizes the point where Hardenbergstraße culminates at Ernst-Reuter-Platz. From the city square, the building is entered by either a terrace of front steps or, from the parking lot's platform, via a bridge through the data processing center. The office floors can be freely divided as 3-level facilities. The slanted surfaces of the parapet bands are made of enameled steel panels.

337

Telefunken skyscraper
1958–60
Charlottenburg, Ernst-Reuter-Platz 3
Architects: Paul Schwebes, Hans Schoszberger
Client: Telefunken

Through the efforts of Bernhard Hermkes and Ernst May, and following a 1955 master plan, a landmark in the form of a 22-storey, 80-m high office building was built at the city's so-called east-to-west axis. Its architectural style and vertically tapering construction make it seem related to the Pirelli skyscaper by Gio Ponti in Milan. In Berlin, though, the pros and cons of skyscraper construction are frequently discussed – and passionately. Are acceptable models to be found in New York or Paris? This skyscraper is currently used by the Technische Universität Berlin diagonally facing it. Into the 1920s, the city square the building stands on was known as "Knie" (knee) square, because the route from the Stadtschloß to Schloß Charlottenburg seemed to "bend at the knee" at this spot.

338

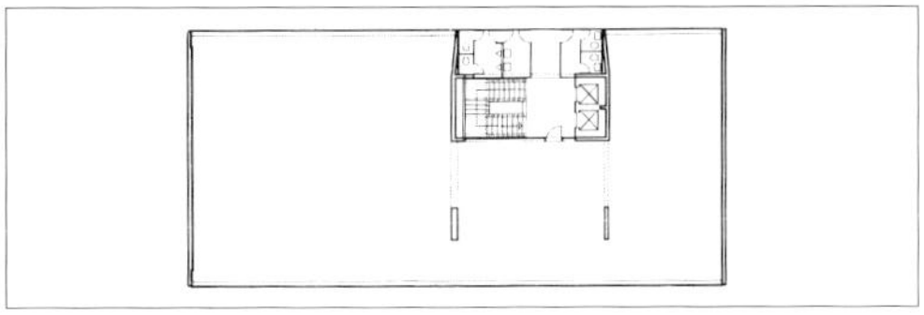

Plan of a standard floor

Ruhrkohle-Haus
1958
Charlottenburg, Bismarckstraße 107
Architect: Paul G. R. Baumgarten

This block development requires two firewalls, which, together with the stairwell and massive parapets, form the load-bearing framework. Located on the upper storeys are office spaces, and on the ground floor the exhibition spaces, lecture rooms, and kitchen. Display windows and glass walls provide views for the ground floor and cellar with heating facilities. The polished plate glass, blue-toned enameled sheet-steel, white enameled insulation profiles, and wooden windows form the simplest of curtain-wall façades endowed with a Berlin charm.

339

Foyer

Deutsche Oper Berlin
1961
Charlottenburg, Bismarckstraße 35–37
Architect: Fritz Bornemann
Entranceway sculpture: Hans Uhlmann

The building emerged from a 1955 competition focussed on reconstructing the 1912 opera house under the condition of incorporating parts of the former stage and workshop facilities. These stipulations led to having to shift a forecourt to the side of the building. However, the entrance to the opera house remained on Bismarckstraße – underneath a much criticized, 70-m long wall made of washed concrete. The building's box-like balcony units are arranged along the auditorium's side and back walls, and the stage tower rises to a height of 35 m.

340

Residential part on Bismarckstraße

Opernviertel
1966/67
Charlottenburg, Bismarckstraße, Krumme Straße, Zillestraße
Architects: Hans C. Müller, Georg Heinrichs with Mosch, Krohn, Burghard Greger
Clients: Mosch, Gewobag

Arranged along Bismarckstraße, the property is subdivided in 4 parallel strips. It features a 3- to 5-storey, street-bordering building part for commercial spaces, behind which lies a purely residential section of 8 to 17 storeys, with the parts staggered in opposing directions. Farther back is the small park-like area, and at Zillestraße a public housing structure. This cross-wall construction made of poured concrete has prefabricated, parapet elements lined with mosaics.

341

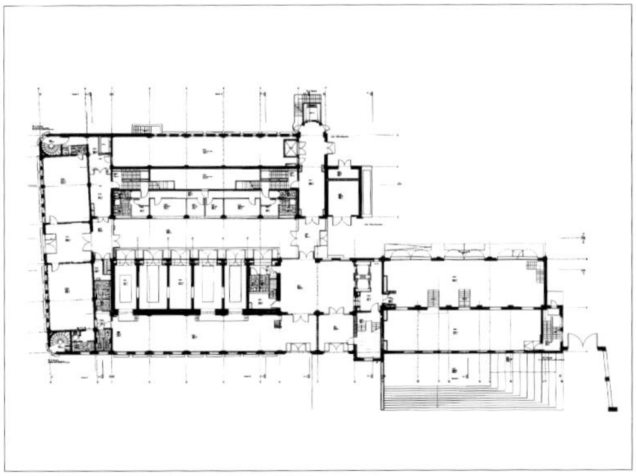

Plan of the ground floor

Metahaus
1927/1999–2001
Charlottenburg, Leibnizstraße at the corner of Niebuhrstraße
Architect: Hans Heinrich Müller
Usage change: Paul Kahlfeldt, Petra Kahlfeldt
Client: Metahaus Leibniz for Meta-Design

At numerous Berlin locations, modern technology has made older constructions usable again and available for other purposes – a good example being the conversion of the old building on Kopenhagener Straße into the Vitra-Museum. The Metahaus is a similar case. The architect Hans Heinrich Müller worked between the 1920s and 1930s (this building dates from 1927), and the newly arranged areas of use for this structure protected by historic preservation laws were transformed into studios, offices, and other work spaces.

342

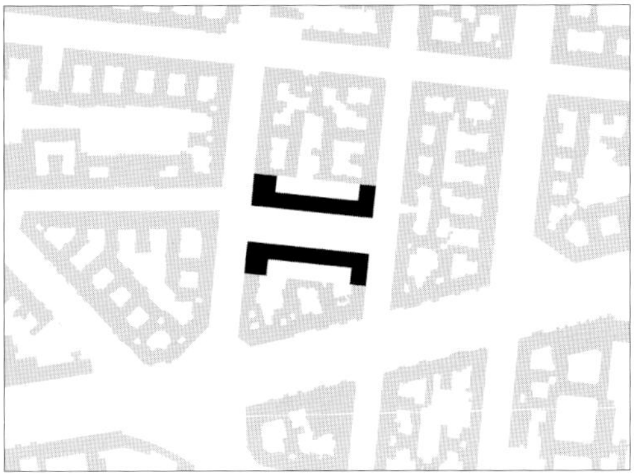

Site plan

Leibnizkolonnaden
1997–2001
Charlottenburg, Walter-Benjamin-Platz, Wielandstraße 19–22, Leibnizstraße 49–53
Architects: Hans Kollhoff, Helga Timmermann
Client: Investitionsgesellschaft Leibnizkolonnaden

After submitting a competition-winning concept in 1984 for a media center in the form of a large greenhouse on property formerly occupied by tennis courts and later by a parking lot, the architects finally developed a public space for grander living – with apartments, office floors, stores inserted in the colonnades' Italian flair, roof-top kindergarten, and 2-level underground garage for 400 vehicles. The plasticity of the façade is made by an ingenious system of thin lamina stone plates.

343

Office building Ku-70
1985–88
Charlottenburg, Kurfürstendamm 70
Architects: Murphy/Jahn Architects
Client: Peter Schiansky

Following the traffic-friendly expansion of Lewishamstraße, architects had tried every possible concept aimed at utilizing a slender leftover plot measuring 54 sqm. The site finally assumed a highly mechanical form: supported on piles, it autonomously developed to eight floors of office spaces that left its address suspended in midair.

344

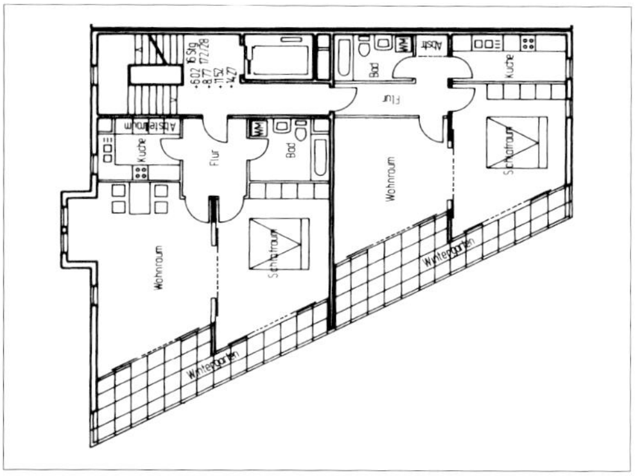

Plan of a standard floor

Four infill buildings
1978–81
Charlottenburg, Lewishamstraße at the corners of Sybelstraße and Mommsenstraße
Architect: Jürgen Sawade
Project manager: Axel Schulz
Client: Südwest-Boden-Gesellschaft

In various sections of Berlin, what qualified as a challenge for Haussmann in Paris, namely a diagonal penetration of the street through a city block, led to the remains of property as well as open rear courtyards. In a manner that is acoustically effective as well what could be achieved here was the re-establishment of the street's spatial integrity using four, identical infill buildings made of prefabricated concrete components and glazed solariums. The rooftop gardens meant to compensate for the missing areas of open (garden) space are just the same fenced in by tall sections of latticework. Garages with 3-m tall ceilings were also for hire by small businesses.

345

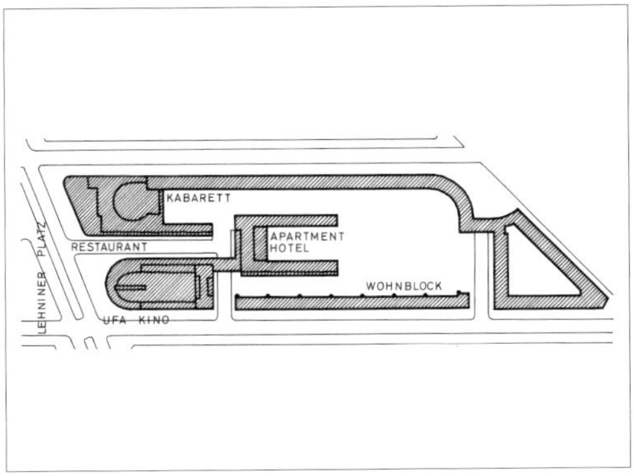

Site plan

Building complex on Lehniner Platz
1926–28
Wilmersdorf, Kurfürstendamm at the corner of Cicerostraße
Architect: Erich Mendelsohn

The traditional West-Berlin boulevard evolved even further: beside row houses arranged along tennis courts, created here was an apartment building, cabaret, and large-scale movie theater typical of that period, everything designed by the same architect. His curved and wavelike constructions fashioned in dark brick and brightly colored, smooth plastered surfaces seemed to reach out to the posters and blinking advertisements and interact with the street. Following the war, some time passed before the popular Italian restaurant "Ciao", the disco "Treibhaus", and bowling alleys appeared in the construction's eastern building part, and the rehearsal stage of the theater known as the Schaubühne **(346)** appeared even later.

346

Apartment development on Cicerostraße

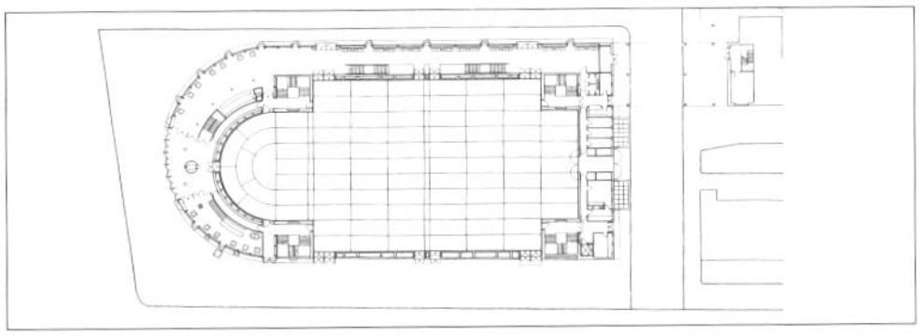

Plan of the ground floor in 1978

Interior of the Universum movie theater, 1926

Neue Schaubühne
1978–81
Wilmersdorf, Kurfürstendamm 153
Architect: Jürgen Sawade
Client: Senator für kulturelle Angelegenheiten

After being left abandoned for many years, the shell of an old movie theater was converted into the new address of the "Schaubühne", a theater/troupe meanwhile established by director Peter Stein, performing until then in a building along the Hallesches Ufer. With the staging of its technically elaborate productions in the new building, the experimental theater created a totally flexible performing space which erased the division between the stage and the audience. This also made it possible to produce a wide range of spatial constellations utilizing two massive, fireproof, roll-up doors and 76 vertically rising platforms. Parallel to finishing the new theater, a workshop building was erected.

347

Kirche am Lietzensee
Church on Lietzensee
1957–59
Charlottenburg, Herbartstraße 5
Architect: Paul G. R. Baumgarten

Two sides of the 5-cornered church open entirely towards the trees encircling Lietzensee and allow the creator's greatest work, nature itself, into the space. The folded, ribbed roof is made of reinforced concrete. At the two points where the structure extends down to the ground, the inclination corresponds with the folding of the roof. The church bells hang between lateral walls on the side of the building housing the entranceway.

348

St.-Canisius-Kirche
2000–02
Charlottenburg, Witzlebenstraße 27–29
Architects: Heike Büttner, Claus Neumann, Georg Braun with Peter Flucke
Outer wall: Joan Waltemat
Client: Kath. Kirchengemeinde St. Canisius

The concept was arrived at after a long search, preceded by concluding an advisory report. Rudolf Schwarz comments: "Ideally, the holy space founded entirely on its community and work would be embraced from within the liturgy and sink back into it again." The original church from the 1950s, designed by Reinhard Hofbauer, caught fire due to a childish prank and now stands totally detached. The new building was to be visible through a "portal situation" behind the edge of an improved, block-system plan.

349

Development courtyard

Engelhardt-Hof
1995/96
Charlottenburg, Danckelmannstraße at the corner of Christstraße
Architects: Paul Kahlfeldt, Petra Kahlfeldt
Project manager: Anja Herold, Christoph Haag
Landscape planning: TOPOS
Client: Engelhardt Grundstücksverwaltung

Since 1850 the building parts adapted to the rudimentary structure of a development plan. But after the former brewery was closed down, enough space appeared in the block interior for an office and commerce building producing a courtyard, and for a residential row construction on Christstraße. What produces the ensemble effect here is the use of the same architectural style; consistently yellow, frost-proof engineering brick, and the incorporation of the restored buildings on Danckelmannstraße.

350

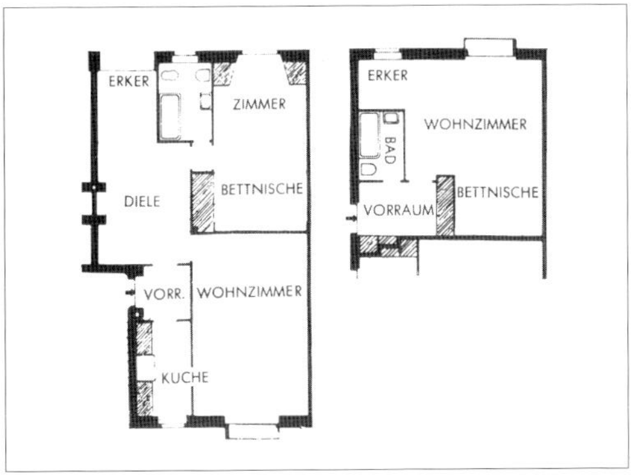

Plans of 1- and 2-room apartments

Apartment building
1928/29
Charlottenburg, Kaiserdamm 25
Architect: Hans Scharoun

This building of flats for singles offers 1- and 2-room apartments, together with a ground-floor restaurant also meant to serve the tenants. Regarding the connections to the older apartment development – despite the neighboring building adhering to a formally more competitive time period with its high-peaked roof and building form – the new development simply continues beyond the gable masonry wall. The smooth white stuccoed surfaces and confident interplay of different window types are typical stylistic elements of the 35-year-old master and newcomer.

351

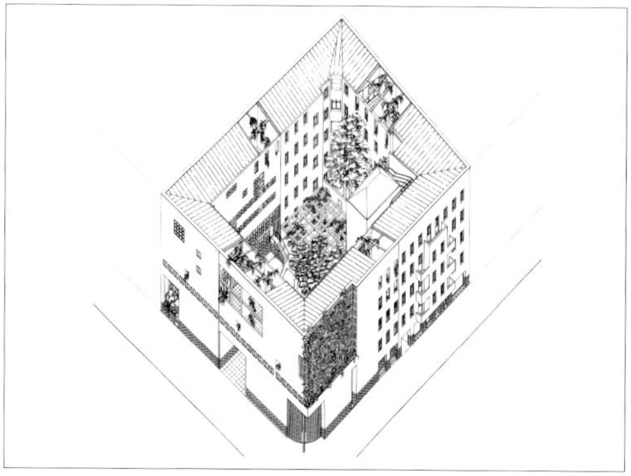

Wohnhof am Goethepark
Residential courtyard at Goethepark
1980–91
Charlottenburg, Kaiser-Friedrich-Straße at the corner of Schillerstraße
Architect: Oswald Mathias Ungers
Client: Klingbeil Gruppe
The end of the block is closed by a courtyard-generating new development, which integrates an existing older building and takes on the dimensional depths of its side wings. The point of orientation for all the apartments is a quiet centralized courtyard with small gardens connected to individual dwellings as well as larger and shared exterior surfaces. On the street-facing side of the building, the orientation provides freely changeable design possibilities using either the wall surfaces, closed for the most part, or an expansive lattice.

352

Plan of the 3rd floor

Office building with two penthouse apartments
1978/79
Charlottenburg, Richard-Wagner-Platz 3
Architect and client: Bernhard Binder
A piece of inner-city property measuring only 256 sqm and considered worthless as a building site for more than three decades had to remain an ugly construction gap until the expression "urban repairs" demanded constructing here, on the neighborhood's weak spot, and made the same property highly functional. "The defining characteristic is an undulating blue façade in which dull-edged bay windows appear on different levels." The wall does more than serve as what connects neighbors; it also replaces the decor of the old constructions.

353

Interior of the hall

Entrance bridge

Sporthalle Charlottenburg
1962
Charlottenburg, Sömmeringstraße 23–31
Architect: Ludwig Leo

The hall is the first-prize winner of a competition. Its dimensions of 52 x 70 m accommodate a handball court and two grandstands for spectators. The flat, overhead vaulting consists of 4-cm-thick poured concrete slabs and an assemblage of rhombus-shaped 2,80-m-long rods made of ready-mixed concrete. At the turn of the century, this form of construction was often used for sports halls and boat houses, but made entirely of wood. Parking is available on the hall's north side, with a connection to an open-air recreational area created to the south. The wooden sculpture is by Heinrich Brummack.

354

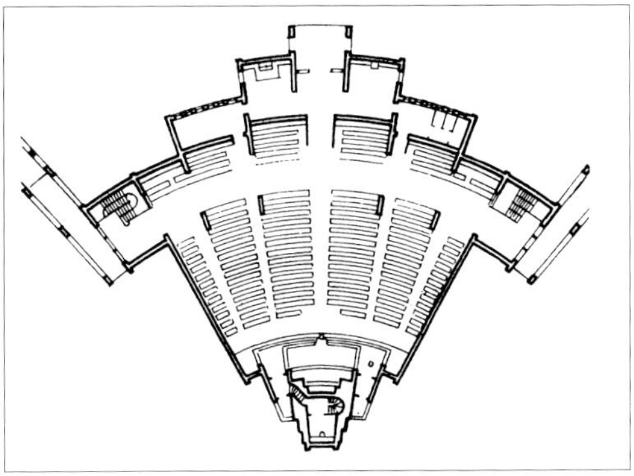

Gustav-Adolf-Kirche
1934
Charlottenburg, Brahestraße, Herschelstraße
Architect: Otto Bartning

The building's reinforced-concrete framework is infilled with masonry brickwork. The church spire rises up at an intersection, where it stands in clear view from four directions. "In this case, this leads to the task of developing not only the space of the church, but also the entire group of buildings from both the tip of the property and from the church spire. The pulpit and altar stand at the foot of the church spire, which also functions as the external sign of a spiritual ordering." (Excerpt from a 1934 construction survey)

355

View from the courtyard

Luisenplatz development
1987
Charlottenburg, Luisenplatz 1–2
Architects: Andreas Brandt, Rudolf Böttcher, with Yadegar Assisi
Client: Hans K. Herr

On the occasion of a 1984 competition, the construction form sought for the eastern edge of the Luisenplatz was to be unmistakably Modern while visually referring to the Baroque palace, and to the pavilion by Schinkel through its proportions. The reduction to 3 storeys, continuous roof over the uniform façade, and passageway to Eosanderstraße represent here a calming down of the otherwise livelier edges of the city square.

356

Housing development at Luisenplatz
1985–87
Charlottenburg, Eosanderstraße, Otto-Suhr-Allee
Architects: Hans Kollhoff, Helga Timmermann
Client: APL

Three terrace building parts with a metropolitan flair complete the existing blocks in a westerly direction – with dark brick, wide glazed surfaces, and a slightly swung sculptural, flying roof. Facing the parterre of Luisenplatz, the building assumes a calm and reserved position. Despite its high quality standards, it could be built using normal funding.

357

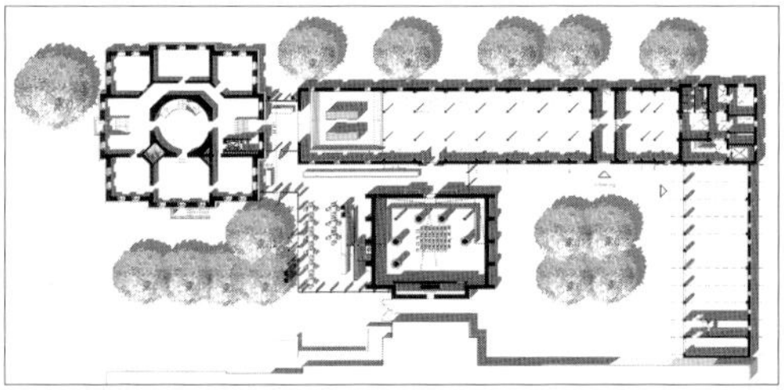

Animated floor plan

Sammlung Scharf-Gerstenberg
The Scharf-Gerstenberg collection
2005–07
Charlottenburg, Spandauer Damm / Schloßstraße
Architect: Georg Sunder-Plasmann

Opposite Schloss Charlottenburg, designed 1702 to 1713 by Eosander von Göthe, are two corner constructions from the year 1855: barracks of the Garde du Corps completed through August Stüler, meanwhile reconstructed to function as museums and housing two private as well as intimate art collections. The pavilion to the west houses the Berggruen collection, featuring exquisite artworks by Klee, Picasso, and Matisse. The east-facing pavilion, with the adjoining stable house, outbuilding, and new information pavilion embedded in a glazed entranceway and cafeteria area, houses the art collection of Dieter Scharf, which devotes itself to a comprehensive ordering of "surrealist worlds". The design for this structure emerged from a 2001 competition process and was the only submission to promote access to the building from its courtyard side.

358

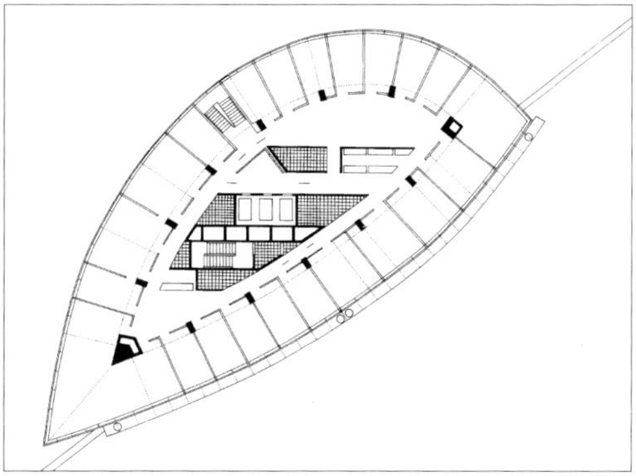

Plan of an office floor

Bürohaus Halensee
1994–96
Wilmersdorf, Halenseestraße, Kronprinzendamm
Architects: Hilde Léon, Konrad Wohlhage
Landscape planning: Karl Thomanek, Hiltrud Duquesnoy
Client: MÜBAU

Conceived during the course of a 1990 competition and executed on a left-over fragment piece of property, this construction form proved satisfactory from both an engineering and an economic standpoint thanks to its high usability, as well as from an ecological standpoint with regard to the effective soundproofing achieved by the raised foundation storey. Created here was an exciting form made of a foundation wall and a sharp-edged, ellipsoidal, glass attachment with a gross floor area of 14,000 sqm. At the same time, this arranges and stabilizes the urban planning situation between the Halensee and the residential district that connects to the east.

359

Epiphanienkirche
1960
Charlottenburg, Knobelsdorffstraße 74
Architects: Konrad Sage, Karl Hebecker

In order to reconstruct the church built in 1906 and destroyed by fire during the war, it was necessary to completely restructure the building. The former access route from the east was no longer available due to a stretch of highway being built so close by. This made it necessary to place the new entrance at the building's south side, and the altar at the north side. As a load-bearing spatial construction, the roof consists of folded plates of aluminum sheet-metal, which produce the triangles also visible as recurring architectural elements.

360

Streetcar depot

Residential buildings

Tramway service station and staff accommodation
1930
Charlottenburg, Königin-Elisabeth-Straße at the corner of Knobelsdorffstraße
Architects: Jean Krämer, Otto Rudolf Salvisberg

The maintenance depot in a steel construction was designed by the same architect responsible for Berlin's transportation authority (BVG) and fills the courtyard spaces of an entire city block. Given the fact that in West-Berlin the abolishment of the city's streetcar lines has been underway since 1967, this service station for the municipal streetcars needs a new function, obvious not the apartments both sides of the Knobelsdorffstraße with their both, big 8-storey head buildings like two doorposts, up to Westend.

The ICC with the old fair buildings in the background

Main foyer

Main lecture hall

Internationales Congress Centrum ICC
1973–79
Charlottenburg, Messedamm
Architects: Ralf Schüler and Ursula Schüler-Witte
Artists: Jean Ipousteguy (sculptural component), Alexander von Ekbatana, Brigitte and Martin Matschinsky-Dennighof (sculptural component), Frank Oehring (light sculpture)
Client: Neue Heimat for Land Berlin

In the middle of the 1960s, what developed from a competition focussed on creating new multifunctional exhibition halls was the idea to create a congress hall. In turn, this led to the idea of creating a congress "center"able to be used in several ways. The competition among congress locations led to organizing a program of superlatives for this construction: congress hall with seating for 5,000 guests; banquet room with seating for 3,000 guests; 7 medium-sized and smaller halls offering seating for 150 to 350 guests; a press center, restaurant, and large-scale kitchen, as well as changing rooms and cloakroom areas; a stage with additional presentation and performance-related spaces, and a parking facility for 630 vehicles. What the architects placed between the highway's serpentine and the trade-fair buildings was a gigantic machine-like construction with a formal language taken from the world of industrial design. It connects to the radio tower on the highway's triangle and spans the Messedamm thoroughfare with a support-free bridge-building. The building consists of structure-giving, steel trusses with supports at its doubled stairwells. The roof and façade are formed as separate outer shells made of aluminum panels. For years now, the spaces for holding congresses have remained permanently booked in advance, but the current need to rid the construction of its asbestos content lures newer investors onto the scene. This building is a longstanding trademark of Berlin as a congress location.

362

Funkturm
Radio tower
1924–26
Charlottenburg, Messedamm
Architect: Heinrich Straumer

A symbol for Berlin since the 1920s, the radio tower has long stood in the shadows of the Eiffel Tower in Paris. Today it competes more so with Berlin's television tower **(105)**. The 150-m tall construction accommodates a 2-storey restaurant elevated at a height of 55 m. The lower floors house the kitchen and social rooms, above which are gastronomical services with seating for 180 guests. A viewing platform stands at a height of 125 m.

363

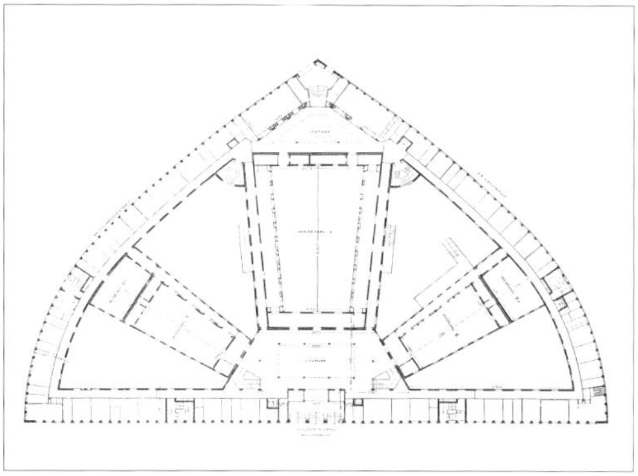

Plan of the ground floor

Haus des Rundfunks
House of broadcasting
1931
Charlottenburg, Masurenallee 8–14
Architect: Hans Poelzig

Radially grouped around the entranceway hall are three broadcasting areas (halls) enclosed by office buildings and well-protected from street-noise. The outer façade is clad with brick and ceramic tiles. Also worthy of notice are the elaborate interior spaces: the centralized, large-scaled entranceway hall is carefully detailed, and the use of diverse and intensely glazed ceramic components lend the foyer a festive quality. The building's concert hall was renovated and fully modernized in 1958. On the right side two white, very clear cubes from 2004 by the architects Jürgen Engel and Klaus Zillich. In 2008 a glazed three-storey studio building was added by Hans-Joachim Tunnat.

364

Trade-fair halls
1969–71
Westend, Jafféstraße
Architect: Harald Franke with Siegfried K. Jaik
Client: Senator für Bau- und Wohnungswesen

Addition to the trade-fair halls of 1935 by Richard Ermisch. This expansion was created in a single building phase and closed the structural ring of the fairgrounds while creating a roofed-over access to the exhibition halls. The required separation in the fire-protection area led to a chamber-like ordering of the halls, but it also granted the needed flexibility, which allowed every building part to be altered when necessary.

365

New entrance hall

Trade-fair halls
1990–99
Westend, Messedamm 22
Architect: Oswald Mathias Ungers with Jörg Lenschow, Walter Noebel
Client: Messe Berlin

The mounting competition among cities serving as trade fair locations made it necessary to expand the exhibition areas by Hans Poelzig and Richard Ermisch, grouped around the Funkturm or "radio tower" **(362)**. These were increased by 72,000 sqm in 1986, and by another 330,000 sqm during this building phase. Finally, a second entranceway by the same architects was developed in a round building at the south side of the fairgrounds, facing the civic hall known as Deutschlandhalle.

366

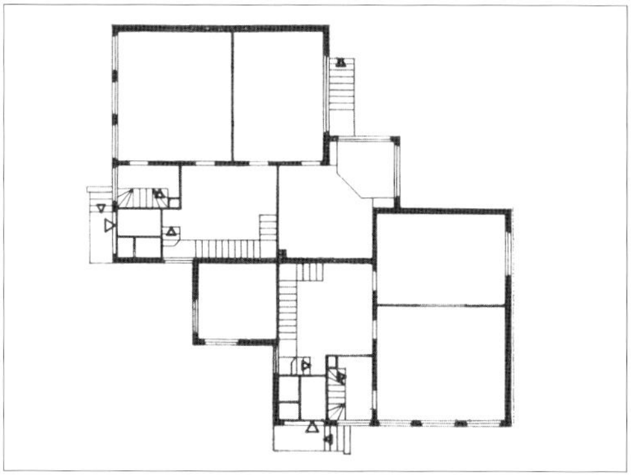

Plan of the ground floor

Double villa
1922
Westend, Karolingerplatz 5a
Architect: Erich Mendelsohn

What characterizes this building is the mirror-image floor plan on the angle segmentation of the street corner, in which one of the apartments has the music room facing the garden, and the other its corner room facing the street. The foundation with basement and ground-floor storey have stuccoed surfaces. The upper part of the building displays strong graphically structured brickwork. The windows function as either contracted bands or emphasize the corners.

367

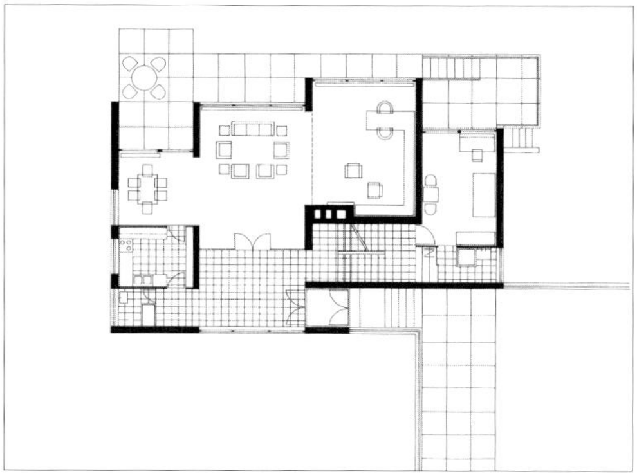

Plan of the ground floor

Haus Müllerburg
1960/61
Charlottenburg, Sensburger Allee 19 A
Architect: Georg Heinrichs

Similar to Haus Karsch, the building is clearly subdivided in powerful cubes. It features a Berlin "Pfeifenkopf" (pipe-bowl) wall component) and a surface made of glazed, white ceramic stone. These are contrasted by large window openings in Prussian-blue and horizontal formats. The form is disturbed by neither drainpipe nor metal sheet covering; the building's entranceway is marked by no more than a quarter-circle. While the floor plan follows the principle of clear subdivisions, the stipulated functions celebrate their orientation towards the garden.

368

Apartment and studio / Georg-Kolbe-Museum
1928/29
Charlottenburg, Sensburger Allee 25
Architect: Ernst Rentsch

This building served as the apartment and studio of the sculptor Georg Kolbe. In 1932, it was further expanded using Paul Linder's design for a ceramics studio and sculpture garden. The 2-storey, cubical, brickwork construction has a flat roof. The apartment and studio spaces face north. In front of these, facing south, is the spacious workshop with overhead lighting and tall lateral windows. On the upper floor are the living quarters, bedrooms, and rooftop garden. The former apartment contained an additional studio. For more than a decade, the building is now used as an intimate museum devoted to sculptural works from Kolbe's creative period.

369

Plan of the living floor

Haus Dr. Sternefeld
1923
Charlottenburg, Heerstraße 109
Architect: Erich Mendelsohn

Like the double villa on Karolingerplatz, this combination of reinforced-concrete and brickwork construction is one of Berlin's first cubical, flat-roofed buildings. The outer walls are surfaced with plaster, and the foundation with iron clinker brick. The 3rd-storey spaces open towards an enclosed patio or solarium. It was slightly reconstructed by Mendelsohn for his client in 1932. During an interim period, the building also served as a private senior citizens residence.

370

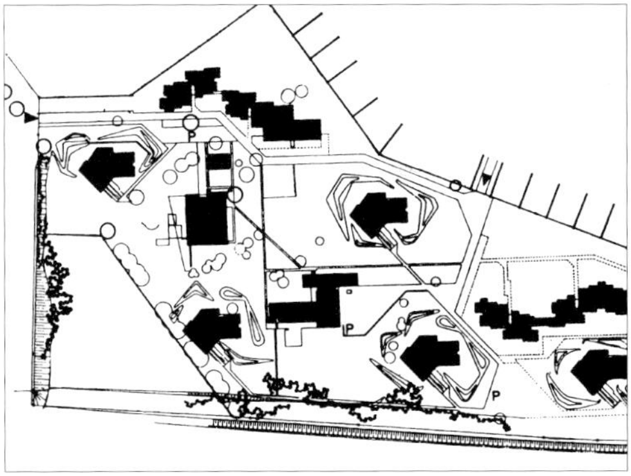

Site plan

Eichkamp student housing colony
1959, 1966/67
Eichkamp, Harbigstraße
Architect: Hans C. Müller with Georg Heinrichs, Ludwig Leo, Daniel Gogel
Project manager: Walter Hötzel
Garden planning: Hermann Mattern

Grouped around the clubhouse from 1950, the apartment houses of the first building phase, each intended for 60 students, are built in a park landscape. At the same time, the floor plan expressively developed around the three-cornered stairwell accentuates the character of each house. Outwardly, the windows of the one-, two-, and three-bed dormitory rooms, and of the maisonnette apartments, form a powerful ornamentation together with the intensely colored plaster facing. Similar to the Mommsen-Stadion **(372)**, other building parts are lined with yellow brick. Later, to satisfy the need for space-making building parts, the facility was consolidated by creating rows of houses which use the same "room type" as before.

371

Building part by Bruno Taut

Building part by Max Taut and Franz Hoffmann

Siedlung Eichkamp
1926/27
Waldschulallee, Lärchenweg, Am Vogelherd
Architect: Bruno Taut
1924/1927/28
Lärchenweg, Buchenweg, Zikadenweg
Architects: Max Taut, Franz Hoffmann
Client: Gehag

After World War I, a small-scale housing colony was conceived for Eichkatzweg (1918/19). Built in the south of the Westend area, it stood close to the car-race course known as the Avus (1921) and featured single-family houses grouped around a village green. It was designed by the brother Bruno Taut. From 1927/28, the colony was expanded with more single-family houses, as well as with duplexes and row houses which preserved the colony's rural character by Max Taut.

372

North-facing staircase tower

Mommsen-Stadion
1930
Eichkamp, Waldschulallee 42–43
Architect: Fred Forbat

A flat-roofed grandstand made of steel stands above a massive, 3-storey foundation which accommodates changing rooms, administrative areas, gymnastics arena, and a restaurant. The grandstand is extended by two, outward spiraling flights of stairs, and the side of the building with the entrance is interrupted by two glazed structures which house staircases

373

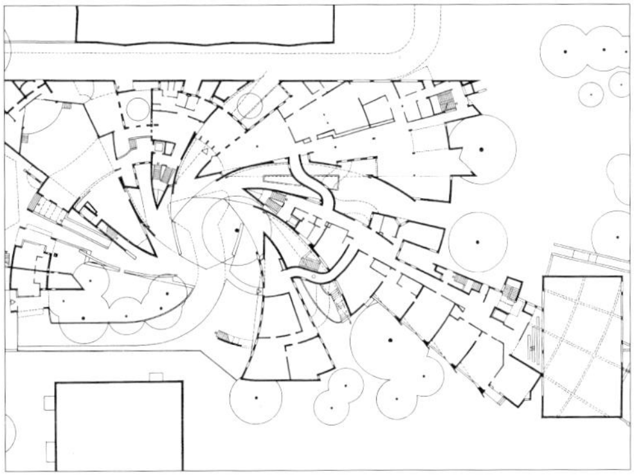

Site plan

Heinz-Galinski-Schule
1992–95
Eichkamp, Waldschulallee 73–75
Architect: Zvi Hecker with Inken Baller, Gerhard Pichler
Client: Jüdische Gemeinde zu Berlin

The elementary school built for children of Jewish families living in West Berlin at the edge of the Grunewald district, near Mommsen-Stadion **(372)**, was quickly accepted by the general public: "The school is designed in the form of a flower, as a gift to Berlin's children. This cosmic 'sunflower form' seemed the ideal structural metaphor for the school. Its blossoms turn to face the sun, and rays of light illuminate all the classrooms."

374

Unité d'habitation "Typ Berlin"
1957/58
Westend, Heilsberger Dreieck
Architect: Le Corbusier

Presented on the occasion of the 1957 International Building Exhibition, this construction represents the third example of the "unité d'habitation" concept already used in Marseilles and Nantes, but now adapted to the conditions and needs of Berlin's citizens. It has a fort-like presence in the surrounding rooftop landscape and profits from it's multi-colored loggia. As a clearance factor between the ceiling and floor, modifying the scale of ratios was achieved here by enlarging the spatial width to 4,00 m and raising its height to 2,50 m. Because of the building's exceptional location, well-situated in the Westend area, the apartments could be converted into owner-occupied flats. Altogether nine "inner-streets" provide access to 527 apartments which offer 1-, 2-, and 3-room living spaces.

375

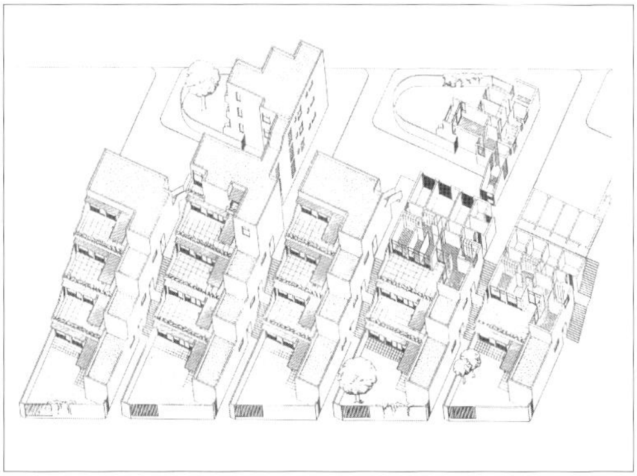

Isometric drawing

Stepped hillside houses on Teufelsberg
1969–72
Westend, Kranzallee, Grethe-Weisser-Weg
Architects: Jan Rave, Rolf Rave with Hans Joachim Knöfel
Garden design: Elisabeth Kutschera
Client: Degewo

A 6-m high elevation justified using a terrace construction method here, the same method used only in mountainous countries until then. This produced alternating larger and smaller rows, so that small courtyard developments emerged on the streets: open spaces for communication. Originally planned to comply with subsidized and socially-oriented housing construction measures, the individual apartments are stepped and twisted away from each other that no inhabitant can view the generously proportioned terraces toward which all the rooms orient themselves: open spaces for contemplation – with a view of "Teufelsberg" (devil's peak), a hill made of Berlin's debris from the air raids.

376

View of "condolence hall" courtyard

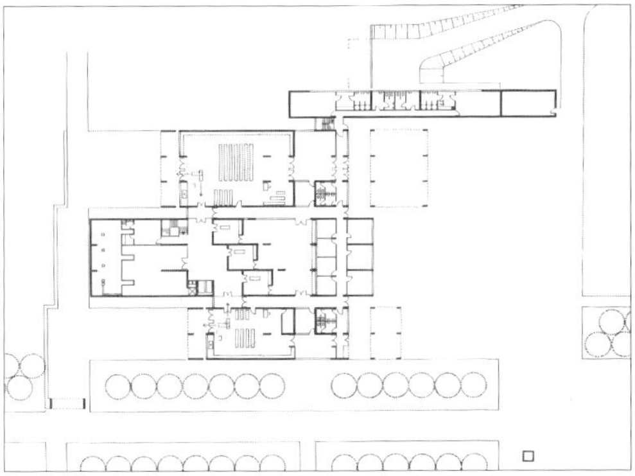

Plan of the main floor

Krematorium Ruhleben
1972–75
Charlottenburg, Am Hain
Architects: Jan Rave, Rolf Rave
Murals: Markus Lüpertz
Client: Bezirksamt Charlottenburg

The way in which this prize-winning structure from a 1962 competition is subdivided respects both the memorial service's order of events and the building's in-house services. It offers large and small halls with anterooms and "condolence" areas, between which lie in-house administration zones with elevators. Attempted here was to instill our cult of the dead with a hint of innovation by avoiding the sinking down of the coffin during the service, and placing the viewing rooms in an inner courtyard. The construction is made of exposed, prefab-blocks, so-called B2-blocks from Holland. Additional details include beams and ceilings made of fair-faced concrete, wooden windows, and copper roofing.

377

Multipurpose hall

Horst-Korber-Sportzentrum
1987–90
Westend, Glockenturmstraße 3
Architect: Christoph Langhof with Thomas Hänni, Herbert Meerstein
Client: Landessportbund Berlin
Architekturpreis Berlin 1992

The multipurpose, sports hall measuring 88 x 40 sqm can be divided twice and slides directly into the slope. Its interior is lit by more than 420 skylights installed on all sides of the ceiling's vaulted shell, which hangs on eight pylons, each of which has five "fingers" anchored to cables outside of the hall. Located just beyond the access ramp is a small building for service facilities and overnight accommodations.

Olympic stadium, 1936

Stadium for swimming events, 1936

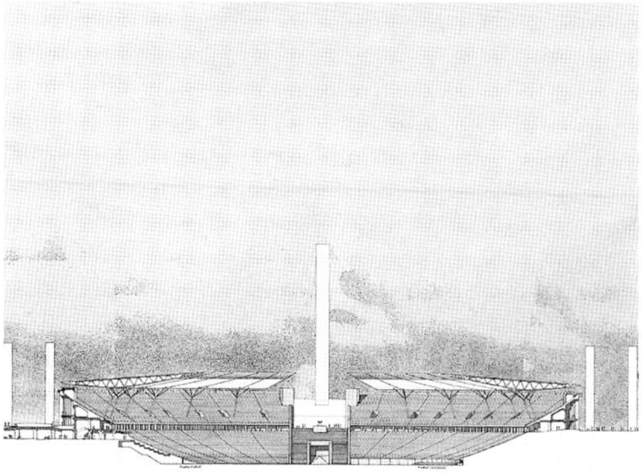

Olympic stadium
1934–36, 2000–04
Westend, Olympischer Platz / Reichssportfeldstraße
Architect: Werner March
Overhead roofing and modernization: von Gerkan, Marg und Partner
Engineers: Schlaich, Bergermann und Partner, Krebs und Kiefer

The central part of the facility is the elliptical stadium offering the original seating capacity for 85,000 guests, as well as standing room spaces for 35,000 spectators. Viewed in cross section the outward opening, stepped seating levels create a parabolic form. The first balcony is made of 40 stepped levels and lies 12 m below the entrance level, so that spectators can enter the stadium at half its height through 16 openings from an encircling pillared hall. In this pillared hall are stairways to the upper balcony level, which provides 31 stepped levels and rises to a height of 16,50 m. Originally, a tripod or three-legged pedestal for the Olympic flame stood at the west-facing side of the marathon gate. Protected by historic preservation laws, the stadium was meant to remain essentially unchanged, yet adapted to meet with present-day standards. Paramount here was the building of a large, continuous roofing which today shelters 76,000 spectators. Using a minimized, slip-on support construction it was possible to make the roofing and high pillars of the ambulatory seem to levitate over the massive stadium. In the diagonal axis of the sports arena, the stadium for swimming events connects to the north with a 20 x 20 m pool for diving events, and another pool measuring 20 x 50 m for relays. At the longer sides of the same area are grandstands for 7,000 spectators.

379

Domed hall

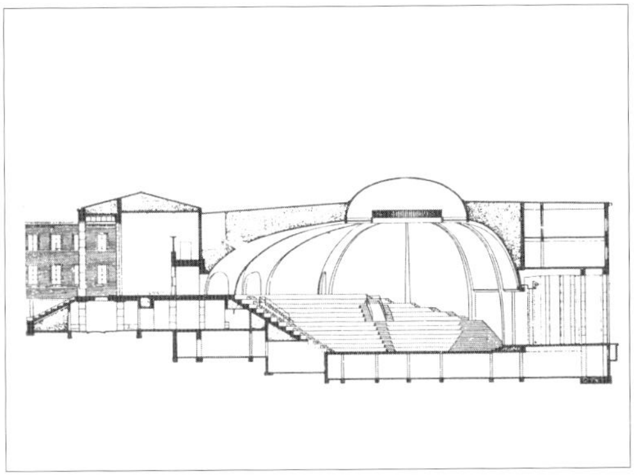

Deutsches Sportforum
1926–28/1934–36
Charlottenburg, Rominter Allee
Architect: Werner March

This first-prize winner in a limited 1925 competition process involved a gymnastics area, a swimming-pool facility, and a student housing complex. In the 1930s, the building added to the ensemble the hall of honor, as well as the lecture and presentation rooms for 1,200 guests underneath an elliptical, ribbed dome made of exposed concrete. Severely damaged during the war, the building was rebuilt by the British military, which then set up its headquarters here.

380

Former stage

Former VIP platform

The "Waldbühne" open-air theater
1934–36
Charlottenburg, Am Glockenturm
Architect: Werner March

Located at the northwest edge of the stadium district, the open-air theater takes full advantage of the slope of a circa 30-m deep ravine on its property, and offers here 88 stepped seating levels for 20,000 spectators: three, large seating areas divided by aisles. Directed at the greenery of the slope, the expansive view over the orchestra, stage platform, and cubical building housing the stage's technical facilities recalls the atmosphere of antique theaters. Today the modernized facilities serve the Pop scene for the most part, often reverberating late into the night.

Großsiedlung Siemensstadt / Paul-Hertz-Siedlung

Großsiedlung Siemensstadt
Nord-Charlottenburg
Paul-Hertz-Siedlung

To the west, the so-called Ring Colony is composed of the Siemensstadt housing colony by Hans Hertlein and the planning for Siemensstadt by Hans Scharoun and Martin Wagner. To the east it includes "Nord-Charlottenburg" and Scharoun's so-called apartment courtyards, and the Paul-Hertz-Siedlung developed by Wils Ebert east of the Kurt-Schumacher-Damm thoroughfare. Viewed from today's perspective, the most dynamic impulses to be witnessed in the development of Berlin's colony constructions are made especially clear in the buildings presented here, which date from 1929 to 1931 and are meanwhile regarded as Modern classics. The Paul-Hertz-Siedlung is an expansation after World War II in the 1950s, east of Kurt-Schumacher-Damm in the 1960s.

Key

1 Hans Hertlein
2 Hans Maurer
3 Hans Scharoun (381)
4/5 Otto Bartning (382)
6 Walter Gropius (383)
7 Hugo Häring (385)
8 Fred Forbat (386)
9 Paul Rudolf Henning
10/12 Hans Scharoun (384)
11 Hans Hoffmann
13 Werner Weber
14 Wils Ebert

381

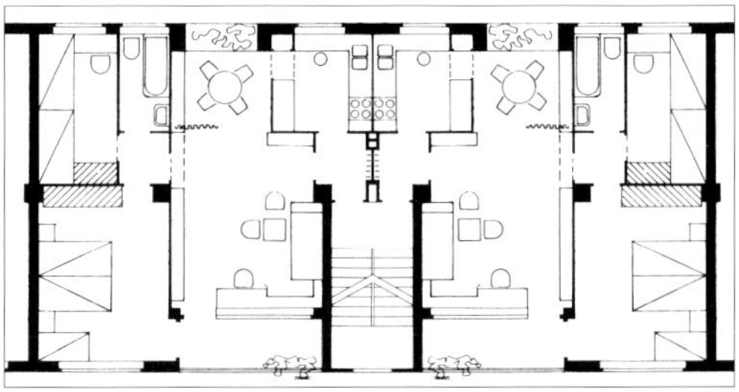

Großsiedlung Siemensstadt
1929–31
Siemensstadt, Jungfernheideweg, Mäckeritzstraße
Architect: Hans Scharoun

Together with the building facing it, the apartment building is composed in a way to form a funnel-like gate to the old Siemensstadt colony which leads to the "Ring" colony featuring buildings by Gropius, Häring, Bartning, Forbat, and Henning. The smooth, white building surfaces and swung balconies soon gave it the nickname "Panzerkreuzer B" (battleship B). What still has an interesting, incentive-giving effect even today are all the efforts made to have the tenants' daily activities (working, cooking, eating, and communicating) exist in a sensible relationship to the space.

382

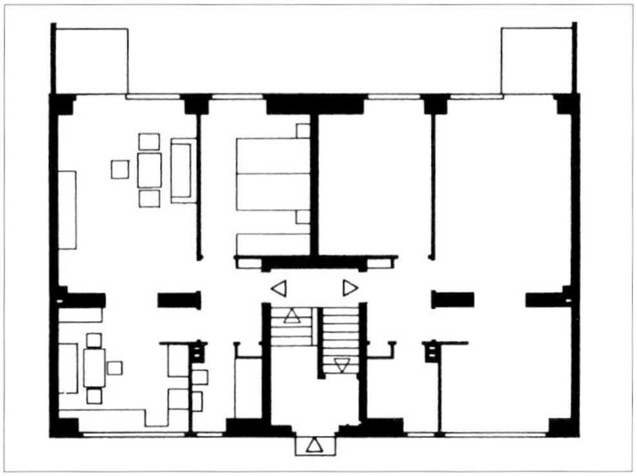

Großsiedlung Siemensstadt
1929–31
Siemensstadt, Goebelstraße
Architect: Otto Bartning
Client: Gemeinnützige Baugesellschaft Berlin-Heerstraße m.b.H.

This long row of apartments formes the edge of the colony to the south, in the direction of the S-Bahn railway line. While its concave curvature extends from Goebelstraße without being interrupted by a single building element, the balconies protrude to the south. The construction offers only small apartments because the building principle concerns purely north–south types: two rooms, bathroom, and eat-in kitchen accessed from a hallway, with the living room and kitchen connected by a generously proportioned doorway opening leading to a living area which altogether profits from being located on the south side of the building. Its nickname "Langer Jammer" means "long desaster".

383

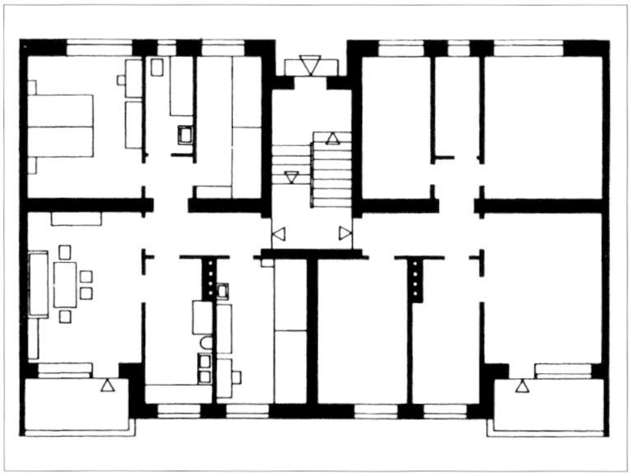

Plan of a $3\,^1\!/_2$-room apartment

Großsiedlung Siemensstadt
1929–31
Siemensstadt, Jungfernheideweg, Goebelstraße
Architect: Walter Gropius

This part of the colony involves north–south rows and a balcony access block with 2-, $2\,^1\!/_2$-, and $3\,^1\!/_2$-room apartments. In a 1930 issue of *Bauwelt* magazine, Gropius states: "With both construction types, the layout of the floor plan is conceived in a way that makes every space accessible from the hallway. Given the diverse needs of apartment seekers, I see this changeable floor as being the most applicable here." Here this could also mean that the areas for living and sleeping are interchangeable.

384

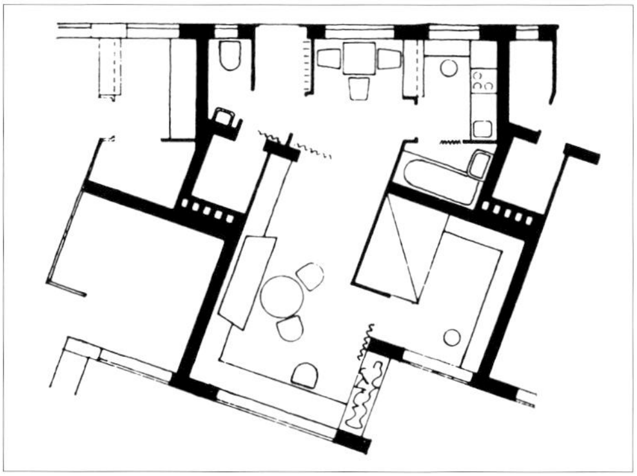

Plan of a 1-room apartment

Addition to the Bartning building
1957
Siemensstadt, Goebelstraße 1–9
Architect: Hans Scharoun

The expansion of the "Langer Jammer" structure by Bartning and as its head this building leads directly into the district from the 1950s, featuring a 4-storey balcony access block with a saw-bladed floor plan. Around the same time, on Heilmannweg, Scharoun conceived so-called housing courts, which developed a courtyard using two rows whose variety of residential forms produced an apartment community here. Most striking is how the design turns towards a strong sense of anthroposophy, as well as the expressively segmented building form which effectively reappears in Scharoun's cultural buildings at Kemperplatz **(207 to 210)**.

385

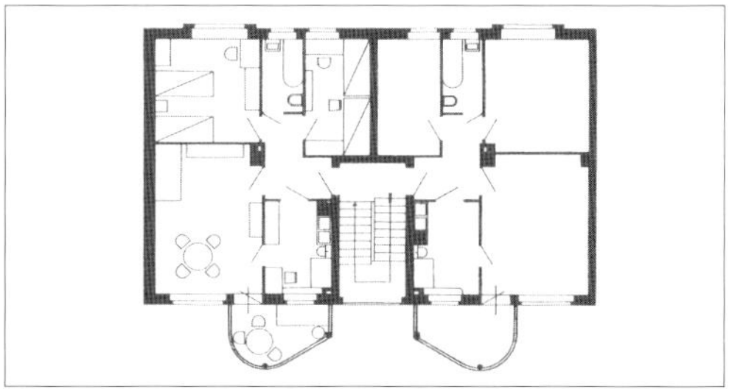

Partial plan of the 1st and the 2nd floors

Großsiedlung Siemensstadt
1929–31
Siemensstadt, Goebelstraße
Architect: Hugo Häring

Erected here were nine approximately 80-m long rows. While one row houses 2-room apartments, the other eight house 2 1/2-room apartments. The apartments have round balconies, which, under ideal spatial conditions, cast few shadows. Like the other building parts, this 5-storey unit, constructed using the simplest of means, contains storage, laundry, kitchen, and dry-room areas. In this way, intricate cellar spaces could be avoided. The façade's visually pleasing yellow brickwork and the parapets of the balconies in particular create a friendlier living atmosphere.

386

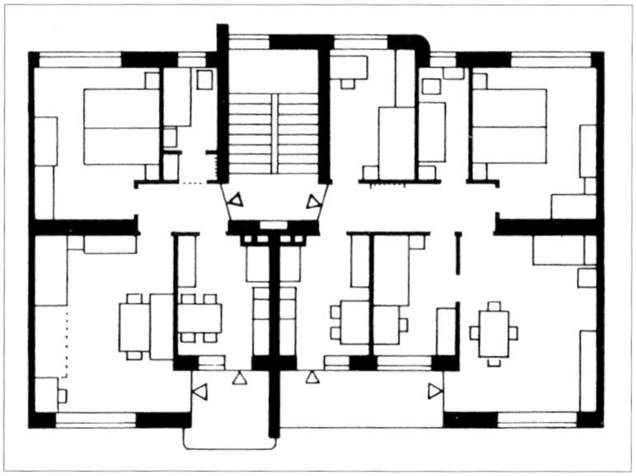

Plan of a 2- and 2 1/2-room apartment

Großsiedlung Siemensstadt
1929–31
Siemensstadt, Geißlerpfad, Goebelplatz
Architect: Fred Forbat

Like the neighboring buildings by Henning (which formerly connected in the south, with four storeys, to buildings by Häring), both rows erected in the north, in 1931, are 3-storey constructions. In the case of the northern row's 2 1/2-room apartments, the shifting of the kitchen beside the bathroom and the ordering of a dining area produce a variation possibility in an apartment the same size as the others. Equally distinctive here is the attic floor built as a full storey.

387

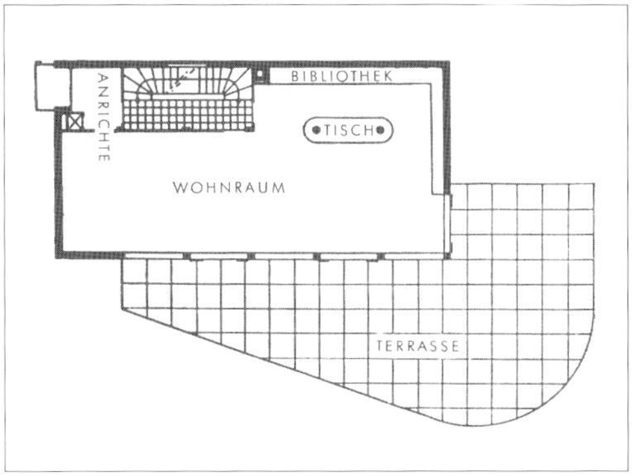

Plan of the living floor

Two villas (1)
1928
Charlottenburg, Heerstraße 55
Architects: Wassili and Hans Luckhardt, Alfons Anker

Of three planned houses, only two were carried out to their completion: a pair of buildings erected as steel-framed constructions. That they have identical architectural elements makes it less surprising than that their interior compositions are so alike: the collected service areas are located in the base floor beneath a large terrace. The living room occupies the entire main

388

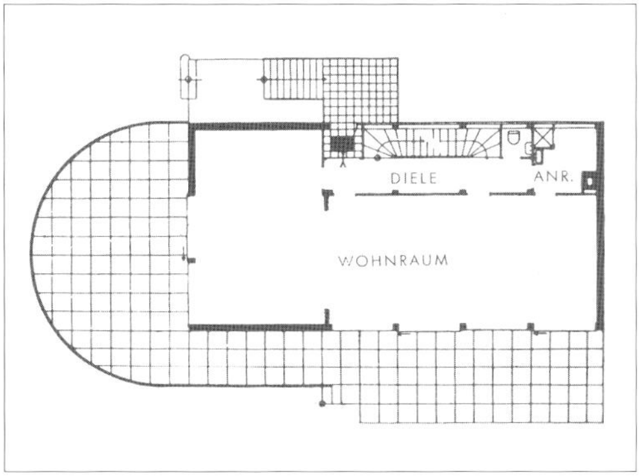

Plan of the living floor

Two villas (2)
1928
Charlottenburg, Am Rupenhorn 24
Architects: Wassili and Hans Luckhardt, Alfons Anker

floor, above which are the bedrooms. Other architectural details which link the two houses are their protruding terraces in the vicinity of the living quarters, and the roof terraces signaled by encircling ring beams. The duplicity of both houses strengthens every aspect, including the prototypical aspect. After the perfect renovation the houses are in a good condition.

389

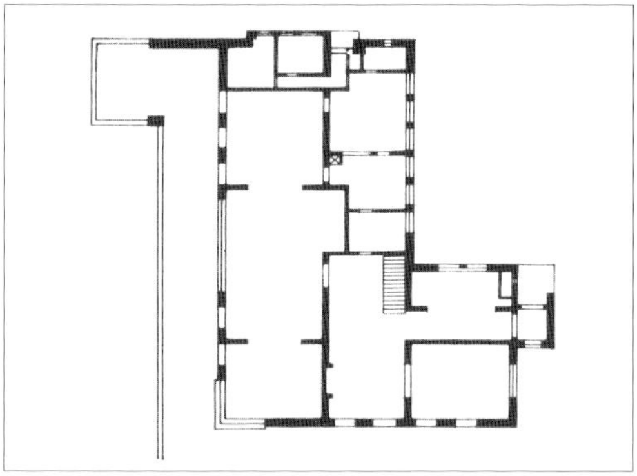

Plan of the ground floor

Haus Lindemann
1929
Charlottenburg, Am Rupenhorn 5
Architect: Bruno Paul

The floor plan shows the original condition of the house: a 2-storey, flat-roofed, brick construction. Arranged side by side on the ground floor are three living spaces with a view over a steep slope that faces the lake. The bedrooms are on the upper floors. In 1935, Ernst Sagebiel carried out a minimum of remodeling measures on the house, and the newly built chauffeur's apartment appeared in 1937. Since World War II, the house accommodated an institute dedicated to youth groups. Later it was used for educational purposes.

390

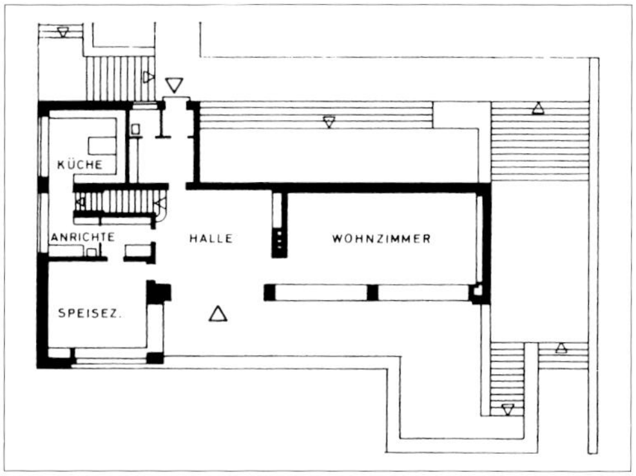

Plan of the ground floor

The architect's private residence
1929
Charlottenburg, Am Rupenhorn 6
Architect: Erich Mendelsohn

Erected at a charmingly rural spot in the Grunewald, the building stands high over the Havel River. All the living spaces face west and enjoy a view of the Havel landscape, while the bedrooms on the upper floor face east. The large ground-floor area was formerly a music room, and the spacious terrace in front of it used for staging small-scale theater and dance productions. "Gesundheit – Schönheit – Komfort" (health, beauty, comfort) was once the motto for an affluent social sector abreast with the zeitgeist of their time. This sector would altogether vanish after 1933 and fail to regain its former popularity up to the present day. In 1937, the house experienced a change of ownership.

391

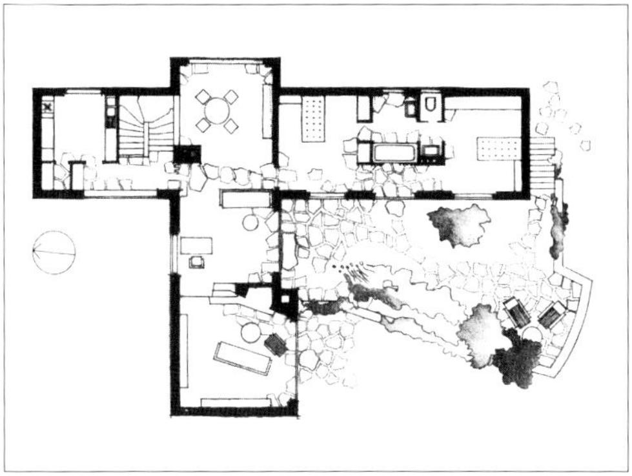

Haus Dr. Steingroever
1937
Charlottenburg, Stallupöner Allee 37
Architect: Egon Eiermann

The inherent liveliness of the property produces the strong connection to the garden on both storeys of the house. The entrance and garage are located on the lower storey, and access to the spacious apartment terrace is on the upper storey. Here too, not unlike in other houses by Eiermann, three wings develop from a centralized entrance and contain service, living, and sleeping functions, and the garden is divided into different functional areas.

392

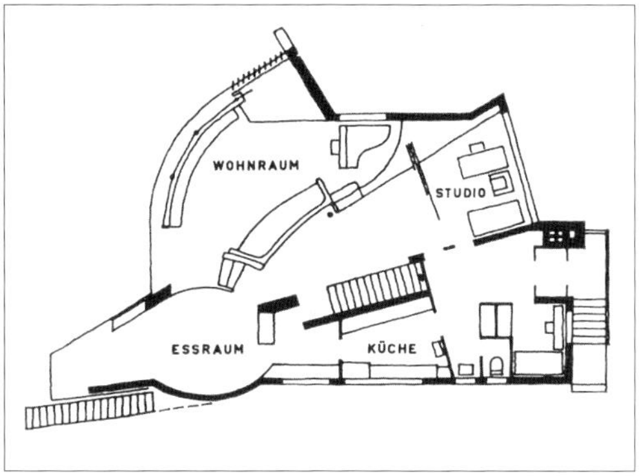

Plan of the ground floor

Haus Dr. Felix Baensch
1934/35
Gatow, Weinmeistershöhe, Höhenweg 19
Architect: Hans Scharoun
Garden design: Hermann Mattern, Karl Förster

The "residence" is a 2-storey, tubular steel-scaffolding construction. Its walls are made of partially plastered, partially clad hollow brick. The silhouette of the reddish-brown main cornice creates the corresponding liveliness to the ground-floor plan and stepped levels of the living spaces, which differentiate between one another as well as flow together. After the year 1933, however, many of those architects suffering under the developing pressures of the National Socialists' regime slowly looked towards only the single-family house.

393

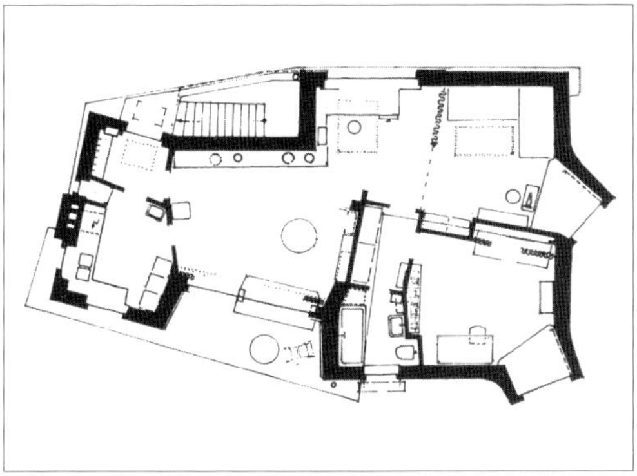

The architect's private residence
1960
Kladow, Kurpromenade 6
Architect: Sergius Ruegenberg

The open form of the house develops from both the sensible orientation of the living and sleeping areas and a turning away from the street. The financial expenditure involved with the building of the construction equaled the usual means employed by colony associations erecting single-family row houses. This was also the central theme of the house's program.

394

The DLRG Berlin headquarters (Siegfried-John-Haus)
1969–71
Spandau, Am Pichelsee 20–21
Architect: Ludwig Leo
Inclined elevator: Fa. Oskar Fritz
Client: Deutsche Lebens-Rettungs-Gesellschaft

From the *Bauwelt* magazine, 37/1972: "Not since the end of the 1920s has Berlin's Havel area witnessed so convincing an architectural undertaking, such a harmony of form and function." Ten levels house 80 boats in a construction which also provides workshops, training rooms, rescue center, and sleeping areas. The mast located at the top of the 30-m high building is both an antenna and outrigger. Typical of Leo is the fundamental questioning of every conventional form, which led to drawing the boats directly out of the water with an inclined elevator and giving the building a triangular form which escalates to the radio tower.

395

Platform area

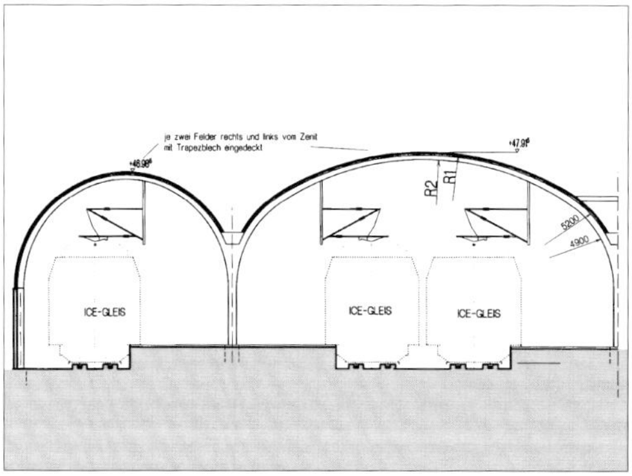

Cross section of two of three sections

Spandau train station
1996–98
Spandau, Klosterstraße at the corner of Seegefelder Straße
Architects: von Gerkan, Marg und Partner with Hubert Nienhoff
Client: DB Immobilien

The 3rd-prize winner of a 1993 competition: with its three 430 m long vaulted sections, parallel to one another but slightly curved lengthwise, and built as a steel and glass construction, the platform area for the suburban railway (S-Bahn) and long-distance lines is roofed-over using the typographic principle common to historical train stations. The load-bearing system uses longitudinal girders supported in a grid of 18,0 m. The entrance hall and loading areas are on the street level.

396

Ward block

Entrance hall

Krankenhaus Spandau
Spandau hospital
1996–99
Spandau-Neustadt, Neue Bergstraße 6
Architects: Heinle, Wischer und Partner; responsible partner: Till Behnke

"The new building of the Spandau hospital, a ward and treatment block, follows the historical development concept of both the garrison infirmary built in 1881, and of the municipal hospital built in 1895. On the one hand, structures are arranged along the streets which surround the block; on the other, the design of the block's interior space is kept free of construction measures and creates a rural setting."

397

Nauener Zeile
Nauen residential row
1994/95
Spandau, Nauener Straße at the corner of Seegefelder Straße
Architects: Wolfgang Scharlach, Rainer Wischhusen
Client: WIR Wohnungsbau

"A block development in heterogeneous surroundings: three constructions come together to create a single large form – a 'sign', with integrated trees as part of the 'window to the courtyard'. At the side facing the street, the row has a membranous brick skin. The plastered courtyard façades are both subdivided and 'individualized' by projected areas. The residential row offers 1- to 6-room apartments (maisonnettes)."

398

Residential blocks
1926
Spandau, Zeppelinstraße and Falkenseeer Chaussee
Architect: Richard Ermisch
Client: Adolf Steil

While sustaining a position second to Ludwig Hoffmann, Martin Wagner, Hans Scharoun, and Karl Bonatz **(113, 311, 364)**, Richard Ermisch influenced and formed the course of Berlin's architectural history for some thirty years (1921–55). Like in all of his early works, here too, one clearly recognizes how the influence of Cubism and the Art Nouveau develops to an impressive form, but also how a rare and unforgettable, overall urban planning concept develops from the structural repetition of four similar corner towers. The shops are arranged along the well-considered space of the intersection. Otherwise, the blocks' greatly subdivided and sensitively-detailed rows accommodate 500 exclusively small-scaled apartments.

399

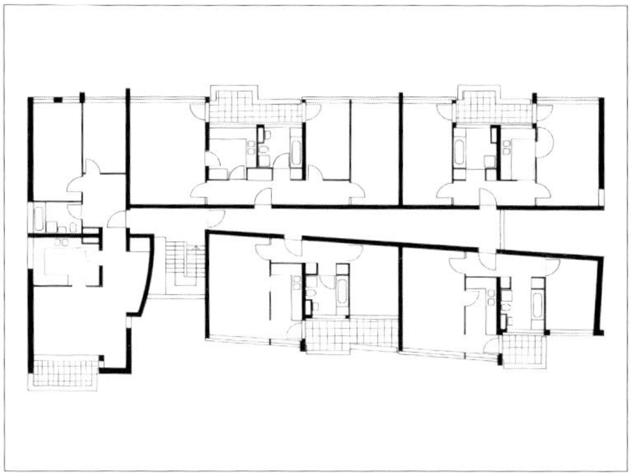

Plan of a standard floor

Apartment building
1993/94
Spandau, Siegener Straße
Architects: Georg Eyl, Werner Weitz, Joachim Würmle
Project partner: J. M. Abcarius
Exterior facilities: Regina Poly
Client: WIR

In a carefree and well-proportioned manner, the staircase, middle wing, apartments, and 4 maisonnettes on both upper floors express a lively and suburban architecture. In addition, the blue-colored shear wall subdividing the building's side and main wings pulls one's gaze deeper into the double loggia at the upper end of the stairwell.

400

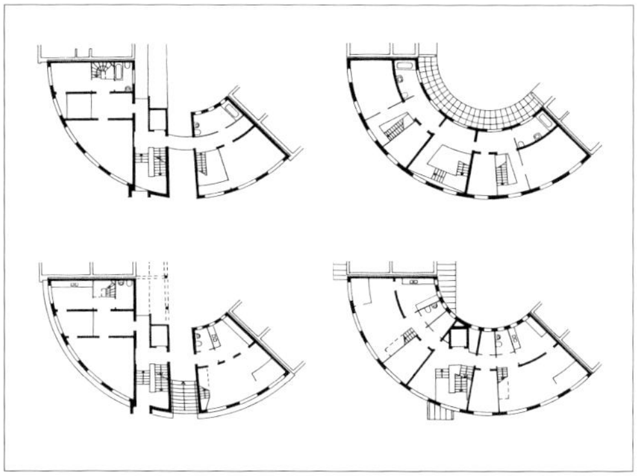

Floor plans of the ground, the 1st, the 4th and the 5th floors

Apartment building
1987/88
Spandau, Streitstraße at the corner of Goltzstraße
Architects: Georg Eyl, Werner Weitz, Joachim Würmle
Client: Immobilien Braun

Curved around the apex corner of both streets, five buildings avoid forming a humdrum circle by having a series of architectural elements perforate and enter the geometry of their long building sides. 4- and 8-storey building parts are inserted one in the other, and a lighthearted composition mixes a sense of order and game-playing as done in the Haus Wieland at the corner of Niebuhrstraße, built around the same time.

401

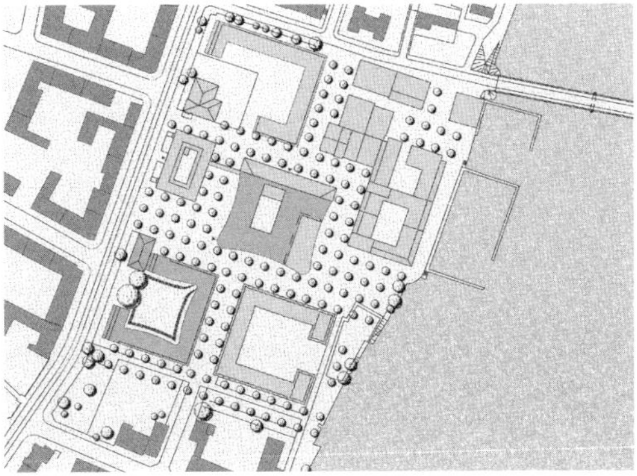

Site plan

Schultheiß-Quartier
1997–99
Wasserstadt Spandau, Neuendorfer Straße
Architect: Benedict Tonon
Client: BBV – Grundstücksgesellschaft

Like elsewhere, a brewery location is abandoned for rationalizing purposes, with attempts made to reutilize its parts in order to complete the area with residential usage. This includes the development of a courtyard around a pair of 500-year old trees. Surfaced with red brick and white floor-bands, the rising walls give a special meaning to corners, and to additional block forms producing here attractive walkways, city squares, and a waterside promenade reaching as far as the Eiswerderbrücke.

402

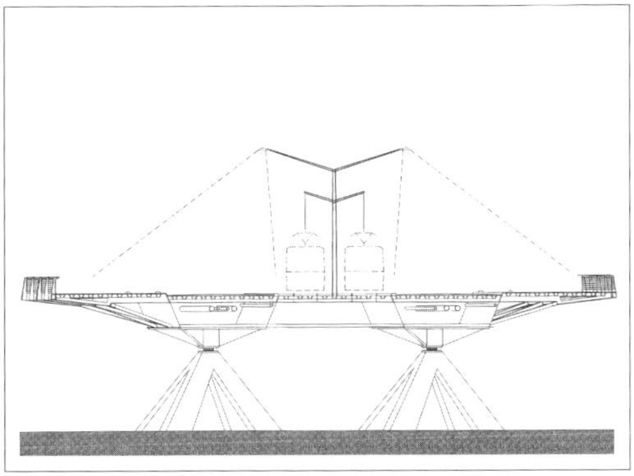

Cross section

Wasserstadtbrücke
1998–2000
Spandau, Rauchstraße, Daumstraße
Architects: Joachim Dörr, Axel Ludolf, Josef Wimmer
Structural engineer: Herbert Fink
Client: Land Berlin

The 300-m long northern bridge, wide enough for streetcar tracks and costing circa 28 million Euro, was constructed as the second connection for both halves of the "Wasserstadt" area. Since the conventional, lateral piers were designed as concrete bucks with pointed, load-bearing tops, people using the waterside routes are given the impression that the bridge is extremely light.

403

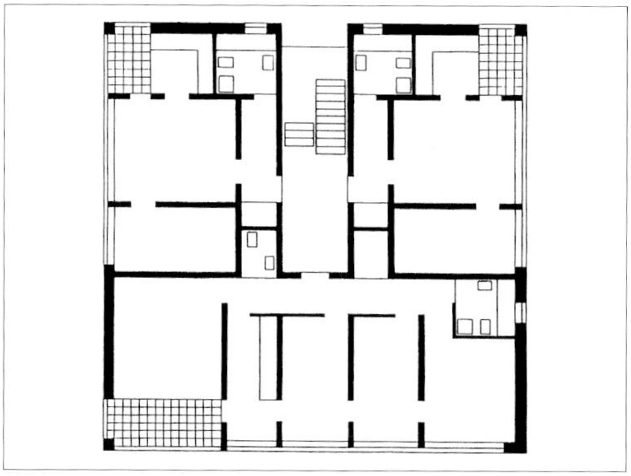

Plan of a standard floor

House for several families
1995–97
Wasserstadt Spandau, Quartier Pulvermühle, Olga-Tschechowa-Straße 18
Architect: Carola Schäfers
Client: GSW

The northern sector of the apartment colony area, known as the "Pulvermühle" (gunpowder factory), was reserved for this multi-floored, detached house for several families – a construction type lovingly referred to as "city villa" in the 1970s and 1980s. With the vanishing of the name, the pathos vanished as well, taking with it the axially aligned symmetry of the entranceway – even though it appears in this floor plan. Measuring 16 x 16 x 16 m, the 5-storey cube follows the guidelines of an urban planning concept by architects Gernot and Johanne Nalbach, whose plan has "... the flexibility best known from old-style apartments".

404

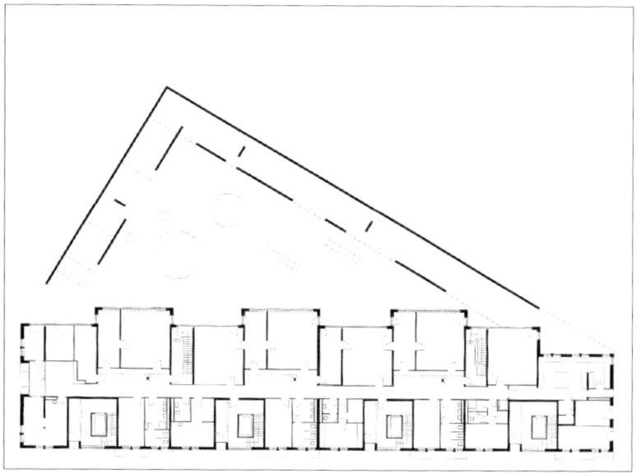

Plan of the ground floor

Apartment building and childcare center
1995–99
Wasserstadt Spandau, Quartier Pulvermühle, Goldbeckweg 1
Architect: Benedict Tonon
Client: GSW

"In this case, the design concept involves a 7-storey apartment building with an integrated childcare center and multipurpose facility. The project is part of an overall urban-planning concept. But while a large portion of the planned building refers to an orthogonal system, the askew positioning and unique location give it a character more like that of a solitary structure."

405

Promenade view

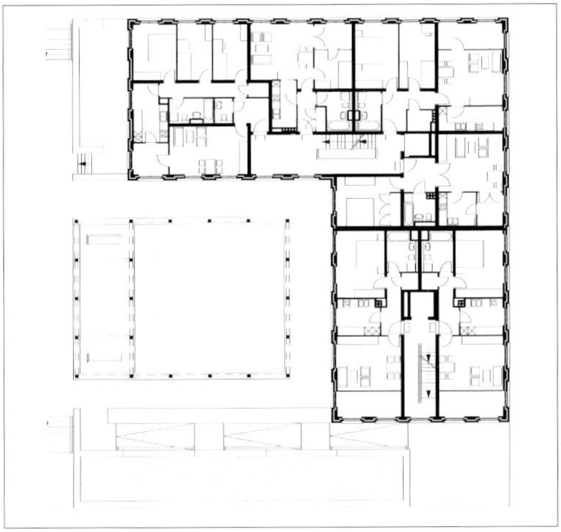

Plan of a standard floor

Apartment and commercial buildings
1996–98
Wasserstadt Spandau, Quartier Pulvermühle, Romy-Schneider-Straße 9–11
Architect: Bernd Albers
Client: GSW

Facing the water, two corner constructions develop the terrace courtyard by offering stores at this level. The window types develop their themes on both sides – one arrangement is city-related, the other landscape-related. Diagonally opposite, at No. 4–6, is another courtyard-producing corner construction type by the same architect.

406

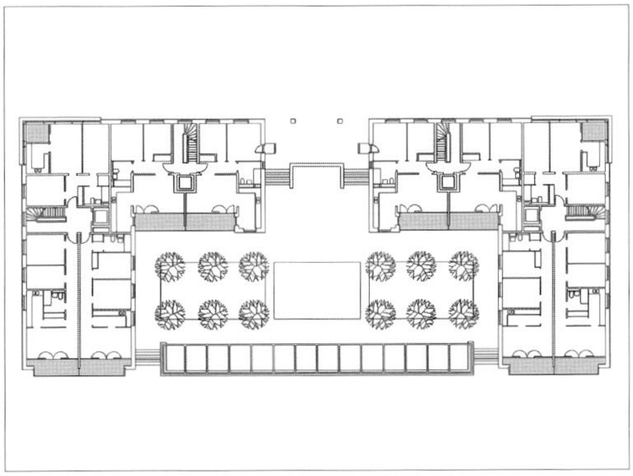

Plan of the ground floor

Wohnen am Spandauer See
Living at Spandauer See
1998
Wasserstadt Spandau, Quartier Pulvermühle, Romy-Schneider-Straße 1–7
Architects: Ingrid Hentschel, Axel Oestreich
Client: GSW

The urban planning concept develops the theme of an orientation towards the water. The approach is effectively completed by the courtyard orientation, raised parterre with pergola, large-scale solariums, and apartment orientation. Each building has four large apartments oriented directly towards the water, the Havel River, and a smaller one indirectly oriented.

407

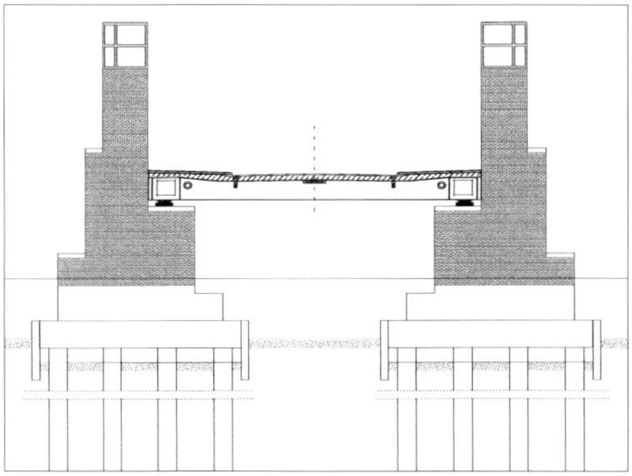

Cross section

Spandauer-See-Brücke
1996–98
Spandau, Rhenania-Straße
Architect: Walter A. Noebel
Structural engineers: Leonhardt, Andrä und Partner; Schmitt, Frühauf und Partner
Client: Land Berlin

The result of a 1994 competition: the elegantly arched bridge, supported by powerful pairs of brick piers (four of each on both sides of its vertex), represents a "spatial thickening". The piers form small outlooks, and the basis for large, glazed light cubes with metal frames like lanterns. In addition, a small viewing terrace appears at the east side.

408

Courtyard view

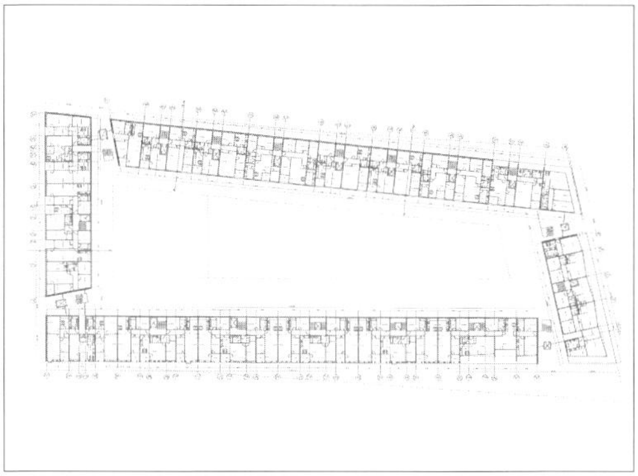

Site plan

Apartment and commercial buildings
1995–97
Wasserstadt Spandau, Havelspitz, Hugo-Cassirer-Straße
Architects: Kees Christiaanse, Peter Berner, Oliver Hall, Markus Neppl with Suter + Suter
Client: Bavaria

The residential quarter around Havel River, the northern part of the "Wasserstadt" project, consists mainly of large, skewed blocks of more or less opened courtyards ranging from 5 to 7 floors. The street spaces facing the Havel become considerably wider at this site, and the openings are arranged to avoid conventional and conflict-laden corners. Each building front is broken open and differently colored.

409

Aerial view – east

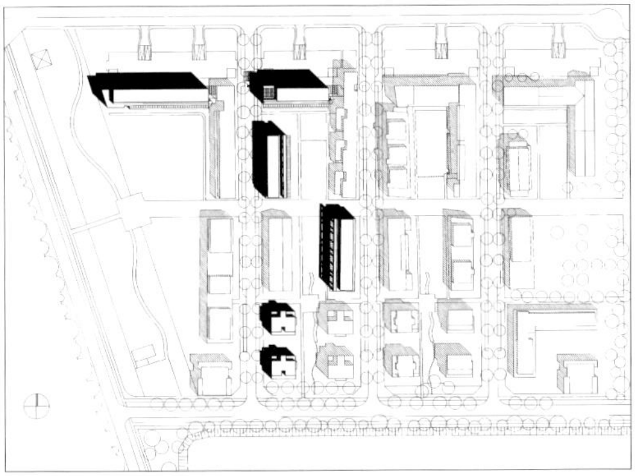

Site plan by Kramm + Strigl

Wasserstadt Aalemannufer
1996–98
Spandau-Hakenfelde, Niederneuendorfer Allee at the corner of Aalemannufer
Master plan: Kramm + Strigl
Client: Bauwert Immobilienverwertung

Located on a green field at a junction canal of the Havel riverbed, the small quarter was planned during a series of 1993 workshops, and the exalted living standard and uniformity are two of its remarkable features. Stipulated here was the building of only 4- to 5-storey white-stuccoed structures. This basic rule makes it easier to compare the individual designs of the various architects' offices: Chipperfield; Feige und Döring; Gregotti; Kramm + Strigl; Martin + Pächter; Nolte.

410

Square – east side

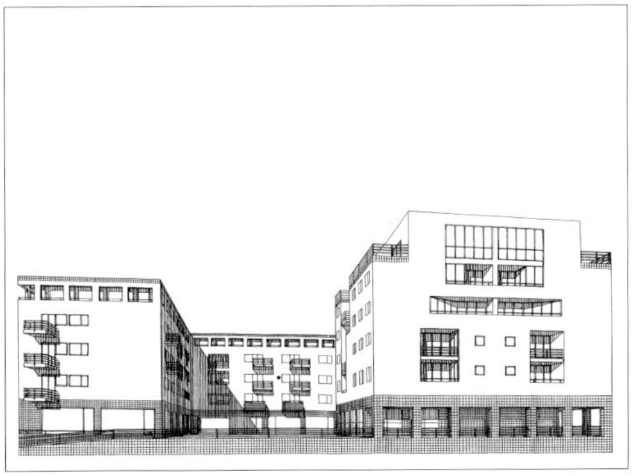

Apartment development
1998
Spandau-Hakenfelde, Aalemannkanalstraße
Architects: Vittorio Gregotti with Augusto Cagnardi, Pierluigi Cerri
Client: Bauwert Immobilienverwertung

In each case, two buildings develop at two locations close to one another on the canal – producing either a row through their linear arrangement, or a square by facing one another. To the south, towards the bank of the canal, appears the identical façade of an almost identical building part. The homogenous, white-plaster coats accentuate the structural vividness of 5- to 6-storey buildings with striking loggia, balconies, and terraces.

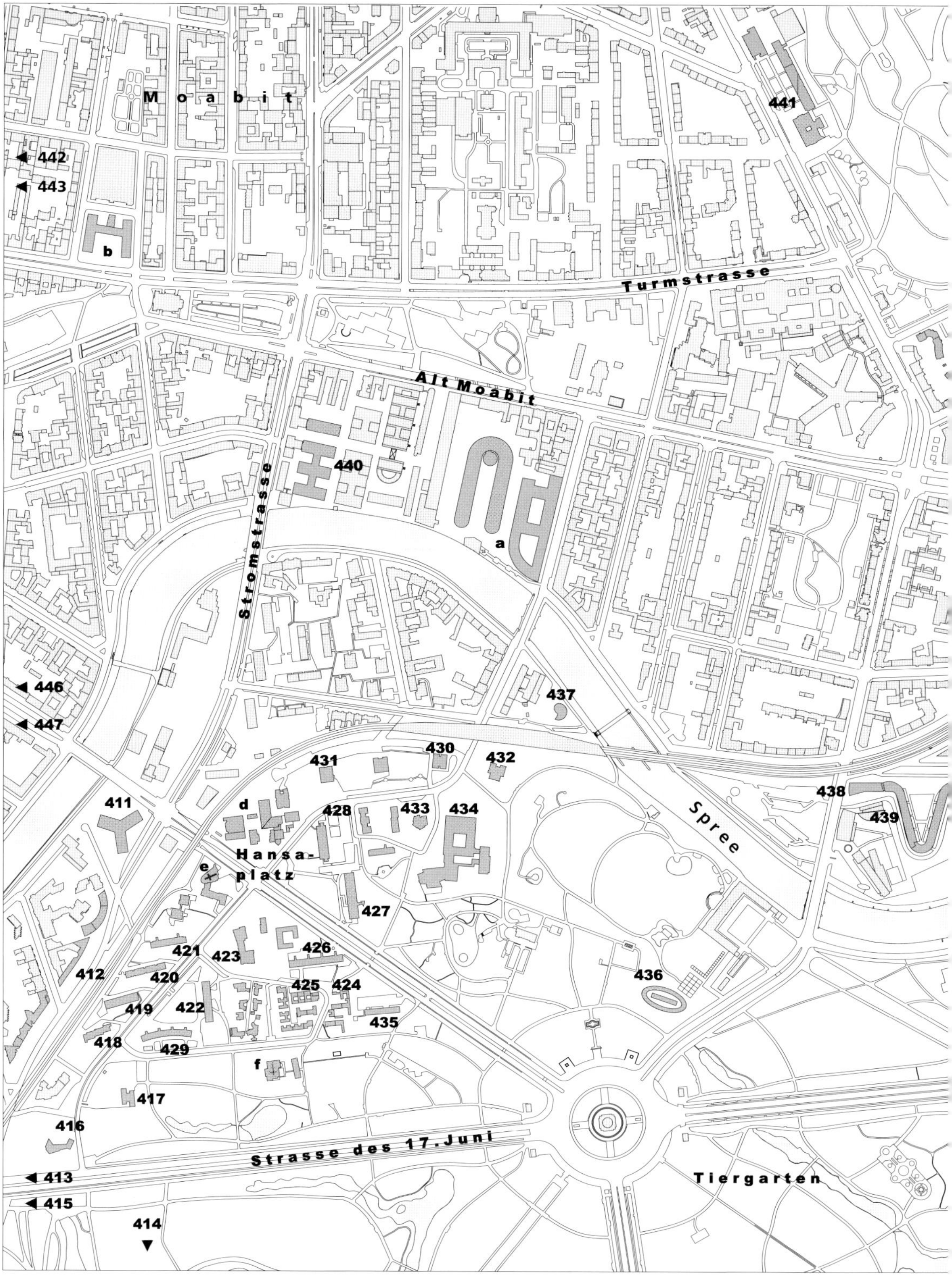
Moabit
Turmstrasse
Alt Moabit
Stromstrasse
Spree
Hansa-
platz
Strasse des 17. Juni
Tiergarten
a
b
d
e
f
411
412
413
414
415
416
417
418
419
420
421
422
423
424
425
426
427
428
429
430
431
432
433
434
435
436
437
438
439
440
441
442
443
446
447

Hansaplatz NW

411	Evangelisches Konsistorium	Georg Heinrichs
412	Apartment development	Hans C. Müller, Moritz Müller
413	Königliche Porzellan-Manufaktur Berlin	von Gerkan, Marg und Partner
414	Canal-circulation facility of TU Berlin	Ludwig Leo
415	Dorint Novotel	Laurids Ortner, Manfred Ortner
416	Berlin-Pavillon / Interbau	Hermann Fehling, Daniel Gogel, Peter Pfankuch
417	Interbau, object 1	Klaus Müller-Rehm, Gerhard Siegmann
418	Interbau, object 4	Hans C. Müller
419	Interbau, object 5	Günther Gottwald
420	Interbau, object 9	Luckhardt, Hoffmann
421	Interbau, object 10	Paul Schneider-Esleben
422	Interbau, object 8	Pierre Vago
423	Interbau, object 16	Alvar Aalto
424	Interbau, object 39	Eduard Ludwig
425	Interbau, object 40	Arne Jacobsen
426	Interbau, object 15	Fritz Jaenecke, Sten Samuelsen
427	Interbau, object 14	Oscar Niemeyer
428	Interbau, object 13	Egon Eiermann
429	Interbau, object 7	Walter Gropius, Wils Ebert
430	Interbau, object 21	J. H. van den Broek, J. B. Bakema
431	Interbau, object 20	Eugène Beaudoin, Raymond Lopez
432	Interbau, object 19	Hans Schwippert
433	Interbau, object 28	Otto H. Senn
434	Akademie der Künste	Werner Düttmann
435	Interbau, object 23	Paul G. R. Baumgarten
436	Bundespräsidialamt	Martin Gruber, Helmut Kleine-Kraneburg
437	Apartmenthaus "Schnecke"	Benedict Tonon
438	Kopfbau	Jörg Pampe
439	Spreeschlange	Georg Bumiller
440	Focus Teleport Berlin	Walter Rolfes, Joachim Ganz
441	Youth center	Gerd Neumann, Dietmar Grötzebach, Günter Plessow
446	Refuse-reloading station	Paul G. R. Baumgarten
447	Spree-Forum	Kleihues + Kleihues

a	Spree-Bogen	Kühn Bergander Bley, 1992–94
b	Rathaus Tiergarten	Richard Ermisch, 1935/36
c	Heinrich-Zille-Siedlung	Volker Theißen, 1979–82
d	Shopping center	Hansrudolf Plarre, 1956
e	St.-Ansgar-Kirche	Willy Kreuer, 1957–58
f	Kaiser-Friedrich-Gedächtniskirche	Ludwig Lemmer, 1957

411

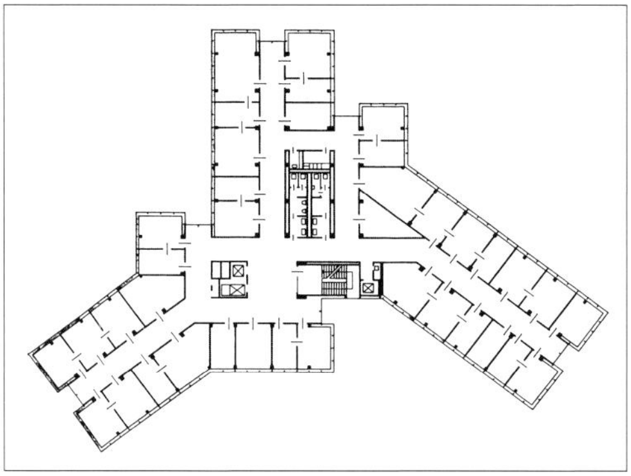

Plan of a standard floor

Former Evangelisches Konsistorium
1964–70
Tiergarten, Bachstraße
Architect: Georg Heinrichs
Project manager: Siegwart Geiger
Site management: Walter Hötzel
Client: Evangelische Kirche Berlin-Brandenburg

Elevated over a parking deck, this Y-shaped office building has three overlapping wings which frame a centralized development core. At the time of its construction, the flush, curtain wall façade made of aluminum, glass and neoprene was considered unusual and innovative. The basic principle of a façade module able to expand when necessary was based on the system first developed by Jean Prouvé, and its wide-ranging variability is continued within the building's easily subdividable floor plan. Despite its architectural significance, the building was threatened to be torn down.

412

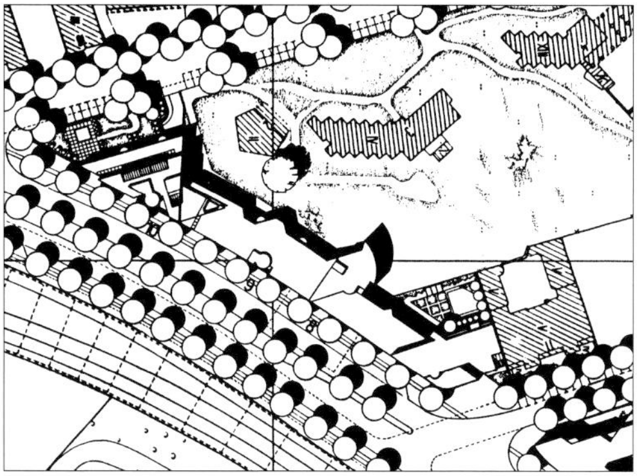

Site plan

Apartment development
1983–86
Tiergarten, Bachstraße at the corner of Siegmundshof
Architects: Hans C. Müller, Moritz Müller
Client: Buschmann

About his project, Hans C. Müller says: "Connecting a new street corridor in the arching presence of the city monument of the elevated railway line creates a new impulse. Instead of a series single buildings, a prominent bar shape was built. With towers and indented areas subdivided by window slits, it defies the imposing, railway embankment; and while defending the intimacy of the living space from the railway's canon of movement, it nevertheless incorporates it in a lively manner."

413

KPM Gallery, upper floor

Königliche Porzellan-Manufaktur Berlin
2001–04
Charlottenburg, Wegelystraße
Architects: von Gerkan, Marg und Partner
Client: KPM

On the one hand, as a cubical structure pushed onto a side-street, the company's exhibition and sales pavilion for its world-famous products – with the KPM scepter on their bottom sides – borders a spacious and bright courtyard, around which the carefully restored production halls are grouped; on the other, in a northerly direction, it borders an ensemble of newer buildings which accommodate a variety of uses.

414

Canal-circulation facility of the Technische Universität Berlin
1975/76
Charlottenburg, Müller-Breslau-Straße
Architect: Ludwig Leo
Client: Senator für Bau- und Wohnungswesen for Technische Universität Berlin

This building – a part of the university's institute of waterway engineering and navigational studies – is located on the Landwehrkanal. By being placed vertically in a typically horizontal situation, the canal circulation facility succeeds in saving an enormous amount of space. The building and its measuring booths are stilted over the canal. Here too, like with the DLRG headquarters **(394)**, "forms follows function" in a manner far more radical than the one suggested in the much-quoted Bauhaus truism.

Lobby

Dorint Novotel
2001–04
Charlottenburg, Straße des 17. Juni at the corner of Bachstraße
Architects: Laurids Ortner, Manfred Ortner
Client: Theseus Immobilienmanagement

"With its 60-m tall tower, the hotel and office building visually marks the eastern entranceway to the newly developed KPM quarter, in whose center resides the tradition-laden facility of the porcelain manufacturer. This ensures the area's urban planning presence along the east–west axis. Along the thoroughfare Straße des 17. Juni, the development is enhanced by a 7-storey building base which functions as a hotel, and incorporates the height of the neighboring Ernst-Reuter-Haus."

Hansaviertel

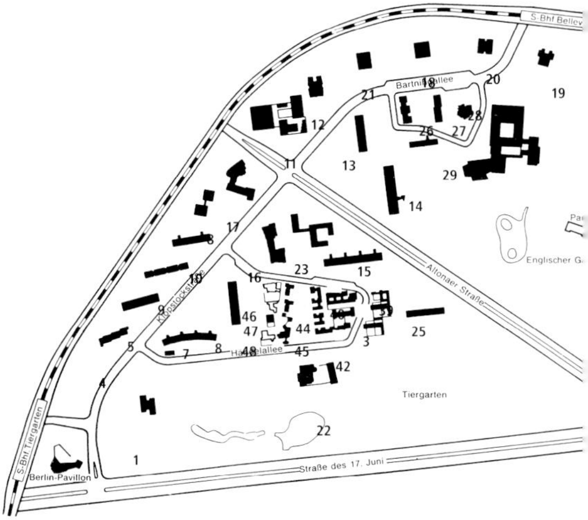

Key

- 1 Klaus Müller-Rehm, Gerhard Siegmann (417)
- 4 Hans Christian Müller (418)
- 5 Günther Gottwald (419)
- 7 Walter Gropius, Wils Ebert (429)
- 9 Wassili Luckhardt, Hubert Hoffmann (420)
- 10 Paul Schneider-Esleben (421)
- 13 Egon Eiermann (428)
- 14 Oscar Niemeyer (427)
- 15 Fritz Jaenecke, Sten Samuelson (426)
- 16 Alvar Aalto (423)
- 19 Hans Schwippert (432)
- 20 Eugène Beaudoin, Raymond Lopez (431)
- 21 J. H. van den Brock, J. B. Bakema (430)
- 23 Paul G. R. Baumgarten (435)
- 28 Otto Senn (433)
- 39 Eduard Ludwig (424)
- 40 Arne Jacobsen (425)

416

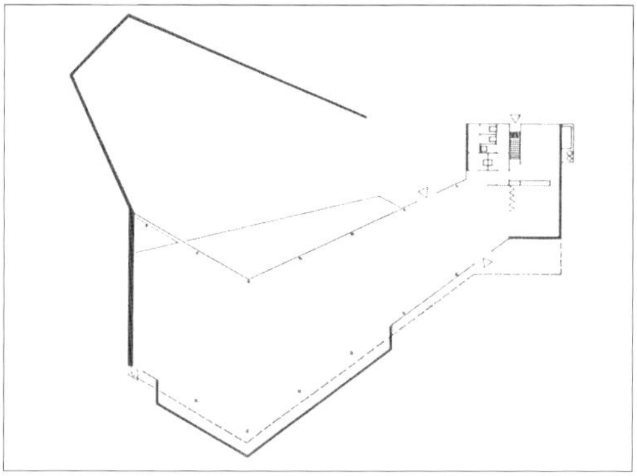

Berlin-Pavillon

1957

Hansaviertel, Straße des 17. Juni, Klopstockstr.

Architects: Hermann Fehling, Daniel Gogel, Peter Pfankuch

Client: Senator für Bau- und Wohnungswesen

This was the first-prize winner of a competition announced in conjunction with the **Interbau**, an expansive project which developed Berlin's Hansaviertel. The pavilion was built to provide visitors with introductory information before proceeding through the rear exit and gradually opening courtyard to the actual building exhibition. Later, the exhibition spaces served to inform the public of developments in the area of urban construction. Shortly before the pavilion's fiftieth birthday, its total reutilization for commercial purposes took place, yet the largest possible amount of its original building substance was preserved through the efforts of Paul and Petra Kahlfeldt.

417

Plan of a standard floor

Interbau, object 1

1957

Hansaviertel, Klopstockstraße

Architects: Klaus Müller-Rehm, Gerhard Siegmann

The almost entirely destructed Hansaviertel was newly restructured in the1950s and intended to act as a role model for future living. Freestanding buildings designed by renowned architects in a park-like environment demonstrated the contemporary modern lifestyle. Otto Bartning undertook the coordination of all planning processes. This object involves an apartment high-rise housing 1-room apartments. On the ground floor is a restaurant, and every storey above it contains ten apartments: four apartments facing east, four facing west, and two south-facing. The balconies are very narrow, but the windows of the living spaces extend down to the floor. Two terrace apartments are installed in the building's attic floor. Emergency stairwells complete the design. The load-bearing walls are constructed using prefabricated concrete slabs.

418

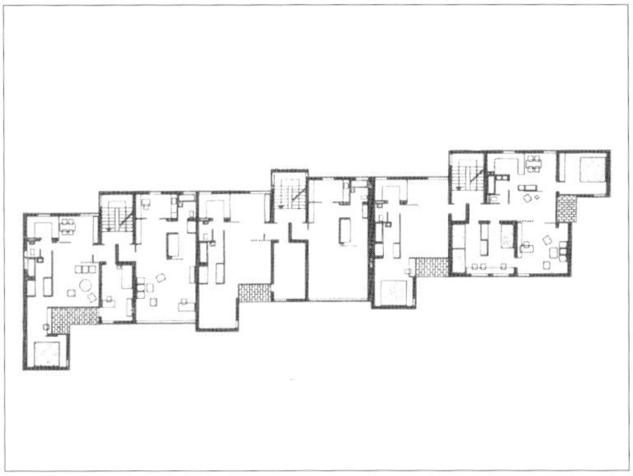

Plan of a standard floor

Interbau, object 4
1957
Hansaviertel, Klopstockstraße 7, 9, 11
Architect: Hans Christian Müller

Here a 4-storey apartment building with three entranceways was constructed as a semi-detached dwelling. To add variety to the apartment communities, several types of flats were created. The ground floor was enhanced with exits on a common level leading into open areas. The floor plan's design sought to shield the building from the S-Bahn railway line and, at the same time, create introverted living and sleeping areas with deeply inset loggia.

419

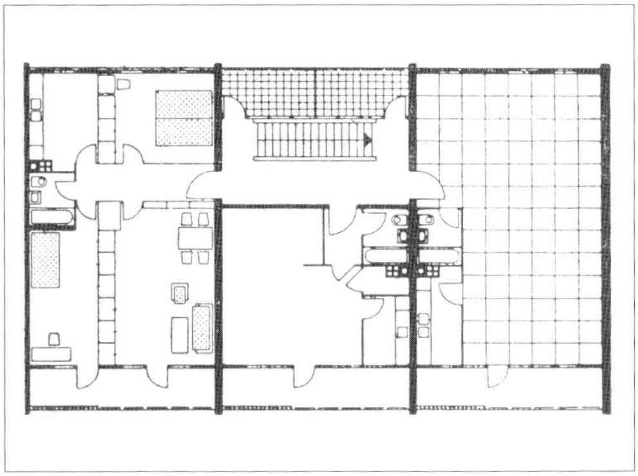

Interbau, object 5
1957
Hansaviertel, Klopstockstraße 13, 15, 17
Architect: Günther Gottwald

The floor plan and elevation are determined by the crushed stone walls that separate the apartments. The storey-high screens which alternate from side to side per storey give the building a modern touch for today's standards. In its entirety, this object involves three stairwells as well as a semi- and 3-way detached structure. The original plan to produce here standardized and freely dividable wall, door, and closet elements was only completed as a model.

420

Plan of the ground floor

Interbau, object 9
1957
Hansaviertel, Klopstockstraße 19, 21, 23
Architects: Wassili Luckhardt, Hubert Hoffmann

The 4-storey residential row is clearly subdivided by the stairwell sections. A series of totally differing apartments and maisonnettes are generated by two recurring load-bearing spans. While architects took rationalization through repetition into account at an early stage, unlike in the East, the construction industry was slow to react.

421

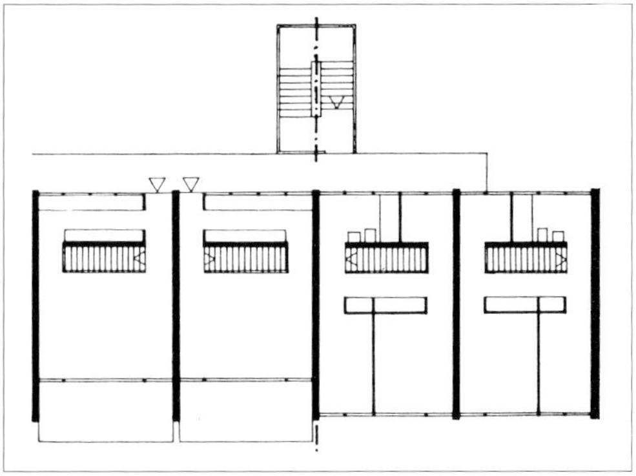

Plans: left, apartment floor; right, bedroom floor

Interbau, object 10
1957
Hansaviertel, Klopstockstraße 25, 27
Architect: Paul Schneider-Esleben

This 1-storey, south-facing building type is a cellular framed construction with a span of 5,50 m. Between traverse crushed stone walls are two apartments stacked one atop the other and reacting like mirror images. Ground-floor living spaces with interior staircases lead to bedrooms on the 1st floor; the 2nd floor contains the sleeping quarters of the upper apartment, whose living room lies directly above it. This results in the living space always facing the garden in one case, and having the better view in the other.

422

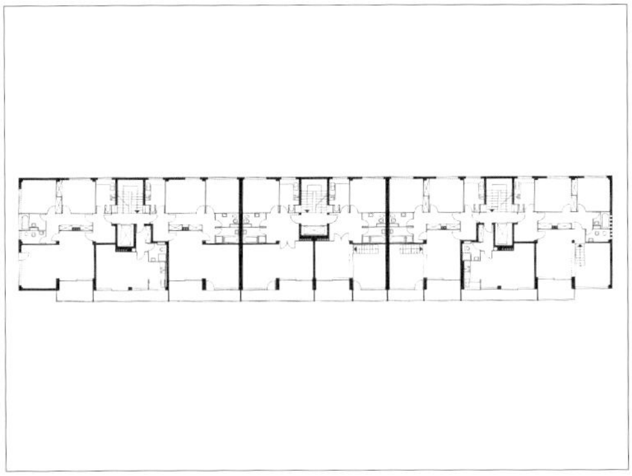

Interbau, object 8
1957
Hansaviertel, Klopstockstraße 14–18
Architect: Pierre Vago

This 8-storey, reinforced concrete construction houses 1- to 4-room apartments oriented to the east, west, and south. In some cases, the living spaces are raised by a half storey or lowered by creating a clearance height of 4.70 m, which shifts the balcony to the building's east side. The west side is lined with colored glass plates.

423

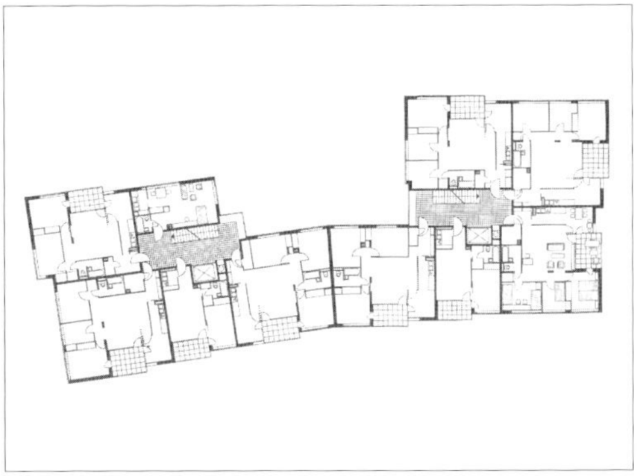

Interbau, object 16
1957
Hansaviertel, Klopstockstraße 30, 32
Architect: Alvar Aalto
Contact architect: Paul G. R. Baumgarten

Both of the 8-storey, five-way-detached buildings stand at a slight angle to one another and form a U which opens to the east. The ten apartments on each floor are composed of six different large-scale apartment types. A centralized entranceway area is created by omitting two apartments on the ground floor. The broken-brick, concrete walls are lined with Leca slabs.

424

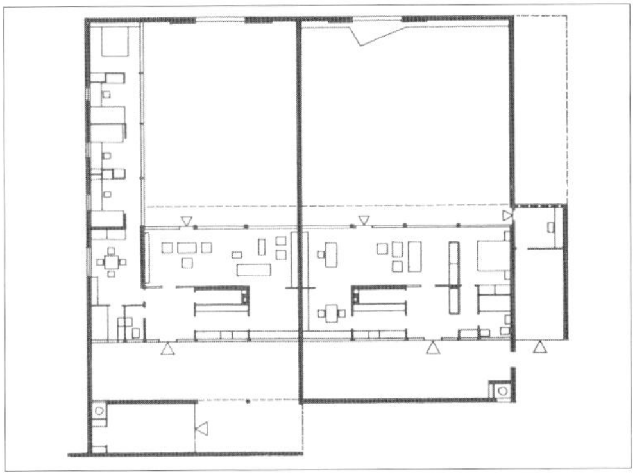

Plan of two types

Interbau, object 39
1957
Hansaviertel, Händelallee 26–30
Architect: Eduard Ludwig

Postwar urban planning of the 1950s is strongly influenced by the theories of the Athens Charter: the typology of building forms is namely 8- to 12-storey rows, point buildings (high-rises), in a north–south or east–west orientation and, to a degree, a single-storey bungalow. Concealed by protective walls, the basic theme of this flat, glazed apartment house is varied five times in the five buildings. The garden enclosure's sheet-pile walls are made of Eternit. The building's walls made of porous concrete slabs are surfaced with Glasal plates.

425

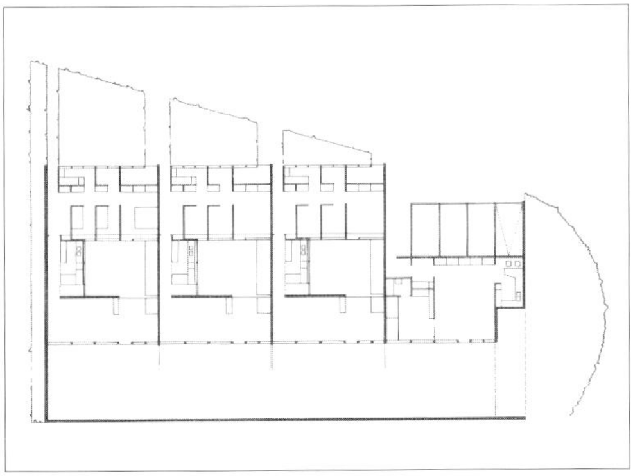

Interbau, object 40
1957/58
Hansaviertel, Händelallee 33–39
Architect: Arne Jacobsen

Three of the houses are atrium houses. In every case, their adjoining courtyards are bordered to the north by the wing of the sleeping quarters; to the west by the eat-in kitchen, and to the east by a wall facing the neighboring object. The eat-in kitchen is the centralized meeting area of the house, and the south-facing living room offers a view of the garden shared by all four houses.

426

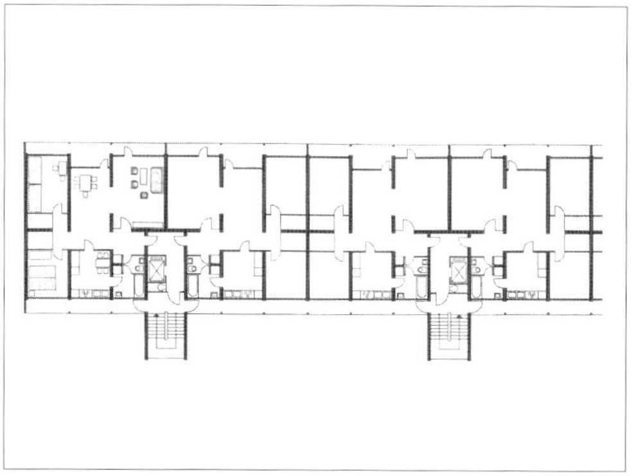

Plan of a section

Interbau, object 15
1957
Hansaviertel, Altonaer Straße 3–9
Architects: Fritz Jaenecke, Sten Samuelson

This 10-storey, reinforced concrete, cross-wall construction with a full-concrete ceiling houses a storey for businesses as well as 69 apartments. On the building's long side, protruding floor slabs which serve as loggia to the south, form emergency escape routes to staircases to the north. The building houses four elevators. The knowledge gained from the Swedish satellite town is put to use here.

427

Est side with elevation tower

Interbau, object 14
1957
Hansaviertel, Altonaer Straße 4–14
Architect: Oscar Niemeyer

Niemeyer is internationally known – especially in Brazil – for the use of clear and expansive geometric forms in his architectural language. The fact that he was always a spokesman for the interests of socially disadvantaged groups makes it hardly surprising that he wanted this object's 5th floor to be used exclusively by groups for social functions. What remains here, however, is an multifunctional room almost never used. The sharp-edged tower housing an elevator connects only at the 5th and a second time at the 8th floor.

428

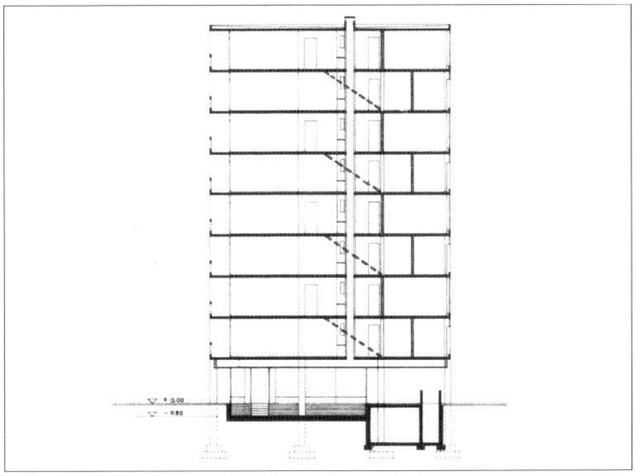

Interbau, object 13
1960/61
Hansaviertel, Bartningallee 2–4
Architect: Egon Eiermann

The building contains 48 2-room and 48 1-room apartments. While the kitchens, bathrooms, and living areas fill out the space to the west, along the building's east side the developing hallways and storage areas close the second rooms of the larger apartments by way of the inserted staircases. A post-office is located on the ground floor. The structure incorporates crushed stone cladding, exposed concrete surfaces, and lined partition fillings in the bonding. Erecting the building lasted longer than planned, and a rumor spread that the post-office tried to be the client.

429

Interbau, object 7
1957
Hansaviertel, Händelallee 3–9
Architects: Walter Gropius, Wils Ebert

After the war, apart from designing the Bauhaus Archiv **(254)** and this object, Gropius did largly only urban planning. Devoting himself to a large-scale housing estate on southeast Berlin led to this area taking on his name: Gropiusstadt: an urban planning concept involving circular apartment houses intended to form centralized squares or so-called "focus points", but never completed due to faulty organization. The building's slightly swung form, accentuated horizontal orientation, and bundled pairs of floors make it possible to perceive the grand gestures of Gropius' urban planning ideas. Wils Ebert, who studied under Gropius, served later as his contact architect in Germany. Thanks to this collaboration, in his countless furniture designs, and even the furnace for the iron foundry in Franken, one continually recognizes the connection to Gropius.

430

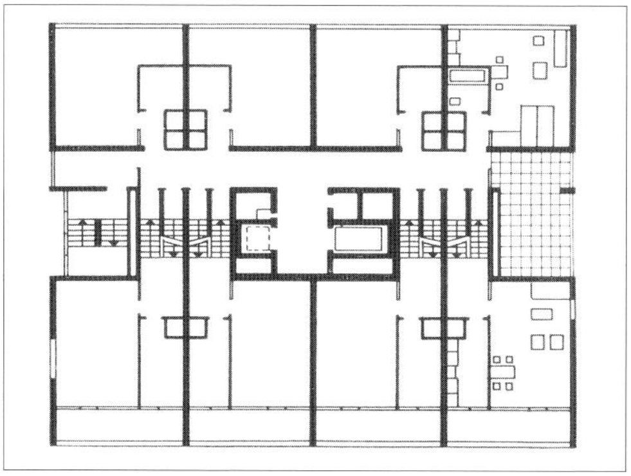

Plan of an apartment entranceway level

Interbau, object 21
1957
Hansaviertel, Bartningallee 7
Architects: J. H. van den Broek and J. B. Bakema

The 73 apartments of this high-rise are closed by six corridors. While 24 1-room apartments appear on the same level, 48 3-room apartments are staggered by a half-landing. Between the corridor storeys, the larger apartments take on the full width of the building and receive cross-ventilation. On the ground floor, reinforced-concrete slabs develop to supports. The cladding consists of prefabricated cement slabs.

431

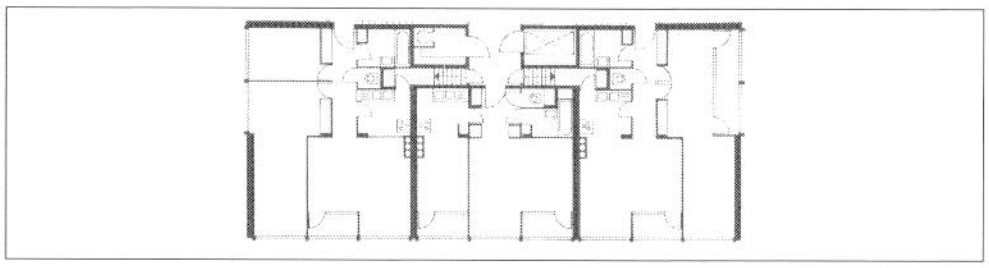

Plan of a standard floor

Interbau, object 20
1957
Hansaviertel, Bartningallee 11–13
Architects: Eugène Beaudoin, Raymond Lopez

The 15-storey high-rise is built using a modular unit of 2.34 m, half the width of a room. The six apartments on each storey are grouped around the junction point. Two apartments respectively, each measuring 40 sqm, lie on the same level as the junction, while four corner apartments, each measuring 61 sqm, spring to the height of the half-landing. This series of 5 buildings seemed the best way to develop apartments along the elevated railway line and to arrange them, to an extent, neither in front of nor behind the railway structure, but rather over it.

432

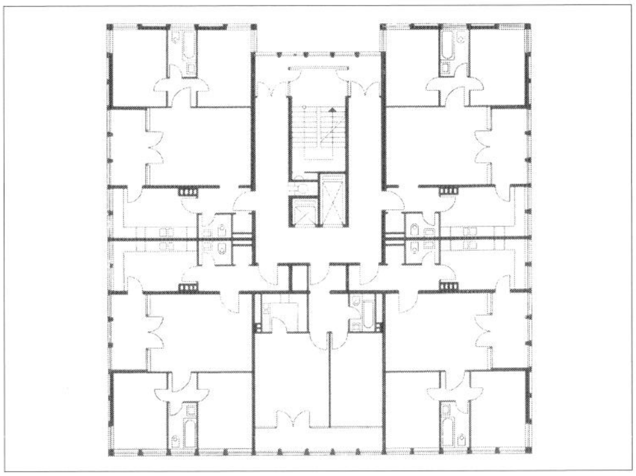

Plan of a standard floor

Interbau, object 19
1957
Hansaviertel, Bartningallee 16
Architect: Hans Schwippert

This represents an exceptional example of a construction with prefabricated, storey-high concrete elements in which the insulating layers and installation are perfectly incorporated. Arranged around the junction core are three, U-shaped, basic units of the same size, varied in such a way to create 27 $1^1/_2$-room apartments, 8 apartments with three bedrooms, and 26 maisonnette apartments. The two levels of the maisonnettes are connected by loggia.

433

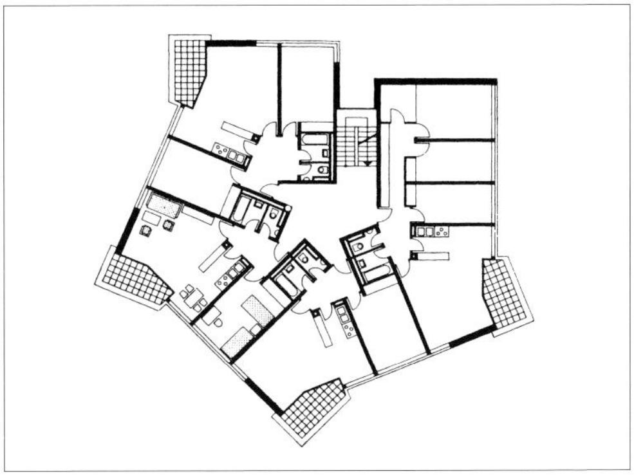

Plan of a standard floor

Interbau, object 28
1957
Hansaviertel, Hanseatenweg 12
Architect: Otto H. Senn

Three standard floors house four apartments each: two 1-room apartments, one 3-room apartment, and one 4-room apartment are grouped around a centralized hallway area at the stairwell. The attic floor provides three $1^1/_2$- to $2\ ^1/_2$-room apartments with a studio-like character. A terrace garden stands in front of the recessed loft apartments. The ground floor contains washroom facilities, drying rooms, and storage areas. The recessed rooftop apartments have a smal terrace garden.

434

Auditorium

Akademie der Künste
Academy of the arts
1960
Hansaviertel, Hanseatenweg 10
Architect: Werner Düttmann
Garden and atrium: Walter Rossow

The form and materials divide the building into three parts. The ground floor contains the rectangle of the exhibition halls constructed around an interior courtyard. A variety of overhead lighting is used in combination with the washed concrete walls. The performing hall made of brick has an irregular, folded copper roof and a seating capacity of 600 guests on both sides of the stage. The 5-storey wing of studio and office spaces is surfaced with blue plaster. After the fall of the Berlin Wall, and the merging together of the city's East and West sectors, with a gesture almost archetypal for Berlin, a second academy of the arts was created on Pariser Platz **(005)**, where this far older institution holds firmly to its former status.

435

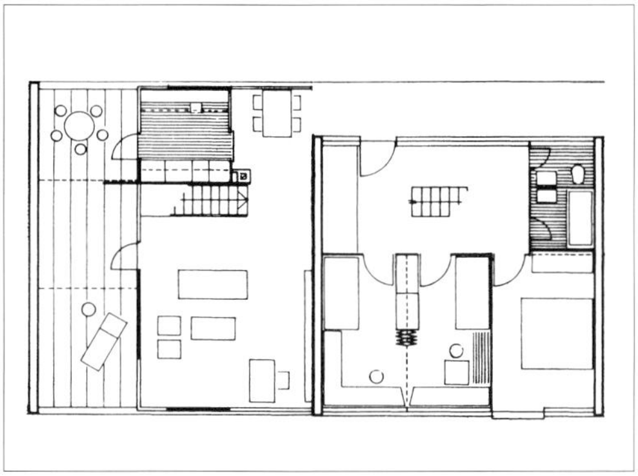

Floor plans of the 2nd and the 3rd floors

Interbau, object 25
1957
Hansaviertel, Altonaer Straße 1
Architect: Paul G. R. Baumgarten
Client: Eternit AG

Over the bedroom storey, each of the seven maisonnette apartments has a roof garden which fills the entire width of the building and lies to the side of the living space. The expansive glazing of the lower storey – formerly used by the Eternit company as a commercial space during the Interbau period – offers an unobstructed view of the Tiergarten city park. Crowning the structure are protruding, roof plates in the form of an inverted ribbed ceiling as well as "Welleternit" roofing. The outer skin is lined with Glasal tiles. In the meantime, the Eternit company has found a replacement for the asbestos-bearing cement fiber plates used in the past, and is well in business again.

436

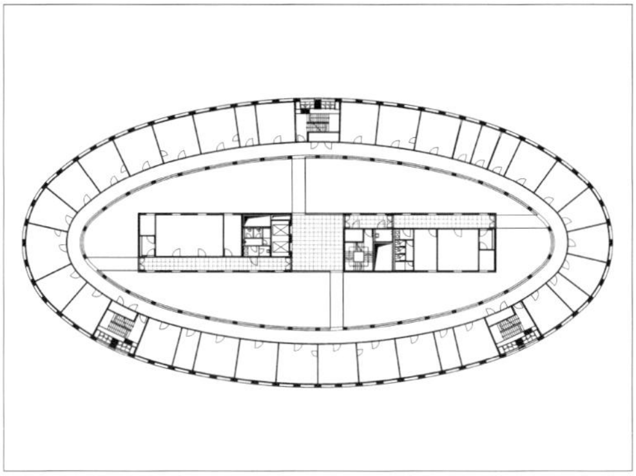

Plan of the 1st floor

Bundespräsidialamt
1996–98
Tiergarten, Spreeweg 1
Architects: Martin Gruber, Helmut Kleine-Kraneburg
Surface coloring: Lothar Baumgarten
Client: Bundesamt für Bauwesen und Raumordnung

The building was placed in the immediate vicinity of Schloß Bellevue, the palace designed by Philipp Michael Boumann in 1785. The intention was to insert in Berlin's city park, Tiergarten, an office building meant as a supplementary and tree-friendly structure with a minimized volume. This was achieved through the oval building form with its polished, nero impala façade. The arrangement of its elements within a shell structure of office spaces, and detached core for the headquarters' mechanical services, offer enough space and light for developing halls, exterior corridors, and bridges. This 3-storey construction with a basement level utilizes a floor area of 12,800 sqm.

437

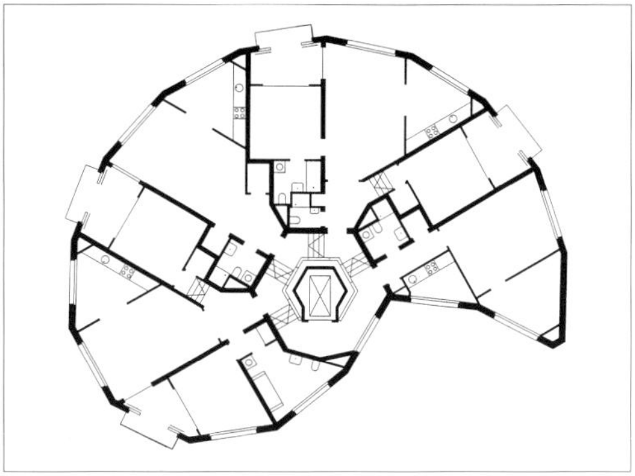

Plan of a standard floor

Apartementhaus "Schnecke"
"Snail" apartement building
2002/03
Tiergarten, Holsteiner Ufer 46
Architect: Benedict Tonon
Client: WIR

"The solitary structure interprets the special quality of this site. With a free-flowing form developed from a successive turning of the ground-floor plan, the building development separates itself from the right-angled structure of its so-called 'grid town' while also freeing itself from the location's three-sided emphasis – lodged between the train station, the corner development leading to the main thoroughfare, and the Spree River. The ground-floor plan is given a rising and terraced segmentation, and all the apartments turn to face the light and open towards the sun's path between the east and the west. The entrance to every apartment is further individualized by small leaps from floor to floor, each composed of 4 stepped segments. Yet the 'snail' generates the atmosphere of a community just the same."

438

Kopfbau
Head building
1998/99
Tiergarten, Joachim-Karnatz-Allee at the corner of Paulstraße
Architect: Jörg Pampe with Irene Keil
Client: Frankfurter Wohnungsbaugesellschaft
The end construction of a snake-like building – a 1991 competition winner focused on Berlin's Moabiter Werder district – spreads out to the west as far as Paulstraße. At this point the "snake", housing predominantly 1-room apartments (11 per storey, and altogether 43 in the 4 upper storeys), changes its direction. The lower half is enhanced with window elements which respect the sunlight conditions for office and business spaces. At the snake's other end (to a certain extent the tail) are three atrium buildings, designed by Müller-Rhode-Wandert and Ariane Röntz.

439

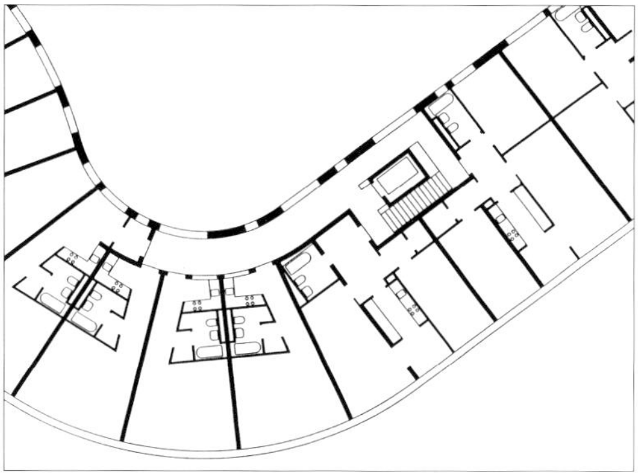

Floor plan (section)

Spree–Schlange
Spree snake
1997–99
Tiergarten, Moabiter Werder, Joachim-Karnatz-Allee
Architect: Georg Bumiller
Client: Deutschbau, Frankfurter Siedlungsgesellschaft
Emerging from a 1995 development competition, on a larger scale the project successfully freed itself from the initial, urban planning guidelines expressed in the competition. It could also consider the meanwhile stabilized plans from the "Kanzlergarten". The 5 to 8 storeys of the building have a homogenous clinker-brick skin between their strips of windows. Originally built for the civil servants about to move to Berlin, the apartments orient themselves toward the Spree River – and can meanwhile be rented by anyone.

440

Façade facing the Spree River

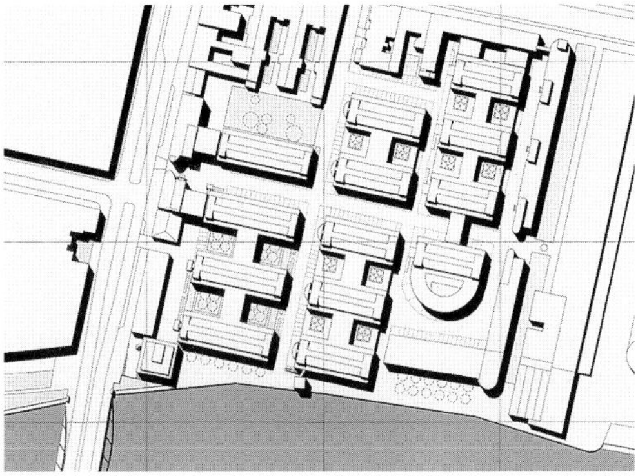

Site plan

Focus Teleport Berlin
1987–2001
Moabit, Stromstraße 1–7, Alt-Moabit 90–96
Architects: Walter Rolfes (until 1993), Joachim Ganz
Landscape planning: Cornelia Müller, Jan Wehberg
Client: ITAG Berlin, DIFA Hamburg

In five construction phases, a workspace offer for firms specializing in new technology was created at a traditional, industrial site in the city district of Moabit. Completing the first phase made available rentable, business spaces that offered, for the first time in Berlin, the necessary in-house technical infrastructure for the rapidly developing new-technology market. With its use of brick and steel, the physical presence of the architecture refers to traditional elements of Berlin's industrial culture. Floor area: 146,000 sqm; building costs: circa 117 million Euro.

441

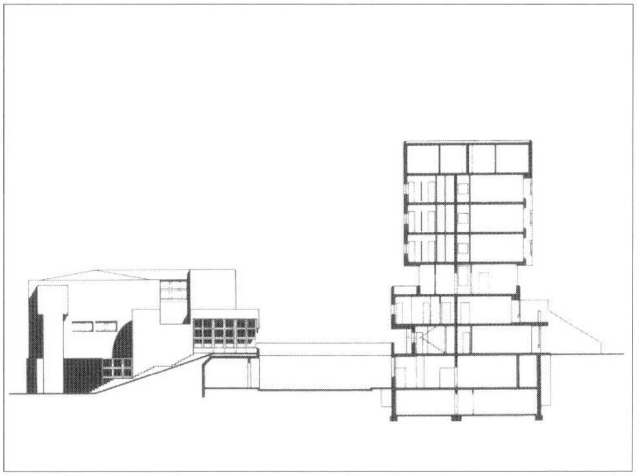

Youth center
1974–78
Moabit, Rathenower Straße 15–18
Architects: Gerd Neumann, Dietmar Grötzebach, Günter Plessow with Eberhard Lucht
Client: Bezirksamt Tiergarten

A childcare center, children's and youth home, and youth recreational center are brought together to form a group of buildings with shared spaces for sports, events, dining, and socializing. The open connecting network leads over a play area, stairs, bridges, ramps, roofed walk, and the passageway to Fritz-Schloß-Park, whose sloped grounds are used here in a variety of ways. Shortly before handling this project, the same architects completed an exciting school building made of exposed concrete on Guerickestraße in the district of Charlottenburg.

442

Base of a triple-hinged girder

Assembly hall of the AEG turbine factory
1909
Moabit, Huttenstraße, Berlichingenstraße
Architect: Peter Behrens

At the hall's east side stand exposed triple-hinged girders and a glass façade which tilts with the inward slant as the supports. In contrast to this, the hall's south-facing front end is flanked by squared, corner pillars. A 2-storey flat construction immediately connects at the building's west side. Later, by extending the construction, the original length of 110 m was archived. One construction element of this steel structure – having the base of the downward tapering supports function here as a visible decorative element on the street – anticipates the "form follows function" notion.

443

Administrative building of Ludwig Loewe AG.
1907
Moabit, Huttenstraße at the corner of Wieberstraße
Architect: Alfred Grenander
Client: Isidor Loewe

The massive, 4-storey brick construction with a wide pillared area takes first prize for its modern disposition regarding the treatment of the two attic floors: reminiscent of a string of pearls, semicircular roof dormers, arranged in a row to an extent crown the building. In the process, the 6-axial central span recedes behind the façade and emphasizes the entranceway flanked with columns. The firm originally founded in 1869 as the manufacturer of mechanical devices, and later insisted on being an "electric company".

444

Wernerwerk

445

Schaltwerk

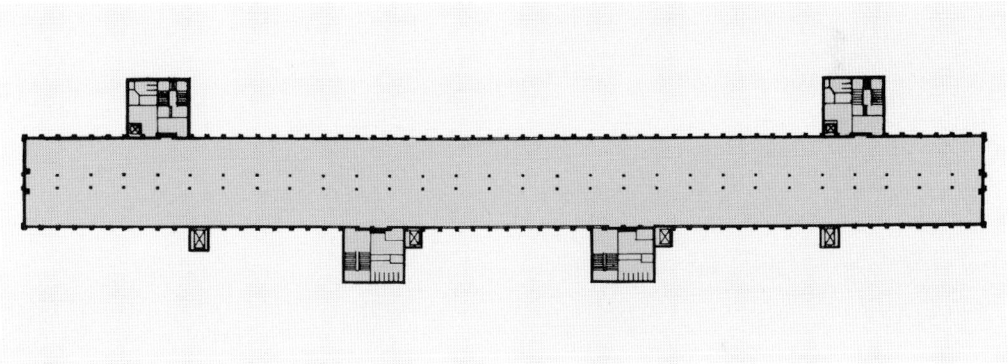

Standard floor of the Schaltwerk, with all vertical functions outside of the manufacturing plants

Wernerwerk of Siemens & Halske AG
1929/30
Siemensstadt, Siemensdamm, Ohmstraße
Architect: Hans Hertlein

Building the Wernerwerk high-rise created a concentrated and clearly-structured administrative wing. Unlike with the Schaltwerk, the supports of the steel skeleton lie behind the building's smooth outer skin. To the southwest stand structural building parts for news services and measurement technology, erected using an easily expandable courtyard system and forming here longitudinal and lateral constructions. Besides being the seat of the German government, Berlin was foremost an industrial city. From the mid-1920s onward, the city received a tremendous boost through the addition of modern technologies and its improved marketing status worldwide. This surge of energy reversed itself during the 1948 blockade period. Since then, the headquarters of Siemens Inc. have been located in Munich.

Schaltwerk of Siemens & Schuckert AG
1926–28
Siemensstadt, Nonnendammallee 101–110
Architect: Hans Hertlein

All the stairwells and auxiliary spaces of this 11-storey high-rise are installed in tower-like structural additions to insure the greatest freedom of movement in the work areas. Both upper storeys house office spaces. The protruding, outer supports of the steel-framed construction are clad in masonry. Two bridges connect the halls of flat-roofed shed structures to the building's west side.

446

Refuse-reloading station
1936/37
Charlottenburg, Helmholtzstraße 42
Architect: Paul G. R. Baumgarten

At this reloading station, a fourth of Berlin's refuse (formerly incinerated in ovens) is dumped into floating barges. Four trash trucks at a time can be unloaded here and immediately driven out again via a revolving platform. The technical details of the station include a dust removal facility, in-house headquarters, as well as waiting and washrooms. The steel-framed construction is infilled with ochre brick. Currently the main level is used by an architect's office, and the lower level for a painter's studio.

447

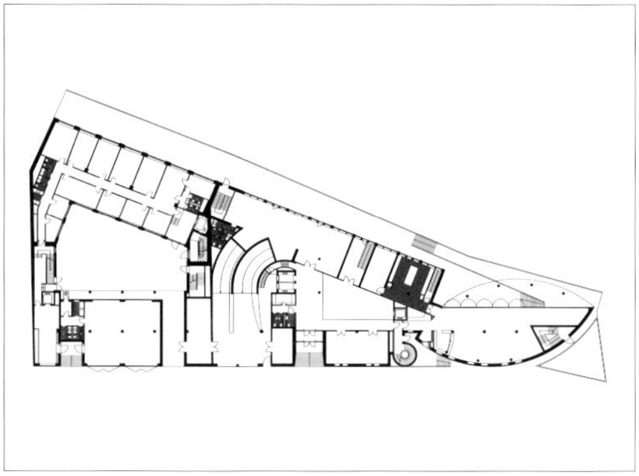

Plan of the ground floor

Spree-Forum
1994–96
Tiergarten, Alt-Moabit 59–61
Architects: Kleihues + Kleihues
Project manager: Götz Kern
Client: Hanseatica

An addition originally planned as the merchandising building on an existing but renovation-needy business complex ended up becoming a conventional, cellular office building. Its creators merely reserved a greater, functional area for the eye-shaped tip construction. Continued along the Spree River, its foundation also serves as a restaurant terrace.

Passenger terminal

Service building

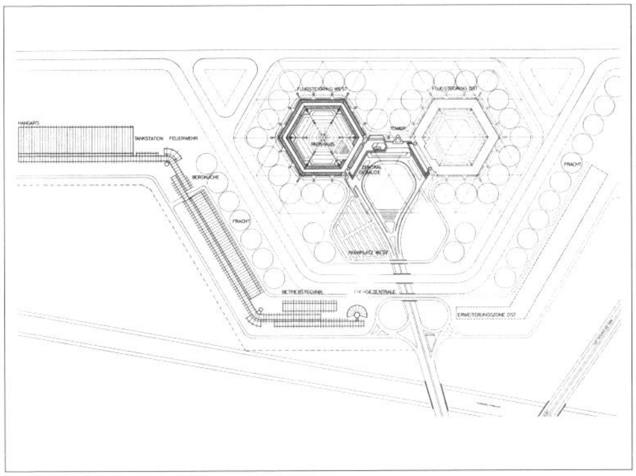

Site plan with second, planned gate-ring

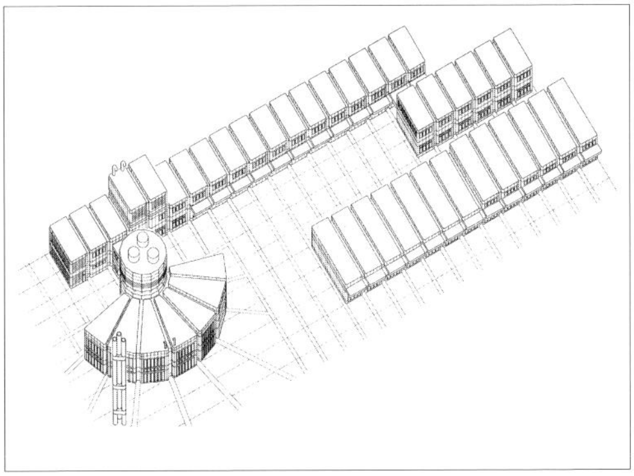

"Container" annex to the service building

Berlin-Tegel Airport
1970–75
Reinickendorf, Kurt-Schumacher-Damm
Architects: Meinhard von Gerkan, Volkwin Marg, Klaus Nickels
Project-managing partners: Karsten Brauer, Klaus Staratzke, Rolf Niedballa
Wolkentor sculpture: Heinrich Brummack
Colored guidance system: Werner Nöfer
Client: Berliner Flughafen-Gesellschaft

This first-prize winner of a nationwide competition is a so-called "drive-in airport" meant to shorten the route from the car to the plane. The hexagonal, ring-like gate containing the check-in areas has a view of the airfield and take-off strips and provides direct access to the planes via movable bridges. In the middle of the airport is the U-shaped main building with offices, restaurants, and customer service zones. The airport's service buildings are accommodated by the linear addition of "building containers" of varying heights and depths, which serve the many uses of the aircraft and form here an energy center, cargo handling facility, fire station, board kitchen, as well as aircraft halls and workshops. This simultaneously creates an "urban planning framework which avoids the usual heterogeneous and side-by-side arrangement of industrial facilities". The highly successful architect's office is involved with the planning of a totally new, international and large-scale airport to replace Berlin's Schönefeld Airport, bearing the initials BBI (Berlin-Brandenburg International).

449

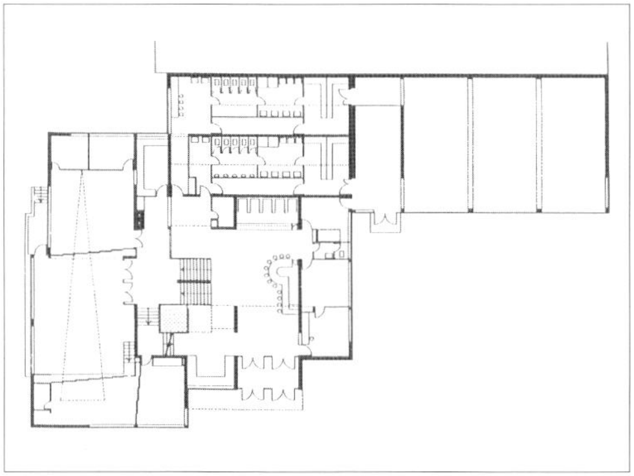

Plan of the ground floor

Youth clubhouse
1964–66
Borsigwalde, Tietzstraße 12
Architects: Jan Rave, Rolf Rave
Sculptural work: Reinhold Hommes
Client: Bezirksamt Reinickendorf

All the building, whether the basement storey conceived to withstand noise, the gymnastics hall, social room with stage, or the quiet zones on the upper floors develops around a centralized hall with areas for sitting, playing, and reading, as well as a bar. At the same time, the different levels shift at a 3rd storey. Standing-brick facing and two sizes of standard prefabrecated sound-control glass latently form the module for the building.

450

Connection to the existing development by B. Taut

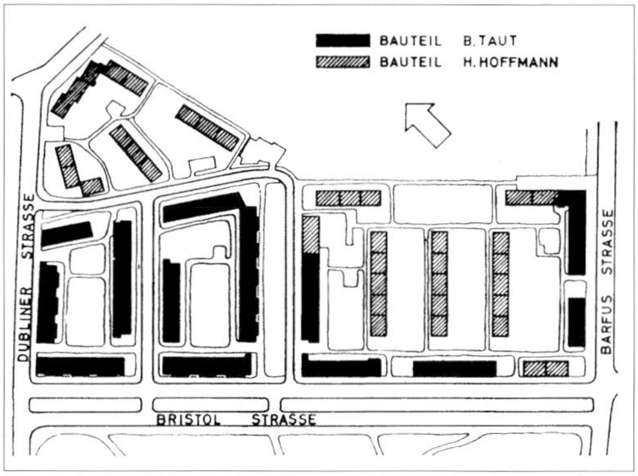

Site plan

Siedlung Schillerpark
Housing colony at Schillerpark
1924–28 / 1954
Reinickendorf, Bristolstraße, Oxfordstraße, Windsorstraße, Dubliner Straße
Architect: Bruno Taut
Connection development: Hans Hoffmann
Client: Berliner Bau- und Wohunungsgenossenschaft von 1892

The ordering of these flat-roofed, 3-storey row constructions reflects the peaceful apartment courtyards of a block perimeter development. The southwest side orients itself towards Schillerpark via Bristolstraße. The different building phases were completed with differentiating façade designs. The structure features red brickwork, plaster, and exposed concrete. The connecting building part from the 1950s appears built by Hoffmann in the same way that Taut might have, that is, were such large windows and glazed surfaces affordable then in apartment construction practices.

451

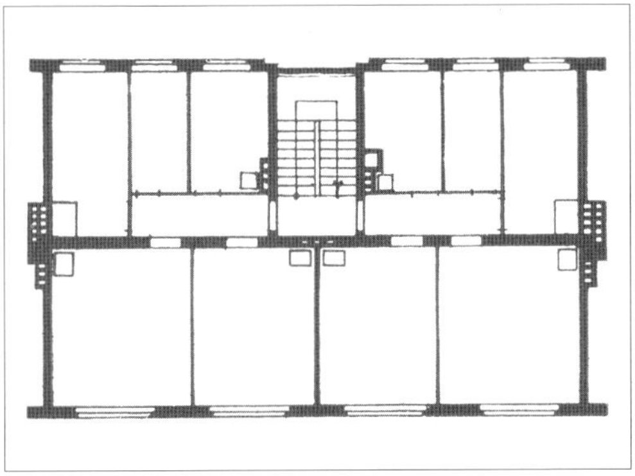

Plan of a standard floor

Apartment block
1928/29
Reinickendorf, Ollenhauerstraße, Kienhorstraße, Waldowstraße, Pfahlerstraße
Architect: Erwin Gutkind

This ranks as a testament to horizontal subdivisions in the language of Modernism. Together with the buildings which diagonally face it, the self-contained block of buildings offers 422 2-room to 3-room apartments. Various surfaces subdivide the construction, which spatially contains the courtyard and the street through its calculated misalignment. Playing areas and a children's home are located in spacious apartment courtyards. Later, a commercial space was attached at Ollenhauerstraße.

452

Entrance hall

Volksschule Wittenau
Wittenau elementary school
1931
Wittenau, Alt-Wittenau
Architect: Jean Krämer

Standing at the south side of a large schoolyard is the curved school building with two pavilions at its ends for two gymnasiums. Also included here is a public library and the caretaker's quarters. Arranged along the building's axis is the entrance hall with two staircases. By operating a lever, the upper and lower window elements can be slid one beside the other in order to ventilate the classrooms.

453

Plan of a typical floor

Rollberge high-rise apartment blocks
1969–71
Waidmannslust, Zabel-Krüger-Damm 50–52
Architect: Hans Scharoun
Client: GSW

At the entrance to the Rollberge housing estate, and end of the footpath following the edge of a slope through the commercial center, this 20-storey construction made of two H-types attached one to the other assumes a dominating spot. The architect's passion for design is evident in the floor plans. Living in high-rises became a much debated topic in the 1970s, especially where it concerned families with children.

454

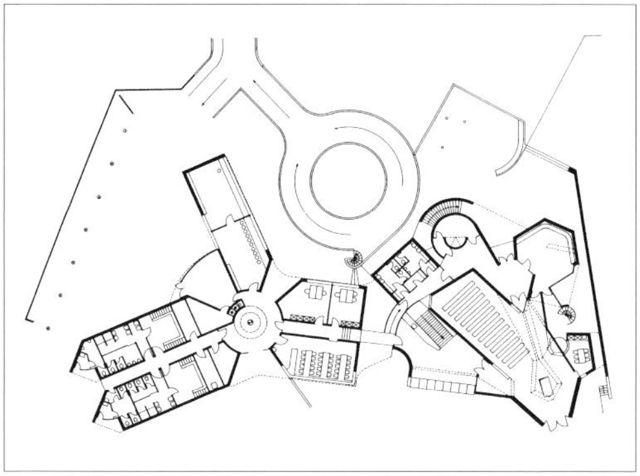

Plan of the ground floor

Cemetery chapel at Fließtal
1971–73
Tegel, Waidmannsluster Damm 13
Architects: Hermann Fehling, Daniel Gogel with Günter Ssymmank
Client: Bezirksamt Reinickendorf

"On the one hand, the walls which encircle and limit the grounds have a protective function in that they create peaceful antechambers; on the other, they architecturally direct visitors into the cemetery's landscape. Through the interconnected ordering of individual spatial elements, as well as through the ordering of light sources, the hall for memorial services is meant to receive the necessary atmosphere for such a space."

The "Scholle" courtyard

Waidmannsluster Damm

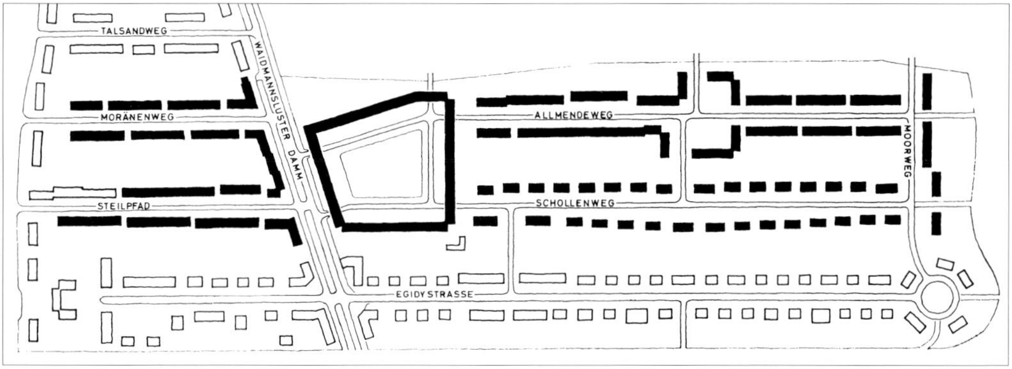

Site plan

"Freie Scholle" housing colony
1924–26, 1929–31
Tegel, Waidmannsluster Damm, Schollenweg, Allmendeweg, Moränenweg, Steilpfad
Architect: Bruno Taut
Restoration: Winfried Brenne
Client: Gehag, "Freie Scholle" GmbH

In August 2001, Thomas Nolte stated: "The name 'Freie Scholle' (free clod) stands for a multifaceted program: not only does it mean being free of the inner-city urban planning dictates of tenement housing, but also the realization of property-forming goals in connection with new living concepts pursued in a consciously liberal-minded community of settlers. This outlook takes into account various living, working, and recreational practices. It addresses a cooperative society that embraces construction and production-related matters. This cooperative society grew out of the self-help-oriented initiatives of 'workers without capital', and the urban gardening concepts conceived in the suburban colony construction were developed in relation to the self-sufficiency of workers." The duplex houses were built on Schollenweg in 1924, and constructing the row houses on Steilpfad lasted until 1926. From 1929 to 1931, in opposition to the pitched roofs in rural developments, 2- to 3-storey row constructions were built, whose flat roofs and courtyard formation gave them an urban accent. The various house types are tied together by a strong sense of coloring.

456

Borsigturm
1927
Tegel, Berliner Straße 35
Architect: Eugen G. Schmohl

The guiding spirit of the industrial company founded in 1837, which manufactured iron castings and steam-engine devices, and built the first locomotive in 1841, was a highly successful individual: August Borsig. The increasing lack of space on the developed grounds of the facility led to the construction of a high-rise for the administration. Because of the small amount of available building property (20 x 16 m), the somewhat omnipotent, 12-storey brick tower creates a trademark at this site. Meanwhile the building has been sold, cleared out, and occupied by the management of different modern services.

457

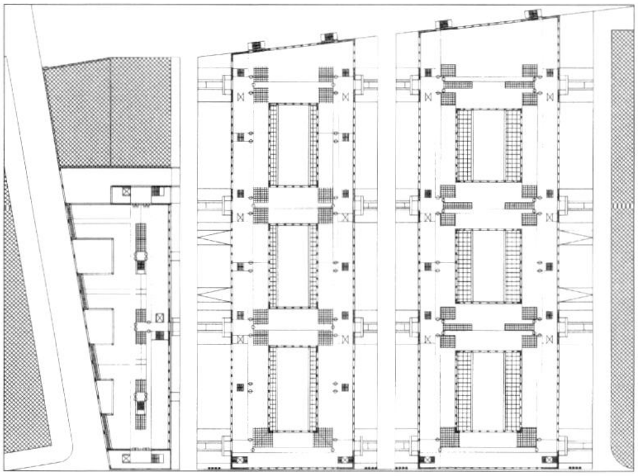

Site plan

Phönix-Gründerzentrum
Phönix technology center
1996–2002
Tegel, Am Borsigturm 42–56
Architect: Walter Rolfes with Klaus Deterding
Landscaping: Seebauer, Wefers + Partner
Client: Herlitz Falkenhöh AG

The technology center is part of an overall concept to revitalize the industrial complex at the site of the former Borsig facilities in the Tegel district. The guiding impulse of the first building phase was to erect the state-funded "Gründerzentrum" dedicated to transportation technology. The ground-floor plan and structural outfitting, including an infrastructure for the center's mechanical services, enable its flexible utilization. The architecture's measurements, proportions, and applied materials refer in part to the still existing Borsig factory buildings.

458

North curved edifice and Borsig Gate

459

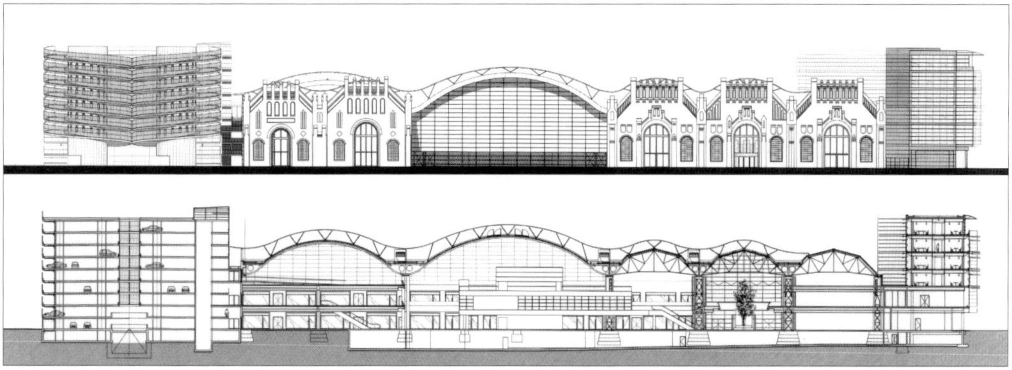

Elevation and cross section of the public garage and the halls

Office park at the Borsigturm
1996–2002
Tegel, Berliner Straße at the corner of Am Borsigturm
Architects: Axel Schultes, Hannelore Deubzer, Jürgen König
Client: RSE, formerly Herlitz Falkenhöh

Assuming a central position in the entire rehabilitation area of the former Borsig factory facilities, the urban development built here terminates in two rounded ends similar to the "strip of government structures". It was meant to be completed in three building phases, for office spaces and a hotel, on a floor area of 45,382 sqm. Incorporated in the construction's overall form is the axis to the old Borsig gate as well as the Borsigturm **(456)** – built in 1927 as one of the first skyscrapers and designed by Eugen Schmohl.

Production halls at the Borsigturm
1997–99
Tegel, Berliner Straße 27
Architect: Claude Vasconi with Dagmar Gross
Structural enginers: Polónyi + Fink
Mechanical services: HL-Technik + Ebert

Costing circa 117 million Euro, incorporating the former halls of 5 factory buildings made it possible to create a floor area of 86,000 sqm to be created for recreational facilities, retail trade, and 9 movie theaters with seating for altogether 2,500 people. The new roofs of the halls connect by way of a magnificent wave-like structuring that aligns with the profiles of the old steel construction, all of which received a coat of iron oxide paint and creates the colorful string of businesses. The adjacent parking facilities accommodate 1,200 vehicles.

460

Humboldt-Mühle
The Humboldt mill
1991/92
Tegel, An der Mühle
Architects: Karl-Heinz Steinebach, Friedrich Weber
Client: Ernst Freiberger

The intention here was to create an ensemble with hotel and office spaces by rebuilding a mill and then creating an expansion with additional buildings: "Walking through the new court complex, the surprising overlapping of forms, set off by the edges of the old buildings and new building elements, reveals an ever newer visual axis and viewing angle. A footbridge leads over the water into another newly designed area – a court with an even greater sense of intimacy – whose appeal is based on the contrasting of three building styles."

461

Control station

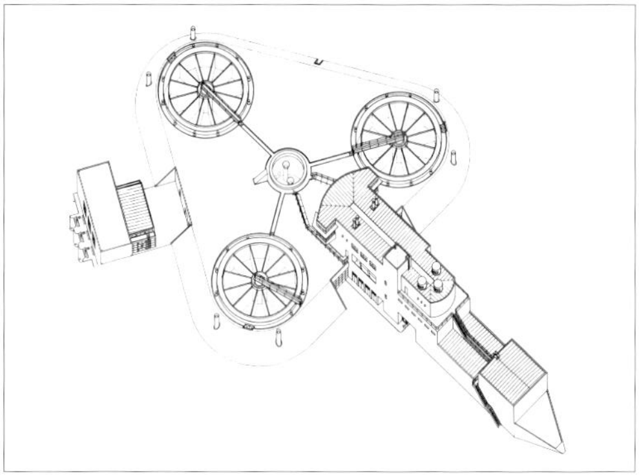

Phosphate elimination facility
1980–85
Tegel, Buddestraße at the corner of Waidmannsluster Damm
Architect: Gustav Peichl
Garden architects: Günther Stache, Cornelia Müller, Elmar Knippschild, Jan Wehberg
Client: Land Berlin/IBA (International Building Exhibiton)

Situated on a grassy field, the building for biologically improving the quality of water presents itself here in the form of a ship – with the central control station as the captain's bridge. A large portion of the technical facilities and storage tanks are located underneath the raised terrain. A neighboring residential building – also painted white and of the same architectural language as the control station – repeats the theme of the ship's bow another three times.

462

Residential housing
1995/96
Tegel, Schloßstraße 7–8
Architects: Fin Bartels, Christoph Schmidt-Ott
Client: Gewiwo

The 4-storey residential row is part of an ensemble made up of other buildings, some of them still in the planning, and two already completed tower buildings, arranged about a slightly raised rotunda. Emerging from an urban planning competition, the "snake" slinks towards the building's southern end in alternating, two or three waves of tension and terminates by having its winding staircase protrude from the north façade.

463

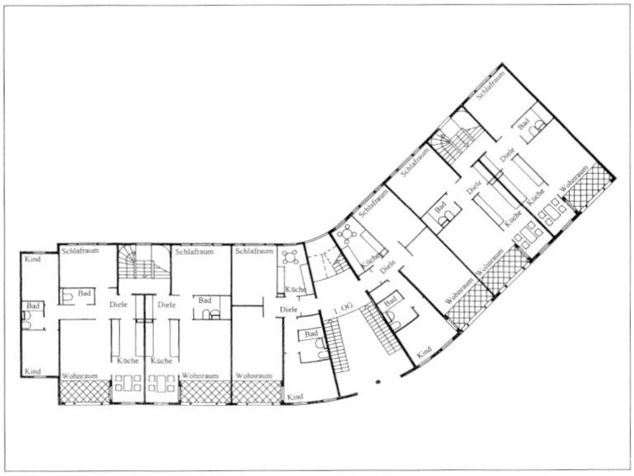

Plan of the 1st and the 2nd floors

Wohnschlange
Residential snake
1986/87
Tegel, Am Tegeler Hafen
Architects: Karl-Heinz Steinebach, Friedrich Weber
Client: Otremba/IBA (International Building Exhibiton)

Not only the form of the floor plan, but also the complete attitude of the building follows the snake approach, as well as that of Bangert, Jansen, Scholz, Schultes, and the "single home" further east of the overall concept by Moore Ruble Yudell – which more or less applies to both marvelously playful examples of a blossoming Postmodernism by Stanley Tigerman and Robert Stern. The adapting of the living rooms and bedrooms makes it possible to enjoy the spatial quality of both – the sunnier side and the harbor side.

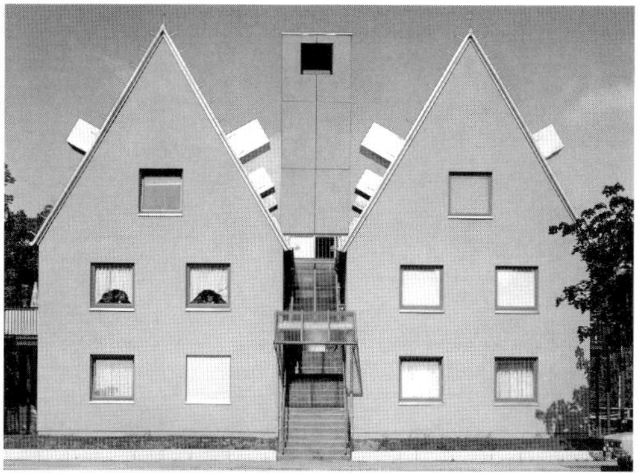

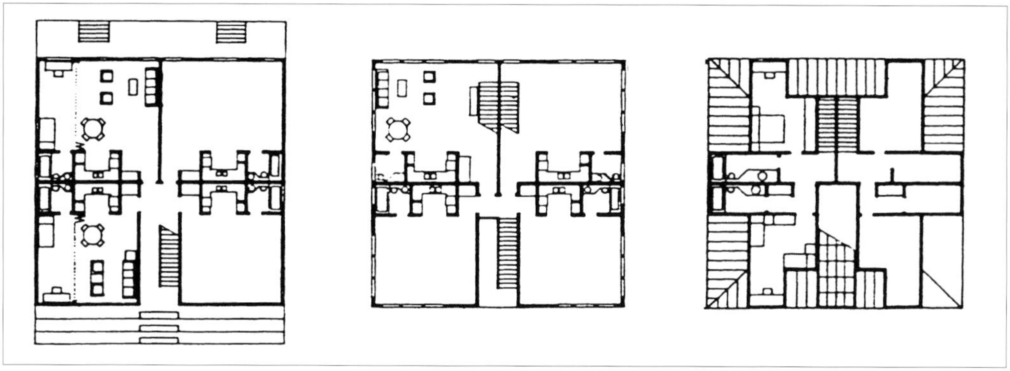

Examples of house types

Single home
1986/87
Tegel, Am Tegeler Hafen
Architect: Robert Stern
Clients: Beta Beteiligungen/IBA (International Building Exhibition)

A fully ripened fruit of Postmodernism, this building indicates a general as well as deeper-reaching retro-concern. Displayed here is the entire palette of design elements from every design era that ever influenced the house type "villa". In addition, an unbearable lightness of being and a shot of Hollywood mix an emotional cocktail that tastes as much of the old hat as it does of the horribly new.

Single home
1986/87
Tegel, Am Tegeler Hafen
Architect: John Hejduk
Clients: Beta Beteiligungen/IBA (International Building Exhibition)

The puritanical counter-design: the fact that this design hardly concerns a home for a single family, but rather for two families joined by only a shared staircase is not kept a secret. The actual house is only the lofty code for a "house", and even in the roof one looks directly into the sky.

465

Courtyard side

Wohnbebauung am Tegeler Hafen
Apartment development on the Tegel waterfront
1986/87
Tegel, Am Tegeler Hafen
Architects: Moore Ruble Yudell with Thomas Nagel, Leon Glodt, and Regina Pizzinini

This development for 165 apartements involved the partial realization of a winning entry submitted on the occasion of a competition aimed at developing the entire waterfront area, and the fact that it met with the public's widespread approval justified the means. As the group of responsible architects stated, "By using prefabricated concrete elements in our design we tried to attain an exceptionally high degree of diversity regarding the construction method, and to have this densely built up 'urban housing-colony' reflect great style and playfulness at the same time." A huge space, in and of itself almost a landscape, borders a small octagon bearing four gates, two of which form the overall impression and view, but also the axis to the water.

466

Perspective section

Humboldt-Bibliothek
1987/88
Tegel, Karolinenstraße
Architects: Moore Ruble Yudell
Client: Bezirksamt Reinickendorf/IBA (International Building Exhibition)

This long, hall construction is part of a planned, cultural ensemble of recreational facilities with a music and primary school. As a state library located on a piece of headland, inserted in front of the old harbor basin, its applied and altered historic, formal elements merge together to create a unified visual whole – especially true of the interior space, producing here a kind of library coziness. Along the other expanse of the harbor, the impressive courtyard complex designed by the same architects rises to a height of eight floors.

Architects, artists, engineers

We have made every attempt here to properly name all photographers of the pictures published in this book. Should we have been unsuccessful at this in the one or the other case, we would like to apologize and request that you notify us and/or contact the responsible architects or their clients.

Ahlers, Hans-Dieter 177
Albrecht, Wolfgang 265, 374
Arche Vision 036
Arena Bild 081a
ATUB 113a

Bach, Hans 395
Barte, Karsten 259
Baugilde 303a
Bauhaus-Archiv Berlin 429
Bauhaus-Archiv Berlin/Foto Hartwig Klappert 254
Benke, Till 396
Bitter, Jan 084
Bitter & Brett cover, 118, 143, 154, 178, 189
Blundell Jones, Peter 208b, 234, 350a, 392
Bohn, Erik 460
Bolduan, Christina 134a, 146a, 157b, 213, 238, 357, 399, 400, 440a
Bolk, Florian 009, 082, 120
Bredt, Marcus 025
Bruckhausen, Jörg von 291
Büker, Siegfried 344, 346a
Bünck + Fehse 190, 378 r
Burtin, Justus 297a+b, 298
Busch-Reisinger Museum 429b

Catchen, Gary L. 335b
CCSC 138b
Classen, Martin 10a

Dankschat, Ebba 413b
Delzios-Popp, Martha 161b
DLRG, Berlin 394a+b

Eicken, Thomas 186
Ermisch, Richard 398a+b
Esch, H.G. 201
Eyl, Georg 223

Faskel, Bernd 094
Forum für Sportgeschichte – Förderverein für das Sportmuseum Berlin 379
Friedrich, Reinhard 209, 207, 210, 211, 272, 276, 318, 352

Gackstatter, Henrik 290
Gagern, Verena von 162
Gahl, Christian 128, 257, 413a
Ganz, Joachim 053, 119
Görner, Reinhard 040, 123, 139, 144, 148, 166, 197, 230a, 236a+b, 239, 252b, 295a, 329a, 406, 463
Grahn, Robert 167b, 409
Greuner, S. 081
Grohe, Robert 125b

Hagemann, Otto (LA) 160, 192a+b, 226
Hahn, Silvia 362
Harder, Reinhold 376
Hattwig, Markus 317
Helle, Jochen 132
Hempel, Jörg 083
Hentschel Oestreich 039
Hilbich, Markus 122a
Huthmacher, Werner 021a, 101a+b, 176, 174, 188, 231, 401, 402, 437, 438, 439

Ibbeken, Hillert 232, 274a+b, 275, 302
Imhof, Michael 072, 076, 109, 124, 142, 204, 206, 253a, 319
Irsburger 161

Jacobs, Karl E. 024, 374, 418, 428, 435
Jansen, Helmut 159a+b

Kanakaris-Wirtl, Inge 414
Kasperski, Edmund (LA) 208, 465a+b
Kassner, Gerhard 187
Kendel, Hermann 251
Kessler, Rudolf (LA) 156, 284, 333, 347, 434, 435
Kiel, Willy (LA) 293b
Knöfel, H.J. 047r, 261, 335a, 375, 450, 455r+l
Kleihues + Kleihues 001, 026, 191
Klimek, Stanislaw 108
Köhler, Rolf 425
Koenig, Wilmar 127, 158, 218, 248, 249, 279, 377a+b
Köster, Arthur 270a+b, 350, 381, 385, 386, 387, 388, 420
Köster, Walter 047, 098, 099a+b, 169, 170, 171, 311a+b, 315, 316, 336, 380a+b, 383, 387, 388, 390
Koppelkamm, Stefan 136
Krase, Waltraud 250a
Kroll, Bernhard 121
Krille 63b
Krüger, Michael 068

Landesarchiv Berlin (LA) 052, 105b, 156, 215, 320, 331, 337, 347, 363, 366, 378a+b, 384, 417, 419, 421, 422, 423, 426, 431, 432, 433
Lehnartz, Klaus (LA) 080, 105a, 107, 152a+b, 322a
Leistner, Dieter 071
Lintner, Linus 015, 173
Lommatzsch, Ingeborg 150, 287, 307

Review and thanks

After the devastating destruction suffered in the Second World War, Berlin first started a public discussion about its urban development in the fifties, with the "Building Exhibition of 1957" which took place on the edge of the idyllic city park called "Tiergarten". This urban discourse was initiated at the same time that a counter model of urban development, the "Stalin-Allee" (today "Karl-Marx-Allee"), a demonstration of power and scale, was being formulated in the eastern, Soviet occupied, half of the city.

It was a time of growing international interest that drew many people from abroad to Berlin. Against this background I felt it especially important to draw attention to the 1920s and recall the architectural developments of the Nazi-banned Bauhaus, and the unique urban housing developments of people like Gropius, Mies von der Rohe, Bartning, Taut or Salvisberg.

Together with a fellow architecture student, Hans Joachim Knöfel, I began to put together an architectural guide, ranging from the beginnings of Modern architecture, which shunned Historicism, up to the "present day", which was in 1963.

With city maps, a notebook and a camera, we began simply to document what had survived the war and to piece together what plans could be found in deeds, archives and publications. Today there is a guidebook for every tourist city, but at that time the only architecture guidebook known to us was *Paris construit*. This gave us the opportunity to develop our own ideal layout for a topographic catalogue, This layout is still used today.

This first book was followed by a second about the 1970s, which I wrote with my brother Jan Rave. The third guide, covering the immense building boom that ensued after a second international building exhibition in 1987 and the fall of the wall in 1989, was published in December 2005. It became obvious that these three books should be compiled, resulting in a guide covering the years 1907 through 2007, or a century of Modern architectural development, reflected in the buildings of Berlin, and be published in English for the international public interest.

As usual, things are not as simple as they appear and this book would not have been possible without a lot of help. For this reason I would like firstly to thank the photographers who graciously allowed us to use their photos and to thank the city department for urban development, which provided us with the eight city maps, graphically reworked by Julia Wolter. My thanks also go to Karl Edward Johnson for his English translation, Rebecca Chestnutt, Nora Krehl-von Mühlendahl and Robert Niess for their monitoring of the translation, and Wolfgang Schäche, who not only described the ever-shifting history of the city in his introduction, but also corrected and supplemented several texts in the main body of the book. Finally I want to thank Edition Axel Menges for checking the whole work once again, for procuring many new photographs – and for publishing the book.

The fact that Edition Axel Menges is able to publish a second edition after only three years may be proof of the successful reception of the book by the public.

Rolf Rave

Bibliography

Architekten- und Ingenieur-Verein zu Berlin (ed.), *Berlin und seine Bauten*, Berlin, 1877 ff.

Borgelt, Christiane, and Regina Jost, *Konstruktion und Kreativität. Die Ingenieure der GSE*, Berlin, 2005.

Günther, Sonja, *Wils Ebert. Ein Bauhausschüler 1909–1979. Die Arbeit eines Architekten und Städtebauers*, Berlin, 1993.

Hegemann, Werner, *Das steinerne Berlin. Geschichte der größten Mietskasernenstadt der Welt*, Berlin 1930, 1963.

Hüter, Karl-Heinz, *Architektur in Berlin 1900–1933*, Dresden, 1988.

Jaeger, Falk, *Zurück zu den Stilen, Baukunst der achtziger Jahre in Berlin*, Berlin, 1991.

Kahlfeld, Paul, *Die Logik der Form. Berliner Backsteinbauten von Hans Heinrich Müller*, Berlin, 2004.

Kleihues, Josef Paul (ed.), *750 Jahre Architektur und Städtebau in Berlin. Die Internationale Bauausstellung im Kontext der Baugeschichte Berlins*, Stuttgart, 1987.

Krüger, Ingo, *Landhäuser und Villen in Berlin und Potsdam*, Bremen, 2008.

Meuser, Philipp, *Vom Plan zum Bauwerk. Bauten in der Berliner Innenstadt nach 2000*, Berlin, 2002.

Posener, Julius, *Berlin auf dem Wege zu einer neuen Architektur: das Zeitalter Wilhelms II.*, Munich, 1979.

Rave, Paul Ortwin, *Berlin in der Geschichte seiner Bauten*, Munich, 1960, 4th ed. 1987.

Rave, Rolf, *Bauen seit 1980 in Berlin. Ein Führer zu 400 Bauten in Berlin von 1980 bis heute*, Berlin, 2005.

Rave, Rolf, and Hans-Joachim Knöfel, *Bauen seit 1900 in Berlin*, Berlin, 1968, 6th ed. 1987.

Rave, Rolf, Hans-Joachim Knöfel and Jan Rave, *Bauen der 70er Jahre in Berlin*, Berlin, 1981, 3rd. ed. 1994.

Ribbe, Wolfgang, and Wolfgang Schäche (eds), *Baumeister, Architekten, Stadtplaner. Biographien zur baulichen Entwicklung Berlins*, Berlin, 1987.

Schäche, Wolfgang (ed.), *75 Jahre Gehag 1924–1999*, Berlin, 1999.

Schulz, Joachim, *Architekturführer DDR. Berlin: Hauptstadt der Deutchen Demokratischen Republik*, Berlin (Ost), 1981.

Teut, Anna, *Portrait Georg Heinrichs*, Berlin, 1984.

Zechlin, Hans Josef, *Landhäuser*, Berlin, 1939.

Zohlen, Gerwin (ed.), *Rudolf Fränkel. Die Gartenstadt Atlantic und Berlin*, Sulgen, 2006.

Memorandum